FO

Historians of the future, flash-frying muskrat snouts with milkweed pods and chanterelles over their campfires, will speak of America's travails in the early twenty-first century with a kind of nauseous, hushed awe, for this was the moment in history when our country became CrazyLand.

I started my blog, *Clusterfuck Nation*, almost twenty years ago to chronicle the week-by-week process of our collapsing civilization as described in my 2005 book *The Long Emergency*. The complex systems we depend on in the everyday life of the nation were beginning to come undone and one needed an agile medium to keep up with events. The internet, in all its untidy profligacy, had shoved the old newspapers and cable TV channels aside in the center ring in the circus of public opinion, so I migrated to the web with this new political blog while continuing to publish books.

What I had not anticipated in *The Long Emergency* was how badly the process of collapse would disorder the minds of the whole American population and, with that, the consensus about reality. A lot of things were going wrong in our country's daily life. The fabulous production economy that had made America the envy of the world was gone, drop-kicked into the Third World. In its place arose a set Ponzi schemes and swindles ("financialization") that stealthily embezzled away the wherewithal of the sore-beset, blindsided middle class. The Federal Reserve commenced the ruinous money-printing operations that were soon dignified under the rubric of Modern Monetary Policy. The arts and the universities got marched through and vandalized by the cultural Marxists. American youth was inveigled into a cult of sexual bamboozlement and race hatred, and politics entered a toxic zone of totalistic polarity. Our nation's motto seemed to change from *E. Pluribus Unum* to *Anything Goes and Nothing Matters*. And then, in 2016, Donald Trump entered the scene.

At first, I regarded him as the sheer oddity he seemed to be, with a bit of outlaw charm. As the entrained energy of his peculiar persona began to look like an implacable force, and the Republicans submitted to nominate him for president, I had considerable sport with him, dubbing him *The Golden Golem of Greatness*. And then, probably because his opponent Hillary Rodham Clinton proved to be both unlikable and perfidious, Trump managed to win the election. The mighty psyop called RussiaGate was already underway, and by the time Trump placed his hand on the inaugural Bible, the malevolent cabal we came to know as *The Deep State* organized itself to overthrow him.

I was on to the game early enough — probably around the time in 2016 that Bill Clinton paid a surprise visit to Attorney General Loretta Lynch's plane idling on the tarmac in Arizona. Something was not right there, and that was exactly when and where the Justice Department became the Left's prime weapon against anyone foolish enough to stand in its way. Poor Mr. Trump didn't know what he was up against. The first prime absurdity they laid on him, and the country, was the plot by FBI Director James Comey and his henchmen to jettison his new national security advisor, General Mike Flynn, for the crime of speaking with the Russian ambassador. Somehow the "Resistance," as the anti-Trumpers styled themselves, put over the idea that diplomats from foreign lands are not here to talk to our government officials. The news media validated that hoodwink and poor General Flynn spent the next three years in court running down his life savings to zero.

The RussiaGate extravaganza was a matrix of lying treachery that should have incriminated several dozen FBI agents, DOJ officials, federal judges, and various Democratic Party operatives in the three-plus years of its odious run. Many alt news reporters and bloggers had the whole scam sussed out in real time, while half the country succumbed to a trance induced by the blinding gaslight thrown off by *The New York Times*, the mendacious Rachel Maddow of MSNBC, and the rest of the old news gang. The criminality was right in your face, especially the special counsel inquiry fronted by a mentally compromised Robert Mueller (while actually run by one lawfare paladin, Andrew Weissmann, renowned for malicious prosecutions). The whole spectacle was exciting to write about.

Within months of the Mueller Report flopping, it was on to Impeachment Number 1, another confection of Deep State scoundrels, led by Rep. Adam Schiff, a CIA mole turned "whistleblower" named Eric Ciaramella, and NSC fraudster Col. Alexander Vindman, with an assist from intel community inspector general (and former DOJ official) Michael Atkinson — who changed the whistleblower regulations to allow for secondhand hearsay in order to falsely accuse Mr. Trump of daring to inquire about the bribery operations in Ukraine of the Biden family, subsequently proven to be true and egregious. The impeachment was fun to write about too as it unspooled and flopped, though at times it was hard on the nerves considering how much rage it induced.

And then it was on to the fantastic mind fuckery of Covid-19 and the phony, useless, harmful vaccinations that have to date killed many people, injured and

❧ CRAZYLAND ❧

DISPATCHES ON
THE GREAT AMERICAN
DERANGEMENT
OF OUR TIME

JAMES HOWARD KUNSTLER

Cover design by Allen Crawford
Interior book design by The Troy Book Makers

Printed in the United States of America
The Troy Book Makers • Troy, New York • thetroybookmakers.com

To order additional copies of this title,
contact your favorite local bookstore
or visit www.shoptbmbooks.com

ISBN: 978-1-61468-846-4

This book is for my girl, Bonnie Furlong, the soul of patience

❧ CRAZYLAND ❧

ALSO BY JAMES HOWARD KUNSTLER

Fiction

The *World Made by Hand* series

The Harrows of Spring

A History of the Future

The Witch of Hebron

World Made by Hand

Maggie Darling, a Modern Romance

Thunder Island

The Halloween Ball

The Hunt

Blood Solstice

An Embarrassment of Riches

The Life of Byron Jaynes

A Clown in the Moonlight

The Wampanaki Tales

Nonfiction

CrazyLand

Young Man Blues

Living in the Long Emergency

Too Much Magic

The Long Emergency

The City in Mind

Home from Nowhere

The Geography of Nowhere

disabled many more, and set up all of Western civilization for an era of medical, financial, and political tyranny. The lying and bad faith entailed in that operation were so rich and remorseless that a blogger could sit at the keyboard 24/7 and never run out of crimes and outrageous affronts to the public interest to record and explicate. And that epic of ill will led to the obviously crooked 2020 election, and all its wicked aftereffects, including the FBI-instigated "insurrection," the Twitter Files revelations of a government at war against the truth, and subsequent malicious prosecutions, including the four cases currently lodged against candidate Donald Trump as he mounts a seemingly impossible campaign to return to power so as to wreak vengeance on his tormenters. Let's not leave out the baleful legacy of "Joe Biden" in the White House and his idiotic war in Ukraine, trifling with World War Three.

Here we stand entering the fateful year 2024. It might be plain in reading these selected blogs of the era that I grew more sympathetic to *The Golden Golem of Greatness* the more travails were dishonestly heaped on him. You had to admire his sheer fortitude if not his personal presentation. But the greater theme running through all this vicissitude has been the gross dishonor of the institutions that we Americans depend on in order to live in a polity based on age-old truths and virtues embedded in a moral basis for human conduct. The obverse of that high-toned medallion is the shrieking face of a nation driven insane by its own astoundingly bad behavior.

It was my paramount objective in this long ordeal by prose to bring some artistry to the composition of political commentary, often so boring, and to introduce notes of comedy where it belonged, which was often. I predicted that tilt toward the antic in Samuel Beckett's droll observation that "nothing is funnier than unhappiness." And so, in this moment of national anguish, I give you . . . *CrazyLand.*

❊ 2016 ❊

SLOWLY, THEN ALL AT ONCE

September 19, 2016

The staggering incoherence of the election campaign only mirrors the shocking incapacity of the American public, from top to bottom, to process the tendings of our time. The chief tending is permanent worldwide economic contraction. Having hit the resource wall, especially of affordable oil, the global techno-industrial economy has sucked a valve in its engine.

For sure there are ways for human beings to inhabit this planet, perhaps in a civilized mode, but not at the gigantic scale of the current economic regime. The fate of this order has nothing to do with our wishes or preferences. It's going down whether we like it or not because it was such a violent anomaly in world history and the salient question is: how do we manage our journey to a new disposition of things. Neither Trump nor Clinton show that they have a clue about the situation.

The quandary I describe is often labeled the *end of growth*. The semantic impact of this phrase tends to paralyze even well-educated minds, most particularly the eminent econ professors, the Yale lawyers-turned-politicos, the *Wall Street Journal* editors, the corporate poobahs of the "C-suites," the hedge fund maverick-geniuses, and the bureaucratic errand boys (and girls) of Washington. In the absence of this "growth," as defined by the employment and productivity statistics extruded like poisoned bratwursts from the sausage grinders of government agencies, this elite can see only the yawning abyss. The poverty of imagination among our elites is really something to behold.

As is usually the case with troubled, overripe societies, these elites have begun to resort to magic to prop up failing living arrangements. This is why the Federal Reserve, once an obscure institution deep in the background of normal life, has come downstage front and center, holding the rest of us literally spellbound with its incantations against the intractable ravages of debt deflation. (For a brilliant gloss on this phenomenon, read Ben Hunt's essay "Magical Thinking" at the Epsilon Theory website.)

One way out of this quandary would be to substitute the word "activity" for "growth." A society of human beings can choose different activities that would produce different effects than the techno-industrial model of behavior. They can organize ten-acre farms instead of cell phone game app companies. They can do physical labor instead of watching television. They can build compact walkable towns instead of suburban wastelands (probably even out of the salvaged detritus of those wastelands). They can put on plays, concerts, sing-alongs, and puppet shows instead of Super Bowl halftime shows and internet porn videos. They can make things of quality by hand instead of stamping out a million things guaranteed to fall apart next week. None of these alt activities would be classifiable as "growth" in the current mode. In fact, they are consistent with the reality of contraction. And they could produce a workable and satisfying living arrangement.

The rackets and swindles unleashed in our futile quest to keep up appearances have disabled the financial operating system that the regime depends on. It's all an illusion sustained by accounting fraud to conceal promises that won't be kept. All the mighty efforts of central bank authorities to borrow "wealth" from the future in the form of "money" — to "paper over" the absence of growth — will not conceal the impossibility of paying that borrowed money back. The future's revenge for these empty promises will be the disclosure that the supposed wealth is not really there — especially as represented in currencies, stock shares, bonds, and other ephemeral "instruments" designed to be storage vehicles for wealth. The stocks are not worth what they pretend. The bonds will never be paid off. The currencies will not store value. How did this happen? Slowly, then all at once.

We're on a collision course with these stark realities. They are coinciding with the sickening vectors of national politics in a great wave of latent consequences built up by the sheer inertia of the scale at which we have been doing things. Trump, convinced of his own brilliance, knows nothing, and wears his incoherence like a medal of honor. Clinton personifies the horror of these coiled consequences waiting to spring — and the pretense that everything will continue to be okay with her in the White House (not). When these two gargoyle combatants meet in the debate arena a week from now, you will hear nothing about the journey we're on to a different way of life.

But there is a clear synergy between the mismanagement of our money and the mismanagement of our politics. They have the ability to amplify each other's disorders. The awful vibe from this depraved election might be enough to bring down markets and banks. The markets and banks are unstable enough to affect the election.

In history, elites commonly fail spectacularly. Ask yourself: how could these two ancient institutions, the Democratic and Republican parties, cough up such human hairballs? And having done so, do they deserve to continue to exist? And if they go up in a vapor, along with the public's incomes and savings, what happens next?

Enter the generals.

Sizing Up the Endgame

October 3, 2016

All Hillary had to do last week was show up and stand at a podium for ninety minutes without swooning while Donald Trump barked and grunted his way through the half-assed press conference we like to call a "debate." It was all I could do to keep watching the nauseating spectacle. It made you want to reach out and whap your TV upside its head, or maybe just shoot the fucker, like Elvis used to do.

The torment of who or what to vote for has become unbearable. I'd considered casting mine for Johnson / Weld, until Gary Johnson demonstrated that the front end of his brain is missing. Aleppo? Wasn't he one of the Marx Brothers? I sense that Jill Stein of the Green Party is more social justice warrior than eco warrior, and the last thing I want is for the rest of America to become one big college campus rife with trigger warnings and microaggression persecutions. Vote for Trump? Not if you chained me to the back bumper of a Toyota Land Cruiser and dragged me over six miles of broken lightbulbs. Hillary? Make that nine miles, and throw down some carpet tacks.

But wait a minute! Here's something to consider: a proposition put out by David McAlvany on his podcast last week: "To Understand Election 2016 You Have to See 2020." The idea is that the winner of the presidential election is sure to be the biggest loser because the global economy is in the process of tanking, Long Emergency style, and the global finance system is going down with it. Whoever presides over this fiasco from the White House is going to be a bigger bag holder than old Herbert Hoover in 1929.

The salutary part of the story is that such an epochal crack-up will sweep the establishment out of power. In the present case, this means discrediting the crony-capitalist, revolving-door grifters of the Wall Street / Washington axis, plus the neocon military empire builders bent on starting World War Three for profit, plus the economic central planners of the Federal Reserve whose desperate meddlings have nearly destroyed the necessary operations and meaning of money. And the cherries on top to get thrown out with the rest of this giant shit sundae would be the campus cultural Maoists. In short, vote for Hillary and let history flush them all out of the system.

A vote for Trump would let the aforesaid villains and bunglers off the hook because supposedly Trump represents free market business interests, and if he got elected they would be blamed for the economic and financial cataclysm that has been in motion for going on for two decades — and has accelerated mightily under the genial Obama. Whatever else you might say about free markets, had they been allowed to operate naturally, a lot of dead wood might have been cleared out of the financial forest by allowing failing institutions and companies to crash and burn. Instead, they were artificially propped up and hosed down with bailouts and other accounting frauds at all costs. The cost turns out to be the coherent workings of markets.

There can be little question that Hillary represents so much that has gone wrong in American public life under the baby boomer regime. The fact that she will be the oldest president ever at inauguration itself says a lot about the limitless cupidity of the boomer political gen. They just don't know when to stop. It's history's job to stop them now, nature's way, by seating them at the banquet of consequences for all their poisonous cookery and quackery.

Watching these lamebrain debates you get the impression that the *folks* running things, including media stars like the debate moderators, lack the slightest clue about the gathering economic storm. They are too busy reading the false weather reports posted by the Fed and the US Bureau of Labor Statistics. Both Hillary and Trump seem to believe that we can winkle our way back to a 1962-style economy if we click our ruby slippers three times. That is not going to happen.

There are too many people onboard the planet and too few resources to keep them all going. It's hard to say whether we might have managed the necessary contraction, say, starting back in the 1970s when the writing was on the wall and a truly honest president (one Jimmy Carter) spelled it out in plain English. We blew it, electing Ronald Reagan to enable the final feeding frenzy of the techno-industrial age.

Now it's up to natural forces — and their galloping horsemen — to get the job done. So let us by all means throw our votes behind Hillary and let her rip so we can move on from there sooner rather than later and find new ways to remain civilized in the coming disposition of things.

THE ODOR OF DESPERATION

October 17, 2016

It must be obvious even to nine-year-old casual observers of the scene that the US national election is hacking itself. It doesn't require hacking assistance from any other entity. The two major parties could not have found worse candidates for president, and the struggle between them has turned into the most sordid public spectacle in US electoral history.

Of course, the Russian hacking blame-game story emanates from the security apparatus controlled by a Democratic Party executive establishment desperate to preserve its perks and privileges. (I write as a still-registered-but-disaffected Democrat.) The reams of released emails from Clinton campaign chairman John Podesta, and other figures in HRC's employ, depict a record of tactical mendacity, a gleeful eagerness to lie to the public, and a disregard for the world's opinion that are plenty bad enough on their own. And Trump's own fantastic gift for blunder could hardly be improved on by a meddling foreign power. The US political system is blowing itself to pieces.

I say this with the understanding that political systems are emergent phenomena with the primary goal of maintaining their control on the agencies of power at all costs. That is, it's natural for a polity to fight for its own survival. But the fact that the US polity now so desperately has to fight for survival shows how frail is its legitimacy is. It wouldn't take much to shove it off a precipice into a new kind of civil war much more confusing and irresolvable than the one we went through in the 1860s.

Events and circumstances are driving the US insane, literally. We can't construct a coherent consensus about what is happening to us and therefore we can't form a set of coherent plans for doing anything about it. The main event is that our debt has far exceeded our ability to produce enough new wealth to service the debt, and our attempts to work around it with Federal Reserve accounting fraud only makes the problem worse day by day and hour by hour. All of it tends to undermine both national morale and living standards, while it shoves us into the crisis I call the Long Emergency.

It's hard to see how Russia benefits from America becoming the Mad Bull of a floundering global economy. Rather, the Evil Russia meme seems a projection of our country's own insecurities and contradictions. For instance, we seem to think that keeping Syria viciously destabilized is preferable to allowing its legitimate government to restore some kind of order there. Russia has been on the scene attempting to prop up the Assad government while we are on the scene there doing everything possible to keep a variety of contestants in a state of incessant war. US policy in Syria has been both incoherent and tragically damaging to the Syrians.

The Russians stood aside while the US smashed up Iraq, Afghanistan, and Libya. We demonstrated adequately that shoving sovereign nations into civic failure is not the best way to resolve geopolitical tensions. Why would it be such a bad thing for the US to stand aside in Syria and see if the Russians can rescue that country from failure? Because they might keep a naval base there on the Mediterranean? We have scores of military bases around the region.

It's actually pretty easy to understand why the Russians might be paranoid about America's intentions. We use NATO to run threatening military maneuvers near Russia's borders. We provoked Ukraine — formerly a province of the Soviet state — to become a nearly failed state, and then we complained foolishly about the Russian annexation of Crimea — also a former territory of the Soviet state and of imperial Russia going back centuries. We slapped sanctions on Russia, making it difficult for it to participate in international banking and commerce.

What's really comical is the idea that Russia is using the internet to mess with our affairs — as if the USA has no cyber-warfare ambitions or ongoing operations against them (and others, such as hacking Angela Merkel's personal phone). News flash: every country with access to the internet is in full hacking mode around the clock against every other country so engaged. Everybody's doing it. It is perhaps a projection of America's ongoing rape hysteria that we think we're special victims of this universal activity.

Slouching Toward Election Day

October 24, 2016

It's getting hard to give a shit about this election, though you might still care about this country. The damage has been done to the two long-reigning political parties and perhaps that's a good thing. They deserved to be dragged into the gutter and now they can either go through a severe rehab or be replaced by as yet unformed coalitions of reality-based interests.

Trump did a greater disservice all-in-all to the faction he supposedly represented. Their grievances about a grift-maximized political economy were genuine, and Trump managed to make them look like a claque of sinister clowns. This cartoon of a rich kid with no internal boundaries was unable to articulate their legitimate complaints. His behavior during the so-called debates verged on psychotic. If Trump loses, I will assay a guess that his followers' next step will be some kind of violence. For the moment, pathetic as it is, Trump was their last best hope.

I'm more comfortable about Hillary — though I won't vote for her — because it will be salutary for the ruling establishment to unravel with her in charge of it. That way, the right people will be blamed for the mismanagement of our national affairs. This gang of elites needs to be circulated out of power the hard way, under the burden of their own obvious perfidy, with no one else to point their fingers at. Her election will sharpen awareness of the criminal conduct in our financial practices and the neglect of regulation that marked the eight years of Obama's appointees at the Department of Justice and the Securities and Exchange Commission.

The "tell" in these late stages of the campaign has been the demonization of Russia — a way more idiotic exercise than the McCarthyite Cold War hysteria of the early 1950s, since there is no longer any ideological conflict between us and all the evidence indicates that the current state of bad relations is America's fault, in particular our sponsorship of the state failure in Ukraine and our avid deployment of NATO forces in war games on Russia's border. Hillary has had the full force of the foreign affairs establishment behind her in this war-drum-banging effort, yet they have not been able to produce any evidence, for instance, in their claim that Russia is behind the Wikileaks hack of Hillary's email. They apparently subscribe to the Joseph Goebbels theory of propoganda: *if you're going to lie, make sure it's a whopper, and then repeat it incessantly.*

The media have been onboard with all this. *The New York Times* especially has acted as the hired amplifier for the establishment lies — such a difference from the same newspaper's role in the Vietnam War ruckus of yesteryear. Today (Monday) it ran an astounding editorial "explaining" the tactical necessity of Hillary's dishonesty. "In politics, hypocrisy and doublespeak are tools," the *Times* editorial board wrote. Oh, well, that's reassuring. Welcome to the George Orwell Theme Park of Democracy.

Of course neither Trump nor Hillary show any signs of understanding the real problems afflicting the USA. They don't recognize the basic energy equation that has made it impossible for industrial economies to keep growing, or the deformities in banking and finance that result from official efforts to overcome these implacable conditions, namely, the piling up of ever greater debt to "solve" the problem of overindebtedness.

The beginning of the way out of this quandary will be recognition that the federal government is the greatest obstacle for America making the necessary adjustments to a world that has changed. If Trump got elected, I'm convinced that he would be removed from office by a military coup inside of a year, which would be an epic smashup of our political machinery per se, comparable to the period 44 BCE in Rome, when the republic crashed. Hillary would bring a more measured discredit to the system with the chance that our institutions might be rehabilitated — with the cherry on top being Hillary's eventual impeachment for lying, a fate that her husband and the late Richard Nixon both wiggled out of one way or another.

HALLOWEEN NATION

October 31, 2016

What was with James Comey's Friday letter to Congress? It looks to me like the FBI director had to go nuclear against his parent agency, the Department of Justice, and Attorney General Loretta Lynch, his boss, in particular. Why? Because the attorney general refused to pursue the Clinton email case when more evidence turned up in the underage sexting case against Anthony Weiner, husband of Hillary's chief of staff, Huma Abedin.

Over the weekend, the astounding news story broke that the FBI had not obtained a warrant to examine the emails on Weiner's computer and other devices after three weeks of getting stonewalled by DOJ attorneys. What does it mean when the director of the FBI can't get a warrant in a New York minute? It must mean that the DOJ is at war with the FBI. Watergate is looking like thin gruel compared to this fantastic bouillabaisse of a presidential campaign fiasco.

One way you can tell is that *The New York Times* is playing down the story Monday morning. Columnist Paul Krugman calls the Comey letter "cryptic." Krugman's personal cryptograph insinuates that Comey is trying to squash an investigation of "Russian meddling in American elections." Senate Minority Leader Harry Reid chimed in with a statement that "it has become clear that you [Comey] possess explosive information about close ties and coordination between Donald Trump, his top advisers and the Russian government." How's that for stupid and ugly? It's the Russians' fault that Hillary finds herself in trouble again?

Earlier this week, lawyers at the DOJ attempted to quash a parallel investigation of the Clinton Foundation. They must be out of their minds to think that story will go away. Isn't it about time that a House or Senate committee subpoenaed Bill Clinton to testify under oath about his June airport meeting with Loretta Lynch. He doesn't enjoy any special immunity in this case.

Speaking of immunity, when will we learn what kind of immunity Huma Abedin may have been granted in previous cycles of the email investigation? Plenty of other Clinton campaign associates got immunity from prosecution earlier this year, rendering bales of evidence on their own laptops inadmissible in the email server case.

Things as yet unknown: Where is US Attorney (for the Southern District of New York) Preet Bharara in this case? He works for the DOJ, but he is known to be an independent operator, and he must be already involved at least in the underage sexting case against Weiner, meaning he's had access to an awful lot of collateral evidence from Weiner's laptop, and he must have obtained some kind of warrants of his own.

What appears to be unraveling is AG Loretta Lynch's effort to protect Hillary Clinton and now, in this Alfred Hitchcock movie of a presidential election, she's trying to make it look like James Comey is stabbing Hillary in the shower. (Film buffs note: in Hitchcock's *Psycho* the character played by Janet Leigh made off with a bundle of money from her place of employment before Norman Bates worked his hoodoo on her at the motel.)

Trump, of course, is playing the escapade up in his usual idiotic way. It would be unfortunate if it ended up getting him elected — but how would it not be unfortunate for Hillary to wind up in the White House under a cloud of possible indictment? She will be doing Chinese fire drills with a special prosecutor the whole time she is in office, tempted at every moment to start a war with the Russians to divert attention from her legal problems.

Soon we will learn what kind of tensions are roiling between the FBI and the DOJ, and internally within each of these agencies. There are too many pissed off people there to prevent leakage, and probably plenty of email memoranda among the officials that would nicely lay out a trail of incrimination leading into the attorney general's office itself.

What a fine mess. And anybody who thinks that any of it might be resolved before November 8 will be disappointed. This story has so many legs, it looks like an Amazonian centipede compared to the lumbering cockroach that was Watergate. The awful proceedings will grind on and on while the US economy and its vampire squid matrix of financial rackets implode in 2017 along with the European Union and global trade. How do you like the Long Emergency now?

THE FAT LADY HAS A SORE THROAT

November 7, 2016

A mighty nausea wells up across the land as the awful day cometh. Who will receive the black spot of fate on Tuesday? I wouldn't want to be him or her on that dreadful day. The flagship of modernity has lost its vaunted mojo and nobody knows what to do about it as the USS *USA* pitches and yaws into the maelstrom.

Much opinion "out there" contends that we will have to suffer an election overtime, with the results contested on every hill and molehill from sea to shining sea. That scenario suggests various outcomes, all of them pretty bad. 1) The election is once again relegated to a Supreme Court case, only this time it ends up a 4–4 tie. Constitutional crisis time. 2) Perhaps as a function of no. 1, it ends up in the US House of Representatives. The catch is: members aren't limited to Trump or HRC. They can vote for whomever they like. 3) A lot of web chatter has President Obama invoking some sort of emergency with the election postponed until some conclave of political viziers can figure a way out of it. Unlikely, but possible.

FBI Director James Comey's eleventh-hour reprieve of Hillary in the email server case sent an odor of rotting carp wafting across the political landscape. Like, his peeps actually vetted 650,000 emails in a week? I'm sure. Of course, the FBI does not issue indictments; that's AG Loretta Lynch's job over at the Department of Justice. The FBI only makes criminal referrals to such. But this puts too fine a point on the matter because the much more serious issue is the Clinton Foundation case, and the arrant sale of influence while HRC ran the State Department.

That currently overshadowed case is not closed. It sends up the odor not of a single rotting carp but of an entire whale pod dead on the beach. Half the emirs in Arabia dropped millions on the foundation to facilitate arms deals or to influence policy at State, and that was only part of what looks exactly like a classic racketeering operation. The Clinton Foundation story is not going away anytime soon and it will suck all the air out of the public arena for as far ahead as anyone can see when Hillary is in the Oval Office.

All of that obscures the gathering calamity in banking and finance that drives the waiting, whirling maelstrom. Thanks to eight years of central bank experiments, the engines of capital are hopelessly gunked up with political additives like QE and ZIRP™. Nothing is priced correctly, especially money. It's all kept running on an ether of accounting fraud. We can't come to grips with the resource realities behind the fraud, especially the end of *cheap* oil. And the bottom line is the already manifest slowdown of global business. The poobahs of banking pretend to be confounded by all this because everything — their reputations, their jobs, their fortunes — depends on the Potemkin narrative that ever greater economic expansion lies just around the corner.

Not so. What waits around the corner is a global scramble for the table scraps of the late techno-industrial banquet. Scrambles like that are liable to foment kinetic conflict. Neither Hillary nor Trump appear to have a clue what this means and so they are likely to misinterpret the true signals amid all the noise and start an unnecessary war. Hillary is already hard at it with her cawing over supposed "Russian hackers" in the election.

The tragedy of Trump is that he represented a roster of legitimate grievances but argued them so poorly and then betrayed them with behavior so oafish and crude that he often looked not sane enough to hold high office. His partisans brushed that aside, saying it was good enough that he personified a giant "fuck you" to the political establishment. No, that wasn't good enough because in the process he delegitimized the issues.

For instance, there are excellent arguments for a "time-out" from immigration. Congress acted on that in 1925, after a half-century flood of immigration needed to man the factories of the early twentieth century. The consensus on that policy change was arrived at with minimal rancor — and just in time, by the way, for the Great Depression, when manufacturing employment crashed. We're also in for a collapse of activity, only this time it won't be the few remaining factory workers. It'll be everyone from the McDonald's counter jockeys to the bond packagers of Goldman Sachs.

The establishment will get its "fuck you" anyway. I do go along with the argument advanced by others that it would probably be better for Hillary to win, because that way the right people (the gang already in power) will be blamed for the descent into the maelstrom and will be expeditiously swept away.

Just about anything may rise up across America after that — the true cornpone Nazi who succeeds Trump in the *meshuggeneh* branch of conservative politics... a second civil war... or a World Made by Hand. I detect a general awareness that the country must pass through some epic ordeal to straighten itself out. Well, here it is, just in time for the holidays.

Me? I'm going to write in my vote for Homey D. Clown, because he don't mess around.

WHAT NOW?

November 14, 2016

Not to put too fine a point on it, America coughed up Hillary Clinton like a hairball last week — the catch being it then had to swallow the Cheeto-colored bolus called Donald Trump. It was worth it to see the fog of Hillary smuggery lift across the cable TV networks since the "I'm With Her / It's Her Turn" fog was a cover for the looting operation that the permanent Washington DC establishment had turned into, including the Clinton Foundation.

Obviously, the nation is reeling from this emetic, struggling to process the meaning of it all. The big tell for me came at a moment in last week's Slate Political Gabfest, a leftish-oriented podcast, when moderator David Plotz asked his sidekicks John Dickerson (of CBS News) and Emily Bazelon (of *The New York Times*) what the Democratic Party might do to regain legitimacy after this electoral disaster. Dead silence on the air. Nothing came to mind.

Something came to my mind as a longtime disaffected (registered) Democrat: jettison the stupid identity politics and get back to reality. Alas, that may be too much to ask. For now, the party lies in ruins without a single figure of stature to represent a coherent set of ideas other than boosting the self-esteem of its favor-seeking constituent groups. Here's my idea: how about forming a credible opposition to the so-called Deep State, the matrix of racketeering and empire building that has drained the life out of this polity. That was impossible with the racketeer in chief leading the blue electoral ticket, but now the dynamic stands naked and obvious, answering the question: *what to do next*?

Another catch, of course, is that opposing the Deep State of Rackets is pretty much what Mr. Trump has promised to do, if "draining the swamp" means anything. He never quite articulated it clearly beyond that metaphor, but you can bet that's what the DC establishment is so alarmed about. Trump's behavior on the campaign trail is now being hailed in the media as a kind of genius. To me, it still seems oafish to an extreme, and it remains to be seen how such a blunderer might finesse our escape from the empire of rackets and the racket of empire. He begins to look like a man in a tunnel staring down the harsh light of the onrushing gravy train.

Mr. Trump might not know it yet, but his chief task will be managing contraction. It would appear to be problematic, since his chief promise — to "make America great again" — is based on restarting the epic expansions of the nineteenth and twentieth centuries. Well, things have changed. This is no longer a virgin continent filled with motherlodes, untapped oil bonanzas, and fabulous soils begging to be exploited. In fact, we're close to being played out where those resources are concerned. And the techno-industrial economy engineered out of those assets is wobbling badly.

There is a Great Wish that this system might be replaced just in time with some as yet unrealized green alt economy of solar-charged driverless electric cars — but, of course, the unchallenged pathetic idiocy of the assumed car dependence at the center of this fantasy ought to tell you how exactly unreal it is. The contraction we face has mandates of its own, and it doesn't include the continuation of Happy Motoring on any terms. I'm quite certain that the Trump forces haven't even imagined it.

I would propose three meta-matters in consideration of how America might survive the disorders of the Long Emergency: the financialization of the economy, the burdens of empire, and the fiasco of our suburban living arrangement.

The financialization of the economy is already playing into its disastrous climax as I write, with bond markets tanking all over the planet. What this means is that the long-ignored chickens of risk associated with debt are coming home to roost. As they do, they are going to shit over everything on the financial landscape. Industrial societies have been borrowing from the future to a grotesque degree for decades, pretending that these debts were assets rather than liabilities. That perception is about to change, and with it an enormous amount of presumed notional wealth is going to disappear. That will manifest in rising bond yields (and falling bond values), cratering currencies, panicked capital flows, banking emergencies, and weird action in markets. If that seems too metaphysical, you can also think of it as contracting economies and the withering of global trade relations. There's also the chance it will express itself in kinetic conflict, i.e., war.

My sense of things is that this meta-predicament alone could overwhelm the Trump government from the very start. We could have problems with money orders of magnitude worse than anything FDR faced in 1933, with bank closures, the seizing of accounts, and the paralysis of everyday business. That would easily lead to civil disorders, a breakdown in law, and the immiseration of most Americans. It could also lead to previously unimagined political outcomes, such as a discontinuity of government. This is connected with the second meta-problem, the burdens of empire.

The USA is squandering its vitality trying to maintain a halfassed global empire of supposed interests, economic, ideological, and existential. Lately, this hapless project has only resulted in wars with no end in places we don't belong. It includes reckless experiments such as the promotion of regime change (Iraq, Libya, Ukraine, Egypt, Syria), and senseless, provocative exercises such as the use of NATO forces to run war games near Russia's border. The monetary cost of all this is off the hook, of course, redounding to the financial mess. Reining in these imperial impulses could be on the Trump agenda, but his own gold-plated imperial pretensions suggest that he might actually make the situation worse by conflating a reduction of our empire with a loss of the very "greatness" he wants to reclaim. As it happens, America may be forced by economic circumstances to yield the burdens of empire. The world is about to become a bigger place again as globalism winds down and the larger nations establish more realistic spheres of influence. We better get with the program.

Thirdly comes the question of how Americans inhabit the terrain: the suburban fiasco and all its accessories and furnishings. You can just stick a fork in that. The great project awaiting this country is how we might redistribute our people into rescaled walkable communities with relocalized economies, including rescaled agriculture. It's going to happen whether we like it or not. It's only a matter of how disorderly the process may be. Obviously all the suburban crapola out there also represents a tremendous load of presumed wealth. The vested "value" in suburban houses alone is the underlayment of structured finance. There is almost no conscious political awareness in any party — including the Greens — as to how we might attempt to work this out.

But, for example, and for a start, Mr. Trump might consider the effect that national chain Big Box shopping has had on Main Street America. It destroyed local commercial economies all over the land, and with it numberless vocational niches and social roles in communities. He can't sign an edict against the Big Box empire, but his people might start imagining the process of rebuilding local networks of commerce and actively deincentivizing the Big Box business model. That model has many other ways to fail, incidentally, and already is failing to some degree between the impoverishment of its customers and the growing problems with global supply lines. But anything that might lubricate the transition would be better than the stark collapse of the current arrangement.

The chatter this week has been all about the upcoming "infrastructure" orgy that Trump will undertake. That depends first of all on how badly the financial sector cracks up. I hope we do not squander more of our dwindling capital on the accessories of car dependence, because that addiction is on the way out. One thing Mr. Trump might get behind is restoring the passenger railroads of America so that we can at least get around the continental nation when the Happy Motoring fiesta grinds to a halt. It would put an awful lot of people to work on something with real long-term benefit — it ties in to the restoration of Main Street towns and their economies — and it is a doable project that might give us the needed encouragement to get on with the many other necessary projects awaiting our attention.

In case you were wondering, I was not jumping up and down cheering the Trump victory, amazing as it was. I figured the good news was that Hillary lost and the bad news was that Trump won. Now, we just have to roll with it.

Boo Hoo

November 21, 2016

America didn't get what it expected, but perhaps it got what it deserved, good and hard. Daddy's in the house and he busted straight into the nursery and now the little ones are squalling in horror. Mommy was discovered to be a grifting old jade who ran the household into a slum and she's been turned out to solemnly await the judgment of the courts, nowhere to run, nowhere to hide. The kids on campus have gone temporarily insane over this domestic situation and some wonder if they'll ever get over it.

Trump as the USA's Daddy? Well, yeah. Might he turn out to be a good daddy? A lot of people worry that he can't be. Look how he behaved on the campaign trail: no behavioral boundaries... *ucchhh*. He even lurches as he walks, like Frankenstein. Not very reassuring — though it appears that somehow he raised up a litter of high-functioning kids of his own. Not a tattoo or an earplug among them. No apparent gender confusion. All holding rather responsible positions in the family business. Go figure.Judging from the internal recriminations among Democratic Party partisans playing out in the newspapers, it's as if they all woke up simultaneously from a hypnotic trance realizing what an absolute dud they put up for election in Hillary Clinton — and even beyond that obvious matter, how deeply absurd Democratic ideology had become with its annoying victimology narrative, the incessant yammer about "diversity" and "inclusion," as if pixie dust were the sovereign remedy for a national nervous breakdown. But can they move on from there? I'm not so sure.

For all practical purposes, both traditional parties have blown themselves up. The Democratic Party morphed from the party of thinking people to the party of the thought police, and for that alone they deserve to be flushed down the soil pipe of history where the feckless Whigs went before them. The Republicans have floundered in their own Special Olympics of the Mind for decades, too, so it's understandable that they have fallen hostage to such a rank outsider as Trump, so cavalier with the party's dumbass shibboleths. It remains to be seen whether the party becomes a vengeful, hybrid monster with an orange head or a bridge back to reality. I give the latter outcome a low percentage chance.

Mommy is all about feelings and Daddy's role is action and that is another reason that Hillary lost and Trump won. We've heard enough about people's feelings and it just doesn't matter anymore. You're offended? Suck an egg. Someone appropriated your culture? Go shit in your sombrero. What matters is how we're going to contend with the winding down of modernity — the techno-industrial orgy that is losing its resource and money mojo. The politics of sacred victimhood has got to yield to the politics of staying alive.

President-elect Trump may not know it yet, but events are now in charge, not personalities, not even his supersized persona. Global trade and economic activity have been winding down all year and it's finally affecting financial markets kept aloft on borrowed money, sending a strong signal through bonds that the borrowed money may never be paid down, and that additional borrowing will cost a whole lot more — so much more that it will bankrupt the nations that issue it.

That alone will make it difficult for a President Trump to scare up the ready cash for the infrastructure-rebuilding fiesta so many expect. And if he does manage to flush the funding out of the banking thickets, it is liable to carry an inflationary bird flu that will end up killing money all around the world. We won't be worrying about Trans-Pacific Partnerships anymore because letters of credit will be unavailable to move large shipments of anything from point A to point B. How long after that will it be before the supermarket shelves empty down? And in the event, what will the dollar buy?

It looks like the shit sandwich President Obama has carefully prepared and left in the White House pantry for his successor will take the form of inflation, the dying of your money — or, at least, paper currency. Or, if it doesn't die outright, prepare for the possibility that you might not be able to get your hands on it, as money markets gate their exits and banks restrict cash withdrawals.

Though it's clearly a loser strategy now, I suspect that the ragged remains of the Democratic Party will persist in amping up their sacred identity grievances to the point of civil strife without ever understanding the economic dynamics in motion. They don't know what else to do. Plus, they are captives of the poverty policy racketeers. I also suspect that neither Mr. Obama nor Mr. Trump will get around to pardoning Hillary Clinton for the racketeering operation of her foundation, of which the private email server was the least issue — rather, the arrant sale of influence and access to the State Department is the heart of the matter, and anyone paying attention knows it, including the incoming attorney general. If that circus comes to town, Trump could benefit from the distraction it offers the public.

There's a lot of talk on the net about Strauss and Howe's "Fourth Turning" taking stage now. Their excellent book, published twenty years ago, posits the turbulent end of eighty-year generational cycles in history. (Blogger Jim Quinn lays it out nicely this week at *The Burning Platform*.) Previous Fourth Turning presidents Lincoln and Franklin Roosevelt took the nation through epic bloodbaths and economic dislocation. Donald Trump in terms of demeanor is no Lincoln and no FDR. But he did raise up those children of his somehow, and that's all we've got to go on for the moment.

THE REDISCOVERY OF MEN

November 28, 2016

This must account, at least in part, for the post-election hysteria among the social justice folk and their mentors at the prog end of politics, especially those bent on suppressing or eliminating men. Of course, it's only been the last year or so that their long-running animus became explicit, their writ against white men in particular. Before, it was all sub rosa, really just a by-product of the campaign to uplift women, people of color, and the many theoretical gender categories vying for supremacy of the moral high ground. Hillary was expected to drive the final wooden stake through masculinity's demonic heart... but something went wrong... and she was disarmed... and now this Cheeto-headed monster in a red necktie is the president-elect. There must have been a clerical error.

Donald Trump was about as far from my sense of the male ideal as anything short of the Golem. His accomplishments in life — developing hotels that look like bowling trophies and producing moronic TV shows — seem as flimsy as the plastic golden heraldry plastered on his casinos. His knowledge of the world appears to be on the level of a fifth grader. He can barely string together two coherent sentences off-teleprompter. I was as astonished as anyone by the disclosure of his "grab them by the pussy" courtship advice to little Billy Bush. In my experience, it seemed a very poor strategy for scoring some action, to say the least. In a better world — perhaps even the America he imagines to have been great once — Donald Trump would be a kind of freak among men, a joke, a parody of masculinity.

But then consider the freak show that American culture has become in our time and it shouldn't be surprising that a cartoon nation has ended up with a cartoon of a man as head of state. In fact, I doubt that there even is any remaining collective idea of what it means to be a man here in terms of the ancient virtues. Honor? Dignity? Patience? Prudence? Fuhgeddaboudit. The cultural memory of all that has been erased. The apotheosis of Trump may remind a few people of all that has been lost, but we're starting from nearly zero in the recovery of it.

Consider also the caliber of the male persons who stepped into the arena last spring when the election spectacle kicked off. Only Bernie Sanders came close to representing honorable manhood — in the form of your irascible old "socialist" uncle from Brooklyn — while the rest of them acted like Elmer Fudd, Mighty Mouse, and Woody Woodpecker. And then when the primary elections ended, Bernie drove a wooden stake into his own heart in a bizarre act of political hara-kiri.

Hillary Clinton's campaign was engineered from the get-go to complete the demolition of American manhood in what turned out to be a reckless miscalculation. "I'm with her (and against him)." Too much in recent American history has been against "him" and a great many of the hims out there began to notice that they were being squeezed out of the nation's life like watermelon seeds. Most particularly, men were no longer considered necessary in whatever remained of the family unit. This went against the truth of the matter, of course, because nothing has been more harmful to everyday life than the absence of fathers. And this was connected to the secondary calamity of men losing their roles in the workplace — and the loss of self-respect connected with that. So the election awakened some sleeping notion that life was wildly out of balance in America. And being so out of balance, it swung wildly in the other direction.

The corrective to all this awaits a fiery passage through the coming tribulation that is about to start in the realm of money. You can be sure that many of the current popular assumptions about how the world works are about to change. It will present opportunities for men to start acting like men again — for instance, being on the side of the truth instead of reflexive mendacity. Some real men could emerge from the smoldering rubble and begin a from-the-ground-up reassembly of the male spirit. Trump may end up being little more than a broken monument amid the rubble, a sort of golden calf the people constructed in desperation as they sought a way out of the wilderness.

But the blowup in banking and finance could represent a final detonation of manhood, since so much testosterone is sequestered in the dark corners of Wall Street and the money centers like it. And when that happens men might be in disrepute for a thousand years.

THE DEEPENING DEEP STATE

December 5, 2016

One amusing angle on the news media broadside about Russia "hacking" the US election is the failure to mention — or even imagine! — that the US incessantly and continually runs propaganda psyops against every other country in the world. And I'm not even including the venerable, old, out-in-the-open propaganda organs like Voice of America and Radio Free Europe (reminder: the Iron Curtain came down a quarter century ago). Do you suppose that nobody at Langley, or the Pentagon, or the NSA's sprawling 1.5-million-square-foot Utah Data Center is laboring night and day to sow confusion among other societies to push our various agendas?

The main offensive started with *The Washington Post's* publication on November 26 of "The List," a story calling out dozens of blogs and web news sites as purveyors of "fake news" fronting for Russian disinformation forces. The list included Zero Hedge, Naked Capitalism, and David Stockman's blog. There were several whack-job sites mixed in the list for seasoning — The Daily Stormer (Nazis), Endtime.com (evangelical apocalyptic), GalacticConnection (UFO shit). The rest range between tabloid-silly and genuine, valuable news commentary. What else would you expect in a society with an internet *and* a completely incoherent consensus about reality?

Pretty obviously, the struggle between mainstream news and web news climaxed over the election, with the mainstream overwhelmingly pimping for Hillary, and then having a nervous breakdown when she lost. Desperate to explain the loss, the two leading old-line newspapers, *The New York Times* and *The Washington Post*, ran with the Russia Hacks Election story — because only Satanic intervention could explain the fall of *Ms. It's-My-Turn / I'm-With-Her*. Thus, the story went, Russia hacked the Democratic National Committee (DNC), gave the hacked emails to Wikileaks, and sabotaged not only Hillary herself but the livelihoods of every myrmidon in the American Deep State termite mound, an unforgivable act.

Also interestingly, these newspapers and their handmaidens on TV were far less concerned as to whether the leaked information was true or not — e.g., the Clinton Foundation donors' influence peddling around arms deals made in the

State Department; the DNC's campaign to undermine Bernie Sanders in the primaries; DNC temporary chair (and CNN employee) Donna Brazille conveying debate questions to HRC; the content of HRC's quarter-million-dollar speeches to Wall Street banks. All of that turned out to be true, of course.

Then, a few weeks after the election, the US House of Representatives passed H.R. 6393, the Intelligence Authorization Act for Fiscal Year 2017. Blogger Ronald Thomas West reports:

> *Section 501 calls for the government to "counter active measures*
> *by Russia to exert covert influence ... carried out in coordination*
> *with, or at the behest of, political leaders or the security services of*
> *the Russian Federation and the role of the Russian Federation has*
> *been hidden or not acknowledged publicly."*

The measure has not been passed by the Senate or signed into law yet, and the holiday recess may prevent that. But it is easy to see how it would empower the Deep State to shut down whichever websites it happened to not like. My reference to the Deep State might even imply to some readers that I'm infected by the paranoia virus. But I'm simply talking about the massive "security" and surveillance matrix that has unquestionably expanded since the 9/11 airplane attacks, creating a gigantic NSA superstructure above and beyond the Central Intelligence Agency, the Department of Defense's DIA, and the hoary old FBI.

A little paranoia about the growing fascist behavior of the US government is a useful corrective to trends that citizens ought to be concerned about — for instance, the militarization of police; the outrageous "civil forfeiture" scam that allows police to steal citizens' cash and property without any due process of law; the preferential application of law as seen in the handling of the Clinton Foundation activities and the misconduct of banking executives; the attempt to impose a "cashless society" that would herd all citizens into a financial surveillance hub and eliminate their economic liberty.

These matters are especially crucial as the nation stumbles into the next financial crisis and the Deep State becomes desperate to harvest every nickel it can to rescue itself plus the cast of "systemically important" (Too Big to Fail) banks and related institutions like Fannie Mae and Freddie Mac, which are about to *once again* be left holding colossal bags of worthless nonperforming mortgages, not to mention the pension funds and insurance companies that will also founder in the Great Unwind that is likely to commence as Trump hangs his golden logo over the White House portico.

❧ 2017 ❧

HE IS RISEN: BUT FOR HOW LONG?

January 23, 2017

If the first forty-eight hours are any measure of the alleged Trumptopia-to-come, the leading man in this national melodrama appears to be *meshuga*. A more charitable view might be that his behavior does not comport with the job description: president. If he keeps it up, I stick to my call that we will see him removed by extraordinary action within a few months. It might be a lawful continuity-of-government procedure according to the Twenty-fifth Amendment — various high officials declaring him "incapacited" — or it might be a straight-up old school coup d'état ("You're fired").

I believe the trigger for that may be an overwhelming financial crisis in the early second quarter of the year. In, the first case, under Section 4 of the Twenty-fifth Amendment, it works like this:

> *Whenever the Vice President and a majority of either the principal officers of the executive departments or of such other body as Congress may by law provide, transmit to the President pro tempore of the Senate and the Speaker of the House of Representatives their written declaration that the President is unable to discharge the powers and duties of his office, the Vice President shall immediately assume the powers and duties of the office as Acting President.*

Or else, it will be an orchestrated cabal of military and intelligence officers — not necessarily evil men — who fear for the safety of the nation with the aforesaid *meshuganer* in the White House, who is summarily arrested, sequestered, and replaced by an "acting president," pending a call for an extraordinary new election to replace him by democratic means. I'm not promoting this scenario as necessarily desirable, but that's how I think it will go down. It will be a sad moment in this country's history, worse than the shock of John Kennedy's assassination, which happened against the background of an economically stable Republic. History is perverse and life is tragic. And shit happens.

Returning to the first forty-eight hours of the new regime, first the ceremony itself: there was, to my mind, the disturbing sight of Donald Trump, deep in the Capitol in the grim runway leading out onto the inaugural dais. He lumbered along, so conspicuously alone between the praetorian ranks front and back, overcoat open, that long red slash of necktie dangling ominously, with a mad gleam in his eyes like an old bull being led out to a sacrificial altar. His speech to the multitudes was not exactly what had once passed for presidential oratory. It was not an "address." It was blunt, direct, unadorned, and simple, a warning to the assembled luminaries meant to prepare them for disempowerment. Surely it was received by many as a threat.

Indeed an awful lot of official behavior has to change if this country expects to carry on as a civilized polity, and Trump's plain statement was at face value consistent with that idea. But the disassembly of such a vast matrix of rackets is unlikely to be managed without generating a lot of dangerous friction. Such a tall order would require, at least, some finesse. Virtually all the powers of the Deep State are arrayed against him, and he can't resist taunting them, a dangerous game. Despite the show of an orderly transition, a state of war exists between them. Anyway, given Trump's cabinet appointments, his "swamp draining" campaign looks like one set of rackets is due to be replaced by a new and perhaps worse set.

Trump was correct that the ruins of industry stand like tombstones on the landscape. The reality may be that an industrial economy is a one-shot deal. When it's gone, it's over. Even assuming the money exists to rebuild the factories of the twentieth century, how would things be produced in them? By robotics or by brawny men paid $15 an hour? If it's robotics, who will the customers be? If it's low-wage workers, how are they going to pay for the cars and washing machines? If the brawny men are paid $40 an hour, how would we sell our cars and washing machines in foreign markets that pay their workers the equivalent of $1.50 an hour. How can American industry stay afloat with no export market? If we don't let foreign products into the US, how will Americans buy cars that are far more costly to make here than the products we've been getting? There's no indication that Trump and his people have thought through any of this.

Trump can pull out the stops (literally, the regulations) to promote oil production, but he can't alter the declining energy return on investment that is bringing down the curtain on industrial society. In fact, pumping more oil now at all costs will only hasten the decline of affordable oil. His oft-stated wish to simply "take" the oil from Middle Eastern countries would probably lead to sabotage of their oil infrastructure and the cruel death of millions. He would do better to prepare Americans for the project of de-suburbanizing the nation, but I doubt that the concept has ever entered his mind.

The problems with Obamacare, and so-called health care generally, are burdened with so many layers of arrant racketeering that the system may only be fixable if it is destroyed in its current form — the overgrown centralized hospitals, the overpaid insurance and hospital executives, the sore-beset physicians carrying six-figure college-and-med-school loans, the incomprehensible and extortionate pricing system for care, the cruel and insulting bureaucratic barriers to obtain care, the disgraceful behavior of the pharmaceutical companies all add up to something no less than a colossal hostage racket, robbing and swindling people at their most vulnerable. So far, nobody has advanced a coherent plan for changing it. Loosing the Department of Justice to prosecute the medical racketeers directly would be a good start. Overcharging and defrauding sick people ought to be a criminal act. But don't expect that to happen in a culture where anything goes and nothing matters. A financial crisis could be the trigger for ending the massive medical grift machine. Then what? Back to locally organized clinic-scale medicine . . . if we should be so lucky.

Saturday afternoon, Trump paid a call at CIA headquarters, ostensibly to begin mending fences with what may be his domestic archenemies. What did he do? He peeved and pouted about press reports of the lowish attendance at his swearing in. Maximum *meshuga*. I'm surprised that some veteran of the Company's Suriname outpost didn't take him out with a blowgun dart garnished with the toxic secretions of tree frogs.

Do you suppose Trump is going to improve? That was the hope after the election: that he'd take on some POTUS polish. No, what you see is what you get. I can only imagine that what's going on behind the scenes in various halls of power would make a Matt Damon *Bourne* movie look like a sensitivity training session — grave professional men and women on all fours with their hair on fire howling into the acoustical ceiling tiles.

Don't forget that it was the dismal failure of Democratic "progressive" politics that gave us Trump. His infantile lies and foolish tweets were made possible by a mendacious political culture that excuses illegal immigrants as "the undocumented," refuses to identify radical Islamic terror by name, shuts down free speech on campus, made Michael Brown of Ferguson a secular saint, claims that there's no biological basis for gender, and allowed Wall Street to pound the American middle class down a rat hole like so much sand.

You think this is the dark night of the national soul? The sun went down only a few minutes ago and it's a long hard slog to daybreak.

FUROR TIME

January 30, 2017

It's only taken a week for President Trump to give the body politic an immigration enema. The aim, perhaps, was to flush out a set of bad ideas that Barack Obama had managed over eight years to instate as "normal." Namely, that it's unnecessary to enforce the immigration laws, or cruel and unusual to do so, or that national borders are a barbarous anachronism, or that federal laws are optional in certain self-selected jurisdictions.

But Trump's staff sure fucked up the details carrying out his refugee and immigration ban, most particularly detaining people with green cards and those already granted visas. The blunder provoked an impressive blowback of airport protests, and finally a stay from a federal judge, which muddied the legality of Trump's executive order — all in all, a tactical stumble for Prez DT, who apparently omitted to consult with an array of government agencies and their lawyers before issuing the decree at close of business Friday. For the record, I'm down with the complaint that Saudi Arabia, Pakistan, Egypt, and Afghanistan were left off the no-come list, since those lands produce more radical Islamic maniacs than anywhere else.

The reader by now probably detects my ambivalent feelings in this bundle of issues and grievances, so let me try to clarify my basic positions: I think borders matter and they need to be protected. I think our immigration law enforcement under Obama has been deeply dishonest and damaging to our politics in ways that go far beyond the question of who gets to come here. I believe we are under no obligation to take in everybody and anybody who wants to move here. I believe we need an official time-out from the high-volume immigration of recent decades. I believe we have good reasons to be picky about who we let in.

The most dishonest and damaging trope of recent years is the widely accepted idea on the Left that illegal immigrants are merely "undocumented" — as if they were the hapless victims of some clerical error made by the government and therefore deserving of a pass. Language matters. The acceptance and repetition of this lie has in effect given permission to the Left to lie whenever it suits their purposes about all kinds of things, for instance, the delusion that Russia stole the election from Hillary Clinton and that Radical Islam doesn't pose a threat to Western values (or even exist). And it is certainly true that they are assisted by legacy media giants such as *The New York Times*, *The Washington Post*, and *NPR*. The *Times*, especially, is keen to provoke a national crisis that might unseat Trump, by simply declaring it so in a three-column headline.

IMMIGRATION BAN PROVOKES CRISIS

'This Is Not About Religion,' Trump Says of Order

By PETER BAKER

• President Trump's Friday directive closing the nation to refugees and people from certain predominantly Muslim countries provoked a crisis just days into his administration.

• The White House reversed a part of the order, allowing people from banned nations who hold green cards to return to the United States.

• Mr. Trump, criticized by some Republican and world leaders, defended the order as not a ban on Muslims but about "terror and keeping our country safe."

■ 2698 Comments

THE DAILY 360

00:47
Protesting the Ban

Video by TIM CHAFFEE, BRITTANY GREESON, MAUREEN TOWEY and JIM WILSON. Photo by Yana Paskova for The New York Times. Technology by Samsung.

Protests continued in response to Mr. Trump's executive order about immigration. See the signs and hear the chants in New York, Detroit and San Francisco.

The furor seemed rather out of proportion to the people inconvenienced by Trump's administrative blundering: about 300 green card holders out of 300,000 travelers admitted over the weekend — even after the White House walked back its green card miscue on Sunday. And it gives the impression even to someone who is allergic to conspiracy theory (yours truly) that some organizing principle is behind it. That principle may be the deep neurosis of the Dem/Prog Left reduced to virtue signaling in their out-of-power echo chamber. Having no coherent ideas about the immigration issue besides resistance to it, they offer only sentimental narratives:

tears on the Statue of Liberty, "dreamers," sanctuary cities, nation-of-open-arms, we're-all-children-of-immigrants, and anyway North America was stolen from the Indians. The hysteria is impressive, as if the Left has come down with ergot poisoning, seeing witches (racists, homophobes, misogynists, white privilege villains, and Russians) behind every juniper shrub in the land.

I'd go as far to say that this neurosis derives from the general psychological boundary problems of the current Dem/Prog ethos. Their zeal to erase categories has resulted in lost categories of thinking — it's all one big soup of victimization out there now and everybody better rush to cash in their victim brownie points while they still can — or as long as Senator Chuck Schumer can keep the crocodile tears flowing. From my vantage, this country would actually benefit from having firmer categories of thinking and certainly firmer categories of behavior.

What really irks the Left is any defense of Western civilization, especially in something so concrete as demographics. This defensive impulse has been deeply suppressed in the recent political life of Europe and America. On the university campuses, it's become the equivalent of original sin. Donald Trump turned out to be a peculiar choice to lead a turnaround from all this, and his oafishness may eventually deter an effort to restore something like a self-respecting common culture. But the turnaround is coming to Europe, too, this year in a set of national elections. Expect more civil strife as the battle is joined.

Fumbling Toward Collapse

February 20, 2017

In all the smoke and fog emitted by Trump and his adversaries, it must be hard to make out the actual issues dogging this society and, even when you can, to find a coherent position on them. This was nicely illustrated in Paul Krugman's fatuous column in Monday's *New York Times*, "On Economic Arrogance" — the title describes Krugman's own attitude to a T.

In it, Krugman attempts to account for the no-growth economy by marshaling the stock-in-trade legerdemain of academic economics: productivity, demographics, and labor metrics. Krugman actually knows zip about what afflicts us in the present disposition of things, namely the falling energy-return-on-energy-investment in the oil industry, which is approaching the point where the immense activity of getting oil out of the ground won't be worth the cost and trouble of doing it. And since most of the things we do and produce in this economy are based on cheap oil — with no reality-based prospect of replacing it with so-called renewables or as yet undiscovered energy rescue remedies — we can't generate enough wealth to maintain anything close to our assumed standard of living. We can't even generate enough wealth to pay the interest on the debt we've racked up in order to hide our growing energy predicament. And that, in a nutshell, is what will blow up the financial system. And when that department of the economy goes the rest will follow.

So the real issue hidden in plain sight is how America — indeed, all the so-called developed nations — is going to navigate to a stepped-down mode of living, without slip-sliding all the way into a dark age, or something worse. By the way, the ole Maestro, Alan Greenspan, also chimed in on the "productivity" question last week to equally specious effect in a *Business Insider* article. None of these celebrated Grand Viziers knows what the fuck he's talking about, and a nation depending on their guidance will find itself lost in a hall of mirrors with the lights off.

So on one side you have Trump and his trumpets and trumpistas heralding the return of "greatness" (i.e., a booming industrial economy of happy men with lunch boxes), which is not going to happen; and on the other side you have a claque of clueless technocrats who actually believe they can "solve" the productivity problem with measures that really only boil down to different kinds of accounting fraud.

You also have an American public, and a mass media, who do not question the premise of a massive "infrastructure" spending project to reboot the foundering economy. If you ask what they mean by that, you will learn that they uniformly see rebuilding our highways, bridges, tunnels, and airports. Some rightly suspect that the money for that is not there — or can only be summoned with more accounting fraud (borrowing from our future). But on the whole, most adults of all political stripes in this country think we can and should do this, that it would be *a good thing*.

And what is this infrastructure reboot in the service of? A living arrangement with no future. A matrix of extreme car dependency that has zero chance of continuing another decade. More Walmarts, Targets, Taco Bells, muffler shops, McHousing subdivisions, and other accoutrement of our fast-zombifying mode of existence? Isn't it obvious, even if you never heard of, or don't understand, the oil quandary, that we have shot our wad with all this? That we have to start down a different path if we intend to remain human?

It's not hard to describe that waiting world, which I've done in a bunch of recent books. We're going there whether we like it or not. But we can make the journey to it easier or harsher depending on how much we drag our heels getting on with the job.

History is pretty unforgiving. Right now, the dynamic I describe is propelling us toward a difficult reckoning, which is very likely to manifest this spring as the political ineptitude of Trump, and the antipathy of his enemies, leaves us in a constitutional maelstrom at the very moment when the financial system comes unglued. Look for the debt ceiling debate and another Federal Reserve interest rate hike to set off the latter. There may be yet another converging layer of tribulation when we start blaming all our problems on Russia, China, Mexico, or some other patsy nation. It's already obvious that we can depend on the Deep State to rev that up.

A HOLE IN THE HEAD

February 27, 2017

We need a new civil war like we need a hole in the head. But that's just it: America has a hole in its head. It's the place formerly known as the Center. It didn't hold. It was the place where people of differing views could rely on each other to behave reasonably around a touchstone called the National Interest. That abandoned place is now cordoned off, a Chernobyl of the mind, where figures on each side of the political margin fear to even sojourn, let alone occupy, lest they go radioactive.

Anyway, the old parties at each side of the political transect are melting down in equivalent fugues of delusion, rage, and impotence — as predicted here through the election year of 2016. They can't make anything good happen in the National Interest. They can't control the runaway rackets that they engineered in legislation, policy, and practice under the dominion of each party, by turns, going back to Lyndon B. Johnson, and so they have driven themselves and each other insane.

Trump and Hillary perfectly embodied the climactic stage of each party before their final mutual sprint to collapse. Both had more than a tinge of the psychopath. Trump is the bluff that the Republicans called on themselves, having jettisoned anything identifiable as coherent principles translatable to useful action. Hillary was an American Lady Macbeth attempting to pull off the ultimate inside job by any means necessary, her wickedness so plain to see that even the voters picked up on it. These two are the old parties' revenge on each other, and on themselves, for decades of bad choices and bad faith.

The anti-intellectual Trump is, for the Right, the answer to the Intellectual Yet Idiots (IYIs) that Nassim Taleb has so ably identified as infesting the Left. It is a good guess that President Trump has not read a book since high school, and perhaps never in his entire life. But are you not amazed at how the IYIs of the Left have savaged the life of the mind on campus and out in the other precincts of culture where free inquiry once flourished? From the craven college presidents who pretend that race-segregated "safe spaces" represent "inclusiveness," to *The New York Times* editors who pretend in headlines that illegal immigrants have done nothing illegal, the mendacity is awesome.

Something like this has happened before in US history and it may be cyclical. The former Princeton University professor and president Woodrow Wilson dragged America into the First World War, which killed over 53,000 Americans (as many as Vietnam) in only eighteen months. He promulgated the Red Scare, a bit of hysteria not unlike the Race and Gender Phobia Accusation Fest on the Left today. Professor Wilson was also responsible for creating the Federal Reserve and all the mischief it has entailed, especially the loss of over 90 percent of the dollar's value since 1913. Wilson, the perfect IYI of that day.

The reaction to Wilson was Warren Gamaliel Harding, the hard-drinking, card-playing Ohio Main Street boob picked in the notorious "smoke-filled room" of the 1920 GOP convention. He invoked a return to "normalcy," which was not even a word (try *normality*), and was laughed at as we now laugh at Trump for his idiotic utterances such as "win bigly" (or is that big league?). Harding is also known for confessing in a letter: "I am not fit for this office and should never have been here." Yet, in his brief term (died in office, 1923), Harding navigated the country successfully through a fierce post–World War One depression simply by not resorting to government intervention.

Something like the same dynamic returned in 1952 when General Eisenhower took over from Harry Truman and the defeated Democratic nominee Adlai Stevenson quipped, "The New Dealers have been replaced by the car dealers." Ha! If he only knew! After all, who was on board as Ike's veep? None other than Tricky Dick Nixon, soon to be cast as America's quintessential used car salesman.

Well, those were the days, and those days are over. So much has gone wrong here in the past thirty years and the game of *salugi* being played by the Dems and the GOP is not helping any of it. And that is why the two parties are heading toward extinction. We're in the phase of intraparty factional conflict for now. Each party has its own preliminary civil war going on. The election of Obama-era labor secretary and party hack Tom Perez as DNC chair yesterday has set the Bernie Sanders Prog troops into paroxysms of animadversion. They're calling out all up and down the Twitterverse for a new party of their own. Trump faces his own mutineers on the Right, and not just the two cheerleaders for World War Three, John McCain and Lindsey Graham. Coming out of the Conservative CPAC meeting last week, just about his whole agenda was written off as (*cough cough*) politically impractical by the poobahs in attendance: reform and replacement of the Affordable Care Act, tax reform, the promised massive infrastructure-building stimulus orgy, the border wall, the trade blockages.

Anon, comes the expiration of the current debt ceiling, at around $20 trillion, in mid-March. Do you imagine that the two parties warring with each other in Congress will be able to come to some resolution over that? Fuhgeddaboudit. The Democrats have every incentive to let President Trump stew in this fatal brine like a Delancey Street corned beef. What it means, of course, is that the US Treasury runs out of ready cash in midsummer and some invoices just don't get paid, maybe even some bigly ones like Social Security checks and Medicare bills. Won't that be a spectacle? That's where Trump becomes a political quadriplegic and the voters start jumping off the dying parties like fleas off of two dead dogs.

By then, plenty of other mischief will be afoot in the world, including the fractious outcome of elections in France and the Netherlands, with the European Union spinning into its own event horizon, and currency instability like the world has never seen before. Enjoy the remaining weeks of normality.

THE PAUSE THAT REFRESHES

March 13, 2017

Let's take a breather from more consequential money matters at hand midweek to consider the tending moods of our time and place — while a blizzard howls outside the window, and nervous Federal Reserve officials pace the grim halls of the Eccles Building.

It is clear by now that we have four corners of American politics these days: the utterly lost and delusional Democratic Party; the feckless Republicans; the permanent Deep State of bureaucratic foot soldiers and errand boys; and Trump, the Golem King of the Coming Greatness. Wherefore, and what the fuck, you might ask.

The Democrats reduced themselves to a gang of sadistic neo-Maoists seeking to eradicate anything that resembles free expression across the land in the name of social justice. Coercion has been their coin of the realm, and especially in the realm of ideas where "diversity" means stepping on your opponent's neck until he pretends to agree with your Newspeak brand of grad school neologisms and "inclusion" means welcome if you're just like us. I say Maoists because just like Mao's Red Guard of rampaging students in 1966, their mission is to "correct" the thinking of those who might dare to oppose the established leader. Only in this case, that established leader happened to lose the sure-thing election and the party finds itself unbelievably out of power and suddenly purposeless, like a termite mound without a queen, the workers and soldiers fleeing the power center in a hysteria of lost identity.

They regrouped briefly after the election debacle to fight an imaginary adversary, Russia, the phantom ghost-bear, who supposedly stepped on their termite mound and killed the queen, but, strangely, no actual evidence was ever found of the ghost-bear's pawprint. And ever since that fact was starkly revealed by former NSA chief James Clapper on NBC's *Meet the Press*, the Russia hallucination has vanished from page one of the party's media outlets — though, in an interesting last gasp of striving correctitude, Monday's *New York Times* features a front page story detailing Georgetown University's hateful traffic in the slave trade two centuries ago. That should suffice to shut the wicked place down once and for all!

The Republican Party, to avoid going full Whig and sliding down the laundry chute of history, made a bad deal for a new figurehead who is liable to make the party look way worse than it could ever accomplish on its own. This golden boy has dragged the party poobahs to the put-up-or-shut-up room of our nation's capital — the place that Senator Rand Paul was searching high and low for last week — where they are charged with reforming the country's health care racket. It looks for now like they will cook up a toxic farrago of new giveaways to their patrons in the hospital cartel, the insurance companies, and pharma. The voting public already detects the odor of thirty-day-old carp in the first tastings of the dish. There's a fair chance that the recipe will end up getting tossed in the Capitol dumpster, and that in itself could finish the party because there's little question that the current system known as Obamacare or the Affordable Care Act (not) is something like a fatal tumor in the nation's craw. If the effort to fix that fails, the Republicans complete their transformation from the Party of No to the Party of Just Go.

The Deep State seems eager to sever its connections to both putrifying parties and attempt to run the groaning colossus of government ad hoc if necessary. The military and intel chains of command remain intact, along with their "assets," and one can easily imagine anxious meetings of scenario running in the back rooms of the Pentagon and the Langley frat house. *What if...?* "What if we just smoke the fucker?" an old agency warrior remarks offhand, and the roomful of colleagues pause in their cogitations to weigh the notion. Some of them nod and make a moue, and others just cough into their sleeves. One young striver in the back mentions "a little something" they've been working on that involves hairspray and a neurotoxin derived from the Gaboon viper....

And then there is our president himself: Donald J. Trump, in the awesome solitude of his Twitterverse dome. A strange destiny brought him to his place in history thus far, and many of us surveying the scene lo these many months kind of get it: the festering disgust with the other three corners of American power; the dismal fall of the middle class into a purgatory of repossession, idleness, opiates, and tattoos; the accelerating purposelessness of the dwindling consumer economy; the matrix of racketeering that systematically drains everyone's financial mojo while adding humiliation to the shoddy service it delivers; the pointless, costly wars in faraway places and their conversion into permanent shitholes; the disgraceful disfigurement of a once grand national landscape into a wilderness of dying malls and freeway ramps.

So, onto the scene strides The Donald, a giant among the squalling midgets of our time, with his promise to bigly re-greatify this suffering land. I suppose he means well in his torturous way. So did a lot of other figures in history who found themselves at the top: Idi Amin, Uncle Joe Stalin, Vlad the Impaler, King Leopold of Belgium, Adolf You-Know-Who, Pol Pot. The list of the well meaning is very long.

THE CURSE OF
THE THINKING CLASS

March 27, 2017

Let's suppose there really is such a thing as the Thinking Class in this country, if it's not too politically incorrect to say so — since it implies that there is another class, perhaps larger, that operates only on some limbic lizard-brain level of impulse and emotion. Personally, I believe there is such a Thinking Class, or at least I have dim memories of something like it.

The far-fetched phenomenon of Trumpism has sent that bunch on a journey to a strange land of the intellect, a place like the lost island of Kong, where one monster after another rises out of the swampy murk to threaten the frail human adventurers. No one back home would believe the things they're tangling with: giant spiders, reptiles the size of front-end loaders, malevolent aborigines! Will any of the delicate humans survive or make it back home?

This is the feeling I get listening to arguments in the public arena these days, but especially from the quarters formerly identified as left of center, especially the faction organized around the Democratic Party, which I aligned with long ago (alas, no more). The main question seems to be: who is responsible for all the unrest in this land? Their answer since halfway back in 2016: the Russians.

I'm not comfortable with this hypothesis. Russia has a GDP smaller than Texas. If it is able to project so much influence over what happens in the USA, it must have some supernatural mojo-of-the-mind — and perhaps it does — but it raises the question of motive. What might Russia realistically get from the USA if Vladimir Putin was the master hypnotist that Democrats make him out to be?

Do we suppose Putin wants more living space for Russia's people? Hmmmm. Russia's population these days, around 145 million, is less than half the USA's and it's rattling around in the geographically largest nation in the world. Do they want our oil? Maybe, but Russia being the world's top oil producer suggests it has already got its hands full with its own operation. Does it want Hollywood? The video game industry? The US porn empire? Do the Russians covet our Chick-fil-A chains and Waffle Houses? Our tattoo artists? Would they like to induce the Kardashians to live in Moscow? Is it NASCAR they're really after?

My hypothesis is that Russia would most of all like to be left alone. Watching NATO move tanks and German troops into Lithuania in January probably makes the Russians nervous, and no doubt that is the very objective of the NATO move — but let's not forget that most of all NATO is an arm of American foreign policy. If there are any remnants of the American Thinking Class left at the State Department, they might recall that Russia lost 20 million people in the dustup known as the Second World War against whom...? Oh, Germany.

Altogether last January the US military deployed thousands of soldiers and heavy weaponry to Poland, the Baltic states, and southeastern Europe in its biggest buildup since the Cold War (Reuters). As they used to say in old film noir Bogart movies: what's the big idea? The State Department would say the big idea was cautioning Russia against annexing any more neighboring states or regions, as it did in Crimea a few years back. Apparently the public is supposed to forget that the State Department sponsored and engineered the conversion of Ukraine into a failed state, prompting Russia to retain its naval bases in Crimea, its only warm-water outlet to the world's oceans. Ask yourself: if for some reason the state of Virginia were plunged into anarchy by foreign mischief, do you think the US would batten down our naval station in Norfolk?

I think the sad truth of the American predicament these days, including the ascension of a narcissistic ninny to the White House, is that we're responsible for our own problems due, most of all, to the destruction of boundaries in virtually all realms of American behavior from the things we put in our bodies to the ridiculous ways that we occupy our waking hours at the expense of getting our own house in order. I would like to join the party dedicated to getting our house in order. Anybody else out there feel that way?

MUSKTOPIA HERE WE COME!

April 3, 2017

It ought to be sign of just how delusional the nation is these days that Elon Musk of Tesla and Space X is taken seriously. Musk continues to dangle his fantasy of travel to Mars before a country that can barely get its shit together on planet Earth, and the Tesla car represents one of the main reasons for it — namely, that we'll do anything to preserve, maintain, and defend our addiction to incessant and pointless motoring (and nothing to devise a saner living arrangement).

Even people with Ivy League educations believe that the electric car is a "solution" to our basic economic quandary, which is to keep all the accessories and furnishings of suburbia running at all costs in the face of problems with fossil fuels, especially climate change. First, understand how the Tesla car and electric motoring are bound up in our culture of *virtue signaling*, the main motivational feature of political correctness. Virtue signaling is a status acquisition racket. In this case, you get social brownie points for indicating that you're onboard with "clean energy," you're "green," "an environmentalist," "Earth-friendly." Ordinary schmoes can drive a Prius for their brownie points. But the Tesla driver gets all that and much more: the envy of the Prius drivers!

This is all horseshit, of course, because there's nothing green or Earth-friendly about Tesla cars, or electric cars in general. Evidently, many Americans think these cars run on batteries. No they don't. Not really. The battery is just a storage unit for electricity that comes from power plants that burn something, or from hydroelectric installations like Hoover Dam, with its problems of declining reservoir levels and aging rebar concrete construction. A lot of what gets burned for electric power is coal. Connect the dots. Also consider the *embedded energy* that it takes to just manufacture the cars. That had to come from somewhere, too.

The Silicon Valley executive who drives a Tesla gets to feel good about him/her/zheself without doing anything to change him/her/zhe's way of life. All it requires is the $101,500 entry price for the cheapest model. For many Silicon Valley execs, this might be walking-around money. For the masses of flyover

Deplorables that's just another impossible dream in a growing list of dissolving comforts and conveniences.

In fact, the mass motoring paradigm in the USA is already failing not on the basis of what kind of fuel the car runs on but on the financing end. Americans are used to buying cars on installment loans and, as the middle-class implosion continues, there are fewer and fewer Americans who qualify to borrow. The regular car industry (gasoline branch) has been trying to work around this reality for years by enabling sketchier loans for ever sketchier customers — like, seven years for a used car. The borrower in such a deal is sure to be "underwater" with collateral (the car) that is close to worthless well before the loan can be extinguished. We're beginning to see the fruits of this racket just now, as these longer-termed loans start to age out. On top of that, a lot of these janky loans were bundled into tradable securities just like the janky mortgage loans that set off the banking fiasco of 2008. Wait for that to blow.

What much of America refuses to consider in the face of all this is that there's another way to inhabit the landscape: walkable neighborhoods, towns, and cities with some kind of public transit. Some millennials gravitate to places designed along these lines because they grew up in the burbs and they know full well the social nullity induced there. But the rest of America is still committed to *the greatest misallocation of resources in the history of the world*: suburban living. And tragically, of course, we're kind of stuck with all that "infrastructure" for daily life. It's already built out! Part of Donald Trump's appeal was his promise to keep its furnishings in working order.

All of this remains to be sorted out. The political disorder currently roiling America is there because the contradictions in our national life have become so starkly obvious, and the first thing to crack is the political consensus that allows business as usual to keep chugging along. The political turmoil will only accelerate the accompanying economic turmoil that drives it in a self-reinforcing feedback loop. That dynamic has a long way to go before any of these issues get resolved satisfactorily.

What Could Go Wrong?

April 14, 2017

"Things fall apart; the center cannot hold." Yeats wrote. The funny thing is, we didn't seem to miss the center all that much after it was gone. America is perfectly satisfied hunkering down at the margins these days. Especially the margins of thinking.

One thing that used to occupy the center was public discussion, debate, and argumentation. Now and again, it featured a coherent exchange of ideas. These days, the main political factions are sunk in hysteria of one kind or another. Their primitive promptings hardly add up to ideas but rather to limbic spasms of fear and rage. And then there is the shadow partner of the two parties called the Deep State, led by the quaintly dubbed "intelligence community." These birds, many of them lifers, are dedicated to making the public discussion of anything as incoherent as possible so as to prevent any change in policy that might curtail the growth of the Deep State, a sort of cancer of the body politic.

Case in point, the recent Syrian aerial gas attack in the town of Khan Sheikhoun. Elected officials were all over the cable networks selling the NSA's story that Syrian president Bashar Assad bombed women and children with sarin gas three days after State Department declared that it had a new policy of letting Assad remain in power after decades of sedulously scheming to shove him out. That might have led to the end of the six-year-long Syrian civil war, which Assad seemed to be winning, finally — with Russian assistance.

But instead the incident has led to new official calls to shove Assad out . . . to be replaced by what? Nobody knows. Because the US Deep State thrives when chaos reigns in foreign lands. So much the better for their looting operations, such as the theft of Libya's 141-ton gold reserves in 2011. And if not looting hard assets directly, the Deep State benefits when its many black box vendors — the private security armies, materials suppliers, arms sellers — are raking in the accounts receivable.

The fascinating part of the Syrian gas bombing story is how easily the public swallowed it. Those elected congressmen and senators infesting the cable stations told the public that the intelligence community "issued a consensus report" that the Syrian air force has dropped sarin gas bombs on the hapless civilians. Nobody offered any actual evidence that this was so. These days, mere assertions rule.

That's how we roll now. I'm still waiting to see some evidence that Trump's campaign "colluded with Russia" to spin the election toward him. Those claims, too, were put out as "a consensus analysis" by the intelligence community. And then in March, months after the disputed election, just-retired NSA director James Clapper told NBC's *Meet the Press* that his agency had no evidence of "Russian collusion" with the Trump forces. That was only a few weeks ago.

For the moment, it may benefit casual observers to adopt the most cynical attitude possible about the "consensus reports" that emanate from these myriad agencies. What it all finally seems to represent is the snowballing incompetence, venality, mendacity, and impotence of the US government in general, in all its layers and branches.

Hence, the idiotic PR stunt the other day of dropping the so-called Mother of All Bombs (MOAB) on some backwater of the once-and-future Mother of All Backwaters, Afghanistan. Did you happen to see a photo of that Mother Bomb? It looked bigger than any airplane that might be assigned to carry it, a cartoon of a bomb, more ridiculous than anything you might see in a Vin Diesel movie. It even had the acronym *MOAB* plastered on its fuselage in case anyone might confuse it with a canister of Roundup. I wonder what it cost. Got to be more than the $1 million plus for a Tomahawk missile. You could probably run the whole Medicaid system of Alabama on what one MOAB invoice comes in at.

Meanwhile, the navy's Aircraft Carrier Strike Group 1 steams off the waters of North Korea and we lately have word that the US might just try to preemptively take out Kim Jong-un's nuclear bomb assembly site. There's a tang of excitement in the air (and on the cable channels). America's back in the game, proving that when all else fails we can be depended on at least to blow some shit up. What could go wrong?

Paris Afterparty

May 8, 2017

First mistake: Emmanuel Macron's handlers played Beethoven's "Ode to Joy" instead of the French national anthem at the winner's election rally. Well, at least they didn't play "Deutschland Über Alles." The tensions in the Euroland situation remain: the 20 percent–plus youth unemployment, the papered-over insolvency of the European banks, and the implacable contraction of economic activity, especially at the southern rim of the EU.

The clash of civilizations brought on by the EU's self-induced refugee glut still hangs over the continent like a hijab. That there was no Islamic terror violence around the election should not be reassuring. The interests of the jihadists probably lie in the continued squishiness of the status quo, with its sentimental multiculture fantasies — *can't we all just get along*? — so En Marche was their best bet. Le Pen might have pushed back hard. Macron looks to bathe France's Islamic antagonists in a nutrient-medium of Hollandaise lite.

The sclerosis of Europe is assured for now. But events are in charge, not elected officials so much, and Europe's economic fate may be determined by forces far away and beyond its power to control, namely in China, where the phony-baloney banking system is likely to be the first to implode in a global daisy chain of financially uncontrolled demolition. Much of that depends on the continuing stability of currencies.

The trouble is they are all pegged to fatally unrealistic expectations of economic expansion. Without it, the repayment of interest on monumental outstanding debt becomes an impossibility. And the game of issuing more new debt to pay the interest on the old debt completely falls apart. Once again, the dynamic relationship between real capital creation and the quandaries of the oil industry lurks behind these failures of economy. In a crisis of debt repayment, governments will not know what else to do except "print" more money, and this time they are liable to destroy faith in the value of "money" the world over.

I put "money" in quotation marks because the dollars, euros, yuan, and yen are worth only what people believe them to be, subject to measurement against increasingly fictional indexes of value, such as interest rates, stock and bond markets, government-issued employment and GDP stats, and other benchmarks so egregiously gamed by the issuing authorities that ole Karl Marx's hoary warning finally comes to pass and *everything solid melts into air*.

For the record, I'm not in favor of political chaos and economic anarchy, but that seems to be the only route that Deep Staters 'round the world want to go down. The convenient protocols of finance in the industrial era that allowed routine borrowing from the future to get today's enterprise up and running have lost their mojo. The short and practical theory of history applies to this: *things happen because they seem like a good idea at the time*.

Revolving credit seemed like a good idea through the twentieth century, and it sure worked to build an economic matrix based on cheap energy, which is, alas, no more. What remains is the wishful pretense that the old familiar protocols can still work their magic. The disappointment will be epic, and the result next time may be political figures even worse than Le Pen and Trump. Consider, though, that what you take for the drumbeat of nationalism is actually just a stair step down on a much-longer journey out of the globally financialized economy. Because the ultimate destination down this stairway is a form of local autarky that the current mandarins of the status quo can't even imagine.

That journey has already begun, though neither the public nor its elected leaders have begun to apprehend it. The first spark of recognition will come in the months ahead when the current cover story on markets, "money," and growth falls away and political leaders can only stand by in wonder and nausea that the world has the impertinence to change without their permission.

A Monster Eating the Nation

May 19, 2017

Is there any question now that the Deep State is preparing to expel President Donald Trump from the body politic like a necrotic organ? The Golden Golem of Greatness has floundered pretty badly on the job, it's true, but his mighty adversaries in the highly politicized federal agencies want him to fail spectacularly, and fast, and they have a lot of help from the *NY Times* / *WashPo* / CNN axis of hysteria, as well as such slippery swamp creatures as Lindsey Graham.

There are more problematic layers in this matter than in a Moldavian wedding cake. America has been functionally ungovernable for quite a while, well before Trump arrived on the scene. His predecessor managed to misdirect the nation's attention from the cumulative dysfunction with sheer charm and supernatural placidity — NoDrama Obama. But there were a few important things he could have accomplished as chief exec, such as directing his attorney general to prosecute Wall Street crime (or fire the attorney general and replace him with someone willing to do the job). He could have broken up the giant TBTF banks. He could have aggressively sponsored legislation to overcome the *Citizens United* SCOTUS decision (unlimited corporate money in politics) by redefining corporate "citizenship." Stuff like that. But he let it slide, and the nation slid with him down a greasy chute of political collapse.

Which we find embodied in Trump, a sort of tragicomic figure who manages to compound all of his other weaknesses of character with a childish impulsiveness that scares folks. It is debatable whether he has simply been rendered incompetent by the afflictions heaped on by his adversaries, or if he is just plain incompetent in, say, the Twenty-fifth Amendment way. I think we'll find out soon enough, because impeachment is a very long and arduous path out of this dark place.

The most curious feature of the current crisis, of course, is the idiotic Russia story that has been the fulcrum for levering Trump out of the White House. This was especially funny the past week with the episode involving Russian Foreign Minister Lavrov and Ambassador Kislyak conferring with Trump in the White

House about aviation security around the Middle East. The media and the Lindsey Graham wing of the Deep State acted as if Trump had entertained Focalor and Vepar, the Dukes of Hell, in the Oval Office.

Why do you suppose nations employ foreign ministers and ambassadors, if not to conduct conversations at the highest level with other national leaders? And might these conversations include matters of great sensitivity, that is, classified information? If you doubt that then you have no understanding of geopolitics or history.

The General Mike Flynn story is especially a crack-up. Did he accept a $20,000 speaking fee from the Russian news outlet RT in his interlude as a private citizen? How does that compare to the millions sucked in by the Clinton Foundation in pay-to-play deals when Madame was secretary of state? Or her six-figure speeches to Goldman Sachs and that ilk. Are private citizens forbidden to accept speaking fees or consulting fees from countries that we are not at war with? I'd like to know how many other alumni of the Bill Clinton, Bush II, and Obama admins have hired themselves out on this basis. Scores and scores, I would bet.

Trump's adversaries might not get any traction on the Russia story, but they may enrage the rogue elephant Trump enough in the process that he will appear sufficiently incompetent to run him over with the Twenty-fifth Amendment, and I think that is the plan for now. Of course, there are some jokers in the deck. A really striking one is the story of murdered DNC staffer Seth Rich last July. He was shot in the back on the street outside his apartment one night by persons as yet unknown, and twelve days later over forty thousand DNC emails landed at Wikileaks. His laptop is reportedly in the possession of the DC cops — if it hasn't been dumped in the Potomac. I'm generally allergic to conspiracy theories, but this looks like an especially ugly story, which might ultimately be clarified if or when Julian Assange of Wikileaks ever divulges the source of that data dump. Anyway, the new special counsel at the DOJ, former FBI director Robert Mueller, may have to venture down that dark trail.

One way or another, though, the Deep State is determined to drive Trump from office. In the final rounds of this struggle, Trump might conceivably undertake a sudden swamp-draining operation: the firing of a great many politicized intelligence community officers, especially the ones legally culpable for leaking classified information to media — another area that Mr. Mueller could also shine a light on. The colossal security apparatus of this country — especially the fairly new giant NSA — has become a monster eating America. Somebody needs to cut it down to size. Perhaps that's the Deep State's main motive in moving heaven and earth to dump Trump.

When they do, of course, they are liable to foment an insurrection every bit as ugly as the dustup that followed the shelling of Fort Sumter. Trump, whatever you think of him — and I've never been a fan, to put it mildly — was elected for a reason: the ongoing economic collapse of the nation, and the suffering of a public without incomes or purposeful employment. That part of the common weal is liable to completely whirl down the drain later this year in something like a currency crisis or a depressionary market meltdown engineered by yet another Deep State player, the Federal Reserve. That and the ejection of Trump could coincide with disastrous results.

Do You, Mr. Jones . . . ?

May 22, 2017

In case you wonder how our politics fell into such a slough of despond, the answer is pretty simple. Neither main political party nor their trains of experts, specialists, and mouthpieces can construct a coherent story about what is happening in this country — and the result is a roaring wave of recursive objurgation and wrath that loops purposelessly toward gathering darkness.

What's happening is a slow-motion collapse of the economy. Neither Democrats nor Republicans know why it is so remorselessly underway. A tiny number of well-positioned scavengers thrive on the debris cast off by the process of disintegration, but they don't really understand the process either — the lobbyists, lawyers, bankers, contractors, feeders at the troughs of government could not be more cynical or clueless.

The nation suffers desperately from an absence of leadership and perhaps even more from the loss of faith that leadership is even possible after years without it. Perhaps that's why so much hostility is aimed at Mr. Putin of Russia, a person who appears to know where his country stands in history, and who enjoys ample support among his countrymen. How that must gall the empty vessels like Lindsey Graham, Rubio, Schumer, Feinstein, Ryan et. al.

So along came the dazzling, zany Trump, who was able to communicate a vague sense memory of what had been lost in our time of American life, whose sheer bluster resembled something like conviction as projected via the cartoonizing medium of television, and who entered a paralysis of intention the moment he stepped into the Oval Office, where he proved to be even less authentic than the Wizard of Oz. Turned out he didn't really understand the economic collapse underway either; he just remembered an America of 1962 and thought somehow the national clock might be turned back.

The industrial triumph of America in the nineteenth and twentieth centuries was really something to behold. But like all stories, it had a beginning, a middle, and an end, and we're closer to the end of that story than the middle. It doesn't mean the end of civilization but it means we have to start a new story that provides some outline of a life worth living on a planet worth caring about.

For the moment the fragmentary stories of redemption revolve around technological rescue remedies, chiefly the idea that electric cars will save the nation. This dumb narrative alone ought to inform you just how lost we are, because the story assumes that our prime objective is to remain car dependent at all costs — when one of the main features in the story of our future is the absolute end of car dependency and all its furnishings and accessories. We can't imagine going there. (How would you, without a car?)

The economy is collapsing because it was based on cheap oil, which is no longer cheap to pull out of the ground — despite what you might pay for it at the pump these days. The public is understandably confounded by this. But their mystification does nothing to allay the disappearance of jobs, incomes, prospects, or purpose. They retreat from the pain of loss into a fog of manufactured melodrama featuring superheroes and supervillains and supernatural doings.

Donald Trump could never be a Franklin Roosevelt or a Lincoln. These were figures who, if nothing else, could articulate the terms that reality had laid on America's table in their particular moments of history. Mr. Trump can barely speak English and his notions about history amount to a kind of funny papers of the mind. A sinister host of adversaries who ought to understand what is happening in this country, but don't, or can't, or won't, are coming after him, and they are going to get rid of him one way or another. They have to. They must. And they will.

And then what?

THINGS TO COME

June 12, 2017

As our politicos creep deeper into a legalistic wilderness hunting for phantoms of Russian collusion, nobody pays attention to the most dangerous force in American life: the unraveling financialization of the economy.

Financialization is what happens when the people in charge "create" colossal sums of "money" out of nothing — by issuing loans, a.k.a. debt — and then cream off stupendous profits from the asset bubbles, interest rate arbitrages, and other opportunities for swindling that the artificial wealth presents. It was a kind of magic trick that produced monuments of concentrated personal wealth for a few and left the rest of the population drowning in obligations from a stolen future. The future is now upon us.

Financialization expressed itself in other interesting ways, for instance, the amazing renovation of New York City (Brooklyn especially). It didn't happen just because Generation X was repulsed by the boring suburbs it grew up in and longed for a life of artisanal cocktails. It happened because financialization concentrated immense wealth geographically in the very few places where its activities took place — not just New York but San Francisco, Washington, and Boston — and could support luxuries like craft food and brews.

Quite a bit of that wealth was extracted from asset stripping the rest of America where financialization was absent, kind of a national distress sale of the flyover places and the people in them. That dynamic, of course, produced the phenomenon of President Donald Trump, the distilled essence of all the economic distress "out there" and the rage it entailed. The people of Ohio, Indiana, and Wisconsin were left holding a big bag of nothing and they certainly noticed what had been done to them, though they had no idea what to do about it, except maybe try to escape the moment-by-moment pain of their ruined lives with powerful drugs.

And then, a champion presented himself, and promised to bring back the dimly remembered wonder years of postwar well-being — even though the world had changed utterly — and the poor suckers fell for it. Not to mention the fact that his opponent — the avaricious Hillary, with her hundreds of millions in ill-gotten wealth — was a very avatar of the financialization that had turned their lives to shit. And then the woman called them "a basket of deplorables" for noticing what had happened to them.

And now the rather pathetic false promises of President Trump, the whole MAGA thing, is unraveling at exactly the same time that the financialized economy is entering its moment of final catastrophic phase change. The monuments to wealth — especially the stock and bond portfolios and the presumed value of real estate investments — will surrender to a process you might call *price discovery from Hell*, revealing their worth to be somewhere between little and nothing. The accumulated monstrous debts of persons, corporations, and sovereign societies will be suddenly, shockingly, absolutely, and self-evidently unpayable, and the securities represented by them will be sucked into the kind of vortices of time/space depicted in movies about mummies and astronauts. And all of a sudden the avatars of that wealth will see their lives turn to shit just like the moiling, Budweiser-gulping, OxyContin-addled deplorables in the flat, boring, parking lot wastelands of our ruined drive-in utopia saw their lives rendered into a brown-and-yellow slurry draining clockwise down the toilet of history.

Nobody in power in this country is paying attention to how close we are to that epic moment — at least, they're not talking about it. If the possibility of all that even occupies some remote corner of their brains, they surely don't know how to prepare the citizenry for it, or what to do about it. The truth is that societies respond emergently to major crises like the imminent unraveling of our financialized economy, often in disorderly and surprising ways. I suppose we'll just have to watch the nauseating spectacle play out, and in the meantime enjoy the Russian collusion melodrama for whatever it's worth — probably more than a ticket to *Wonder Woman* or the new Tom Cruise mummy movie.

ABSENT WITHOUT LEAVE

June 19, 2017

It ain't bragging if it's true. I've said repeatedly on this blog for years that the federal government would only become more impotent, more incompetent, and more ineffectual as the Long Emergency rolled out. And here we are now, at just such a pass in history.

The process has been well underway since the beginning of the century. Even the attempts to expand its scope and reach — such as the post-9/11 addition of God knows how many new intelligence services — has only produced an epic clusterfuck of cross-purposed mission creep that threatens the federal government's existential legitimacy.

After nearly a year of investigating, the FBI, the CIA, the NSA, the DIA, the DHS et. al. haven't been able to leak any substantial fact about "Russian collusion" with the Trump election campaign — and, considering the torrent of leaks about all manner of other collateral matters during this same period, it seems impossible to conclude that there is anything actually there besides utterly manufactured hysteria.

Now, one might imagine that this *intelligence community* could have *manufactured* some gift-wrapped facts rather than just waves of hysteria, but that's where the incompetence and impotence come in. They never came up with anything besides Flynn and Sessions having conversations with the Russian ambassador — as if the ambassadors are not here to have conversations with our government officials. You'd think that with all the computer graphics available these days they could concoct a cineplex-quality feature film–length recording of Donald Trump making a "great deal" to swap Kansas for Lithuania, or Jared Kushner giving piggyback rides to Vladimir Putin in the Kremlin. But all we've really ever gotten was a packet of emails from the Democratic National Committee and John Podesta of the Clinton campaign gloating about how nicely they fucked over Bernie Sanders — and that doesn't exactly reflect so well on what has evolved to be the so-called Resistance. The net effect of all this sound and fury is a government so paralyzed that it can't even pass bad legislation or execute its existing (excessive) duties. That might theoretically be a good thing, except what we're seeing are individual departments just veering off on their own, especially the military, which now operates without any civilian control. Apparently General Mattis, the secretary of defense, pretty much decided on his own to dispatch another 8,000 US troops to Afghanistan to move things along there in the war's sixteenth year. Or did he get President Trump to look up from his Twitter window for three seconds to explain the situation and get a nod of approval?

Perhaps you also didn't notice the news item over the weekend that a US-led fighter plane coalition shot down a Syrian air force plane in Syrian airspace. In an earlier era that could easily be construed as an act of war. Who gave the order for that, you have to wonder. And what will the consequences be? Reasonable people might also ask: haven't we already made enough deadly mischief in that part of the world?

With the US military gone rogue in foreign lands, and the intelligence community off the reservation at home, and the Trump White House all gummed up in the tar baby of RussiaGate, and the House and Senate lost in the shuffle, you also have to wonder what anybody is going to do about the imminent technical bankruptcy of the USA as the Treasury Department spends down its dwindling fund of remaining cash money to pay ongoing expenses — everything from agriculture subsidies to Medicare. That well is going dry in the middle of the summer, and without any resolution to the debt ceiling debate, the country will not be able to borrow more to pretend that it's solvent.

I don't see any indication that the House and Senate will be able to bluster their way through this. Instead, the situation will compel extraordinary new acts of financial fraud via the central banks and its cadre of Too Big to Fail associates. In the event, the likely outcome will be a spectacular fall in the value of the US dollar, and, perhaps consecutively, the collapse of the equity and real estate markets.

The public may not give a shit about Syria, Afghanistan, or federal dairy supports, but they'll sure perk up and notice that their money is going worthless. I doubt they'll be clamoring for Hillary Clinton to be installed as the first US Caesar to fix it all.

THE TECHNICOLOR SWAN

June 26, 2017

When I think of the Democratic Party these days, the image instantly comes to mind of little Linda Blair playing the demon-possessed child in the classic horror movie *The Exorcist* (1973), most particularly the scene in which she spews a stream of pea soup–like projectile vomit into the face of kindly old Max von Sydow, as Father Merrin, the priest come to rescue her.

The pea soup represents the sort of ideology that the Democratic Party has spewed out in recent years — a toxic mush of racial identity politics, contempt for men, infantile entitlement tantrums, corporate whoring, and a demonic quest for war with the Russian Federation. Father Merrin, the priest, stands for incorruptible American men, who have been, at last, killed off by this barrage of diabolical idiocy.

Can you think of a single figure in the Democratic faction who dares to oppose the lethal nonsense this party has been sponsoring and spewing? Who are its leaders? Chuck Schumer in the Senate — a mendacious errand boy for Wall Street? Nancy Pelosi in the House, who wears her cluelessness like a laminate of pancake makeup? Got anyone else? Uncle Joe (Biden)? That's rich. Bernie? (Looks like his wife is about to be indicted on a federal bank fraud rap for running a small Vermont college into the ground. Whoops.)

Who else you got? Governor Andrew Cuomo of New York. I live near Albany, the state capital, and I can assure you that Governor Cuomo is ripely loathed and detested by anyone who has had actual dealings with him. Insiders tell me he makes Nixon look like Mr. Rogers. And this is apart from the fact that he seems to stand for nothing.

I registered as a Democrat in 1972 — largely because good ole Nixon was at the height of his power (just before his fall, of course), and because he was preceded as party leader by Barry Goldwater, who, at the time, was avatar for the John Birch Society and all its poisonous nonsense. The Democratic Party was still deeply imbued with the personality of Franklin Roosevelt, with a frosting of the recent memory of John F. Kennedy and his brother Bobby, tragic, heroic, and glamorous. I was old enough to remember the magic of JFK's press conferences

— a type of performance art that neither Bill Clinton nor Barack Obama could match for wit and intelligence — and the charisma of authenticity that Bobby projected in the months before that little creep shot him in the kitchen of the Ambassador Hotel. Even the lugubrious Lyndon Johnson had the heroic quality of a southerner stepping up to abolish the reign of Jim Crow.

Lately, people refer to this bygone era of the 1960s as "the American High" — and by that they are not talking about smoking dope (though it did go mainstream then), but rather the post–World War Two economic high, when American business might truly ruled the planet. Perhaps the seeming strength of American political leaders back then was merely a reflection of the country's economic power, which since has been squandered and purloined into a matrix of rackets loosely called *financialization* — a criminal magic act whereby wealth is generated without producing anything of value.

Leaders in such a system are bound to be not just lesser men and women but something less than human. Hillary Clinton, for instance, lost the 2016 election because she came off as demonic, and I mean that pretty literally. To many Americans, especially the ones swindled by the magic of financialization, she was the reincarnation of the little girl in *The Exorcist*. Donald Trump, unlikely as it seems — given his oafish and vulgar guise — was assigned the role of exorcist. Unlike poor Father Merrin, he sort of succeeded, even to his very own astonishment. I say *sort of succeeded* because the Democratic Party is still there, infested with all its gibbering demons, but it has been reduced politically to impotence and appears likely to soon roll over and die.

None of this is to say that the other party, the Republicans, has anything but the feeblest grip on credibility or even an assured continued existence. First of all there is Trump's obvious plight as a rogue only nominally regarded as party leader (or even member). Then there is the gathering fiasco of neither Trump nor his party being able to deliver remedies for any of the ills of our time that he was elected to fix. The reason for that is simple: the USA has entered Hell, or at least a condition that looks a lot like it. This is not just a matter of a few persons or a party being possessed by demons. We've entered a realm that is populated by nothing but demons — of our own design, by the way.

Our politics have become so thoroughly demonic that the sort of exorcism America needs now can only come from outside politics. It's coming, too. It's on its way. It will turn our economic situation upside down and inside out. It's a Technicolor swan, and you can see it coming from a thousand miles out. Wait for it. Wait for it.

WE ARE GOOD PEOPLE,
REALLY WE ARE!

July 10, 2017

The disgrace of America's putative intellectual class is nearly complete as it shoves the polity further into dysfunction and toward collapse. These are the people Nassim Taleb refers to as "intellectual yet idiots." Big questions loom over this dynamic: How did the thinking class of America sink into this slough of thoughtlessness? And why – what is motivating them?

One path to understanding it can be found in a sober essay by Neal Devers, "The Overton Bubble," published two years ago on TheFuturePrimaeval.net — a friend turned me on to it the other day (dunno how I missed it). The title is a reference to the phenomenon known as the Overton window. Wikipedia summarizes it:

> *The Overton window, also known as the window of discourse, is the range of ideas the public will accept.... The term is derived from its originator, Joseph P. Overton (1960–2003), a former vice president of the Mackinac Center for Public Policy.*

Devers refines the definition:

> *The Overton window is a concept in political sociology referring to the range of acceptable opinions that can be held by respectable people. "Respectable" of course means that the subject can be integrated with polite society. Respectability is a strong precondition on the ability to have open influence in the mainstream.*

This raises another question: who exactly is in this corps of "respectable people" who set the parameters of acceptable thought? Primarily, the mainstream media — *The New York Times*, *The WashPo*, CNN, etc. — plus the bureaucratic functionaries of the permanent government bureaucracy, a.k.a. the Deep State, who make and execute policy, along with the universities that educate the "respectable people" (the thinking class) into the prevailing dogmas and shibbo- leths of the day, and finally the think tanks and foundations that pay professional "experts" to retail their ideas.

The Overton window can be viewed as a mechanism of political control, demonizing anyone who departs from the consensus of respectable thought, and especially if they express their heresies in public speech. This has consequences.

Devers explains:

> *The trouble with the Overton window as a mechanism of political control, and with politicization of speech and thought in general, is that it causes significant collateral damage on the ability of your society to think clearly. If some thoughts are unthinkable and unspeakable, and the truth happens in some case to fall outside of polite consensus, then your ruling elite and their society will run into situations they simply can't handle.... An unwise political elite is one incapable of thinking clearly about their strategic situation, acting in concert, or sticking to a plan.... An insecure political elite is one which has either no sufficient mechanisms of political power short of the politicization of speech and thought, or is faced by such powerful but somehow never decisively powerful enemies that they need to permanently escalate to a state of vigorous politicization of speech and thought. We can compare this state to "intellectual martial law" for its structural similarity to the physical-security equivalent.*

We're now living under that condition of "intellectual martial law." The con- sequent degradation of thinking means that the polity can't construct a coherent consensus about what is happening to it (or devise a plan for what to do about it). This is exactly the point where the Overton window turns into an Overton bubble, as described by Devers. The bubble comprises ideas that are assumed to be self-evident (though they actually aren't) and notions that are potentially de- structive of society, even suicidally so. Here is a partial list of the current dogmas and shibboleths inside today's Overton bubble.Russia hacked the election of 2016 (no evidence required).

Russia (Vladimir Putin in particular) is bent on destroying the USA.

All immigrants, legal or illegal, have equal status before the law.

National borders are inconvenient, cruel, and obsolete.

Western civilization is a malign force in human history.

Islam is "the religion of peace," no matter how many massacres of "infidels" are carried out in its name.

Men are a negative force in society.

White men are especially negative.

Brownie points given for behaviors under the rubric LBGTQ.

All discussion about race problems and conflicts is necessarily racist.

The hijab (head covering worn in public by some Muslim women) is a device of liberation for women.

There should be a law against using the wrong personal pronoun for people who consider themselves neither men nor women (recently passed by the Canadian parliament).

A unifying common culture is unnecessary in national life (anything goes).

Colonizing Mars is a great solution to problems on Earth.

That list defines the general preoccupations of the thinking classes today — to the exclusion of other issues. Here is an alternative list of matters they are not generally concerned about or interested in.The energy quandary at the heart of our economic malaise.

The enormous debt racked up to run society in the absence of affordable energy inputs.

The dangerous interventions and manipulation in markets by unelected officials of the Federal Reserve.

The extraordinary dysfunction of manipulated financial markets.

The fragility of a banking system based on accounting fraud.

The dysfunction and fragility of the American suburban living arrangement.

The consequences of a catastrophic breakdown in the economy due to the above.

The destruction of planetary ecology, threatening the continuation of the human race, and potentially all life.

Now, the question of motive. Why does the thinking class in America embrace ideas that are not necessarily, and surely not self-evidently, truthful, and even self-destructive? Because this class is dangerously insecure and perversely needs to insist on being right about its guiding dogmas and shibboleths *at all costs*. That is why so much of the behavior emanating from the thinking class amounts to virtue signaling — *we are the good people on the side of what's right, really we are*! Of course, virtue signaling is just the new term for self-righteousness. There is also the issue of careerism. So many individuals are making a living at trafficking in, supporting, or executing policy based on these dogmas and shibboleths that they don't dare depart from the Overton bubble of permissible, received thought lest they sacrifice their status and incomes.

The thinking classes are also the leaders and foot soldiers in American institutions. When they are unable or unwilling to think clearly, then you get a breakdown of authority, which leads to a breakdown of legitimacy. That's exactly where we're at today in our national politics — our ability to manage the polity.

Boomerangski

July 17, 2017

The strenuous effort of "Resistance" passengers in the Limousine of State to shove Donald Trump out of the driver's seat continues into what would normally be the news wasteland of midsummer. Last week it was the smoking popgun of Trump Junior's meeting with a Russian lawyer purported (by British music promoter Rob Goldstein) to be associated with the "Russian Crown Prosecutor" (no such office in a country without a monarch).

The news caused the usual commotion among the very media mouthpieces who publish anti-Trump allegations as a staple for their "Resistance" readerships. By the way, this blog might be described as anti-Trump, too, in the sense that I did not vote for him and regularly inveigh against his antics as president — but neither is *Clusterfuck Nation* a friend of the Hillary-haunted Dem-Prog "Resistance," in case there's any confusion about where we stand. If anything, we oppose the entirety of the current political regime in our nation's capital, the matrix of rackets that is driving the aforementioned Limousine of State off the cliff of economic collapse. Just sayin'.

"Resistance" law professors, such as Lawrence Tribe at Harvard, were quick to holler "treason" over Junior's meet-up with Russian lawyer Natalia Veselnitskaya and Russian-American lobbyist Rinat Akhmetshin. Well, first of all, and not to put too fine a point on it, don't you have to be at war with another nation to regard any kind of consort as "treason"? Last time I checked, we were not at war with Russia — though it sure seems like persons and parties inside the Beltway would dearly like to make that happen. You can't call it espionage either, of course, because that would purport the *giving* of secret information, not the *receiving* of political gossip.

Remember, the "Resistance" is not going for impeachment, but rather Section 4 of the Twenty-fifth Amendment. That legal nicety makes for a very neat and clean surgical removal of a whack-job president, without all the cumbrous evidentiary baggage and pain-in-ass due process required by impeachment. All it requires is a consensus among a very small number of high officials, who then send a note to the leaders in both houses of Congress stating that said whack-job president is a menace to the polity — and out he goes, snippety-snip like a colorectal polyp, into the hazardous waste bag of history. And you're left with a nice clean asshole, namely Vice President Mike Pence.

Insofar as Pence appears to be a kind of booby prize for the "Resistance," that fateful reach for the Twenty-fifth Amendment hasn't happened quite yet. It is hoped, I'm sure, that the incessant piling on of new allegations about "collusion" with the Russians will get the Twenty-fifthers over the finish line and into the longed-for end zone dance. More interestingly, though, the meme that has led people to believe that any contact between Russians and Americans is ipso facto nefarious vectors into the very beating heart of the "Resistance" itself: the Clintons.

How come the Clintons have not been asked to explain why — as reported on *The Hill* blog — Bill Clinton was paid half a million dollars to give speech in Russia (surely he offered them something of value in exchange, pending the *sure thing* Hillary inaugural), or what about the $2.35 million "contribution" that the Clinton Foundation received after Secretary of State Hillary allowed the Russians to buy a controlling stake in the Uranium One company, which owns 20 percent of US uranium supplies, with mines and refineries in Wyoming, Utah, and other states, as well as assets in Kazakhstan, the world's largest uranium producer? Incidentally, the Clinton Foundation did not "shut down," as erroneously reported early this year. It was only its Global Initiative program that got shuttered. The $2.35 million is probably still rattling around in the Clinton Foundation's bank account. Don't you kind of wonder what they did with it? I hope Special Prosecutor Robert Mueller wants to know.

The Value of Everything

July 24, 2017

We are looking more and more like France on the eve of its revolution in 1789. Our classes are distributed differently, but the inequity is just as sharp. America's "aristocracy," once based strictly on bank accounts, acts increasingly hereditary as the vapid offspring and relations of "stars" (in politics, showbiz, business, and the arts) assert their prerogatives to fame, power, and riches — think the voters didn't grok the sinister import of Hillary's "it's my turn" message?

What's especially striking in similarity to the court of the Bourbons is the utter cluelessness of America's entitled power elite to the agony of the moiling masses below them and mainly away from the coastal cities. Just about everything meaningful has been taken away from them, even though many of the material trappings of existence remain: a roof, stuff that resembles food, cars, and screens of various sizes.

But the places they are supposed to call home are either wrecked — the original small towns and cities of America — or replaced by new "developments" so devoid of artistry, history, thought, care, and charm that they don't add up to communities, and are so obviously unworthy of affection that the very idea of "home" becomes a cruel joke.

These places were bad enough in the 1960s and '70s, when the people who lived in them at least were able to report to paying jobs assembling products and managing their distribution. Now those people don't have that to give a little meaning to their existence, or cover the costs of it. Public space was never designed into the automobile suburbs, and the sad remnants of it were replaced by ersatz substitutes, like the now-dying malls. Everything else of a public and human associational nature has been shoved into some kind of computerized box with a screen on it.

The floundering nonelite masses have not learned the harsh lesson of our time that the virtual is not an adequate substitute for the authentic, while the elites who create all this vicious crap spend millions to consort face-to-face in the Hamptons and Martha's Vineyard telling each other how wonderful they are for providing all the artificial social programming and glitzy hardware for their paying customers.

The effect of this dynamic relationship so far has been powerfully soporific. You can deprive people of a true home for a while, and give them virtual friends on TV to project their emotions onto, and arrange to give them cars via some financing scam or other to keep them moving mindlessly around an utterly desecrated landscape under the false impression that they're going somewhere — but we're now at the point where ordinary people can't even carry the costs of keeping themselves hostage to these degrading conditions.

The next big entertainment for them will be the financial implosion of the elites themselves as the governing forces of physics finally overcome all the ruses and stratagems of the elites who have been playing games with money. Professional observers never tire of saying that the government can't run out of money (because they can always print more of it) but they can certainly destroy the value of that money and shred the consensual confidence that allows it to operate as money.

That's exactly what is about to commence at the end of the summer when the government runs out of cash-on-hand and Congress finds itself utterly paralyzed by party animus to patch the debt ceiling problem that disables new borrowing. The elites may be home from the Hamptons and the Vineyard by then, but summers may never be the same for them again.

The Deep State may win its war against the pathetic President Trump, but it won't win any war against the imperatives of the universe and the way that expresses itself in the true valuation of things. And when the moment of clarification arrives — the instant of cosmic price discovery — the clueless elites will have to really and truly worry about the value of their heads.

Narratives Are Not Truths

July 31, 2017

The polity is a social organism, of course, meaning that it adds up to more than the sum of its parts, a *body of politics*, if you will, just as each of us adds up to more than just our bodies. It's alive as we are alive. We have needs. We have intentions in the service of those needs. Those intentions animate us and turn us in one direction or another to stay alive and, even more than that, to thrive.

The American polity is not thriving. It has been incrementally failing to meet its needs for quite a while now, playing games with itself to pretend that it is okay while its institutional organs and economic operations decay. It turns this way and that way ever more desperately, oversteering like a drunk on the highway. It is drunk on the untruths it tells itself in the service of playing games to avoid meeting its real needs. Narratives are not truths.

Here is a primary question we might ask ourselves: do we want to live in a healthy society? Do we want to thrive? If so, what are the narratives standing in the way of turning us in the direction?

Let's start with health care, so called, since the failure to do anything about the current disastrous system is so fresh. What's the narrative there? That "providers" (doctors and hospitals) can team up with banking operations called "insurance companies" to fairly allocate "services" to the broad population with a little help from the government. No, that's actually not how it works. The three "players" actually engage in a massive racketeering matrix — that is, they extract enormous sums of money dishonestly from the public they pretend to serve and they do it twice: once by extortionary fees and again by taxes paid to subsidize mitigating the effects of the racketeering.

The public has its own narrative, which is that there is no connection between their medical problems and the way they live. The fact is that they eat too much poisonous food because it's tasty and fun, and they do that because the habits of life that they have complicitly allowed to evolve in this country offer them paltry rewards otherwise. They dwell in ugly, punishing surroundings, spend too much time and waste too much money driving cars around it in isolation, and have gone along with every effort to dismantle the armatures of common social exchange that afford what might be called a *human dimension* of everyday living.

So the medical racket ends up being nearly 20 percent of the economy, while the public gets fatter, sicker, and more anxiously depressed. And there is no sign that we want to disrupt the narratives.

A related narrative: the US economy is "recovering" — supposedly from a mysterious speed bump that made it swerve off the road in 2008. No, that's not it. The US economy has entered a permanent state of contraction because we can't afford the fossil fuel energy it takes to continue expanding our techno-industrial activities (and there are no plausible adequate substitutes for the fossil fuels). We tried to cover up this state of affairs by borrowing money from the future, issuing bonds to "create money," and now we've reached the end of that racket because it's clear we can't pay back the old bonded debt and have no prospect for "making good" on issuing new bonded debt. Recently, we have been issuing new debt mainly to pay back the old, and any twelve-year-old can see where that leads.

Reality wants us to manage the contraction of that failing economy, and because that is difficult and requires changing familiar, comfortable arrangements, we just pretend that we can keep expanding the old system. Of course, all the workarounds and games only increase the fragility of the system and set us up for a kind of sudden failure that could literally destroy civilized society.

Another popular narrative of the moment — a dominant preoccupation among the "educated" elites these days — is that we can change human nature, especially human sexuality and all the social behaviors that derive from mammals existing in two sexes. This set of narratives is deeply entwined with fashion and status seeking, with the greatest status currently being conferred upon those opting out from being either one sex or the other, along with the biological imperatives associated with one or the other. This has been identified by the essayist Hugo Salinas Price as an updated form of Gnosticism and is now the official reigning ideology of the college campuses. Some call it "cultural Marxism," but it is really a form of religion. It offers colorful distraction from the more difficult adult tasks of managing contraction and rebuilding the political economy with its social armatures.

These conditions might prompt us to ask the more general question: how much longer do we, as a polity, want to pretend that narratives are the same as the truth? As I've averred previously, I think reality itself has to force the issue by delivering circumstances so compelling that it is no longer possible to keep telling yourself the same old stories. And that reckoning is not far off.

Just Wait a Little While

August 7, 2017

The trouble, of course, is that even after the Deep State (a.k.a. "The Swamp") succeeds in quicksanding President Trump, America will be left with itself — adrift among the cypress stumps, drained of purpose, spirit, hope, credibility, and, worst of all, a collective grasp on reality, lost in the fog of collapse.

Here's what you need to know about what's going on and where we're headed.

The United States is comprehensively bankrupt. The government is broke and the citizenry is trapped under inescapable debt burdens. We are never again going to generate the kinds and volumes of "growth" associated with techno-industrial expansion. That growth came out of energy flows, mainly fossil fuels, that paid for themselves and furnished a surplus for doing other useful things. It's over. Shale oil, for instance, doesn't pay for itself and the companies engaged in it will eventually run out of accounting hocus-pocus for pretending that it does, and they will go out of business.

The self-evident absence of growth means the end of borrowing money at all levels. When you can't pay back old loans, it's unlikely that you will be able to arrange new loans. The nation could pretend to be able to borrow more, since it can supposedly "create" money (loan it into existence, print it, add keystrokes to computer records), but eventually those tricks fail, too. Either the "nonperforming" loans (loans not being paid off) cause money to disappear or the authorities "create" so much new money from thin air (money not associated with real things of value like land, food, manufactured goods) that the "money" loses its mojo as a medium of exchange (for real things), as a store of value (over time), and as a reliable index of pricing — which is to say *all* the functions of money.

In other words, there are two ways of going broke in this situation: money can become scarce as it disappears so that few people have any; or everybody can have plenty of money that has no value and no credibility. I mention these monetary matters because the system of finance is the unifying link between all the systems we depend on for modern life, and none of them can run without it.

So that's where the real trouble is apt to start. That's why I write about markets and banks on this blog.

The authorities in this nation, including government, business, and academia, routinely lie about our national financial operations for a couple of reasons. One is that they know the situation is hopeless but the consequences are so awful to contemplate that resorting to accounting fraud and pretense is preferable to facing reality. Secondarily, they do it to protect their jobs and reputations — which they will lose anyway as collapse proceeds and their record of feckless dishonesty reveals itself naturally.

The underlying issue is the scale of human activity in our time. It has exceeded its limits and we have to tune back a lot of what we do. Anything organized at the giant scale is headed for failure, so it comes down to a choice between outright collapse or severe rescaling, which you might think of as managed contraction. That goes for government programs, military adventures, corporate enterprise, education, transportation, health care, agriculture, urban design, basically everything. There is an unfortunate human inclination to not reform, revise, or rescale familiar activities. We'll use every kind of duct tape and baling wire we can find to keep the current systems operating, and we have, but we're close to the point where that sort of cob-job maintenance won't work anymore, especially where money is concerned.

Why this is so has been attributed to intrinsic human brain programming that supposedly evolved optimally for short-term planning. But obviously many people and institutions dedicate themselves to long-term thinking. So there must be a big emotional override represented by the fear of letting go of what used to work that tends to disable long-term thinking. It's hard to accept that our setup is about to stop working — especially something as marvelous as techno-industrial society.

But that's exactly what's happening. If you want a chance at keeping on keeping on, you'll have to get with reality's program. Start by choosing a place to live that has some prospect of remaining civilized. This probably doesn't include our big cities. But there are plenty of small cities and small towns out in America that are scaled for the resource realities of the future, waiting to be reinhabited and reactivated. A lot of these lie along the country's inland waterways — the Ohio, Mississippi, Missouri river system, the Great Lakes, the Hudson and St. Lawrence corridors — and they also exist in regions of the country where food can be grown.

You'll have to shift your energies into a trade or vocation that makes you useful to other people. This probably precludes jobs like developing phone apps, day trading, and teaching gender studies. Think: carpentry, blacksmithing, basic medicine, mule breeding, simplified small retail, and especially farming, along with the value-added activities entailed in farm production. The entire digital economy is going to fade away like a drug-induced hallucination, so beware the current narcissistic blandishments of computer technology. Keep in mind that being in this world actually entitles you to nothing. One way or another, you'll have to earn everything worth having, including self-respect and your next meal.

Now, just wait a little while.

SMOKE AND FIRE

August 14, 2017

Cue the cornpone Nazis. Enter, stage left. Well, what did you expect?

With the various authorities in this culture incessantly applying "white priv-ilege" noogies to the public's skull, sooner or later they were sure to provoke a lizard-brain response from the more limbic-oriented low orders of honkeydom. Of course, you couldn't stage manage a more stupidly arrant provocative act in the State of Virginia, guaranteed to bring out the raging yahoos, than threatening to remove a statue of Robert E. Lee.

There's a depressingly tragic overtone to this whole affair that suggests the arc of history itself is driving this story — a dark animus in the national soul struggling to resolve its contradictions. And the Charlottesville incident, which left a woman dead and many others badly injured from a car ramming, has the flavor of a "first shot" in a new civil war.

The echo civil rights campaign of the moment — a strange brew of *Black Lives Matter*, "Antifa" (antifascist), latest-wave feminism, illegal immigrant sanc-tuary politics, and LGBTQQ agitation — emanates from the college campuses and creeps through the culture at large like a miasma, poisoning group against group, in an orgy of victimization claims of the sort that inevitably lead to vio-lence. This is how tribal and religious wars start in primitive societies.

There is also a funk of phoniness about this campaign that should alert the higher centers of judgment in the brain. The Michael Brown killing in Ferguson, MO, that kicked off the BLM movement was never a convincing case of injustice, but has been widely regarded as if it was, despite state and federal inquiries (under Obama's DOJ) that concluded otherwise. The figment of "white privilege" is not responsible for the extraordinary black-on-black homicide rates in Chicago and Baltimore or the black teen flash mobs in malls around the country. What is sus-piciously at the bottom of it all is the spectacular failure of the original civil rights campaign of the 1960s to alter the structures of poverty in black America, as well as the grinding guilt among white Democratic Progressives over the failures of their own well-intentioned policies — converted perversely into racial self-flagellation.

The latest iteration of feminism comes out of campuses that have been largely taken over by female boomer pedagogues, especially the non-STEM departments, and is now *fait accompli*, so that the grievances still pouring out seem manufactured and hysterical. It also has a strong odor of simple misandry, and the whole package of ideology is wrapped in impenetrable grad school jargon designed to give it an intellectual sheen that is unearned and dishonest. The grim fact is that sooner or later even some intelligent men might notice this, and get pissed off about it.

The Antifa movement would be funny if it wasn't itself prone to violence, since it espouses exactly the same kind of despotism against free thought that it pretends to fight against. It wants to shut down and stamp out debate in the public arena and trample over principles that make it uncomfortable, for instance, the First Amendment asserting the right to free speech. It makes a mockery of the battle cry for "diversity" (*diversity* only for Antifa-approved ideas). That so many current college students subscribe to the movement ought to make thoughtful people very uneasy about the politics of the coming generation. In their black battle garb and masks, they resemble the very fascist mobs of the 1930s that the name "Antifa" supposedly evokes as its enemy.

The illegal immigrant sanctuary movement is just plain insane, starting with the refusal by officials to even make a distinction between citizens and noncitizens. There is every reason to think that mayors of "sanctuary cities" and administrators on "sanctuary campuses" should be prosecuted under federal law. It has reached such a pitch in California, where state college deans are shepherding "undocumented" students into special programs, that they are sure to provoke the cutoff of funds and perhaps the destruction of their own institutions. The movement is the very essence of lawlessness and a disgrace to the supposedly thinking class.

The LGBTQQ movement, an offshoot of Feminism 3.0, seeks to erase biology itself as applied to human mammalian sexuality, at the same time that it wants to create new special social and political entitlements — based on various categories of sexual desire that they insist are biologically driven, such as the urge of a man to equip himself via surgery to behave like a woman. The movement has now gone so far as to try to shame people who place themselves in the original biological categories ("cisgender," another grad school metaphysical jargon clot), and especially heterosexual men. Everybody else gets brownie points for being "cutting edge." One really has to wonder how long this nonsense goes on before it provokes a reaction among the biology-literate.

If we're entering a new civil war, don't make the mistake of thinking that it is the product solely of extreme right-wing yahooism. These Nazi and KKK bozos are rising up because the thinking-enabled people of the center have been too cowardly to stand up against the rising tide of idiocy festering at both ends of the spectrum, and particularly on the Left with its direct wiring to the policymaking centers of American life, dictating how people must think and act, and what they should care about.

What we can't really tell yet is whether these battles will remain joined and even escalate after the financial clusterfuck that the nation is sleepwalking into, or if the financial crisis will overwhelm them like a tsunami and leave all the stupid, tattered battle flags washed up on a lonely beach.

TOTAL ECLIPSE

August 18, 2017

First they came for the statues . . .What do you know, long about Wednesday, August 16, 2017, House Minority Leader Nancy Pelosi (D-Cal.) discovered that the United States Capitol building was infested with statues of Confederate dignitaries. Thirty years walking those marbled halls and she just noticed? Her startled announcement perked up Senator Cory Booker (D- NJ) who has been navigating those same halls only a few years. He quickly introduced a bill to blackball the offending statues. And, of course, the congressional black caucus also enjoyed a mass epiphany on the bronze and stone delegation of white devils.

I'd like to hear an argument as to why the Washington Monument should remain dedicated to that vicious slave driver and rebellious soldier, and indeed the name of the city that is the federal seat of government. Or the District of Columbia (after Columbus, who initiated the genocide of Native Americans). Or America, cribbed out of Amerigo Vespucci, the wicked Florentine cartographer who ascertained that the place called Brazil today was not the east coast of Asia but actually a New World — and so all our troubles began!

Well, there has been a lot of idle chatter the past half century about the *root causes* of this-and-that, and it seems that we have located one at last. I expect that scientific studies out of our best universities will soon confirm that occult transmissions from the statue of Jefferson Davis (a double devil named after an earlier devil) are responsible for the murder rate in Chicago.

Just as empires tend to build their most grandiose monuments prior to collapse, our tottering empire is concocting the most monumentally ludicrous delusions before it slides down the laundry chute of history. It's as if the Marx Brothers *colluded* with Alfred Hitchcock to dream up a melodramatic climax to the American Century that would be the most ridiculous and embarrassing to our posterity.

In the meantime, many citizens await Monday's spectacle of a total solar eclipse in parts of the country. They apparently don't realize that another eclipse has been underway for months: the total eclipse of reality across the entire landscape of the USA. Now *that* has been an event to behold, not just some twenty-minute freak of astronomy. What's being blacked out is the perilously fragile condition of the financial system — a great groaning Rube Goldberg contraption of accounting fraud, grift, statistical deceit, and racketeering that pretends to support the day-to-day activities of our national life.

For months, the recognition of this oncoming financial monster has been blocked by the hallucination of gremlins from the Kremlin infiltrating the recent presidential election. But just as that mirage was dissolving, along comes the treacherous invasion of the Confederate statues. It begins to look like the final piece of the puzzle in the Deep State's quest to eject Donald Trump from the Oval Office. His response to the deadly statue situation ("...why not Washington and Jefferson...?") was deemed so obtuse and unfeeling that even the rodents of his own nominal Republican Party want to jump his ship of state.

So the setup could not be more perfect! The country will now get down to the business of a months-long Twenty-fifth Amendment circle jerk at the very moment that the financial system flies apart. The damage from the financial clusterfuck will be much more real, and much worse, than anything that might be spun out of the anti-statue crusade hogging the headlines today. It will be interesting to see whether the old legacy media even reports on it as it happens, or whether they will cook up new and more bizarre entertainments to distract the public from what might be the ultimate swindling of a lifetime.

DIMINISHING RETURNS

August 21, 2017

These two words are the hinge that is swinging American life — and the advanced techno-industrial world, for that matter — toward darkness. They represent an infection in the critical operations of daily life, like a metabolic disease, driving us into disorder and failure. And they are so omnipresent that we've failed to even notice the growing failure all around us.

Mostly, these diminishing returns are the results of our overinvestments in making complex systems more complex, for instance, the replacement of the 37-page Glass-Steagall Act that regulated American banking, with the 848-page Dodd-Frank Act, which was only an outline for over 22,000 pages of subsequent regulatory content — all of it cooked up by banking lobbyists, and none of which replaced the single most important rule in Glass-Steagall, which required the separation of commercial banking from trafficking in securities. Dodd-Frank was a colossal act of misdirection of the public's attention, an impenetrable smoke screen of legal blather in the service of racketeering.

For Wall Street, Dodd-Frank aggravated the conditions that allow stock indexes to move in only one direction, up, for nine years. During the same period, the American economy of real people and real stuff only went steadily down, including the number of people out of the workforce, the incomes of those who still had jobs, the number of people with full-time jobs, the number of people who were able to buy food without government help, or pay for a place to live, or send a kid to college.

When that morbid tension finally snaps, as it must, it won't only be the hedge funders of the Hamptons who get hurt. It will be the entire global financial system, especially currencies (dollars, euros, yen, pounds, renminbi) that undergo a swift and dire repricing, and all the other things of this world priced in them. And when that happens, the world will awake to a new reality of steeply reduced possibilities for supporting 7-plus billion people.

The same overinvestments in complexity have produced the racketeering colossus of so-called health care (formerly "medicine"), in case you're wondering why the waiting room of your doctor's office now looks exactly like the motor vehicle bureau. Meanwhile, it's safe to say that the citizens of this land have never been so uniformly unhealthy, even as they're being swindled and blackmailed by their "providers." The eventual result will be a chaotic process of simplification, as giant hospital corporations, insurance companies, and overgrown doctors' practices collapse, and the braver practitioners coalesce into something resembling Third World clinics.

We're still struggling to even apprehend the damage being done to people by cell phones — and I'm not even referring to whatever microwaves actually do to brain cells. Many find it amusing to see whole streets and campus byways filled with young people staring into their phones. Whatever they're gaining in endorphin hits from "being connected" is undermined by the immense losses they're suffering in real social skills and the sinister effects of behavioral conditioning by the programmers of web-based social networks. These failures are being expressed in new social phenomena like flash mobs and the manipulation of college students into Maoist thought police — and these are only the most visible manifestations. A more insidious outcome will be a whole generation's failure to develop a sense of personal agency in a long emergency of civilization that will require exactly that aptitude for survival.

Among the more popular and idiotic strains of diminishing returns is the crusade to replace gasoline-powered cars with electric-powered vehicles. And for what? To promote the illusion that we can continue to be car-dependent and live in suburbia. Neither of those wishful notions is supported by reality. Both of them will soon yield to the fundamental crisis of capital scarcity. In the meantime, hardly anyone is interested in the one thing that would produce a better outcome for Americans: a return to walkable communities scaled to economic reality.

The convulsions over President Trump's vivid clowning are just a symptom of the concealed rot eating away at the foundations of American life. What they demonstrate most of all is the failure of this society's sensory organs — the news media — to ascertain what is actually happening to us. And the recognition of that failure accounts for the current state of the media's disrepute, even if its critics are doing a poor job of articulating it.

IN THE DARK

September 11, 2017

The stock market is zooming this morning on the news that only 5.7 million people in Florida will have to do without air-conditioning, hot showers, and Keurig mochaccinos at dawn's early light, Monday, September 11, 2017. I'm mindful that the news cycle right after a hurricane goes kind of blank for a day or more as dazed and confused citizens venture out to assess the damage. For now, there is very little hard information on the web waves. Does Key West still exist? Hard to tell. We'll know more this evening.

The one-two punch of Harvey and Irma did afford the folks in charge of the nation's affairs a sly opportunity to get rid of that annoying debt ceiling problem. This is the law that established a limit on how much debt the Federal Reserve could "buy" from the national government. Some of you may be thinking: *Buy debt? Why would anybody want to buy somebody's debt?* Well, you see, this is securitized debt, i.e., bonds issued by the US Treasury, which pay interest, and so there is the incentive to buy it. Anyway, there used to — back in the days when the real interest rate stayed positive after deducting the percent of running inflation. This is where the situation gets interesting.

The debt ceiling law supposedly set limits on how much bonded debt the government could issue (how much it could borrow) so it wouldn't go hog wild spending money it didn't have. Which is exactly what happened despite the debt limit because the "ceiling" got raised about a hundred times through the twentieth century into the twenty-first so that the accumulated debt stands around $20 trillion.

Rational people recognize this $20 trillion for the supernatural scale of obligation it represents, and understand that it will never be paid back, so what the hell? Why not just drop the pretense, but keep on working this racket of the government borrowing as much money as it wants, and the Federal Reserve creating that money (or "money") on its computers to infinity. Seems to work so far.

Rational people would also suspect that at some point something might have to give. For instance, the value of the dollars that the debt is issued in. If the value of dollars goes down, then the *real* value of the bonds issued in dollars goes down, and as that happens the many various holders of bonds already issued — individuals, pension funds, insurance companies, sovereign wealth funds of foreign countries — will have a strong incentive to dump the bonds as fast as possible. Especially if backstage magic by the Fed and its handmaidens, the "primary dealer" banks, keeps working to suppress the interest rates of these bonds at all costs.

Would the Federal Reserve then vacuum up every bond that others are dumping on the market? It would certainly try. The Bank of Japan has been doing just that with its own government's bonds to no apparent ill effect, though you kind of wonder what happens when a snake eating its own tail finally reaches its head. What's left, exactly, after it eats that, too? My own guess would be three words: you go medieval. I mean literally. No more engines, electric lights, central heating...

In this land, we face a situation in which both the value of money and the cost of borrowing money would be, at last, completely detached from reality — reality being the real cost and value of all goods and services exchanged for money. Voilà: a king-hell currency crisis and the disruption of trade on the most macro level imaginable. Also, surely, a massive disruption in government services, including Social Security and Medicare, but extending way beyond that. And then we go medieval, too. The mule replaces the Ford F-150. And *The New York Times* finds something to write about besides Russia and trannies.

The value of money and the cost of borrowing it is about as fundamental as it gets in a so-called *advanced economy*. You can screw around with a lot of things running a society, but when that goes, you're flirting seriously with anarchy. In the meantime, we'll see how the social glue holds things together in those parts of Florida that are entering a preview of medieval attractions in the electrical blackout days ahead.

DREAMERS DREAMING DREAMS

September 15, 2017

Hurricanes Harvey and Irma are so out of the news now that people not listening to the mold grow in their sweltering bedrooms probably think these events had something to do with the Confederate defeat. Both *The New York Times* and the *WashPo* are much more concerned this morning with doings on the planet Saturn, and the career moves of fashion icon Chelsea Manning, which is perhaps how things should be in Attention Deficit Nation. Standing by on developments there.In the meantime, personally, I think it would be cruel to deport fully acculturated and *Americanized* young adults to Mexico and Central America. But there should be no question that it's up to Congress to figure out what to do about the DACA kids, and put it into coherent law. The Golden Golem of Greatness was correct to serve the ball into Congress's court. The suave and charming Mr. Obama only punted the action on that problem, and rather cynically too, I suspect, since he knew the next president would be stuck with it.

It's hard to overcome the sentimental demagoguery this quandary fetches up. The so-called Dreamers are lately portrayed in the media as a monoculture of spectacularly earnest high achievers, all potential Harvard grads, and future Silicon Valley millionaires working tirelessly to add value to the US economy. This, again personally, I doubt, and there's also room to doubt that they are uniformly acculturated and Americanized as claimed by the journalists cherry-picking their *stories* to support the narrative that national borders and immigration laws are themselves cruel anachronisms that need to be opposed.

That Dem / Prog narrative has been suspiciously hypocritical for years — the insistence on referring to anybody here illegally as "undocumented," as if their citizenship status was due to a mere clerical error, and also the obvious pandering for votes among the fast-growing Hispanic demographic by pretending that boundaries shouldn't matter. Trump's infamous "wall" is actually just a metaphor for a political faction that believes boundaries do matter, especially in law, where ambiguity is a vice.

That narrative is also at odds with the Left's multicultural principle, since their plea for the DACA kids rests on the idea that they've assimilated successfully into the very American common culture that multiculturalism opposes. The DACA poster kids exhibited on the cable news networks speak English as fluently as Anderson Cooper and Don Lemon. Yet the Left so strenuously opposes the idea that speaking English correctly has any importance that they have allowed several generations of American black ghetto kids to fail academically in inner city schools where language skills are deliberately neglected to avoid offending the underspeeched. In fact, these days anyone who proposes that correct English speech matters in America is automatically branded with the scarlet "R" for *racist*. Except, now it matters where the Dreamers are concerned.

Deplorable as they may be, sunk in job loss, anomie, opiate addiction, obesity, and tattoo collecting, the Trumpsters have a legitimate case that they've been shoved out of work and livelihoods by immigrants both legal and illegal, and nobody should be surprised at the animus this generates. It's right and proper that Congress should resolve the fate of the DACA kids by legislation, and that they should actively address reform of the 1965 immigration act, too. Things have changed. This isn't your great-grandad's America of burgeoning factories beckoning to the downtrodden abroad. This is a sunset industrial economy not really knowing where it's headed, but indulging in grandiose fantasies of perpetual robotic leisure where actual work is obsolete but somehow everybody gets rich.

Trump was also correct to set a six-month deadline for Congress to act. It is clearly their responsibility to do so, and the deadline is exactly the sort of *boundary* in thought and act that this lazy-ass nation needs to begin accomplishing anything on its long and neglected to-do list of pressing issues.

#Take the Knee

September 25, 2017

There's a lot to complain about in this deranged republic — if it even still is one — but the burdens of being a multimillionaire football player would not be at the top of my list. Personally, I find it a little peculiar that we have to play the national anthem before *any* sporting event. All it really shows is how insecure we are as a nation that we have to display our *love of country* in this obsessive manner. Same with congressmen and their stupid flag lapel pins, or the flag in front of Denny's chain restaurants. Are eaters of the "lumberjack slam" so disoriented when they leave the place that they need to be reminded what country they're in? "*Oh, look hon, were in the USA after all.*"

What burns my ass is seeing baseball players in camo uniforms, as if they were an extension of the US military. What's up with that? Is San Diego suddenly a theater of war? And why do US soldiers need to wear camo uniforms when shopping for eyeglasses? There used to be a distinction between battle dress and what you wore the rest of the time, even during a world war. And why on earth is it necessary to fly air force fighter jets over the stadium before the Super Bowl? Who authorizes the spend for that? Who are we trying to scare?

Of course, this new gale of ill-feeling stirred up by our intemperate president, the Golden Golem of Greatness, is driven by the oceanic currents of racial animus that are drowning the country more ruinously than the recent spate of hurricanes. The #Take the Knee campaign was already there, and getting hotter, even before Mr. Trump chimed in. At least he didn't issue the usual sort of vapid nostrum about "diversity" and *all of us getting along*. In his blunt, blundering way, he may force the nation to clarify exactly what the beef is.

Surely it's not about the woes of professional athletes. They are representing the grievances of a different realm in black America, perhaps the places they came from, the city ghettos or the rural backwaters of Dixieland, or maybe even boring black suburbs like Prince George County, Maryland. And the lingering question, to be equally blunt, is: how much is non-black America keeping black America down?

I say non-black because there are plenty of other ethnic groups in the mix besides the dwindling majority of "white folks." I daresay there is as much, perhaps more real animus between Asian Americans and black Americans than between white and black. But Asian Americans did not enslave black Africans, so they're off the hook for that original sin.

Mostly what Asian newcomers do is demonstrate that it's possible to succeed economically and educationally in this country even if you start out with a culture and language completely alien to American ways. This is especially noticeable in places of exacting achievement like Silicon Valley. If anything, Asians complain that they do so well in school the universities have to tamp down their admission numbers to give other ethnic groups a chance.

There seems to be so much psychological displacement in the feelings between black and white America that it is next to impossible to sort out what to do next. White Dem Progs (formerly "liberals") appear to be so consumed with anxious consternation over the outcome of the long civil rights struggle that they are ready to commit a sort of hara-kiri to atone for their unforgivable cis-whiteness. To some extent, they have attempted to compensate by campaigning for an ever growing list of other "marginalized" groups in the hopes of showing some positive results for social change — it's just easier to get significant numbers of homosexuals into the corporate executive suites than to get blacks in there — but the Dem Progs are still left with the grinding reality of a large, dysfunctional black underclass. They certainly can't admit that their own contrived "remedies," such as subsidizing out-of-wedlock births, has anything to do with it, or the devastating effect of "multiculturalism" on some sort of unifying common culture based on values that everybody can agree on.

Similarly, black America displaces their *oppositionality* to whatever remains of a national common culture into the memes of "systemic racism and injustice." It has evolved insidiously in their own culture since the 1960s, probably (I believe) as a reaction to the anxiety provoked by the civil rights legislation of 1964–65. It's really about behavior, especially in school. Are you interested in speaking English? Believe me, that would help a lot in this society. Consider this: Ella Fitzgerald was not singing black or white back in the day. She was just singing.

Fall of the Great Pumpkin

October 2, 2017

Welcome to the witching month when America's entropy-fueled death wish expresses itself with as much Halloween jollity and merriment as the old Christmas spirit of yore. The outdoor displays alone approach a Babylonian scale, thanks to the plastics factories of China. I saw a half-life-size T-rex skeleton for sale at a garden shop last week surrounded by an entire crew of moldering corpse Pirates of the Caribbean in full costume ho-ho-ho-ing among the jack-o-lanterns. What homeowner in this sore-beset floundering economy of three-job gig workers can shell out four thousand bucks to decorate his lawn like the set of a zombie movie?

The overnight news sure took on that Halloween tang as the nation woke up to what is now confirmed to be a national record for a civilian mad-shooter incident. So far, fifty-eight dead and over five hundred injured in Las Vegas at the Route 91 Harvest Festival. (Nine up in fatalities from last year's Florida Pulse nightclub massacre, and way more injured this time.)The incident will live in infamy for maybe a day and a half in the US media. Stand by today as there will be calls far and wide, by persons masquerading as political leaders, for measures *to make sure something like this never happens again*. That's rich, isn't it? Meanwhile, the same six a.m. headlines declared that S &P futures were up in the overnight markets. Nothing can faze this mad bull, apparently. Except maybe the $90 trillion combined derivatives books of CitiBank, JP Morgan, and Goldman Sachs, who have gone back whole hog into *manufacturing* the same kind of hallucinatory collateralized debt obligations (giant sacks of nonperforming loans) that gave Wall Street a heart attack in the fall of 2008.

Europe's quaint doings must seem dull compared to the suicidal potlatch of life in the USA but, believe me, it's a big deal when the Spanish authorities start cracking the heads of Catalonian grandmothers for nothing more than casting a ballot. The video scenes of mayhem at the Barcelona polls looked like something out of the 1968 Prague uprising. And now that the Catalonia secession referendum passed with a 90 percent "yes" vote, it's hard to imagine that a good deal more violent mischief will not follow. So far, the European Union stands dumbly on the sidelines. (For details, read the excellent Roel Ilargi Meijer column on today's *TheAutomaticEarth*.)

Next in the cavalcade of October traumas: the USA versus the nuclear weapons ambitions of North Korea. This has been ramping up all year, of course, but it looks to be headed for a climax now that the Golden Golem of Greatness is at the helm. Truly astounding, though, is America's new method for conducting the most sensitive matters of foreign policy. The day after Secretary of State Rex Tillerson declared that his office was in contact with North Korean officials, the secretary's boss, You-Know-Who, tweeted out: "I told Rex Tillerson, our wonderful Secretary of State, that he is wasting his time trying to negotiate with Little Rocket Man."

Could this possibly be a cleverly orchestrated good cop / bad cop effort to bamboozle Kim Jong-un? Or is the US government just completely dysfunctional? Or maybe something else is afoot. Under normal circumstances, Mr. Tillerson would just resign after such a gross insult, but we must suppose that a patriotic sense of duty compels him to remain in office in case the need suddenly arises in this witching month to run over Mr. Trump with the Twenty-fifth Amendment — the clause in the Constitution that allows a consensus of a pretty small number of national political leaders to toss out a sitting president on the grounds of derangement and incompetence. Stay tuned on that one.

Finally — well, who knows what else may pop up now — there is the matter of Puerto Rico. Halloween there is not like New England, with our nippy fall mornings, steaming mugs of hot cider, and quickening fall color. It will remain 90-degrees-plus in the fetid, stinking ruins, with lots of still-standing water, broken communications, shattered supply lines, and very little electricity. FEMA and the US military may be doing all they can now, but they must be on watch for the ominous blossoming of tropical disease epidemics. The story there is far from over. Trump travels there this week. That may be exactly the moment that the Deep State moves to take him down.

INTO THE COLD AND DARK

October 20, 2017

It amuses me that the nation is so caught up in the sexual mischief of a single Hollywood producer when the nation as a whole is getting fucked sideways and upside down by its own political caretakers.

Behind all the smoke, mirrors, Trump bluster, Schumer fog, and media mystification about the vaudeville act known as The Budget and the Tax Cut, both political parties are fighting for their lives and the Deep State knows that it is being thrown overboard to drown in red ink. There's really no way out of the financial conundrum that dogs the republic and something's got to give.

Many of us have been waiting for these tensions to express themselves by blowing up the artificially levitated stock markets. For about a year, absolutely nothing has thwarted their supernatural ascent, including the threat of World War Three, leading some observers to believe that they have been rigged to perfection. Well, the algo-bots might be pretty fine tuned, and the central bank inputs of fresh "liquidity" pretty much assured, but for all that, these markets are still human artifacts and Murphy's Law still lurks out there in the gloaming with its cohorts, the diminishing returns of technology (a.k.a. "blowback") and the demon of unintended consequences.

Many, including yours truly, have expected the distortions and perversions on the money side of life to express themselves in money itself: the dollar. So far, it has wobbled down only about 10 percent. This is due perhaps to the calibrated disinformation known as "forward guidance" issued by this country's central bank, the Federal Reserve, which has been threatening — pretty idly so far — to raise interest rates and shrink down its vault of hoarded securities — a lot of it janky paper left over from the misadventures of 2007–2009.

I guess the lesson is that when you have a pervasively false and corrupt financial system, it is always subject to a little additional accounting fraud — until it's not. And the next thing you know, you're sitting in the rubble of what used to be your civilization.

The ever more immiserated schnooks who make up the former middle class know that their lives are crumbling, and may feel that they're subject to the utterly overwhelming forces of a cruel destiny generated by a leviathan state that hates and despises them. And of course that is exactly why they turned to the Golden Golem of Greatness for salvation.

Alas, Mr. Trump has not constructed a coherent strategy for defeating the colossus of fakery that drives the nation ever deeper toward the cold and dark. He has a talent for distraction and disruption, though, and so far that gave cover to a whole lot of other people in power who have been able to stand around with their hands in their pockets doing nothing about the sinking state of the nation.

Now, the vaudeville act is coming to a spectacular conclusion as the trappings of Halloween go back in the closet and the pulsating, LED-studded Santas go up on the rooftops. Every ceremony of American life seems drained of meaning now, including the machinations of government over the budget and taxes. The revolution to come out of this frozen swamp of irresponsibility will be the messiest and most incoherent in world history. Nobody will have any idea what is going on outside the geo-storm of failure.

About the only thing one can say for sure is that the American life which emerges from this maelstrom will not look a whole lot like what we're living in today. I remain serenely convinced that when it finally passes, the air will be fresh again and the sun will shine, and a lot more people will know what is real and what is not.

What Could Go Wrong?

November 2, 2017

Everybody and his uncle, and his uncle's mother's uncle, believes that the stock markets will be zooming to new record highs this week, and probably so, because it is the time of year to fatten up, just as the Thanksgiving turkeys are happily fattening up — prior to their mass slaughter.

President Trump's new Federal Reserve chair, Jerome "Jay" Powell, "a low-interest-rate kind of guy," was obviously picked because he is Janet Yellen minus testicles, the grayest of gray go-along Fed gofers, going about his lifelong errand-boy duties in the thickets of financial lawyerdom like a bustling little rodent girdling the trunks of every living shrub on behalf of the asset-stripping business that is private equity (eight years with the Deep State-ish Carlyle Group) while subsisting on the rich insect life in the leaf litter below his busy little paws.

Powell's contribution to the discourse of finance was his famous utterance that the lack of inflation is "kind of a mystery." Oh, yes, indeed, a riddle wrapped in an enigma inside a mystery dropped in a doggie bag with half a pastrami sandwich. Unless you consider that all the "money" pumped out of the Fed and the world's other central banks flows through a hose to only two destinations: the bond and stock markets, where this hot-air-like "money" inflates zeppelin-sized bubbles that have no relation to on-the-ground economies where real people have to make things and trade things.

Powell might have gone a bit further and declared contemporary finance itself "a mystery," because it has been engineered deliberately so by the equivalent of stage magicians devising ever more astounding ruses, deceptions, and misdirections as they enjoy sure-thing revenue streams their magic tricks generate. This is vulgarly known as "the rich getting richer." The catch is, they're getting richer on revenue streams of pure air, and there is a lot of perilous distance between the air they're suspended in and the hard ground below.

Powell noted that the economy is growing robustly and unemployment is supernaturally low. Like his colleagues and auditors in the investment banking community, he's just making this shit up. As the late Joseph Goebbels used to say describing his misinformation technique, if you're going to lie, make sure it's a whopper.

The economy isn't growing and can't grow. The economy is a revenant of something that used to exist, an industrial economy that has rolled over and died and come back as a moldy ghoul feeding on the ghostly memories of itself. Stocks go up because the unprecedented low interest rates established by the Fed allow company CEOs to "lever up" issuing bonds (i.e., borrow "money" from, cough cough, "investors") and then use the borrowed "money" to buy back their own stock to raise the share value, so they can justify their companies' boards of directors jacking up their salaries and bonuses — based on the ghost of the idea that higher stock prices represent the creation of more actual things of value (front-end loaders, pepperoni sticks, oil drilling rigs).

The economy is actually contracting because we can't afford the energy it takes to run the things we do — mostly just driving around — and unemployment is not historically low, it's simply misrepresented by not including the tens of millions of people who have dropped out of the workforce. And an epic wickedness combined with cowardice drives the old legacy news business to look the other way and concoct its good times "narrative." If any of the reporters at *The New York Times* and *The Wall Street Journal* really understand the legerdemain at work in these "mysteries" of finance, they're afraid to say. The companies they work for are dying, like so many other enterprises in the nonfinancial realm of the used-to-be economy, and they don't want to be out of a paycheck until the lights finally go out.

The "narrative" is firmest before its falseness is proved by the turn of events, and there are an awful lot of events *out there* waiting to present, like debutantes dressing for a winter ball. The debt ceiling . . . North Korea . . . Mueller . . . Hillarygate . . . the state pension funds . . . That so many agree the USA has entered a *permanent plateau* of exquisite prosperity is a sure sign of its imminent implosion. What could go wrong?

ABRACADABRA

December 11, 2017

And so, as they say in the horror movies, *it begins*! The unwinding of the Federal Reserve's balance sheet. Such an esoteric concept! Is there one in ten thousand of the millions of people who sit at desks all day long from sea to shining sea who has a clue how this works? Or what its relationship is to the real world?

I confess, my understanding of it is incomplete and schematic at best — in the way that my understanding of a Las Vegas magic act might be. All the flash and dazzle conceals the magician's misdirection. The magician is either a scary supernatural being or a magnificent fraud. Anyway, the audience "out there" for the Federal Reserve's magic act — x-million people preoccupied by their futures slipping away, their cars falling apart, their kid's $53,000 college loan burden, or the $6,000 bill they just received for going to the emergency room with a cut finger — wouldn't give a good goddamn even if they knew the Fed's magic show was going on.

So the Fed has this thing called a balance sheet, which is actually a computer file, filled with entries that denote securities that it holds. These securities, mostly US government bonds of various categories and bundles of mortgages wrangled together by the mysterious government-sponsored entity called Freddie Mac, represent about $4.5 trillion in debt. They're IOUs that supposedly pay interest for a set number of years. When that term of years expires, the Fed gets back the money it loaned, which is called the principal. Ahhhh, here's the cute part!

You see, the money that the Fed loaned to the US government (in exchange for a bond) was never there in the first place. The Fed prestidigitated it out of an alternate universe. It gave this money to a "primary dealer" bank in exchange for the bond, which the bank *abracadabraed* up for the US Treasury. Well, not really. In fact, the Fed just made a notation on the bank's "reserve" account that the money from the alternate universe appeared there. Somehow that money was sent via a virtual pneumatic tube to the US Treasury, where it was used to pay for drones to blow up Yemeni wedding parties, and for the Secret Service to visit pole dancing bars when the president traveled to foreign lands.

Here's the fun part. The Fed announces that it is going to shed this nasty debt, at about $10 billion worth a month starting this past October. The stated goal is to reach an ultimate wind down velocity of $50 billion a month (cue laugh track). If it ever gets there (cue laugh track) it would take twenty years to complete the wind down. The chance of that happening is about the same as the chance that Janet Yellen will come down your chimney on December 24 with a sackful of chocolate Bitcoins. But never mind the long view for the moment.

One way they plan to accomplish this feat is to "roll off" the bonds. That is, when the bonds mature — i.e., come to the end of their term — they will cease to exist. *Poof!* Wait a minute! When a bond matures, the issuer has to send the principal back to the lender. After all, the Fed lent the US Treasury x-billion dollars, the US Treasury paid interest on the loan for x years, and now it has to fork over the full value of the loan (hopefully in dollars that have magically inflated over the years and are now worth less than when they were borrowed — another magic trick!). But that doesn't happen.

Instead, when the theoretical principal is returned to the Fed, the Fed disappears the money, like the girl in a bikini onstage who enters the magician's sacred box and vanishes. Now you see her, now you don't. The explanation, of course, might be that the money was never really there in the first place, so it makes sense to fire it back to the alternative universe it came from. Well, uh, I guess . . .

The catch is: for a while it was here on earth and folks were doing stuff with it, such as the aforementioned drone strikes and pole dancers. Not only that, but the "primary dealer" banks were allowed to loan out ten times the *reserve* minimum denoted on their Fed accounts for participating in the scheme. Who did they lend all that money to? Apparently, a lot of it went to corporations who borrowed it at ultra-low interest rates in order to buy back their own stock, which paid dividends way higher than the interest rate they borrowed at to buy the stuff, and which also pumped up the share value of the stocks, which also happened to make the executives of the corporations way richer in terms of their stock options and bonuses (awarded for boosting the share value of the stock!).

And so *shazzam*: I give you the one percent! And a bankrupt United States of America.

And don't even ask about all those bundles of janky Freddie Mac mortgages fobbed off on the Fed. The reason they did that in the first place was because those mortgages weren't being paid off, and the banks and insurance companies that held them were choking to death on them. So they parked them in a crawl space under the Fed's Eccles Building in Washington, hoping they would just turn to compost. And guess what: they're no more valuable now than they were then. File that one under *Necrophilia*.

THE DARKEST HOURS

December 13, 2017

The Tax "Reform" bill working its way painfully out the digestive system of Congress like a sigmoid fistula ought be renamed the US Asset-stripping Assistance Act of 2017, because that's what is about to splatter the faces of the waiting public, most of whom won't have a personal lobbyist / tax lawyer by their side holding a protective tarpulin during the climactic colonic burst of legislation.

Sssshhhh . . . The media have not groked this, but the economy is actually collapsing, and the nova-like expansion of the stock markets is exactly the sort of action you might expect in a system getting ready to blow. Meanwhile, the more visible rise of the laughable scam known as crypto currency is like the plume of smoke coming out of Vesuvius around 79 AD — an amusing curiosity to the citizens of Pompeii below, going about their normal activities, eating pizza, buying slaves, making love — before hellfire rained down on them.

Whatever the corporate tax rate might be, it won't be enough to rescue the Ponzi scheme that governing has become, with its implacable costs of empire. So the real aim here is to keep up appearances at all costs just a little while longer while the table scraps of a four-hundred-year-long New World banquet get tossed to the hogs of Wall Street and their accomplices. The catch is that even hogs busy fattening up don't have a clue about their imminent slaughter.

The centerpiece of the swindle, as usual, is control fraud on the grand scale. Control fraud is the misuse of authority in applying Three Card Monte principles to financial accounting practice, so that a credulous, trustful public will be too bamboozled to see the money drain from their bank accounts and the ground shift under their feet until the moment of freefall. Control fraud is at work in the corporate C-suites, of course, because that is its natural habitat — remember that silver-haired CEO swine from Wells Fargo who got off scot-free with a lifetime supply of acorns after scamming his account holders — but their errand boys and girls in Congress have been superbly groomed, pampered, fed, and trained to break trail and cover for them.

The country has gotten used to thinking that the game of pretend is exactly the same as what is actually going on in the world. The now seminal phrase coined by Karl Rove, "we make our own reality," is as comforting these days to Republicans from Idaho as it is to hairy, "intersectional" professors of poststructural gender studies in the bluest ivory towers of the Ivy League. Nobody in this Republic really wants to get his-hers-zhe's-they's reality on.

Ah, but reality wants to do its thing regardless of our wishes, hopes, and pretenses, and you can kind of see how these moves taken in the dark waning hours of 2017 will play out in the quickening weeks of 2018. Long about March or April, something's got to give. Other players around the world are surely eager to assist shoving this mad bull of a polity toward the critical state it deserves to enter, though we are doing quite enough on our own to put ourselves at ground zero of financial and political implosion.

The addiction metaphor does apply to America. We are simply addicted to our own bullshit. But like all floundering addicts, we have to hit bottom before anything like clarity returns to our daily doings. When that does happen, it will be as far from intoxicating as you can imagine. The smoldering wreckage of *The World's Highest Standard of Living* will be visible in a 360-degree panorama. A lot of familiar faces will be among the suddenly missing. But we're already prepped for this by the sexual purges of the season. One day, the reassuring figure of ole Garrison Keillor is there to remind you of the exquisite taste of Midwestern sweet corn on an August night; and the next morning, you're up to your eyeballs in the colonic explosion of unintended consequences engineered by the least reassuring cast of characters ever assembled under one capitol dome.

❧ 2018 ❧

"Fire and Fury"

January 5, 2018

It's told that Richard Nixon, during the endgame weeks of Watergate, wandered the west wing hallways in the wee hours, fueled on scotch whiskey, conversing with portraits of notable Americans, including many of his predecessors. "Whaddaya say, Millard? Should I stay or should I go?" He was a trapped animal, after a long, grueling hunt, and he knew the hounds were closing in. Perhaps he took some consolation in hearing that old Abe Lincoln was even more depressed in the final, victorious days of the Civil War than he, Nixon, was at the sheer cruelty of history. In the end, he marshaled the remaining shreds of his dignity, and mounted the helicopter to — his pursuers hoped — an oblivion more fathomless than the mystery of the grave.

And now here is Mr. Nixon's latest successor, the Golden Golem of Greatness, Donald J. Trump, haunting those hallways with the political equivalent of a sucking chest wound, Big Mac in one hand, Big Gulp in the other, wondering who all the people in those oil paintings are . . . and what are they looking at, anyway, as he storms back to his lonely private quarters for a few last tweets of anguish.

It's beginning to look like the last roundup at the O.K. Corral for this somewhat accidental president, product of a decrepitating polity that otherwise grudges up a leadership of fretful, craven, corporate catamites and call girls. Michael Wolff's juicy book *Fire and Fury* would be a career ender for any self-respecting politician, but the narcissism of Trump is altogether a different mental state. Speaking of which, it sounds like some of the amateur psychologists in Congress are taking a deep Talmudic dive into the Twenty-fifth Amendment to see if they can pound the square peg of Trump's head through that particular round hole in the Constitution.

Is he fit for office? This question hangs in the air of the DC swamp like a necrotic odor that can't be seen while it can't be ignored. In a way, the very legitimacy of the republic comes into question — if Trump is the best we can do, maybe the system itself isn't what it was cracked up to be. And then why would we think that removing him from office would make things better? How's that for an existential quandary?

We're informed in *The New York Times* today that "Everyone in Trumpworld Knows He's an Idiot," though "moron" (Rex Tillerson) and "dope" (General H. R. McMaster) figure in there as well. Imagine all the energy it must take for everyone in, say, the cabinet room to pretend that the chief executive belongs in his chair at the center. It reminds me of that old poker game "Indian," where each player holds a hole card pressed outward from his forehead for all to see but him.

Ill winds are blowing and dire forces are converging. Do you think that it's a wonderful thing that the Dow Jones Industrial Average just bashed through the 25,000 gate? The president obviously thinks so. And, of course, he's egged on by all the fawning economic viziers selling stories about a booming economy of waiters, bartenders, and espresso jockeys. But I tell you as sure as there is a yesterday, today, and tomorrow, those stock indexes, grand as they seem, are teetering on the brink of something awesomely sickening. And when they go over that no-bid Niagara cascade into the maelstrom, Mr. Trump's boat will be going over the falls with them.

It's an unappetizing spectacle to watch such a tragic arc play out. After all, these are the lives of fragile, lonely, human creatures trying hard to fathom their fate. You have to feel a little sorry for them as you would feel sorry even for a sad little peccary going down one of those quicksand holes in the Okefenokee Swamp. Surely, many feel that these are simply evil times in which goodness and mercy are AWOL. I'm not sure exactly how this story ends, but it is beginning to look like a choice between a bang and a whimper.

FEVER PITCH

January 13, 2018

In case you're worked up about the looming federal government shutdown, this is exactly how we're supposed to roll in the Long Emergency: everything organized at the gigantic scale is going to wobble and fail. It's nature's way of saying, "get smaller, get realer, scale down, and get local." The catch is, we probably won't listen to nature. Instead, we'll just behave like bystanders and do nothing until the full force of failure is upon us, just as we're doing with climate change — the *tragedy of the commons* at planetary scale.

The failure of national party politics is deep and systemic, as you would expect from activities nurtured in a shithole called Washington, corruption being the manifestation of sepsis. The lethal vector of this illness is money. There's the money flowing into the "campaign funds" (so-called) of congressmen and senators, of course, but there's also the "money" that is flowing in and out of the leviathan government — a whole lot of it is not really there. It's a figment of promises to pay back loans on top of a monumental heap of past promises that will never be kept. The threatened government shutdown is just a symptom of the illness: a society doing things out of scale, trying to run its excessive activities by check kiting and accounting fraud. What could go wrong?

Not the stock and bond markets, I'm sure. Though . . . wait a minute . . . that hockey-stick surge in equities looks a little bit like the action of a thermometer measuring the rising body temperature of a very sick patient. From 25,000 to 26,000 on the Dow — in what? seven days? — is kind of like the flu victim going from 98.6 to 105 after onset. And we know what happens to humans up around the 105 Fahrenheit body temperature level: the brain starts to sputter and smoke. Soon, it's lights out and don't let your karma smack you on the butt going through the exit.

Will a government shutdown be the final insult to the matrix of extreme fragility that holds itself together on little more than inertia and faith? (*Oh, you'll get paid back, don't worry.*) The hubris around this delusional state of affairs seeped over the swampy Washington landscape this week like one of those malaria-laden miasmas of old. The president crowed about the lowest unemployment in decades and the lobotomized media just swallowed it like a wad of masticated pepperoni. Nobody notices the roughly 100 million adults out of the workforce. Do they even figure into the statistical picture? Lowest black and Hispanic unemployment ever. You're kidding, right? Well, we make our own reality. Karl Rove and Oprah agree on that.

I had a lot of fun last night, after the Thursday evening fiddle jam, clicking back and forth between CNN, Fox, and MSNBC. Anderson Cooper was trying — with flagging conviction — to sell another "Trump Dossier" story. Over at MSNBC, Rachel Maddow was in full snide fulmination mode about Russians infiltrating the NRA to get to Trump. Rachel's clarion call *"we now know"* is beginning to sound like Senator Joseph McCarthy's battle cry, "I have in my hand a list of fifty-three communists...!" On Fox, Sean Hannity almost busted a cerebral blood vessel over the unspooling shenanigans in the top ranks of the FBI-DOJ. With each click of the remote control I felt like I was arriving and departing different planets.

Expect the turmoil to get a whole lot worse before it gets better. The Mueller investigation is festering into a constitutional crisis. The bond market is having a heart attack with the Ten Year shooting above the 2.6 percent interest rate line. The dollar is flirting with a sub-90 DXY hashmark. Risk has supposedly been banished — only to come screaming out of the attic like Norman Bates's mother at the last moment, slashing your misplaced confidence to shreds.

HAPPY LANDINGS

January 26, 2018

The blowoff orgy in the stock markets is supposedly America's consolation prize for what many regard as the electoral bad acid trip of the Trump presidency. Sorry to tell you, it's just another hallucination, something you're going to have to come down from. Happy landings!

While the markets have roared parabolically up, in Technicolor, with sugar on top, that ole rascal Reality is working some hoodoo in the other rings of this psychedelic circus: namely the dollar and the bond market. The idiots on NPR's *Marketplace* and the cable TV financial shows haven't noticed the dollar tanking the past several months or the interest rates creeping up in the bond markets. Well, isn't that the point of living as if anything goes and nothing matters, the mantra of the age?

Alas, things are connected and consequences await. It would be rich if a flash crash ripped the Dow, S & P, and Nasdaq to shreds twenty minutes after the Golden Golem of Greatness finished schooling the weenies of Davos on the bigly wonderfulness of his year in office. In fact, it would be a crowning comic moment in human history. I can imagine Trump surrounded by the fawning Beta Boys of Banking as the news comes in. *Poof!* Suddenly, he is alone in the antechamber backstage, nothing left of his admirers but the lingering scent of aftershave. The world has changed. The dream is over. In the mirror he sees something that looks dimly like Herbert Hoover in a polka-dot clown suit, with funny orange wig...A financial smashup is really the only thing that will break the awful spell this country is in: the belief that everyday life can go on when nothing really adds up. It seems to me that the moment is close at hand. Treasury Secretary Mnuchin told the Davos crowd that the US has "a weak dollar" policy. Is that so? Just as his department is getting ready to borrow another $1.2 trillion to cover government operations in the year to come. I'm sure the world wants nothing more than to buy bucketloads of sovereign bonds backed by a falling currency — at the same time that the Treasury's partner in crime the Federal Reserve is getting ready to dump an additional $600 billion in bonds on the market out of its overstuffed balance sheet. I'd sooner try to sell snow cones in a polar bomb cyclone.

When folks don't want to buy bonds, the interest rates naturally have to go higher. The problem with that is your country's treasury has to pay the bond holders more money, but the only thing that has allowed the Treasury to keep borrowing lo these recent decades is the long-term drop of interest rates to the near-zero range. And the Fed's timid 25-basis-point hikes in the overnight Fed Fund rate have not moved the needle quite far enough so far. But with the benchmark ten-year bond rate nosing upward like a mole under the garden toward the 3.00 percent mark, something is going to give.

How long do you think the equity indexes will levitate once the bond market implodes? What vaporizes with it is a lot of the collateral backing up the unprecedented margin (extra borrowed money) that this rickety tower of financial Babel is tottering on. A black hole is opening up in some subbasement of a tower on Wall Street, and it will suck the remaining value from this asset-stripped nation into the vacuum of history like so much silage.

Thus will begin the harsh era of America screwing its head back on and commencing the salvage operation. We'll stop ricocheting from hashtag to hashtag and entertain a few coherent thoughts, such as, "Gee, it turns out you really can't get something for nothing." That's an important thought to have when you turn around and suddenly discover you've got nothing left.

YET ANOTHER YEAR
OF MAGICAL THINKING

February 12, 2018

A peculiar feature of the human condition is that a society in distress will call forth intellectual witch doctors to put on a colorful show that distracts the supposedly thinking class from the insoluble quandaries that portend serious trouble ahead. This feature is on display these days in the person of freelance space pioneer Elon Musk. He intends to establish a human colony on Mars of one million people by 2040.

Musk, who is also developer of the Tesla line of electric cars and businesses that make solar-electric gear and batteries, has tested a series of space vehicles, most recently last week's celebrated launch of his Falcon Heavy Rocket, said to be the most powerful in the world. It is just the precursor of the soon-to-come colossus Musk calls the BFR ("Big Fucking Rocket") that will convey as many as two hundred people at a time to their new home on the Red Planet.

NPR reporter Ari Shapiro was rhapsodizing about this Space X project last week on the airwaves, lending it the media stamp of approval. And since NPR is a major news source for the US thinking class especially, you can be sure this meme of colonizing Mars is now embedded in the brains of the Pareto distribution ("the law of the vital few") who affect to be thought leaders in this land.

There's an old gag about the space race of yore that goes something like this (trigger warning to the ethnically hypersensitive):

The UN convenes a General Assembly session on space travel. The ambassadors of various nations are asked to talk about their space projects. The Russians and the Americans tick off their prior accomplishments and announce plans to explore the planets. Finally, the ambassador from Poland takes his turn at the rostrum. "We intend to land a man on the sun," he declares. There is a great hubbub in the assembly, cries of "Say, what?" and "Wait a minute now . . ." The secretary-general turns to the Polish ambassador and says, "Your scientists must be out of their minds. It's six thousand degrees up there! How can you possibly land a spacecraft on it?" A hush falls over the assembly. The Polish ambassador looks completely relaxed and serene. "We are going to do it at night!" he announces triumphantly.

NPR's Shapiro interviewed blogger Tim Urban of the *Wait But Why* blog for the segment on Musk's space program. Here's a sample of their conversation.

> URBAN: *If humanity is, you know, like a precious photo album you've got, the Earth is like a hard drive you have it on. And any sane person would obviously back it up to a second hard drive. That's kind of the idea here – is all of our eggs are currently on one planet. And if we can build a self-sustaining civilization on Mars, it's much harder for humanity to go extinct.*

> SHAPIRO: *And a million people is about how many people he thinks it would take for a population to be self-sustaining.*

> URBAN: *Right, self-sustaining meaning if something catastrophic happened on Earth during some world war or something that has to do with, you know, a really bad-case scenario with climate change, maybe some – I don't know – the species went extinct on Earth but ships stopped coming with supplies and anything else, a million people is enough that Mars' population would be fine.*

Not to put too fine a point on it, I never heard so much fucking nonsense in my life. There's absolutely nothing that might make Mars a "sustainable" habitat for human beings, or probably any other form of earthly life. The journey alone would destroy human bodies. If you think that living in Honolulu is expensive, with most daily needs of the population shipped or flown in, imagine what it would be like sending a cargo of provisions (Doritos? Pepperoni sticks? Mountain Dew? Fabreeze?) to a million "consumers" up on Mars. Or do you suppose the colonists will "print" their food, water, and other necessities?

Elon Musk's ventures have reportedly vacuumed in around $5 billion in federal subsidies. Mr. Musk is doing a fine job of keeping his benefactors entertained. Americans are still avid for adventures in space, where just about every other movie takes place. I suppose it's because they take us away from the awful conundrums of making a go of it here on Earth, a planet that humans were exquisitely evolved for (or designed for, if you will), and which we are in the process of rendering uninhabitable for ourselves and lots of other creatures.

This is our home. Can we talk about the necessary adjustments and arrangements we have to make in order to continue the human project here? Just based on our performance on this blue planet, we are not qualified to infect other parts of the solar system.

RESIST THAT

February 23, 2018

Perhaps because a weary public was underwhelmed by his indictment last week of thirteen ham sandwiches with Russian dressing, Special Prosecutor Robert Mueller has returned to an old baloney sandwich with American cheese named Paul Manafort, and slathered on some extra mayonnaise to lubricate his journey to federal prison.

The additional charges specify tax evasion and money-laundering shenanigans around Manafort's activities in Ukraine between 2006 and 2015, a period that included the USA's active participation in the overthrow of Ukraine's elected president Viktor Yanukovych, who had declared a desire to join the Russian Customs Union instead of being shanghaied into an expanded NATO.

Scrupulous observers may note that all this took place well in advance of the 2016 US presidential election, when Manafort was candidate Donald Trump's campaign manager for several months before being thrown overboard for reasons still publicly unknown — but probably the awareness that Manafort's personal financial affairs were a smoldering wreck. Meanwhile, Manafort's business colleague Rick Gates has also been charged by Mueller, and this week an associate of Gates, one Alex Van Der Swaan, son-in-law of a Russian billionaire, was persuaded to plead guilty to lying to the FBI about his contacts with Gates.

All of this suggests that there were fabulous opportunities for American profiteering in the sadsack, quasi failed state of Ukraine, and that the feckless Manafort circle will be doing Chinese fire drills in the federal courts until the cows come home, but it doesn't say a whole lot about Russian interference in the 2016 US election. One might surmise that there is enough pressure on Manafort and company to get them to say anything now to save their asses. On the other hand, it could lead in open court to the airing of all sorts of dirty laundry about surreptitious US meddling in Ukraine, and about the corps of camp-following moneygrubbing American grifters who raced in after 2014 to steal anything that wasn't nailed down there by the homegrown kleptocrats.

But it also raises the question whether Mr. Mueller was invited on the scene to prosecute any old thing that fell in his path. Or why he is ignoring the much more obvious smoking mess around his old FBI colleagues who seemed to have committed manifold acts of criminal misconduct in their pursuit of FISA warrants to gather intel on candidate Trump.

In the end — if this extravagant melodrama ever does end — we are stuck with ourselves and our many serious problems here in the USA, which include especially an unraveling financial system that may leave the nation as economically broken and desolate as Russia was in 1991— but ironically with a far less resilient population unused to real travail, as the Russians were after seventy years of soviet Deep State-ism.

Our own Deep State has rapidly become an entity as sinister as the old Soviet nomenklatura. It is interesting and dismaying to see so many public intellectuals swallow its self-serving claims when it was not so many years ago that a healthy and natural skepticism about government lying was the order of the day, especially when it came to the dark towers of US intel.

ANOTHER QUANDARY

March 9, 2018

That crusty ole rascal Gov. Jerry Brown, of California, seems to be enjoying his sunset journey into Civil War Two or maybe the destination is more like *Blade Runner* (since we know that history only rhymes but does not repeat). Anyway, it's not a good place. The once golden state begins to look something like what one federal official recently called — dare I say it? — a shithole.

> *A mix of used hypodermic needles, human feces, and other trash litters the streets and sidewalks in a large section of downtown San Francisco, a local news outlet reported Sunday night. It's a problem that has grown by epic proportions in recent years and has many concerned for the health and safety of some the city's youngest residents.*
> *— The Blaze*

Yes, quite literally. This particular failure of the political Left started in the 1970s when states began aggressively shuttering their large mental hospitals. Many of these institutions dated from the late nineteenth century — ghastly old gothic revival warehouses for the mentally ill, fraught with overtones of abuse and neglect, scenes out of Vincent Price movies . . . lightning flashes through the barred windows . . . a scream in the night . . . hysterical laughter echoing down the dark, tiled hallways. They were an embarrassment, for sure, and certainly an affront to liberal sensibilities. But, of course, they fucked up the remedy for that. Instead of replacing the giant old state insane asylums with smaller, better-managed institutions, they just released the inmates under the rationale that they were a *politically oppressed minority group*. And there it ended.

And so here we are, going on a half century later, with an economy that manufactures failure and immiseration at a greater volume than its other finished products, and many more lost souls out on the city streets, and now we are an even more ideologically inflamed society than we were in 1973, with the ranks of *intersectional* oppressed minorities and aggrieved victim groups grown into virtual armies of the night — and the mentally ill just lost in the crowd.

It never seems to occur to anyone that a mental hospital can be run humanely, at an appropriate scale, and that these poor, sad creatures might, at least, be better off there with a bed, a bathroom, and somebody to check in on them daily than they are wallowing in the gutters of San Francisco and other cities. Surely there are up-to-date models in other lands for this kind of caretaking — if maybe we sent a few bureaucrats overseas to have a look.

But that's not how we roll in this exceptionally greatest of great polities. After all these years, it's hard to avoid concluding that Americans just prefer melodrama to any other form of behavior, including problem solving. Melodrama is colorful, fun, and absorbing. It's just another kind of show business for a people conditioned to see everyday life as a TV series they star in. So kick back and enjoy the homeless show, because it's more entertaining than doing the right thing.

Likewise, the sanctuary city show, a shamelessly sentimental exercise in virtue signaling at the grand scale, larded with little bits of dishonesty, such as the tag "undocumented" for people here illegally, as though their status was the result of some clerical error. Gov. Brown declared war, more or less, on the federal government last week after a fracas in Oakland where the mayor Libby Schaaf rode through town like Paul Revere crying that the ICE teams were coming to make arrests. That riled Attorney General Jeff Sessions enough to start filing lawsuits against this nonsense.

But the Department of Justice faces a big quandary. How are they going to make a big stink over enforcing US immigration laws while they ignore US drug laws vis-à-vis the twenty-nine states that have legalized marijuana use in one way or another? In a number of these states, marijuana production is now a major industry, with substantial political influence. AG Sessions has made noises about cracking down on the marijuana trade, but he hasn't done a damn thing about it because he can't. The state tax revenue alone is too large to be meddled with, never mind popular opinion.

If the AG had a brain in his head instead of the CB radio that's implanted there, he'd realize that the answer is to lean on Congress to delist marijuana as a *Schedule 1 controlled substance*. Or to write a simple law leaving the question to the states. Of course, the intelligent thing would be to put an end to the melodrama called "The War on Drugs." Just like the intelligent thing would be to place the homeless mentally ill in caretaking sanctuaries, call them what you like.

I really don't see how Mr. Sessions can assert federal jurisdiction over illegal immigration without resolving the marijuana question.

IF YOU COME TO A FORK
IN THE ROAD, TAKE IT

March 19, 2018

Various readers, fans, blog commenters, Facebook trolls, and auditors twanged on me all last week about my continuing interest in the RussiaRussiaRussia hysteria, though there is no particular consensus of complaint among them — except for a general "shut up, already" motif. For the record, I'm far more interested in the hysteria itself than the Russia-meddled-in the-election case, which I consider to be hardly any case at all beyond 13 Russian Facebook trolls.

The hysteria, on the other hand, ought to be a matter of grave concern, because it appears more and more to have been engineered by America's own intel community, its handmaidens in the Department of Justice, and the twilight's last gleamings of the Obama White House, and now it has shoved this country in the direction of war at a time when civilian authority over the US military looks sketchy at best. This country faces manifold other problems that are certain to reduce the national standard of living and disrupt the operations of an excessively complex and dishonest economy, and the last thing America needs is a national war dance over trumped-up grievances with Russia.

The RussiaRussiaRussia narrative has unspooled since Christmas and is blowing back badly through the FBI, now with the firing (for cause) of Deputy Director Andrew McCabe hours short of his official retirement (and inches from the golden ring of his pension). He was axed on the recommendation of his own colleagues in the FBI's Office of Professional Responsibility, and they may have been influenced by the as yet unreleased report of the FBI inspector general Michael Horowitz, due out shortly.

The record of misbehavior and "collusion" between the highest ranks of the FBI, the Democratic Party, the Clinton campaign, several top political law firms, and a shady cast of international blackmail peddlers is a six-lane Beltway-scale evidence trail compared to the muddy mule track of Trump "collusion" with Russia. It will be amazing if a big wad of criminal cases are not dealt out of it, even as *The New York Times* sticks its fingers in its ears and goes, "La-la-la-la-la . . ."

It now appears that Mr. McCabe's statements post-firing tend to incriminate his former boss FBI Director James Comey — who is about to embark, embarrassingly perhaps, on a tour for his self-exculpating book *A Higher Loyalty: Truth, Lies, and Leadership.*

A great aura of sanctimony surrounds the FBI these days. Even the news pundits seem to have forgotten the long, twisted reign of J. Edgar Hoover (1924–1972), a dangerous rogue who excelled at political blackmail. And why, these days, would any sane American take pronouncements from the CIA and NSA at face value? What seems to have gone on in the RussiaRussiaRussia matter is that various parts of the executive branch in the last months under Mr. Obama gave each other tacit permission, wink-wink, to do anything necessary to stuff HRC into the White House and, failing that, to derail her opponent, the Golden Golem of Greatness.

The obvious lesson in all this hugger-mugger is that the ends don't justify the means. I suspect there are basically two routes through this mess. One is that the misdeeds of FBI officers, Department of Justice lawyers, and intel agency executives get adjudicated by normal means, namely, grand juries and courts. That would have the salutary effect of cleansing government agencies and shoring up what's left of their credibility at a time when faith in institutions hangs in the balance.

The second route would be for the authorities to ignore any formal response to an ever more self-evident trail of crimes, and to allow all that political energy to be funneled into manufactured hysteria and eventually a phony provocation of war with Russia. Personally, I'd rather see the US government clean house than blow up the world over an engineered hallucination.

STATE OF FAILURE

April 9, 2018

BEIRUT, Lebanon — Days after President Trump said he wanted to pull the United States out of Syria, Syrian forces hit a suburb of Damascus with bombs that rescue workers said unleashed toxic gas.

Fool me once, shame on you; fool me twice, shame on me, the old saying goes. So tread carefully through the minefields of propaganda laid for the credulous in such low organs as *The New York Times*. There are excellent reasons to suppose that the American Deep State wishes strenuously to keep meddling all around the Middle East. The record so far shows that the blunt instruments of US strategic policy produce a consistent result: failed states.

Syria was well on its way to that sorry condition — prompted by an inflow of Jihadi maniacs fleeing our previous nation un-building experiment in Iraq — when the Russians stepped in with an arrantly contrary idea: to support the Syrian government. Of course, the Russians had ulterior motives: a naval base on the Mediterranean, expanded influence in the region, and a Gazprom concession to develop and manage large natural gas fields near the Syrian city of Homs, for export to Europe. The latter would have competed with America's client state Qatar, a leading gas exporter to Europe.

But the US objected to supporting the government of Bashar al-Assad, as it had previously with Saddam Hussein and Muammar Gaddafi, as well as Russia's presence there in the first place. So the US cultivated antigovernment forces in the Syrian civil war, a hodgepodge of Islamic psychopaths variously known as ISIS (Islamic State of Iraq and the Levant), Daesh, al-Qaeda, al-Nusra, Ansar al-Din, Jaysh al-Sunna, Nour al-Din al-Zenki, and what have you.

As it happened, US policy in Syria after 2013 became an exercise in waffling. It was clear that our support for the forces of Jihad against Assad was turning major Syrian cities into rubble fields, with masses of civilians caught in the middle and ground up like so much dog food. President Barack Obama famously drew a line in the sand on the use of chemical weapons. It was well known that the Syrian army had stockpiles of chemical poisons. But the US also knew that our Jihadi consorts had plenty of their own. Incidents of chemical atrocities were carried out by . . . somebody . . . it was never altogether clear or proven . . . and Mr. Obama's line in the sand disappeared under dust storms of equivocation.

Finally, a joint mission of the United Nations Human Rights Commission (UNHRC) and the Organization for the Prohibition of Chemical Weapons (OPCW) was called in to supervise the destruction of the Syrian government's chemical weapons, and certified it as accomplished in late 2014. Yet poison gas incidents continued — most notoriously in 2017 when President Donald Trump responded to one with a sortie of cruise missiles against a vacant Syrian government airfield. And now another incident in the Damascus suburb of Douma has provoked Mr. Trump to tweetstormed threats of retaliatory violence, just days after he proposed a swift withdrawal from that vexing corner of the world.

Surely by now the American public has developed some immunity to claims of nefarious doings in foreign lands ("weapons of mass destruction" and all). The operative sentence in that *New York Times* report is "Syrian forces hit a suburb of Damascus with bombs that rescue workers said unleashed toxic gas." Yeah, well, how clear is it that the toxic gas was contained in the bombs, or rather that the bombs dropped by the Syrian military blew up a chemical weapon depot controlled by antigovernment Jihadis? Does that hodgepodge of maniacs show any respect for the UN, or the Geneva Convention, or any other agency of international law? As in many previous such incidents, we don't know who was responsible — though there is plenty of reason to believe that parties within the US establishment are against Mr. Trump's idea of getting the hell out of that place and might cook up a convenient reason to prevent it.

Lastly, how is it in Bashar al-Assad's interests to provoke a fresh international uproar against him and his regime? I'd say it is not the least in his interest, since he is on the verge of putting an end to the awful conflict. He may not be a model of rectitude by Western standards, but he's not a mental defective. And he has very able Russian support advising him in what has been so far a long and difficult effort to prevent his state from failing — or being failed for him.

That Collapse You Ordered…?

April 30, 2018

I had a fellow on my latest podcast, released Sunday, who insists that the world population will crash 90-plus percent from the current 7.6 billion to 600 million by the end of this century. Jack Alpert heads an outfit called the Stanford Knowledge Integration Lab (SKIL) which he started at Stanford University in 1978 and now runs as a private research foundation. Alpert is primarily an engineer.

At 600 million, the living standard in the USA would be on a level with the post-Roman peasantry of fifth-century Europe, but without the charm, since many of the planet's linked systems — soils, oceans, climate, mineral resources — will be in much greater disarray than was the case 1,500 years ago. Anyway, that state of life may be a way station to something more dire. Alpert's optimal case would be a world human population of 50 million, deployed in three "city-states," in the Pacific Northwest, the Uruguay / Paraguay border region, and China, that could support something close to today's living standards for a tiny population, along with science and advanced technology, run on hydropower. The rest of world, he says, would just go back to nature, or what's left of it. Alpert's project aims to engineer a path to that optimal outcome.

I hadn't encountered quite such an extreme view of the future before, except for some fictional exercises like Cormac McCarthy's *The Road*. (Alpert, too, sees cannibalism as one likely by-product of the journey ahead.) Obviously, my own venture into the fictionalized future of the *World Made by Hand* books depicted a much kinder and gentler reset to life at the circa-1800 level of living, at least in the USA. Apparently, I'm a sentimental softie.

Both of us are at odds with the more generic techno optimists who are waiting patiently for miracle rescue remedies like cold fusion while enjoying reruns of *The Big Bang Theory*. (Alpert doesn't completely rule out as yet undeveloped energy sources, though he acknowledges that they're a low-percentage prospect.) We do agree with a basic premise that the energy supply is mainly what supports the way we live now, and that it shows every evidence of entering a deep and destabilizing decline that will halt the activities necessary to keep our networks of dynamic systems running.

A question of interest to many readers is how soon or how rapid the unraveling of these systems might be. When civilizations crumble, it tends to fast-track. The Roman empire seems to be an exception, but in many ways it was far more resilient than ours, being a sort of advanced Flintstones economy, with even its giant-scale activities (e.g., building the Colosseum) being accomplished by human-powered work. In any case, the outfit really fell apart steadily after the reign of emperor Marcus Aurelius (161–180 AD).

The Romans had their own version of a financialized economy: they simply devalued their coins by mixing in less and less silver at the mint, so they could pretend to pay for the same luxuries they had grown accustomed to as resources stretched thin. Our financialized economy — like everything else we do — operates at levels of complexity so baffling that even its supposed managers at the central banks are flying blind through fogs of debt, deception, and moral hazard. When that vessel of pretense slams into a mountaintop, the effects are likely to be quick and lethal to the economies on the ground below.

In our time, the most recent crash of a major socioeconomic system was the fall of the Soviet Union in 1990–91. Of course, it happened against the backdrop of a global system that was still revving pretty well outside the USSR, and that softened the blow. Ultimately, the Russians still had plenty of oil to sell, which allowed them to reset well above the fifth-century peasant level of existence. At least for now. The Soviet Union collapsed because it was a thoroughly dishonest system that ran on pretense and coercion. Apparently, the US intel community completely missed the signs that political collapse was underway.

They seem to be pretty clueless about the fate of the USA these days, too. If you consider the preoccupations of two very recent intel chiefs — John Brennan of CIA and James Clapper, DNI — who now inveigh full time on CNN as avatars of the Deep State against the wicked Golden Golem of Greatness. Personally, I expect our collapse to be as sudden and unexpected as the USSR's, but probably bloodier because there's simply more stuff just lying around to fight over. Of course, I expect the collapse to express itself first in banking, finance, and markets — being so deeply faith-based and so subject to simple failures of faith. But it will become political and social soon enough, maybe all at once. And when it happens in the USA, it will spread through the financial systems the whole world round.

GATE OF GATES?

May 18, 2018

When historians of the future finish their meal of rat à la moutarde at the camp-fire, and pass around the battered plastic jug of wild raisin wine, they will kick back and hear the griot sing of John Brennan, the fabled chief of an ancient order called the CIA, and how he started the monkey business aimed at bringing down the wicked Golden Golem of Greatness, chief of chiefs in the land once known as America. Alas, the hero's journey of Brennan ends in a jail cell at the storied Allenwood Federal Penitentiary, where he slowly pined away between games of Ping-Pong and knock hockey, dreaming of a cable network retirement package that never was...One gets the feeling more and more that Mr. Brennan is at the center of this ever mushrooming matrix of scandals around the 2016 election. "Bigger Than Watergate?" the headline in today's *New York Times* asks? The mendacity of this once proud newspaper is really something to behold. Take the following paragraph, for instance. *Depending on what is eventually proven, the core scandal could rival Watergate, in which a "third-rate burglary" of Democratic National Committee headquarters ultimately revealed a wide-ranging campaign of political sabotage and spying to influence the 1972 presidential election and undercut perceived rivals. In the current case, a hostile foreign power sought to sway the 2016 election and there is evidence that at least some people in Mr. Trump's circle were willing to collaborate with it to do so.* You have to really wonder how the *Times* editors overlooked the other relevant details *in the current case* pertaining to goings-on initiated by Mr. Brennan and involving obviously criminal misbehavior among the US intelligence services, and especially the Federal Bureau of Investigation, in their effort to undo the election that put the Trump creature in the White House instead of the enchantress known as Hillary. I did like the trope "a hostile foreign power." Apparently they were too embarrassed to just say "Russia," since by now it has become the most threadbare hobgoblin in all of US political history.

Rumors are flying that the long-awaited (so long it is nearly forgotten) Department of Justice inspector general's report contains a rather severe interpretation of what actually has been going on for the last couple of years in this far-rago of charge and countercharge that the legacy news media has been doing its best to garble and deflect — namely, that the highest officers of the government conspired to tamper with the 2016 election. The latest twist is news — actually reported by the *Times* Thursday — that the FBI placed a "mole" inside the Trump campaign. If the mole discovered anything, then it is the only morsel of information that hasn't been leaked in two years, which leads the casual observer to infer that *the mole* found really nothing.

On the other hand, a great deal is already known about the misdeeds surrounding Hillary and her supporters, including Mr. Obama and his inner circle, and some of those incriminating particulars have been officially certified — for example, the firing of FBI Deputy Director Andrew McCabe on recommendations of the agency's own ethics committee, with overtones of criminal culpability. There is also little ambiguity left about the origin of the infamous Steele Dossier. It's an established fact that it was bought and paid for by the Democratic National Committee, which is to say the Hillary campaign, and that many of the dramatis personae involved lied about it under oath. Many other suspicious loose ends remain to be tied. Those not driven insane by Trumpophobia are probably unsatisfied with the story of what Attorney General Loretta Lynch was doing, exactly, with former president Bill Clinton during that Phoenix airport tête-à-tête a few days before FBI Director Jim Comey exonerated Mr. Clinton's wife in the email server "matter."

One can see where this tangled tale is tending: to the sacred chamber known as the grand jury. Probably several grand juries. That will lead to years of entertaining courtroom antics at the same time that the USA's financial condition fatefully unravels. That event might finally produce the effect that all the exertions of the so-called Deep State have failed to achieve so far: the discrediting of Donald Trump. Alas, the literal *discrediting* of the USA and its hallowed institutions — including the US dollar — may be a much more momentous thing than the fall of Trump.

Personally, I won't be completely satisfied until the editors of *The New York Times* have to answer to charges of sedition in a court of law.

NOTES ON HEARTACHE AND CHAOS

May 31, 2018

I was interviewing a couple of homesteaders on an island north of Seattle at twi-light last night when they noticed that the twelve-year-old family dog, name of Lacy, had not come home for dinner as ever and always at that hour. A search ensued and they soon found her dead in the meadow a hundred feet behind the house with two big puncture wounds in her body. Nobody had heard a gunshot. We'd just been talking inside and a nearby window was open. They suspect the dog met up with a black-tailed deer buck out there and was gored to death. We hadn't heard a yelp, or anything. A week ago, an eagle got one of their geese, and some land-based monster got its companion just the other day.

Nature is what it is, of course, and it's natural for human beings to think of its random operations as malevolent. That aspersion probably inclines us to think of ourselves as beings apart from nature (some of us, anyway). We at least recognize the tragic side of this condition we're immersed in, and would wish that encoun-ters between its denizens might end differently — like maybe that two sovereign creatures meeting up by sheer chance on a mild spring evening would exchange pleasantries, ask what each was up to, and go on their ways.

Malevolent nature visited me the night before, back home in upstate New York. Something slit the screened window of my henhouse, got inside, and slaughtered two of my birds. Big Red was missing altogether except for a drift of orange feathers. I found Little Blue just outside in a drift of her own feathers, half eaten. I suspect a raccoon got them, slitting the window screen cleverly with its dexterous handlike paws — yes, so much like our own clever hands. (In classic after-the-fact human style, I fortified the window with steel hardware cloth the next day.)

It's the time of year when the wild critters of field and woodland are birthing their young and anxious to procure food for them. Who can blame them for that. Chicken is an excellent dish. I eat it myself, though never my own hens. I actually rescued Little Blue from the clutches of a red-tailed hawk last year as the hawk struggled to get airborne with her and let go as I screeched at it. Blue recovered from the talon punctures and had a good year — one good year on this earth with all its menace, when it is not busy being beautiful.

I worry about my chickens inordinately, though my friends who've been immersed in country doings much longer than me find this ludicrous. Despite our yearnings and pretenses to bethink ourselves specially holy beings, we're specialists at carnage when we're not composing string quartets or carrying out God's work on Wall Street.

The next morning, I motored down Interstate 5 to the Seattle airport to board a giant aluminum and plastic simulacrum of a bird for a rapid journey to Oakland, California. The fantastic violence of an interstate highway is hard to detect when a) you're hermetically sealed in the capsule of your rent-a-car, and b) when you've been driving on interstate highways so many years that it seems like a normal human environment. And the fury of a jet airplane rending the fabric of the sky is hardly noticeable when you're in seat 21-D being served iced drinks and pretzels. Somewhere in this universe — maybe everywhere in it — a skeptical intelligence may be wondering at our doings here.

Something lethal is waiting *out there* to get you and me, too — some carnivore perhaps, a one-celled demon, a venture capitalist with a snootful of Cabo Wabo "thick cut" tequila behind the wheel of a Chevy Tahoe. It's not so hard to meet heartache and chaos in this world, and yet love and beauty still abide. Treasure them when you find them. They explain everything.

THE SUMMER OF DISCONTENT

June 8, 2018

The ill-feeling among leaders of the G-7 nations — essentially, the West plus Japan — was mirrored early this morning in the puking financial market futures, so odious, apparently, is the presence of America's Golden Golem of Greatness at the Quebec meet-up of First World poobahs. It's hard to blame them. The GGG refuses to play nice in the sandbox of the old order.

Like many observers here in the USA, I can't tell exactly whether Donald Trump is out of his mind or justifiably blowing up out-of-date relationships and conventions in a world that is desperately seeking a new disposition of things. The West had a mighty good run in the decades since the fiascos of the mid-twentieth century. My guess is that we're witnessing a slow-burning panic over the impossibility of maintaining the enviable standard of living we've all enjoyed.

All the jabber is about trade and obstacles to trade, but the real action probably emanates from the energy sector, especially oil. The G-7 nations are nothing without it, and the supply is getting sketchy at the margins in a way that probably and rightfully scares them. I'd suppose, for instance, that the recent run-up in oil prices from $40 a barrel to nearly $80 has had the usual effect of dampening economic activity worldwide. For some odd reason, the media doesn't pay attention to any of that. But it's become virtually an axiom that oil over $75 a barrel smashes economies while oil under $75 a barrel crushes oil companies.

Mr. Trump probably believes that the USA is in the catbird seat with oil because of the so-called shale oil miracle. If so, he is no more deluded than the rest of his fellow citizens, including government officials and journalists, who have failed to notice that the economics of shale oil don't pencil out — or are afraid to say. The oil companies are not making a red cent at it, despite the record-breaking production numbers that recently exceeded the previous all-time peak set in 1970. The public believes that we're "energy independent" now, which is simply not true because we still import way more oil than we export: 10.7 million barrels incoming versus 7.1 million barrels a day outgoing (US EIA).

Shale oil is not a miracle so much as a spectacular stunt: how to leverage cheap debt for a short-term bump in resource extraction at the expense of a future that will surely be starved for oil. Now that the world is having major problems with excessive debt, it is also going to have major problems with oil. The quarrels over trade arise from this unacknowledged predicament: there will be less of everything that the economically hyperdeveloped nations want and need, including capital. So what's shaping up is a fight over the table scraps of the banquet that is shutting down.

That quandary is surely enough to make powerful nations very nervous. It may also prompt them to actions and outcomes that were previously unthinkable. At the moment the excessive debt threatens to blow up the European Union, which is liable to be a much bigger problem for the EU than anything Trump is up to. It has been an admirably stable era for Europe and Japan, and I suppose the boomers and X gens don't really remember a time not so long ago when Europe was a cauldron of tribal hatreds and stupendous violence, with Japan marching all over East Asia, wrecking things.

There is also surprisingly little critical commentary on the notion that Mr. Trump is seeking to "reindustrialize" America. It's perhaps an understandable wish to return to the magical prosperity of yesteryear. But things have changed. And if wishes were fishes, the state of the earth's oceans is chastening enough to give you the heebie-jeebies. Anyway, we're not going back to the Detroit of 1957. We'll be fortunate if we can turn out brooms and scythes twenty years from now, let alone flying Teslas.

This will be the summer of discontent for the West especially. The fact that populism is still a rising force among these nations is a clue of broad public skepticism about maintaining the current order. No wonder the massive bureaucracies vested in that order are freaking out. I'm not sure Mr. Trump even knows or appreciates just how he represents these dangerous dynamics.

CONFLICT ESCALATION

June 25, 2018

My website was down early this morning, and I'm just a little suspicious that it had something to do with me expressing an opinion outside the Overton window of what is considered acceptable discourse on illegal immigration. Namely, that it's illegal, with all that implies. At least I wasn't thrown out of a restaurant over the weekend, though the fact is I didn't even try to eat out.

Now my particular problem may turn out to be no more than a cockroach chewing through some wires in the Jersey server farm where this blog dwells — we'll find out soon enough — but there are obviously other signs that "the Resistance" is tuning up the antagonism against its perceived enemies.

I'm in the peculiar position of not being a partisan of President Trump, and yet being a publicly avowed enemy — if there's any doubt — of the Resistance, especially these days its institutional branch known as the Democratic Party. What a ragtag and bobtail of mendacious cowards it has become.

The truth, I believe, is that the party wants to bring as many Mexicans and Central Americans as possible across the border, by any means necessary, to fortify its future voter base. And so they are acting to ensure that it happens. Of course, this might also be viewed as a suicidal course of action for the party, since it puts them in opposition to the rule of law as a general principle, which is a pretty sketchy basis for any claim to govern. That being the case, the outcome for the Democratic Party may be its own demise as a legitimate political bloc. It's one thing to ignore the economically foundering, traditional working-class constituency of actual US citizens who are having a tougher time every year making a living; it's another thing to bring in a several-millionfold population of noncitizens to replace them.

Anyway, it's a pretty poor strategy for success in the coming midterm election. The effort got a boost over the weekend from Congresswoman Maxine Waters (D-Cal.) who called for Trump administration employees to be thrown out of department stores and other retail establishments as well as restaurants. Why stop there? Why not enslave Trump employees and supporters? Force them to work without pay in the Chick-fil-A regional distribution warehouses? One wonders what House Minority Leader Nancy Pelosi thinks of Ms. Waters's proposal. Other Democratic party leaders zipped their pieholes about it.

It may also be the case that the majority Republicans in Congress are cowed and anxious about doing anything legislatively to clarify the disheveled US immigration laws. If that's true, they might pause to consider that their own party is not so far from whirling around the drain, too, from a consistent demonstrated lack of principle — as well as its uncomfortable association with the maverick president who only nominally leads the party.

The trouble is that the entities waiting to replace both the useless, careless, feckless Democrats and Republicans are chaos and violence, not reconstituted parties with coherent political programs. The US, and really all the so-called advanced nations on earth, are heading into an era of scarcity and austerity that is likely to present as mortal conflict.

Bill Maher could easily get his wish of an economic crisis before many more months go by. The financial markets have never been under so much lethal stress. Everybody and every institution is drowning in debt that can't possibly be repaid. The supposed remedies for that — like, inflating the debt away with official monetary policy — would be ruinous for the 99 percenters already struggling to lead normal lives. And the looming novelty of a cashless society would be even worse in terms of personal liberty.

Ah! We somehow miraculously got the website back up and running to post at the usual time today. Last week, I was awash in censure and obloquy for dissing the Resistance stand on illegal immigration, the alleged "torture" of children separated from their parents (or plain parentless) at the US / Mexico border. Much of the published opprobrium against Trump and the federal authorities under him proved to be quite false — such as the weeping child on the cover of *Time* magazine, who was, in fact, not separated from her mother (a previous deportee who abandoned her husband and several other children in Honduras). As far as I know, *Time* has not offered an explanation or an apology for this attempt to misrepresent reality to an already confused American public.

Twelve Ham Sandwiches
with Russian Dressing

July 16, 2018

So former FBI lawyer Lisa Page declined to testify before a congressional committee because she didn't feel like it. Apparently we're now a rule of law–optional nation. Until recently, we were merely reality-optional. That was fun, but when officers of the country's leading law enforcement agency go optional on standard legal procedure, like answering subpoenas, then we're truly in the land where anything goes (and nothing matters).

After two years of Trump-inspired hysteria, it's pretty obvious what went on in the bungled Obama-Hillary power handoff of 2016 and afterward: the indictable shenanigans of candidate Hillary and her captive DNC prompted a campaign of agitprop by the US intel "community" to gaslight the public with a Russian meddling story that morphed uncontrollably into a crusade to make it impossible for Mr. Trump to govern. And what's followed for many months is an equally bungled effort to conceal, deceive, and confuse the issues in the case by Democratic Party partisans still in high places. It was very likely begun with the tacit knowledge of President Obama, though he remained protected by a shield of plausible deniability. And it was carried out by high-ranking officials who turned out to be shockingly unprofessional, and whose activities have been disclosed through an electronic data evidence trail.

Mr. Trump's visit to confer with Russian president Putin in Helsinki seems to have provoked a kind of last-gasp effort to keep the increasingly idiotic Russian election meddling story alive — with Robert Mueller's ballyhooed indictment of twelve "Russian intel agents" alleged to have "hacked" emails and computer files of the DNC and Hillary's campaign chairman John Podesta. The gaping holes in that part of the tale have long been unearthed so I'll summarize as briefly as possible. 1) The bandwidth required to transfer the files has been proven to be greater than an internet hack might have conceivably managed in the time allowed and points rather to a direct download into a flash drive device. 2) The DNC computer hard drives, said to be the source of the alleged hacking, disappeared while in the custody of the US intel community (including the FBI). 3) The authenticity of the purloined emails by Mr. Podesta and others has never been disputed, and they revealed a lot of potentially criminal behavior by them. 4) Mr. Mueller must know he will never get twelve Russian intel agents into a US courtroom, so the entire exercise is a joke and a fraud. In effect, he's indicted twelve ham sandwiches with Russian dressing.

Tragically, the American public is led to take this ploy seriously by a morally compromised news media, especially CNN and the *The New York Times*. The latter outfit is so afflicted with a case of the Russian meddling vapors that it ran this laughable headline at the top of its front page yesterday: "Just Sitting Down with Trump, Putin Comes Out Ahead." Gosh, what's the message there? Don't even bother talking to foreign heads of state, especially in the interest of improving relations?

The salient question that persons in authority might ask out loud is how come so many officers of the intel community have not been hauled in front of grand juries to answer for their obviously incriminating behavior. Mr. Mueller is perhaps too busy chasing Russian phantoms to draw up a bill of particulars against characters such as former CIA chief (now CNN shill) John Brennan, who apparently orchestrated the early chapters of the Russian meddling ruse; Bruce and Nellie Ohr, who ushered the DNC's Steele Dossier into the FBI's warrant machinery; fired FBI Deputy Director Andrew McCabe, who managed the Steele Dossier and its spinoff mischief as an "insurance policy" against Mr. Trump; Peter Strzok, who executed the "insurance policy"; and, of course, Ms. Page, Strzok's paramour, who decided that testifying before Congress was beneath her dignity. These and probably many others.

Tragically, also, these matters can only be fully corrected by the very Department of Justice that includes under its management the rogue FBI. Who else can formally and legally bring these cases before grand juries? The DOJ appears intent on preventing that from ever happening. Congress has so far omitted enforcing its subpoenas or using its impeachment power to dislodge obdurate DOJ officials. Mr. Trump, for now apparently, has declined to use his inherent executive powers to clean out this rats' nest, say by removing secrecy shields from many of the documents at issue in the DOJ's possession — most likely because he can't afford to be seen "meddling" in the tangled proceedings. The net result of all this subterfuge, inaction, and gaslighting is the defeat of the rule of law generally in American life. This ought to be taken seriously. If it's asking too much of the system, then the system itself will eventually not be taken seriously, and that will be the end of the republic as we knew it.

Postscript: I'm advised that Lisa Page did finally testify in closed session while I was out of the country last week. However, it took an extraordinarily long time for her to comply with the request, as detailed in this Tweet from Rep. Mark Meadows.

Remarkably, we learned new information today suggesting the DOJ had not notified Lisa Page of Congress' outstanding interview requests for over 7 months now. The DOJ/FBI appear to be continuing their efforts to keep material facts, and perhaps even witnesses, from Congress.

Post-postscript: Cable TV turned into a madhouse Monday night with CNN's Erin Burnett and MSNBC's Chris Matthews beating the war drums like Comanches waiting on a wagon train. Putin, they screamed, is the criminal head of a hostile foreign power. If they say so, it must be true. John Brennan, ex-CIA chief, calls Mr. Trump's behavior "treasonous" for doubting the veracity of seventeen intelligence agencies. To me, this suggests that the US has got too many intelligence agencies and that they may be a bigger threat to liberty in America than anything Russia has done or is doing to us.

RUSSIA ATTACKED US

July 23, 2018

This idiotic fantasy congealed in the political matrix last week as everyone across the spectrum of parties and factions scrambled for patriotism brownie points in what is shaping up as an epic game of Capture the Flag for the midterm elections. *Listen to me for a moment*, as our arch-nemesis Vlad the Putin said to Fox News knucklehead Chris Wallace in an interview aired Sunday night — when Wallace interrupted Mr. Putin for perhaps the fourth time, saying, "I don't want to interrupt you, sir, but . . ."

"Listen to me. Be patient," Mr. Putin repeated dolefully, like a second-grade teacher struggling with an ADD kid.

The interview was trying my Christian patience, too. And my own personal fantasy was that Mr. Putin would whip out 30 inches of rebar and whap Chris Wallace upside the head with it. But he only repeated, "Be patient . . ."

So, listen to me: Russia did not "attack" us. Trolling on Facebook is not an attack on the nation. The allegation that Russia "hacked" Hillary's email and the DNC server is so far without evidence, and computer forensics strongly suggests that the information was transferred onto a flash drive on its journey to Wikileaks. And, of course, the information itself, concerning embarrassing unethical hijinks among Democratic Party officials, was genuine and truthful — they "meddled" in their own primary elections.

This lingering Russia hysteria got a big reboot last week following Mr. Trump's impressively awkward performance onstage with the nimble Mr. Putin, whose self-possession only reinforced Mr. Trump's lumbering oafishness and amazing verbal incoherence. It's hard enough for Americans to understand what the Golden Golem of Greatness is trying to say; imagine the torment of the translators untangling his tortured utterances!

I daresay that some of the American observers secretly wished that we could swap over Mr. Trump for Mr. Putin so as to have a national leader with some decorum and poise, but alas . . . And one can't help but wonder how Mr. Putin sizes up POTUS among his intimates inside the Kremlin. I'd love to be a fly on that wall.

The Helsinki summit meeting has the look of a turning point in Mr. Trump's political fortunes. One irony is that he may escape his enemies' efforts to nail him on any Russia "collusion" rap only to be sandbagged by financial turmoil as the dog days of summer turn nervously toward autumn. Events will cancel the myth that his actions as president have produced a booming economy. If anything, the activities that make up our economy have only become more vicious rackets, especially the war industries, with all their inducements to counter the imagined Russia threat.

The financial markets are the pillars of the fantasy that the US economy is roaring triumphantly. The markets are so fundamentally disabled by ten years of central bank interventions that they don't express the actual value of any asset, whether stocks, or bonds, or gold, oil, labor, currencies, or the folly known as crypto currency. We await the fabled "moment of truth" when the avenging angel of price discovery returns and shatters the illusion that accounting fraud equals prosperity.

The revelation that Mr. Trump is not an economic genius will spur a deeper dive by chimerical Democrats into nanny state quicksand. They will make the new fad of a Guaranteed Basic Income the centerpiece of the midterm election — even though many Democrats will not really believe in it. They are pretending not to notice how broke the USA actually is, and how spavined by unpayable debt. The lurking suspicion of all this is surely behind fantasies such as *Russia attacked us*, the displacement of abstruse and impalpable fear onto something simple and cartoonish, like the president of the United States.

THE THREE-HEADED MONSTER

August 17, 2018

The faction that used to be the Democratic Party can be described with some precision these days as a three-headed monster driving the nation toward danger, darkness, and incoherence. Anyone interested in defending what remains of the sane center of American politics take heed.The first head is the one infected with the toxic shock of losing the 2016 election. The illness took hold during the campaign that year when the bureaucracy under President Obama sent its lymphocytes and microphages in the intel community — especially the leadership of the FBI — to attack the perceived *disease* that the election of Donald Trump represented. The "doctors" of this Deep State diagnosed the condition as "Russian collusion." An overdue second opinion by doctors outside the Deep State adduced later that the malady was actually an autoimmune disease.

The agents actually threatening the health of the state came from the intel community itself: Mr. Brennan, Mr. Clapper, Mr. Comey, Mr. Strzok, Mr. McCabe, Mr. Ohr, Ms. Yates, Ms. Page et al. who colluded with pathogens in the DNC, the Hillary campaign, and the British intel service to chew up and spit out Mr. Trump as expeditiously as possible. With the disease now revealed by hard evidence, the chief surgeon called into the case, Robert Mueller, is left looking ridiculous — and perhaps subject to malpractice charges — for trying to remove an appendix-like organ called *the Manafort* from the body politic instead of attending to the cancerous mess all around him. Meanwhile, the Deep State can't stop running its mouth — *The New York Times*, CNN, *WashPo* et al. — in an ever more hysterical reaction to the truth of the matter: the Deep State itself colluded with Russia (and perhaps hates itself for it, a sure recipe for mental illness).

The second head of this monster is a matrix of sinister interests seeking to incite conflict with Russia in order to support arms manufacturers, black box "security" companies, congressmen on the take, and an army of obscenely rewarded Washington lobbyists in concert with the military and a rabid neocon intellectual think-tank camp wishing to replay the cold war and perhaps even turn up the temperature with some nuclear fire. They are apparently in deep confab with the first head and its Russia collusion story line. Note all the current talk about Russia already meddling in the 2018 midterm election, a full-fledged pathogenic hallucination.

This second head functions by way of a displacement-projection dynamic. We hold war games on the Russian border and accuse them of "aggression." We engineer and pay for a coup against the elected government of Ukraine and accuse Russia of aggression. We bust up one nation after another in the Middle East and complain indignantly when Russia acts to keep Syria from becoming the latest failed state. We disrupt the Russian economy with sanctions, and the Russian banking system with a cut off of SWIFT international currency clearing privileges, and accuse them of aggression. This mode of behavior used to be known as "poking the bear," a foolish and hazardous endeavor. The sane center never would have stood for this arrant recklessness. The world community is not fooled, though. More and more, they recognize the USA as a national borderline personality, capable of any monstrous act.

The third head of this monster is the one aflame with identity politics. It arises from a crypto-gnostic wish to change human nature to escape the woes and sorrows of the human condition — for example, the terrible tensions of sexuality. Hence, the multiplication of new sexual categories as a workaround for the fundamental terrors of human reproduction as represented by the differences between men and women. Those differences must be abolished, and replaced with chimeras that enable a childish game of pretend, men pretending to be women and vice versa, in one way or another: LBGTQetc. Anything *but* the dreaded "cis-hetero" purgatory of men and women acting like men and women. The horror . . .

Its companion is the race hustle and its multicultural operating system. The objective has become transparent over the past year, with rising calls to punish white people for the supposed "privilege" of being Caucasian and pay "reparations" in one way or another to *underprivileged* "people of color." This comes partly from the infantile refusal to understand that life is difficult for everybody, and that the woes and sorrows of being in this world require fortitude and intelligence to get through — with the final reward being absolutely the same for everybody.

The Winners Will Lose
and the Losers Will Win

August 20, 2018

Who doesn't want to think that they are a good human being? That they are a person of good intentions, clear conscience, fair minded, generous, loving, and merciful? On the other hand, who wants to be a loser?

The current political predicament in the USA has America's winners turned losers and the consequent pain of that flip-flop has propelled the new designated losers into a fury of moral indignation. The deplorable Trump insurgents were supposed to be put in their place on November 8, 2016 — stuffed back into their reeking Walmarts — but instead, their champion with his gold-plated hairdo presides over the nation in the house where Lincoln, the Roosevelts, and Hillary lived. "Winning...!" as the new president likes to tweet.

What a revoltin' development, as Chester A. Riley used to say on *The Life of Riley* TV show back in 1955, when America was great (at least that's the theory). Riley was an original deplorable before the concept even emerged from the murk of early pop culture. He worked in an aircraft factory somewhere in southern California, which only a few decades prior was the mecca of an earlier generations of losers: the Okies and other Dust Bowl refugees who went west to pick fruit or get into the movies.

Chester A. Riley supported a family on that job as a wing riveter. All the male characters in the series had been through the Second World War, but were so far removed from the horror that the audience never heard about it. That was the point: to forget all that gore and get down with the new crazes for backyard barbecue, seeing the USA in your Chevrolet, enjoying that *healthful* pack of Lucky Strikes in the valley of the Jolly Green Giant . . . double your pleasure, double your fun . . . and away go troubles down the drain.

As Tom Wolfe pointed out eons ago, the most overlooked feature of postwar American life was the way that the old US peasantry found themselves living higher on the hog than Louis the XVI and his court at Versailles. Hot and cold running water, all the deliciously engineered Betty Crocker cake you could eat, painless dentistry, and Yankees away games on Channel 11, with Pabst Blue Ribbon by the case! By 1960 or so along came color TV and air-conditioning, and in places like Atlanta, St. Louis, and Little Rock you barely had to go outside anymore, thank God! No more heat stroke, hookworm, or chiggers.

It was a helluva lot better than earlier peasant classes had it, for sure, but let's face it: it was kind of a low-grade nirvana. And a couple of generations beyond *The Life of Riley* the whole thing has fallen apart. There are few hands-on jobs that allow a man to support a family. And what would we even mean by that? Stick the women back in kitchen and the laundry room? What a waste of human capital (even for socialists who oppose capital). The odd thing is that there is increasingly little for this class of people to do besides stand near the door of the Walmart, and if the vaunted tech entrepreneurs of this land have their way with robotics, you can be sure there would be less than nothing for them to do . . . except crawl off and die quietly, without leaving an odoriferous mess.

What political commentator has failed to notice that the supposed savior of this peasant class is himself a sort of shabby version of Louis XVI, with his gilded toilet seats, brand-name pomp, and complex hair? A happy peasantry needs a good king, and that is the role Mr. Trump seems to have cast himself in. I assume that he wants very earnestly to be considered a good person, though all his efforts to demonstrate that have been startlingly clumsy and mostly ineffective.

The one thing he has truly accomplished is driving his opponents in the overclass out of their gourds with loathing and resentment. (The term "overclass" was minted, I believe, by the excellent essayist Michael Lind.) It's a wonderfully *inclusive* term in that it describes basically everyone who is not in the underclass — that now dreadful realm of tattooed diabetics moiling in the war memorial auditoriums and minor league ballparks for their hero and leader to descend like deus ex machina in the presidential helicopter to remind them how much they're winning.

Meanwhile, the class of former winners-turned-losers — the Silicon Valley executives, the Hollywood movers and shakers, the Brooklyn hipsters, the Ivy League faculties, the Deep State guideline writers, the K Street consultants, the yoga ladies of Fairfield County, Connecticut, the acolytes of Oprah Winfrey and Elizabeth Warren — resort to righteous litigation in their crusade to restore the proper order of rule in this land. When they come to power, the shining city will be at hand . . .

I kind of doubt it. The truth is, all current winners and losers are living in the shadow of a financial system that doesn't really work anymore, because it doesn't represent the reality of wealth that is no longer there. The consolation, perhaps, is that there will be plenty for all those who survive the collapse of that system to do when the time comes. But it will be in a disposition of things and of power that we can't possibly recognize from where we stand these days.

THE UNCOMFORTABLE HIATUS

September 3, 2018

And so the sun seems to stand still this last day before the resumption of business as usual, and whatever remains of labor in this sclerotic republic takes its ease in the ominous late summer heat, and the people across this land marinate in anxious uncertainty. What can be done?

Some kind of epic national restructuring is in the works. It will either happen consciously and deliberately or be forced on us by circumstance. One side wants to magically reenact the 1950s; the other wants a Gnostic transhuman utopia. Neither of these is a plausible outcome. Most of the arguments ranging around them are what Jordan Peterson calls "pseudo issues." Let's try to take stock of what the real issues might be.

Energy: The shale oil "miracle" was a stunt enabled by supernaturally low interest rates, i.e., Federal Reserve policy. Even *The New York Times* said so yesterday ("The Next Financial Crisis Lurks Underground"). For all that, the shale oil producers still couldn't make money at it. If interest rates go up, the industry will choke on the debt it has already accumulated and lose access to new loans. If the Fed reverses its current course — say, to rescue the stock and bond markets — then the shale oil industry has perhaps three more years before it collapses on a geological basis, maybe less. After that, we're out of tricks. It will affect everything.

The perceived solution is to run all our stuff on electricity, with the electricity produced by other means than fossil fuels, so-called alt energy. This will happen only on the most limited basis and perhaps not at all. (And it is apart from the question of the decrepit electric grid itself.) What's required is a political conversation about how we inhabit the landscape, how we do business, and what kind of business we do. The prospect of dismantling suburbia — or at least moving out of it — is evidently unthinkable. But it's going to happen whether we make plans and policies or we're dragged kicking and screaming away from it.

Corporate tyranny: The nation is groaning under despotic corporate rule. The fragility of these operations is moving toward criticality. As with shale oil, they depend largely on dishonest financial legerdemain. They are also threatened by the crack-up of globalism, and its 12,000-mile supply lines, now well underway. Get ready for business at a much smaller scale.

Hard as this sounds, it presents great opportunities for making Americans useful again, that is, giving them something to do, a meaningful place in society, and livelihoods. The implosion of national chain retail is already underway. Amazon is not the answer, because each Amazon sales item requires a separate truck trip to its destination, and that just doesn't square with our energy predicament. We've got to rebuild main street economies and the layers of local and regional distribution that support them. That's where many jobs and careers are.

Climate change is most immediately affecting farming. 2018 will be a year of bad harvests in many parts of the world. Agribiz-style farming, based on oil and gas plus bank loans, is a ruinous practice, and will not continue in any case. Can we make choices and policies to promote a return to smaller-scale farming with intelligent methods rather than just brute industrial force plus debt? If we don't, a lot of people will starve to death. By the way, here is the useful work for a large number of citizens currently regarded as unemployable for one reason or another.

Pervasive racketeering rules because we allow it to, especially in education and medicine. Both are self-destructing under the weight of their own money-grubbing schemes. Both are destined to be severely downscaled. A lot of colleges will go out of business. Most college loans will never be paid back (and the derivatives based on them will blow up). We need millions of small farmers more than we need millions of communications majors with a public relations minor. It may be too late for a single-payer medical system. A collapsing oil-based industrial economy means a lack of capital, and fiscal hocus-pocus is just another form of racketeering. Medicine will have to get smaller and less complex and that means local clinic-based health care. Lots of careers there, and that is where things are going, so get ready.

Government overreach: The leviathan state is too large, too reckless, and too corrupt. Insolvency will eventually reduce its scope and scale. Most immediately, the giant matrix of domestic spying agencies has turned on American citizens. It will resist at all costs being dismantled or even reined in. One task at hand is to prosecute the people in the Department of Justice and the FBI who ran illegal political operations in and around the 2016 election. These are agencies that use their considerable power to destroy the lives of individual citizens. Their officers must answer to grand juries.

As with everything else on the table for debate, the reach and scope of US imperial arrangements has to be reduced. It's happening already, whether we like it or not, as geopolitical relations shift drastically and the other nations on the planet scramble for survival in a postindustrial world that will be a good deal harsher than the robotic paradise of digitally "creative" economies that the credulous expect. This country has enough to do within its own boundaries to prepare for survival without making extra trouble for itself and other people around the world. As a practical matter, this means close as many overseas bases as possible, as soon as possible.

As we get back to business tomorrow, ask yourself where you stand in the blather storm of false issues and foolish ideas, in contrast to the things that actually matter.

MONSTERS ALL THE WAY DOWN

September 17, 2018

Robert Mueller's fishing crew was out trawling for Manafort, a blubbery swamp mammal valued for its lubricating oil when, by happenstance, a strange breed of porpoise called a Podesta got caught up in the net. Turns out it was a traveling companion of the Manafort. Back in 2014, the pair swam all the way to a little country called Ukraine via the Black Sea where the Podesta used some Manafort SuperLube on then president of Ukraine, Viktor Yanukovych.

The objective was to grease the wheel of NATO and the EU for Ukraine to become a member. But the operation went awry when Yanukovych got a better offer from the Eurasian Customs Union, a Russian-backed trade-and-security org. And the next thing you know, the US State Department and the CIA are all over the situation and, whaddaya know, the Maidan Square in Kiev fills up with screaming neo-Nazis and Mr. Yanukovych gets the bum's rush — and despite the major screwup, the Manafort and the Podesta swim off with a cool few million in fees and return to the comforts of the swamp where they finally part ways.

Mr. Mueller is apparently concerned about just what happened with those fees. Possibly the loot ended up getting washed and rinsed through an international banking laundromat, and somehow went unreported to the federal tax authorities. Of course, the charge raises some interesting questions, such as: were Manafort and Podesta over in Ukraine as opportunistic freelancers, or were they part of phase one of a US government effort to get Ukraine to sign up for Team West against its old Uncle Russia, the manager of Team East? Kind of seems like that was exactly what they were doing, so it will be interesting to see whether Mr. Mueller may have stepped into a big pile of dog shit on his way to the Manafort plea session in federal court.

I like the theory that it suits Mr. Mueller's purpose to land the porpoise in his net of legal entrapment. After all, Tony Podesta of the swamp influence-peddling company called the Podesta Group is brother of John Podesta, once President Bill Clinton's chief of staff and more recently chairman of the 2016 Hillary Clinton presidential campaign. So Mr. Mueller can now brag that he is an "equal opportunity" fisherman for both Republican and Democratic species. The only problem is that the 2014 Ukraine monkey business is basically a sordid tale of the USA meddling in another country's election affairs, one which had quite a more severe effect on Ukraine and Russia than a handful of Russian Facebook trolls managed against the USA's 2016 election. Does anybody think that Manafort and Podesta were over in Ukraine without the knowledge of the US government? If so, we surely have the most incompetent intel community on earth. It will be interesting to see what kind of 'splainin that will lead to in court. If Mr. Mueller's motive is to embarrass the Deep State, he's well on his way to mission accomplished.

A few other good-sized fish got trawled up the net along with Manafort and Podesta, namely the spiny bottom feeders called Skadden, Arps, Slate, Meagher & Flom, who live on the K Street reef feeding on debris dropped from the mouths of the bull sharks feeding in the lagoon above. They're all flopping around on the deck of Mr. Mueller's trawler and one begins to think that the whole aquatic eco-system is breaking down. If they're not careful, they could conjure up something like a red tide that will kill everything in the DC swamp.

One might ask, though: was Mr. Mueller's ship launched in order to catch blubbery Manaforts, poisonous Podestas, and spiny Skadden Arps? I was under the impression that they were out for whale. There happens to be one, a rare golden humpback, lurking in the depths under Mr. Mueller's trawler, waiting, waiting, to sound and bring down his flukes on the scurvy crew. Somewhere close by, a bassoon is playing ominous notes. Other monsters of the deep may be revealed before this is all over. Monsters over monsters, all the way down.

Feeling the Heat Yet?

October 19, 2018

The loyal opposition is the party out of power in a polity that stands divided into two factions — assuming the polity can still function as such, which, apparently, it no longer can. Historically in the USA, this used to allow for the tempered regulation of changing conditions during two hundred years of a rapidly evolving techno-industrial economy that pumps out more goodies year after year while the population grows and grows.

Much of America, political leaders especially, assume that this arc of growing goodies and more people will just keep trending up forever. They are just plain mistaken about that. Rather, the whole industrialized, wired-up world is rolling over into the greatest contraction ever witnessed. The only thing that's postponed the recognition of this reality is the profligate borrowing of money, or shall we say "money" — data entries that pretend to represent secure wealth. This amounts to borrowing from the future to pay for how you live today. Of course, the act of borrowing is based on the supposition that there will enough future productive activity to allow you to pay back your borrowings with interest. This is obviously not the case now, in the face of epochal contraction, especially of affordable energy to keep things running hot.

Thus, the US has decided to get through the approaching winter by setting its house on fire. The two political parties alternately in charge of things are driving around the burning house, stopping at intervals to run Chinese fire drills. We call these "elections." Both parties pretend that the burning house is not a problem. Mr. Trump, aka the Golden Golem of Greatness, has taken "ownership" of the rising temperature in the burning house. *"Hey, at least you're not freezing now."* He and his party have been piling all the furniture inside the house on the fire, to keep the heat up, rather heedless that flames are starting to shoot out of the attic.

The other party has no quibble with burning down the house. In fact, this has been the Democratic Party's sovereign remedy for problems since the war in Vietnam, when it was explicit policy to burn down villages in order to save them. Seemed to work, until it didn't — and then we just tried to forget about the whole sorry exercise. It still haunts them, though. So these days they've decided to destroy the culture that abided inside the burning house. They're taking down the draperies and collecting all the clothing and tchotchkes and framed photographs of loved ones, and piling them on top of the burning furniture, doing their bit to keep the heat up.

You might infer from all this that no matter whatever else the Republican and Democratic parties might do now is not going to prevent the house from burning down. In a month, or six months, or eighteen months, they will be left standing stunned in the ashes. *How'd this happen*!?! Even the clown cars they were riding around in will be smoldering wrecks. And then the rest of the people of this land can sift through ruins, seeking a few trinkets or useful tools with some remaining value. These people will be entitled to call themselves "survivors." And they will act like survivors should act: by earnestly assessing how the house happened to burn down, and using what few assets and resources they still have at hand to shelter in place, while they draw up plans for a more sensible house.

If there was a true loyal opposition in this land, they would have called the fire department long ago. But they were too busy texting out their contrived grievances and sending cute Instagrams of each other in pussy hats to friends and allies while the flames of the burning house reflected off the screens of their iPhones. The vaunted technology did not save the day. It only stole their attention.

If it happens that the Democrats lose the midterm elections a few weeks ahead, they will jump up and down and holler that the elections were stolen from them, that somebody meddled and colluded to deprive them of victory, and that will amount to throwing just enough gasoline on the still-burning house for one final glorious burst of heat and flame before the rafters crash through the floor. Welcome to the Long Emergency.

Lost in Translation

October 22, 2018

Saturdays, when fewer eyeballs see the paper, *The New York Times* likes to publish its most extreme ventures into social unreality. Last week's prank was the story at the top of page one that declared: *#WontBeErased: Transgender People and Allies Mobilize Against Trump Administration Proposal.* (The accompanying photo featured a rainbow flag, of course, denoting that there was a pot of gold awaiting true believers.) This was a response to a Trump administration policy memo calling for "strict definition of gender based on a person's genitalia at birth," the *Times* said.

The dishonesty at work here ought to impress those observing the slow-motion collapse of culture in the USA. The political Left has taken its lessons in the abuse of language straight from the campus "poststructuralist" workshops, where novelties of narcissism get churned out by striving grad students in the ceaseless pursuit of cutting-edge prestige (and academic career advancement). The game is to produce a never-ending chain of self-referential, status-enhancing worldviews as a replacement for consensual reality. The more "marginalized" one can claim to be, the more deserving of high status (including tenure, grants for attending echo-chamber conferences and symposia, and a claque of attending assistants to actually teach those pain-in-the-ass classes). The goal is to get to feel special, and especially deserving of special privileges based on special grievances.

The net effect is to destroy whatever remains of an American common culture, to divide and conquer the polity in the hope that society might advance into a state with no rules and no boundaries — except for whatever capricious actions the "progressive" authorities might choose, based on how they feel at any particular time. It must be obvious that this all comes down to a vicious sort of sentimentality. It's exactly what turned the governments of the Bolsheviks and the Nazis into killing machines. It's Kafka's nightmare of the murderous bureaucratic state that disposes with the rule of law.

I suspect that neither *The New York Times* nor the Democratic Party actually cares about so-called transgender people, who are merely being used as stalking horses to provoke conflict. The Left's main beef these days is that Mr. Trump is in the White House, signifying that *Daddy's in the House,* an intolerable condition. The Left is desperate to get rid of that particular Daddy and Daddyism per se and altogether. Daddyism represents rules and boundaries. The Left prefers chaos. It's clearly a juvenile disposition, since that point of view fails to apprehend that the universe is chaotic enough without additional help from them. And they are still in despair over the failure of "mommy" (HRC) and her disappearance into the darkling woods of political ignominy.

The rule at hand is that the word "gender" is not a substitute for the word "sex," and that in the world of real things, you don't actually get to declare what sex you are. You can engage in all kinds of behaviors, such as enjoying intimate relations with members of your same sex. You can pretend to be a member of the opposite sex. In statistically very rare instances, you can come into this world with genital abnormalities that present developmental problems, but most of the people currently pretending to some kind of "intersex" status do not fall into that category. The game of pretend can be very personally intense, I'm sure. But it's still just a game of pretend.

I propose the perhaps novel idea that there is a place for everything and that the correct place for the marginal is . . . on the margins! The argument lately, especially on the progressive side, has been that the marginal ought to occupy the center (of American life). That is surely the argument of *The New York Times*. It is a foolish and even dangerous argument, popular only with those determined that the center should not hold. In the process, they have come close to replacing the political center with a black hole. Now they want to drag the country across the event horizon into what they hope is a transhuman paradise of rainbows and unicorns. I wouldn't be so sure that awaits us there.

Welcome to GenderWorld

November 19, 2018

The defeat of Hillary, and the elevation of the vulgar Mr. Trump, loosed a fury of women against men in America that now verges on a kind of all-consuming chaos, like those western wildfires turning every product of human endeavor in the burn path to smoke and ash. All the sorrows of our national life are assigned lately to the wicked white male patriarchy that must be defeated to usher in a satori of female sharing-and-caring.

A case in point is Sam Harris's dialogue on his *Waking Up* (#141) podcast with Rebecca Traister of *New York* magazine, author of the new book *Good and Mad: The Revolutionary Power of Women's Anger*. There is no better interlocutor of the current right-think about men and women than Ms. Traister. She puts it across as though her brain was shot out of a cannon from a graduate seminar on "Engendering the Intellectual Space" as if there are no other points at issue in our national life than the power valences between the two sexes — and, of course, even suggesting that the human mammal comprises two sexes is a punishable offense these days.

To get a sense of the true chaos behind her argument, just have a look at the cover of *Good and Mad*. Notice that the bloodred title stands against a gray field of the word "F*CK" (asterisk hers) repeated 120 times on a 5 x 24 grid. Deconstruct that. Is it the generative act of copulation itself that she is inveighing against? Should it be gotten rid of? Will that solve the problems of a foundering hypercomplex industrial society?

Ms. Traister might have used the word "power" five hundred times in her conversation with the excessively gallant Sam Harris. The choo-choo train of poststructuralist ideology that pulled into the college scene in the 1990s, when she was a student, is based on the idea that all relations between men and women — and all human endeavor, for that matter — come down to questions of who has power over whom. The result, naturally enough, has been an escalating power struggle between men and women that has the potential to tear this society apart.

It has already damaged our understanding of what men and women are supposed to be, and the outcome so far is that men are not sufficiently female and vice versa. Thus the consecration of "transgender, intersex, nonbinary, gender nonconforming" states of being as heroic, and the demonizing cries of "toxic masculinity" ringing through the ivory towers, the halls of Congress, and the corporate C-suites.

Much of this stems from the fact that only in the past half century have men and women tried to occupy the same work spaces, especially in political bureaucracies. Until fairly recently, men and women existed in rather separate work- and social worlds, with behaviors that seem weird and quaint today — for instance, the practice of men and women retiring to different rooms for conversation after a dinner party, based on the idea, possibly true, that they had categorically different interests (as suggested by James Damore in his notorious Google memo).

Now, to suggest that there was anything to these divisions of sexual space amounts to another punishable offense, but that is probably the least of the dreary consequences in this contest. The worst part is that we're burning all our political capital in this foolishly contrived war at the expense of all the other actual tasks we face. If the US Senate put one-tenth of its attention to rebuilding the passenger rail system as it put into the furor raised by Christine Blasey Ford, we might have addressed the awful problem of our soon to be obsolete mass-motoring matrix. But then trains are such a male concern. They have so little to do with . . . feelings!

Apropos of the war between men and women itself, something really bugs me: the deliberate and convenient overlooking of women's sexual power over men. That is what has been absent in the #MeToo movement, and quite dishonestly so. It's really something to see the various indignant women of cable news coming onto the flatscreen every night to inveigh against men while dressed, coiffed, and made up like thousand-dollar Las Vegas call girls — except for Rachel Maddow, of course, who opts to present as the nation's guidance counselor.

In fact, women have tremendous sexual power over men, and it is exactly that which provokes so much of the idiotic behavior that has come to be categorized as "abuse" where men and women intersect and the mists of pheromones perplex the air. It is at least as potent as the power that men supposedly exert in politics and the workplace. And it incorporates a range of behaviors that are subtle and insidious. (Classic literature certainly understands this, but it's being removed from the curriculum for doing that.) The failure to even acknowledge female sexual power or to dismiss it as inconsequential is just plain dirty fighting — though it's proclaimed unself-consciously on the cover of Rebecca Traister's book: "F*CK, F*CK, F*CK, F*CK, F*CK." See for yourself.

Murphy's Law to the Rescue!

November 26, 2018

What can go wrong *will* go wrong. It's so fundamental to the operation of the universe that Sir Isaac Newton should have installed it between his second and third laws of motion — but he had his hands full losing a fortune in Britain's South Sea bubble circa 1721, after muttering to a colleague that he "could calculate the motions of the heavenly bodies, but not the madness of the people." Note to all you hedge fund cowboys out there: old Isaac was probably smarter than you (and all the algos you rode in on).

Was it a fretful Thanksgiving this year, a family feud of political recrimination with a lot of teeth gnashing through mouthfuls of candied sweets? Well, yes, coming after the extraordinary fiasco of the Kavanaugh hearings and the disputed midterm elections, but the glide path to Yuletide looks kind of bumpy, too, so here's a short bill or particulars of things tending to go wrong.Ukraine verges on martial law after a naval incident with Russian ships in the waters off Crimea. Say what? Martial law? They might as well declare a Chinese fire drill. Details of the actual incident around the Kerch Strait between the Black Sea and the Sea of Azov remain murky besides the fact that two Ukrainian gunships and a tug disobeyed orders from Russian ships to stand down in Russian maritime waters and shots were fired. Who knew that Ukraine even had a navy, and how can they possibly pay for it? But now NATO is trying to get into the act, meaning the USA will get dragged into just the sort of unnecessary and idiotic dispute that kicks off world wars. Note to the Golden Golem of Greatness (a.k.a. Mr. Trump): this dogfight is none of our goddamn business. Russia, meanwhile, asked the UN Security Council to convene over this, which is the correct response. What could go wrong?

Late Monday update: I've heard reports this afternoon that Russia had intel Ukrainian ships were transporting an explosive device supplied by NATO, which they suspected was intended to be deployed to blow up the strategic bridge across the Kerch Strait. Still unconfirmed chatter. Developing story . . .

Tuesday morning update: It's worth reading the blog *The Saker* on the situation. He writes: "*Considering the current single-digit popularity rating of [President] Poroshenko and the fact that he has no chance in hell to be re-elected (at least not in minimally credible elections) it is pretty darn obvious of why the Ukronazi regime in Kiev decided to trigger yet another crisis and then blame Russia for it.*"

Sunday, about five hundred Central American migrants rushed the border at Tijuana. The US Border Patrol teargased them and they backed off. Bad optics for those trying to make the case for open borders. Naturally, *The New York Times* portrayed this as *an assault on families*, defaulting to its stock sob story, though the mob assembling down there is overwhelmingly composed of young men. Complicating matters, a new Mexican president, Andrés Manuel López Obrador, takes over next Saturday, a Left-wing populist and enemy of *Trumpismo*. Tijuana is now choking on the thousands of wanderers who were induced to march north to test America's broken immigration policies. What could go wrong?

Congressional Democrats are said to be "loading the cannons" with subpoenas for Trumpsters to get raked over the coals in a circus of committee hearings when they take over the majority in January. They'll be matched by senators firing back in hearings controlled by Republicans, setting up the worst political pissing match since the Civil War. In a fair universe, enough dirt would come out on either side to disable the most sinister forces of the Deep State — especially the seditious "intelligence community." But life is unfair, as Jimmy Carter once observed, and the exercise will only fan the flames of already extreme antipathy. What could go wrong?

The engine pulling that choo-choo train of grievance is Robert Mueller's Russian collusion investigation. I expect him to produce mighty rafts of charges against Mr. Trump, his family and associates, and anyone who ever received so much as a souvenir mug from his 2016 campaign. But I doubt that any of it will have a bearing on Russian election "meddling." And in that case, the charges will be met by countercharges of an illegitimate investigation, meaning welcome to that constitutional crisis we've been hearing about for two years. That's a mild way of describing anything from a disorderly impeachment to troops in the American streets. What could go wrong there?

Finally, there's the elephant in the room with the 800-pound gorilla riding on its back: the economy and its diabolical engine the financial markets. Anyone notice on the lead-up to Thanksgiving and Black Friday that the markets have been going south (and not on holiday to Cozumel)? Stocks are roaring back up again as I write. The TBTF banks and their ringleader, the Federal Reserve, have had a few days to engineer a rally, and the sharper it goes up, the more remaining "greater fools" will get roped in for eventual slaughter. Bond rates are charging back up too, meaning the price is skidding down. Bad combo. The poison cherry on top is Bitcoin, which has plunged about 40 percent in ten measly days to a 3000 handle and is headed to zero. So sad, as the Golden Golem might put it. It seemed like such a sure thing less than a year ago. What could have gone wrong?

THE GHOST OF CHRISTMAS PRESENT

December 3, 2018

Apparently one additional world leader turned up in Buenos Aires without fanfare this weekend. The General Secretary of the North Pole, known popularly as Santa Claus, took his latest-model hypersonic sleigh to the G-20 meeting and made sure that the global financial elite would find their Christmas stockings stuffed with sugarplums one last time before the great reflation bull market dies of incredulity.

Something drastic was required as so many enterprises were skidding into a ditch last month, especially FAANGs, cars, house sales, and oil, while the Grand Old Man of the Dow Jones, General Electric, was singing its death song like an old Arikara chief in the prairie twilight. The US threat of 25 percent tariffs on Chinese exports was shunted ahead 90 days, giving the almighty algos and their human errand boys one last shot at looting the future.

How exactly will this change the basic equation of China sending its industrial output to Walmart in exchange for American IOUs, while the trade deficit mounts ever higher and the last holdouts of the US middle class sink into debt, addiction, and hopelessness? It won't, of course, because Americans have to find another reason to get up in the morning besides reporting to the national demolition derby. I don't know about you, but it doesn't warm my heart to hear about x hundred thousand "housing starts" every month, knowing that it represents the destruction of x thousand acres of meadow, field, and forest, and that what's being laid down on the landscape *out there* is soul-crushing infrastructure with no future.

It's not hard to see why US life expectancy is going down, driven by the two new leading causes of death: opiate drugs and suicide — the former often in the service of the latter. The citizens of this land have exchanged just about everything that makes life worth living for the paltry rewards of "bargain shopping" and happy motoring. But the worst sacrifice is the loss of any sense of community, of face-to-face human transactions with people you know, people who have duties and obligations to one another that can be successfully enacted and fulfilled. Instead, you get to do all your business with robots, even including the robots fronting for companies that seek to ruin you. "Your call is important to us," says the telephone robot at the hospital billing office dunning you to fork over $7,000 for the three stitches Little Skippy got when his best friend flew the drone into his forehead. "Please hold for the next available representative." Who wouldn't want to shoot themselves?

Interestingly, it's the people of France who are going apeshit at this moment in history and not the much more beaten down Americans. For all the deformities of the EU, France still maintains a general quality of life so far above what is found in the US these days that we look like some left-behind evolutionary dead end here in this wilderness of strip malls and muffler shops. They live in towns and cities that are designed to bring people together in public. They support small business in spite of the diktats of Brussels. They maintain an interest in doing things well for their own sake. The French are rioting these days not simply over the cost of diesel fuel but because they've had enough impingements on their traditional ways of life and seek to arrest the losses.

Americans, by contrast, seem to passively accept their new status as world-class losers. You can deprive them of whatever is meaningful, whatever makes life worth living, and sell them depressing simulacra to replace those things, and they never notice. Even the revolts ongoing in this land only seek to make relations between us worse, for instance, the new super-Puritanism that wants to criminalize the most elementary mating ceremonies, like asking for date, or even paying attention to someone of the opposite sex. This is what the Democratic Party, formerly the party of the working people, has dedicated itself to all year. That's your "Resistance." They've managed to ruin one of the few consolations for being on this planet.

Maybe you-all have had enough of that foolishness. Maybe when Christmas is over something will turn in that old proverbial widening gyre, and the anarchy loosed by that turn will not be "mere."

❧ 2019 ❧

AND THE CIRCUS CAME TO TOWN

January 4, 2019

It's Nancy Pelosi's smile that gets me . . . oh, and not in a good way. It's a smile that is actually the opposite of what a smile is supposed to do: signal goodwill and good faith. Nancy's smile is full of malice and bad faith, like the smiles on representations of Shiva the Destroyer and Huitzilopochtli, the Aztec sun god who demanded thousands of human hearts to eat, lest he bring on the end of the world.

It's not exactly the end of the world in Washington DC but as the old saying goes: you can see it from there! It's out on the edge of town like one of those sinister, broken-down circuses from the Ray Bradbury story bag, with its ragtag cast of motheaten lions, crippled acrobats, a crooked wagon full of heartbroken freaks, and a shadowy ringmaster on a mission from the heart of darkness.

The new Democratic majority Congress has convened in the spirit of a religious movement devoted to a single apocalyptic objective: toppling the Golden Golem of Greatness who rules in the House of White Privilege. They're all revved up for inquisition, looking to apply as many thumbscrews, cattle prods, electrodes, waterboards, and bamboo splinters as necessary in pursuit of rectifying the heresy of the 2016 election.

The simpleton California congressman Brad Sherman (D-30th dist.) couldn't contain his glee, like a seven-year-old boy about to pull the wings off a fly. As soon as the Democratic majority was sworn in, he filed his articles of impeachment to impress his wokester San Fernando Valley constituents out for deplorable blood. That was even a bit too much for Madam Speaker who reminded Sherman that some scintilla of a predicate crime was required — but surely would be available when Special Counsel Robert Mueller hurls down his tablets of accusation from on high.

As for their quarry, the Golden Golem, a.k.a. D.J. Trump, I'm not convinced that he is a mere hapless yegg waiting to be sliced, diced, and skewered. He's POTUS, after all, and has access to quite a bit of information and expertise. He'll shortly have a new attorney general on board, William Barr, who might just ask the question that has been hanging in the air like a pulsating zeppelin for two years, viz: has Mr. Mueller paid even a casual glance at the shenanigans going on all around him in the Department of Justice and the FBI lo these many many months of prosecuting Trump factotums on rinky-dink process charges? And might all that monkey business in politicizing the agencies and scheming to undo Mr. Trump even turn up as a footnote in that holy grail of the Mueller report awaited so eagerly by the inquisitionists?

It would be just and logical if Mr. Mueller had paid attention to the misconduct of the highest officials in the DOJ and FBI beginning in the winter of 2016, since there is an evidence trail as broad as the DC Beltway right out there in the public record. Maybe Mr. Mueller will surprise many of us and actually include the already documented misdeeds of his protégé Mr. Comey, Mr. Strzok, Ms. Page, Mr. Rosenstein, Mr. McCabe, Mr. Ohr, Mrs. Ohr, Mr. Brennan, Mr. Clapper, Ms. Lynch, Ms. Yates, and sundry servants of the Obamas and Clintons, involved in the government-sponsored coup attempt. They will eventually have to answer to somebody. I believe that somebody will be Mr. Barr, who will finally have the authority to ignite a counterinquisition.

It's important to set these matters aright, if you want to keep the Constitution. Under the narcoleptic Jeff Sessions, the institutional rot turned into a possibly fatal gangrene. Did certain parties want to send patsies like George Papadopoulos to prison for a couple weeks, or break, defame, and bankrupt General Flynn under a recklessly malicious prosecution — because that was all that they had to show for two years of looking under every rock and rotten log between the Potomac River and the Kremlin? Has Mr. Mueller even noticed the established fact that Hillary Clinton supplied the inquisition with its founding, false documentary evidence?

So, let the circus begin on Capitol Hill. Let them kick out the jams, as we used to say back in the Woodstock era. Let Nancy Pelosi finish the work that the Democratic Party started with the election of 2016 — its own destruction as a viable political force. Let all the darkness and malice be wrung out of it so the country can return to its senses and start paying attention to things that really matter, backed by institutions that people of good faith can believe in.

In the Deep Midwinter

January 25, 2019

Ill winds sweep across the fruited plain in the cruel heart of winter. America can resolve nothing. The state of the union is a kind of hysterical nausea, and the nation hunkers into its crib of toxic *diverse* identities waiting for history to bitch slap it back on its feet. History's big sister Reality stands by, witnessing all. Spring . . . is . . . coming . . .

Things break up in spring. Nature unlocks what was frozen. The bodies emerge from the melting ice and ripen. The air is electric and thunderbolts frighten the gathering mobs in the public square, the Walmart parking lot, with rumors of war. The earth shakes and monuments fall. That's how it's shaping up for 2019.

Sometimes nations just lose their shit. The complex collapse of American life proceeds as the public and its leaders fail to comprehend the forces in play. What the Federal Reserve actually accomplished with its ten years of extend-and-pretend policy was not an economic "recovery," but a degenerative disease of the social contract. If you look more closely, you can sense what will be unleashed when the ground thaws.

There will be a reckoning in the financial markets. Something ominous is rumbling over in bonds. No more high yield for you! Among the victims of a credit freeze in "junk" (high risk) lending: the shale oil industry. Watch it start to roll over this spring as money becomes unavailable for the exorbitant operations that comprise fracking. The swift collapse of the shale oil industry will shock the country, but it is really just the downside of its improbably rapid and acrobatic rise since 2005 on the false premise that profits don't matter in a business venture. Only the fall will be even sharper than the rise: a few measly years. And, of course, the bond market represents the supreme untruth of the age: that debts can be racked up forever and never paid back.

Mr. Trump will be left holding a bag so large that observers may mistake him for a bizarro Santa Claus. But the baggage within will not consist of sugarplums. It is actually stuffed with bankruptcy filings and pink slips. A year from now, there may be no such thing as a hedge fund left on the planet Earth. Or a job opening, unless you're really good at weeding or picking fruit. Mr. Trump will attempt a rescue, but so did Herbert Hoover, who had a good three years to try this and that while the Depression stole over the land like a deadly fungus. The difference, of course, is that Mr. Hoover was acknowledged as a most brilliant mind of his era, and yet Reality had her wicked way with him, anyway.

The Democratic Party should have been tossed into the rubber room two years ago, but it's still out there shrieking in its straitjacket of bad faith. Kamala, Liz, and Kirsten will mud wrestle for dominance, but so far the only cards they can show are the race-and-gender jokers in the deck. Meanwhile, the government shutdown standoff may not be the "winner" move that Nancy Pelosi thought it would be. Why do you suppose she thought that the voters would blame only the Golden Golem of Greatness? She could be gone as Speaker when we're back in shirtsleeve weather.

Also in the background: the likely shocking reversal of the long, dreary RussiaGate affair as about twenty-odd former officials of the FBI, Department of Justice, CIA, State Department, and other dark corners of the Deep State answer charges of sedition in federal court. Many of them are connected, one way or another, to Hillary Clinton, who may be targeted herself. Robert Mueller is also liable to be smacked with a malicious prosecution charge in the matter of General Michael Flynn when he withdraws his guilty plea in March. A significant moment will be when Dean Baquet is fired as editor of *The New York Times*, after years of running the "newspaper of record" as an exercise in nonstop PMS.

Financial crack-up and RussiaGate reversal will leave both major parties gasping in the mud as the tide goes out. And just in time for the Yellow Vest movement to cross the ocean and bring out the street mobs to slug it out on the National Mall in lovely weather. Finally, a protest you can believe in! By June, it will be clear that the old order is being swept away. The fight over the new order struggling to be born will be even harsher and deadlier. But we may not be as confused about what's at stake.

Mistaken Futures

February 11, 2019

And so the Democratic Party has gone and hoisted the flag of "socialism" on the mizzenmast of its foundering hulk as it sets sail for the edge of the world. Bad call by a ship without a captain, and I'll tell you why. Socialism was the response to a particular set of circumstances in time that drove the rise of industrial societies. Those circumstances are going, going, gone.

The suspicion of industry's dreadful effects on the human condition first sparked in the public imagination with William Blake's poem "Jerusalem" in 1804 and its reference to England's newly built "dark satanic mills." Industry at the grand scale overturned everyday life in the Euro-American "West" by the mid-nineteenth century, and introduced a new kind of squalor for the masses, arguably worse than their former status as peasants.

And thus it was to be, through Karl Marx, Vlad Lenin, and the rest of the gang, ever strategizing to somehow mitigate all that suffering. Their Big Idea was that if government owned the industry (the *means of production*), then the riches would be distributed equally among the laboring masses and the squalor eliminated. You can't blame them for trying, though you can blame them for killing scores of millions of people who somehow got in the way of their plans.

Nobody had ever seen anything like this industry before, or had to figure out some way to deal with it, and it was such an enormous force in everyday life thereafter that it shattered human relationships with nature and the planet nature rode in on. Of course, the history of everything has a beginning, a middle, and an end, and we're closer to the end of the industrial story than we are to the middle.

Which opens the door to a great quandary. If industrial society is disintegrating (literally), then what takes its place? Many suppose that it is a robotic utopia powered by some as yet unharnessed cosmic juice, a nirvana of algorithms, culminating in orgasm without end (Ray Kurzweil's transhumanism). Personally, I would check the "no" box on that outcome as a likely scenario.

The self-proclaimed socialists are actually seeing the world through a rearview mirror. What they are really talking about is divvying up the previously accumulated wealth, soon to be bygone. Entropy is having its wicked way with that wealth, first by transmogrifying it into ever more abstract forms, and then by dissipating it as waste all over the planet. In short, the next time socialism is enlisted as a tool for redistributing wealth, we will make the unhappy discovery that most of that wealth is gone.

The process will be uncomfortably sharp and disorientating. The West especially will not know what hit it as it emergently self-reorganizes back into something that resembles the old-time feudalism. We have a new kind of mass squalor in America: a great many people who have nothing to do, no means of support, and the flimsiest notions of purpose in life. The socialists have no answers for them. They will not be "retrained" in some imagined federal crusade to turn meth freaks into code writers for Google.

Something the analysts are calling "recession" is ploughing across the landscape like one of those darkly majestic dust storms of the 1930s, only this time we won't be able to refight anything like World War Two to get all the machines running again in the aftermath. Nor, of course, will the *Make America Great Again* fantasy work out for those waiting in the squalid ruins of the postindustrial Rustbelt or the strip-mall wastelands of the Sunbelt.

Most of the beliefs and attitudes of the present day will be overturned with the demise of the industrial orgy, like the idea that humanity follows an unerring arc of progress, that men and women are interchangeable and can do exactly the same work, that society should not be hierarchical, that technology will rescue us, and that we can organize some political workarounds to avoid the pain of universal contraction.

There are no coherent ideas in the political arena just now. Our prospects are really too alarming. So, jump on board the socialism ship and see if it makes you feel better to sail to the end of the earth. But mind the gap at the very edge. It's a doozie.

GREAT EXPECTATION

February 22, 2019

The #Resistance has been losing bigly in recent days as each new "bombshell" it manufactures turns out to reveal only its modus operandi, which is that *the end justifies the means* — the end being to evict the wicked Mr. Trump from office and the means being dishonesty and bad faith in its use of the government's prosecutorial machinery. *The New York Times* has a Friday op-ed, "The Mueller Report Is Coming. Here's What to Expect," declaring, "A concise report will probably act as a 'road map' to investigation for the Democratic House — and to further criminal investigation by other prosecutors."

Translation: prepare to be disappointed by Mr. Mueller's report and microwave a giant tub of popcorn for an extravaganza of sequels and reboots. Beware of what you wish for. If the baton is passed to House committee chairs Jerrold Nadler, Maxine Waters, and Elijah Cummings, then in Act Two of the show, the country will be treated to something like the Spanish Inquisition as performed by Moe, Larry, and Curly.

Meanwhile, their antics may be eclipsed by the now inevitable inquiry around the misdeeds carried out by public officials in Act One of the show: the Russia Collusion Ruse. Based just on the current Andy McCabe book tour, there will be an awful lot to get to, and it is liable to be far more compelling than the nonsense conjured up by the Three Stooges. Mr. McCabe, in his quest to hand off the hot potato of culpability to his former colleagues, and to sell enough books to pay his lawyers' retainers, has neatly laid out the case for his orchestrating a coup d'état within the FBI.

It's an ugly story, and it's all out there now, like so much spaghetti hurled against the wall, and it won't be ignored. There are many other spaghetti wads already plastered on that wall ranging from Hillary Clinton's Fusion GPS hijinks, to Loretta Lynch's written assurances to the Clinton campaign that the email server matter would be dropped, to the rather complete failure of the FISA process, and much much more that needs to be ventilated in a court of law.

I suspect that Barack Obama and his White House confidants will enter the picture, too, sooner later, and to the great dismay of his partisans who do not want to see his legacy tarnished. Whatever your view of all these dark events, it would be pretty awful for the country to have to see him in a witness chair, but it may be unavoidable. Ditto Hillary, who is liable to go all Captain Queeg-y when she finally has to answer for her campaign's turpitudes.

Most of this cast of characters has seemingly gone to ground in recent months, laying low, staying out of the news, probably spending much of their time conferring with their attorneys — Brennan, Clapper, Comey et al. are keeping their traps shut in recent days as Andy McCabe takes his hangdog road show around the cable networks and the NPR fluff chamber, spelling out the "stress" that prompted the FBI's desperate attempt to cover its ass following the unbelievable 2016 election results.

I don't pretend to know what the new attorney general William Barr might do. He must realize that if he lets all this slide, the institutional damage will be permanent and severe. He is reputed to be a good friend of Special Prosecutor Mueller. Mr. Mueller's reputation as the straightest of straight arrows seems at odds with the actual exercise of his office: generating rinky-dink "process" crimes against bit players in the story, often via malicious prosecutorial tactics. The likely truth is that he was brought into the scene to protect the very characters who misused the terrible powers of the FBI and the Department of Justice. His investigation has been hermetically sealed against leakage. For all I or anyone else knows, he has spent some time preparing a case against the very officers who cooked up the Russia story in the first place. Perhaps not a high-percentage bet, but there it is for consideration.

It's going to be an interesting month. Have you forgotten that General Michael Flynn will be returning to Judge Emmet Sullivan's courtroom after three months in the doghouse that the judge sent him to for the purpose of reconsidering his guilty plea? Perhaps Gen. Flynn rediscovered that he has a spine this winter and will venture into a trial of the Mickey Mouse charge against him: that, as incoming national security advisor to the president, he had preliminary discussions with the Russian ambassador — in all other transitions of power, a completely normal procedure — and supposedly lied about it to the FBI. To the very people orchestrating a coup against his boss, the chief executive.

IDES AND TIDES

March 11, 2019

Just as presidents are expected to act presidentially, Federal Reserve chairpersons are expected to act oracularly — as semi-supernatural beings who emerge now and again from some cave of mathematical secrets to offer reassuringly cryptic utterances on mysteries of the economy. And so was Jerome Powell wheeled out on CBS's *60 Minutes* Sunday night, like a cigar store Indian at an antique fair, so vividly sculpted and colorfully adorned you could almost imagine him saying something.

Maybe it was a hallucination, but I heard him say that "the economy is in a good place," and that "the outlook is a favorable one." Point taken. Pull the truck up to the loading dock and fill it with Tesla shares! I also thought I heard "Inflation is muted." That must have been the laugh line, since there is almost no single item in the supermarket that goes for under five bucks these days. But really, when was the last time you saw a cigar store Indian at Trader Joe's? It took seventeen Federal Reserve math PhDs to come up with that line, *inflation is muted*.

What you really had to love was Mr. Powell's explanation for the record number of car owners in default on their monthly payments: "not everybody is sharing in this widespread prosperity we have." *Errrgghh Errrgghh Errrgghh.* Sound of klaxon wailing. What he meant to say was, hedge funders, private equity hustlers, and C-suite personnel are making out just fine as the asset-stripping of flyover America proceeds, and you miserable, morbidly obese, tattooed gorks watching this out on the Midwestern buzzard flats should have thought twice before dropping out of community college to drive a forklift in the Sysco frozen food warehouse (where, by the way, you are probably stealing half the oven-ready chicken nuggets in inventory).

Interlocutor Scott Pelley asked the oracle about "those half a million people who have given up looking for jobs." Did he pull that number out of his shorts? The total number out of the workforce is more like 95 million, and when you subtract retirees, people still in school, and the disabled, the figure is more like 7.5 million. There was some blather over the "opioid epidemic," the upshot of which was *learn to code, young man.* Personally, I was about as impressed as I was ten years ago when past oracle Ben Bernanke confidently explained to Congress that the disturbances in Mortgageland were "contained."

David Leonhardt of *The New York Times* had a real howler in his Monday column on the state of the economy:

> *Americans are saving more and spending less partly because the rich now take home so much of the economy's income — and the rich don't spend as large a share of their income as the poor and middle class.*

Suggestion to Mr. Leonhardt: learn to code.

Here's what's actually going on in that beast known as the Economy: Globalism is winding down as a decade of Central Bank machinations reach their limits of deception, leaving the major trading nations with little more than comparative disadvantages. Europe is dissolving into political chaos. Japan is cannibalizing itself in preparation for its return to the Tokugawa shogunate. China is groaning with factories that turn out too much stuff; America is groaning with so much of that stuff that it's turning into Yard Sale Nation. In the background of all that are the problematic flows of oil on tankers through dangerous choke points like the Strait of Malacca and the Strait of Hormuz, with a looming horizon on the supply as US shale oil production chokes to death on unpayable debt.

It has been easier to maintain the pretense of economic stability while all the perversities of finance and banking are being acted out in the current fiascos of government. But the tide is surely going out now and, as another ersatz oracle, Warren Buffett, once observed about such situations: pretty soon you get to see who's been swimming naked. In the American lagoon, you will soon behold the awful spectacle of the beached whale known as President Trump flopping helplessly around the mud flats, emitting inchoate threnodies from his blowhole. Ironically, he'll be flopping and gasping at the same time that his antagonists are stricken by a red tide of indictments, perhaps including even the Captain Ahab of the Resistance: Robert Mueller. The Ides of March are upon us.

THE BLIND LEADING
THE DEAF AND DUMB

March 15, 2019

You had to wonder why it took Nancy Pelosi so long to figure out that maybe impeachment was not the big rock candy mountain that, for "the resistance," marked the gateway to a Trump-free nirvana. It became obvious this week, through the release of the Bruce Ohr and Lisa Page transcripts, that RussiaGate was birthed entirely by persons in the employ of Hillary Clinton, with then CIA Director John Brennan as midwife, and the DOJ / FBI avidly assisting — all of them fully aware that the predicate was false. What's more, the evidence timeline makes it clear that Democratic Party leadership, including Nancy Pelosi, knew it was false. Hence, the pained smile she's been wearing these many months.

In the event of an impeachment proceeding in the House, all that would be revealed, especially if it got as far as a trial in the US Senate, where the defense is allowed to mount a case under rules of evidence. Imagine the howls of embarrassment on late-night TV when even ex-comedian Stephen Colbert would have to admit that he was gulled into acting as a shill for a seditious con.

I suppose Ms. Pelosi also made the calculation that any impeachment ginned up by the likes of Jerrold Nadler and Maxine Waters would be superseded by a slew of actual indictments among the abovementioned former law enforcement officialdom, including perhaps former attorney general Loretta Lynch and persons in the Obama White House. You might even include the enigmatic Robert Mueller, who appears to be liable for the destruction of evidence in his own inquiry, as well as malicious prosecution.

All the actual evidence in the public arena indicates that any "collusion" to interfere with the 2016 election involved agents of the Clinton campaign and US government employees, not Russians. Of course, it will not be so easy for Mr. Nadler and Ms. Waters to call off the committee exercises they've been rehearsing, but it will be fun to watch them pissing into the wind as the indictments roll out.

In his new book *Peak Trump*, David Stockman called the RussiaGate affair "a Democratic Party Bereavement Ritual," an excellent diagnosis. The breast-beating and garment-rending have gone on for more than two years, inducing a generalized hysteria that has made it impossible for this country to govern itself, and opening the door to some really serious mischief as the party's new Jacobin wing sets up for the advent of an American failed state.

All of this is a prelude to equally serious tribulation roaring down the two-lane pike of finance and economy that will combine with the engineered destruction of institutional authority from RussiaGate to bring on the greatest crisis since the Civil War. The money is not there to perform any of the miracles of redistribution promised by AOC and Bernie Sanders — unless the Federal Reserve is coerced into printing a whole lot more money out of thin air, in which case the consequence will be that everybody gets to have a lot of worthless money that has lost its value.

If Congress wants to play committee games, it might want to investigate how the USA is going to rack up another $2 trillion in debt to finance its operations before the 2020 election. They're the ones who will have to vote to allow that to happen. The disorders of money coming down in the months ahead, RussiaGate aside, are sure to discredit both political parties. I doubt that Mr. Trump will survive it politically and the revenant Republican Party behind him is so devoid of credible leadership that it could dissolve altogether like an evening mist preceding the cold darkness of night. By then, the whole American political establishment will be, as Mencken quipped, like *a blind man stumbling around a dark cellar looking for a black cat that isn't there.*

Hysterias don't last forever, but the economic depression ahead will last a long, long time, and the nation will have to find some way to adjust to a lower standard of living. None of the nostrums currently in the air — the Guaranteed Basic Income, Medicare for all, the Green New Deal — will avail to alter that fate. The big question is just how disorderly and violent the journey through that will have to be.

BIBLICAL ANXIETIES

April 1, 2019

The sore beset people of this land may be good and goddamn sick of politics, RussiaGate, and Trump-inspired social strife, but they may soon have something more down to earth to worry about: biblical floods and plagues.

Media hysteria around the Mueller Report has nearly eclipsed news of historic flooding in the Midwest that has already caused $3 billion in damage to farms, homes, livestock, and infrastructure. With spring rainfall already at 200 percent of normal levels, the National Oceanic and Atmospheric Administration (NOAA) issued a statement in late March saying, "This is shaping up to be a potentially unprecedented flood season, with more than 200 million people at risk for flooding in their communities."

More to the point, two major western dams show disturbing signs of potential failure that may bring on unprecedented disasters. The Oroville Dam on the Feather River north of Sacramento — the highest earthen dam in the US — nearly blew out in February 2017 when record rains damaged the main spillway, threatening to send a 30-foot wall of water downstream toward California's capital and towns along the way. When that spillway was closed to assess the damage, which was significant, the secondary emergency spillway was opened for the first time since the dam was built in 1968. It too started disintegrating and before long Lake Oroville began flowing over the top of the dam itself. The state had to order evacuation of 188,000 people in three counties. Frantic efforts to drop sandbags from helicopters stabilized the damage and, luckily, the rain stopped.

Subsequent lawsuits against the state's Department of Water Resources revealed shoddy maintenance, theft of equipment, and poor record keeping. Now, two years later, new cracks have appeared in the repaired Oroville Dam main spillway. The Sierra Nevada snowpack stands at 153 percent above average, and the National Weather Service predicts that weak El Niño conditions with above-average Pacific Ocean temperatures are likely to produce above-average rainfall this spring along with the snowpack melt.

The Fort Peck Dam on the upper Missouri River in Montana is likewise troubling experts watching a record snowpack in the Rocky Mountains. It too is an earthen dam — the world's largest by volume — filled with hydraulic slurry. Because it is located on the flat high plains, the dam is extremely long, running 21,000 feet — about four miles — from end to end. Behind it is a reservoir that is the fifth-largest man-made lake in the nation.

Concern is rising because the coming snow melt coincides with seismic activity around the Yellowstone Caldera, one of the world's supervolcanoes. The slurry construction of the dam inclines it to liquification when the ground shakes. Failure of the Fort Peck Dam would send the equivalent of a whole year's flow of the Missouri River downstream in one release that could potentially wash away the other five downstream dams in the Missouri River Mainstem Reservoir System, along with every bridge from Montana to St. Louis, an unimaginable amount of farm and town infrastructure, and several nuclear power installations. It would be the greatest national disaster in US history. Just sayin'.

A shy, science-nerd correspondent writes: "Epidemiologists speculate that a flooding event in Central Asia steppes triggered the 1347 Eurasian plague outbreak. Rumors of a mass human die-off in India reached Europe in the mid-1340s. The Mongols besieging the coastal city of Trebizond on the shore of the Black Sea catapulted plague infested corpses over the city walls and Italian merchant ships fleeing Trebizond carried the infestation to Genoa which foolishly permitted the dying crew to land. . . . Rodents hosting plague spreading fleas typically inhabit arid grassland regions such as the Great Plains of America and the semi deserts of California and New Mexico. The current flooding of the American Mid-West and the mass dumping of flood tainted wheat, corn and soybeans will likely spark a rodent population explosion in the region, which in the context of rat-swarming homeless encampments may yield a 1347 repeat event in North America during the 2020s. What happened before can happen again."

The homeless camps around Los Angeles have turned up cases of other medieval-type diseases typical of human settlements before public sanitation became a standard feature of civilized life. Many are spread through feces (as well as drug use): hepatitis A, typhus, shigellosis (or trench fever, spread through body lice), and tuberculosis. Gawd knows what is coming across the border into America's proudly leading "sanctuary state." Wait for it. Just sayin'.

FREE FOR ALL

May 17, 2019

WASHINGTON — House Democrats, frustrated by President Trump's efforts to stonewall their investigations and eager to stoke public anger about the president's behavior, are pinning their diminishing hopes on Robert S. Mueller III yet again. . . . Mr. Mueller, who was invited to testify by the chairmen of the House Judiciary and Intelligence Committees a month ago, has not agreed to do so. — *The New York Times*

Oh? Is that so? Do you wonder why Mr. Mueller might not want to open his aching heart to any House committee in the desperate, last-ditch effort to wring some impeachment joy juice from the already wrung-out narrative of his disappointing report? For the excellent reason that the minority Republican members of said committees get to ask questions too, and they are sure to be embarrassing questions, perhaps placing the special counsel in legal jeopardy.

For instance: why did Mr. Mueller not reveal publicly that his team, and the FBI, both knew from the very start that the predicating "corpus of evidence" for the two-year inquisition was cheap fiction written by Glenn Simpson and his hirelings at Fusion GPS, the Hillary Clinton campaign's disinformation contractor — including "Russia specialist" Nellie Ohr, wife of then Deputy Attorney General Bruce Ohr? I could go on, but the above fact nugget alone is enough to inform any sentient adult that the Mueller investigation was an entirely political act of seditious subterfuge, and there are many other actionable nuggets of blatant mendacity in the 444-page report to inspire the convening of grand juries against a great many officials in orbit around Mr. Mueller. So don't expect Mr. Mueller to show up in any congressional witness chair, though he may occupy one in a courtroom around the time that the next major election is in full swing.

Here's what will actually happen. These House majority committee chiefs are going to quit their blustering over the next week or so as they discover there is no political value — and plenty of political hazard — in extending the RussiaGate circus. In the meantime, a titanic juridical machine, already a'grinding, will discredit the whole sordid affair and send a number of hapless participants to the federal Ping-Pong academies. And by then the long-suffering citizenry will barely give a shit because we will have entered the climactic phase of the Fourth Turning (or Long Emergency, take your pick), in which the operations of everyday business and governance in this country seriously crumble.

The Golden Golem of Greatness will be blamed for most of that. The internal contradictions of globalism were already blowing up trade and financial relations between the US and China. The Trump tariffs just amount to a clumsy recognition of the fatal imbalances long at work there. As a 25 percent tax on countless Chinese products, the tariffs will punish American shoppers as much as the Chinese manufacturers. Trade wars have a way of escalating into more kinetic conflicts.

The sad truth is that both China and the US are beset by dangerous fragilities. Both countries have borrowed themselves into a Twilight Zone of unpayable debt. Both countries are sunk in untenable economic and banking rackets to cover up their insolvency. China's fate hangs on distant energy supply lines that run through bottlenecks like the Strait of Hormuz and the Strait of Malacca. The US has been producing torrents of shale oil at a net financial loss — a business model with poor long-term prospects. The temperament of the Chinese people is conditioned historically by subservience to authority, which tends to blow into anarchic rage quickly and catastrophically when things go wrong. The US populace, sunk in decadence, despair, distraction, and delusion, moves sluggishly toward unrest — and for the time being expresses its discontent only in ceremonial narcissistic grievance.

The quarrel between the US and China now threatens to suck the rest of the world into a global business depression, which is what you might expect when globalism seizes up and the global players start scrambling desperately to keep any kind of economy going. The danger then will be that the disgruntled populations of these many lands could become as delusional as Americans, and equally inclined to international violence. There could be all kinds of fighting in all sorts of places while everybody goes broke and hungry. And meanwhile, Robert Mueller meets his protégé Jim Comey for the Ping-Pong championship of the Allenwood federal penitentiary.

THE ZEITGEIST KNOWS

June 3, 2019

Who said the global economy was a permanent installation in the human condition? The head cheerleader was *The New York Times'* Tom Friedman, with his 1999 book *The Lexus and the Olive Tree*, the trumpet blast for the new order of things. Since then, we partied like it was 1999, with a few grand mal seizures of the banking system along the way, some experiments in creating failed states abroad, and the descent of America's middle class into a Disney version of Hieronymus Bosch's *Last Judgment* — which is kind of what you see on the streets of Los Angeles these days.

Guess what: the global economy is winding down, and pretty rapidly. Trade wars are the most obvious symptom. The tensions underlying that spring from human population overshoot with its punishing externalities, resource depletion, and the perversities of money in accelerated motion, generating friction and heat. They also come from the fact that techno-industrialism was a story with a beginning, a middle, and an end — and we're closer to the end than we are to the middle. There will be no going back to the prior party, whatever way we pretend to negotiate our way around or through these quandaries.

The USA-China romance was bound to end in divorce, which Mr. Trump is surreptitiously suing for now under the guise of a negotiated trade rebalancing. The US has got a chronic financial disease known as the Triffin dilemma, a set of disorders endemic to any world reserve currency. The disease initially expressed itself in President Nixon's ditching the US dollar's gold backing in 1971. By then, the world had noticed the dollar's declining value trend line, and threatened to drain Fort Knox to counter the effects of holding those dollars. Since then, all world currencies have been based on nothing but the idea that national economies would forever and always pump out more wealth.

It turns out that they pump out more debt in the pursuit of that chimerical wealth until the economic viziers and banking poohbahs begin to declare that debt itself is wealth — and now all the major players around the world are choking to death on that debt, especially the USA and China, but also Japan and the dolorous commune known as the EU. Everybody's broke, one way or another, even though they are up to their eyeballs in products designed to fall apart in a few years. Better learn how to fix stuff, especially machines, because a lot of it won't be replaced going forward.

Notice that Mr. Nixon's escape from the dollar gold standard coincided with America's first oil production peak. It was actually more than a coincidence, though it is unclear that anyone but James Schlesinger (then head of the Atomic Energy Commission, and later secretary of defense, secretary of energy, and CIA director) understood what that signified. Now America is back at a second and even higher production peak thanks to the illusory boom of shale oil. The difference now is that only 10 percent of the companies producing it make a red cent. For the rest, the main result is just more and more debt, contributing to the larger global debt fiasco. It's now down to a race between the sensational depletion rate of the shale oil wells and the country's flagging capacity to generate more debt with a dim prospect of it ever being paid back.

Who knows whether the Golden Golem of Greatness and the people advising him in the White House get where all this is taking us in the history of the future. One might suppose it's behind Mr. Trump's wish to *Make America Great Again*, the vision of a return to the economy of 1955, of men toting lunch boxes through the factory gates, and seventy million boomer schoolchildren dreaming of trips to the moon, and the hard-fought, transient blessings of Pax Americana. All that is a comfort to simpletons, no doubt, but not wholly consistent with what can be observed actually going on — which is a culture and a political system seemingly bent on suicide.

The zeitgeist knows something that we don't. The arc of this story follows the breakup of old arrangements, including trade relations, alliances, nation-states, and widespread expectations about what ought to be. Some observers claim the US will be the "last man standing" in this journey to the post-global economy. (We surely would want to avoid a situation where nobody is left standing.) But all the participants in the orgy now ending will be left at least cross-eyed and flummoxed in the new cold dawn of a world without the old mojo. If the center is not holding, better look for a place on the margins as far from the emerging economic black hole as possible.

GOING WHERE, EXACTLY?

June 7, 2019

In response to what has become a nation of shameless racketeering, vivid wealth disparity, and shocking destitution on display in city streets, the party of the common man seeks remedies in the redistribution of capital. Seems more than fair to many. It's not for nothing that they style it "social justice," the cutting edge of an economic system called socialism — with overtones, of course, of settling racial and gender scores for good measure.

Socialism might seem to be the answer to all this unfairness and indignity. And naturally it focuses on the two activities that have turned into the worst rackets in America: higher education and health care, a.k.a. "eds and meds." Both are now cruel bloated parodies of what they used to be, turning their customers into debt serfs and bankrupts, apart from their dismal failures of basic mission: to prepare developing minds for reality and to *first do no harm.*

The proposed remedy is for the national government to take responsibility for running them and to make their services free to all. That would do nothing, of course, to reform the patent idiocies of the gender studies departments; or rescue the sorry victims of obesity and diabetes from their toxic consumption of whoppers, pizza, and slurpees. Those dynamics operate on feedback wheels of futility for which there is no happy ending outside of drastic changes in thought and behavior.

The Left now promises redemption from these great quandaries with the tag team of Robin Hood and Santa Claus ushering in a new golden era of free stuff. It's understandable perhaps, considering how desperate so many citizens of this land are, and how desperation feeds rescue fantasies. And the Left may even get a chance to try this wizardry after the next election. But it's really not where history is taking us. America is not going to go socialist, it's going medieval. Why is that?

To put it simply, the money is not there. But the "money" is only an abstract representation of material wealth of one kind or another — energy, goods, resources, and delivery systems — and all that is becoming more of a fugitive presence in reality-based civilization. We don't have the mojo anymore to nationalize and centralize these sprawling activities. It must be obvious that government is not only fatally beyond bankruptcy, but that it has also reached the stage of diminishing returns from overinvestment in complexity that translates into generalized incompetency. It's hardly just Mr. Trump alone that is responsible for the chaotic paralysis all around us.

Societies are self-organizing, emergent phenomena. They respond to the circumstances that reality presents, and they take us in unexpected directions. The general expectation in the USA since the Second World War has been for ever increasing material comfort provided by an inexhaustible techno-industrial cornucopia, kind of a cosmic goodie machine. Well, we'd better adjust our thinking to the fact that the horn of plenty is shockingly out of goodies, and that no amount of financial hocus-pocus is going to refill it. Valiant attempts to redistribute the already existing wealth are liable to prove disappointing, especially when the paper and digital representations of that wealth in "money" turn out to be figments — promises to pay that will never be kept because they can't be kept.

So, instead of fantasizing about free PhD programs for everybody, and free insulin for the multitudes, consider instead the vista of a reduced population working in the fields and pastures to bring enough food out of the long-abused land to live through the next winter. Consider a world in which, if we are lucky, the electricity runs for a few hours a day, but possibly not at all. Imagine a world in which men and women actually function in different divisions of labor and different social spaces because they must, to keep the human project going. Imagine a world in which the ideas in your head about that world actually have to comport with the way that world really works — and the severe penalty for failing to recognize that. That's the more likely world we're heading into. It won't put an end to dreams of utopias and cosmic rewards, but it will be a sobering moment in history.

THINGS TO COME

July 29, 2019

"American exceptionalism has led to a country that is exceptionally un-self-aware."
                                                            — Peter Thiel

The economic contraction ahead will put this borderline psychotic country through some interesting ch-ch-ch-changes. Mr. Trump now fully owns the Potemkin status quo of record stock markets poised against a withering rot of human capital at the core of an industrial society in sunset mode. Leadership at every corner of American life — politics, business, media — expects an ever higher tech magical updraft of fortune from an increasingly holographic economy of mere fugitive appearances in which everybody can get more of something for nothing. The disappointment over how all this works out will be epic.

Globalism is wobbling badly. It was never what it was cracked up to be: a permanent new plateau of exquisitely tuned international economic cooperation engineered to perfection. It was just a set of provisional relations based on transient advantage. As it turned out, every move that advantaged US-based corporations blew back ferociously on the American public and the long-term integrity of the social order. Sinister as it seems, the process was simply emergent: a self-organizing evolution of forces previously set in motion. And, like a lot of things in history, it seemed like a good idea at the time.

"Offshoring" US industry jacked up corporate profits while it decimated working-class livelihoods. In return, that large demographic got "bargain shopping" at Walmart, a life of ever upward revolving debt, and dead downtowns. The country got gigantic trade deficits and government debt loads. In effect, globalism compelled America to borrow as much as possible from the future to keep running things the way they were set up to run. Now, there is just suspicion that we've reached the limits of borrowing. Soon it will be a fact and that fact will upend everything we've been doing.

You can see how this is playing out in politics, especially the proposed government-enforced redistribution of whatever wealth is supposed to be left. Of course, much of that wealth is a figment, represented in abstract financial instruments pegged to "money" that may have a lot less value than presumed. The Democratic Party detects opportunity in the gross imbalances of this notional capital and so it is promising every conceivable form of grift to voters from a guaranteed basic income and free medical care and college education to reparations for the descendants of slaves.

They certainly might win the 2020 election on the basis of that proffer, but good luck scaring up the actual financial mojo to make it happen without destroying whatever value remains in the US dollar. The predicament may be aggravated by foreign capital seeking refuge in US financial markets as the banking systems in China and Euroland unwind, giving politicians the false impression that other people's money belongs to Americans. And anyway, what will these foreigners actually be investing in here? Collateralized loan obligations based on seven-year used-car payment schemes?

The American Left just can't grok the fact that we missed the window of opportunity for setting up a national health system. That was a mid-twentieth-century thang: cheap oil and industrial growth. Please note: it was the Democratic Party under Mr. Obama that turned the college loan industry (and higher ed with it) into the appalling racket it's become, because it fit the template of a society pretending to prosper by racking up debt. That demographic of debtors will be seeking magical debt relief. If they get it, it will be at the expense of the government that took on the guaranteed backing of all that debt, now well over a trillion dollars.

Industrial growth is over, and with it the expectation that all the old debts can be paid back. A few economic commentators are predicting "stagflation." We'd be lucky if that's all it turned out to be. But we're unlikely to get a replay of the 1970s. That was an era of geo-financial disturbance that resolved for a while with new oil from Alaska and the North Sea. That's not going to happen again this time. Stagflation was just a matter of going nowhere for a decade. The contraction ahead will be brutal, not going nowhere but rather going down hard to a lower and harsher standard of living.

It's also hard to calculate how disturbing and disruptive the prosecution of the RussiaGate perps will be. If the Democratic Party is acting batshit crazy about it now after the Mueller testimony fiasco, how will it react when dozens of its partisans are marched into court to face charges of sedition. That ugly business looks on track to collide with the coming financial distress. The result will be much more severe political turbulence than the thinking class expects. It's easy to imagine circumstances in which normal institutions get suspended and the old major parties are superseded by "emergency" seizures of power by other parties as yet unknown.

LOST AT SEA

August 23, 2019

In these horse latitudes of late summer, with the seas becalmed and the riggings a'creak, the Resistance's ship of the line (a.k.a. the Democratic Party) drifts ever farther out of sight of land. Even so, a few of its crew members have jumped ship: New York's mayor, stowaway Bill de Blasio, may have been shoved overboard. Former Colorado governor Hickenlooper walked the plank clutching the life buoy of a sure-thing Senate seat. Washington State Gov. Jay Inslee went mad drinking seawater and dove in after hallucinating a school of beckoning mermaids. Months from now, the accursed vessel may be discovered mysteriously deserted, prompting tales of mutiny and cannibalism, like the brigantine *Mary Celeste* of legend.

That's how lost and far out the party looks more than a year from the general election. Back on dry land, the resourceful Golden Golem of Greatness made another flanking maneuver around the Resistance's left, disarming the so-called Flores Rule from 1994 that underlay the racket of using children to evade the immigration laws. Now the kids can remain with their parents awaiting deportation, which is the natural consequence of sneaking across the border illegally. The Resistance cannot grok the reality that federal law actually applies in cases of border jumping. Shrieks of "racism" rise from coastal yoga studios and cappuccino bars. Uncle Sam is racist through and through, from his run-down boot heels to his chin whiskers.

The New York Times, America's journal of double-plus goodthink, is proving this week with its "1619 Project" that the NBA is actually the legitimate governing body of this land, contrary to the racist document purporting to be the "Constitution." How many three-pointers could that roly-poly little math freak Ben Franklin shoot? Don't you understand that the Civil War was fought over the attempt by damnable whites to suppress basketball, the *Times* imputes. Can't anybody play "The Star-Spangled Banner" blues anymore in its original form as a field holler, before that cad Francis Scott Key stole it and quashed all the flatted notes?

Elizabeth Warren set the stage for anointing herself America's race hustler in chief by addressing the niggling matter of her former claim to be a Cherokee Indian, since disproven by a DNA test. There was loose talk, you see, that she used the Cherokee ruse to bamboozle her overseers on the Harvard Plantation, where she got to work in the Big House known as the Harvard Law School based on her "diversity" bona fides — a "minority hire"! The claim was so transparently idiotic and dishonest that she was desperate to walk it back as delicately as possible, in order to keep up with the race hustling of her fellow pols chasing the nomination. A rain dance was arranged in the aptly named heartland town of Sioux City.

"Like anyone who's being honest with themselves, I know that I have made mistakes," said Ms. Warren, who was met with a standing ovation when she took the stage [the Times *reported]. "I am sorry for harm I have caused. I have listened and I have learned a lot, and I am grateful for the many conversations that we've had together."*

Was a more disingenuous political statement ever contrived? A bundle of devious platitudinous promises of the sort that white people always offered the indigenous folk at a thousand crooked treaty councils? It would have been a little more satisfying, perhaps, if Ms. Warren had specified the mistakes made, e.g., *I was falsely claiming a racial identity for career advancement.* Now *that's* an apology! "Listening and learning"? I dunno . . . sounds a little like groveling and pandering. Anyone can choke down a few bites of humble pie but please don't make me eat that shit sandwich!

The Democratic contest may be peaking way too early. And Joe Biden hasn't even had a chance to claim he is the out-of-wedlock grandson of W. C. Handy. There are indications that the political center is already a little tired of the Everything Is Racist trope that the party ran up the flagpole this summer. For *The New York Times*, it became the publicly acknowledged official editorial slant when newsroom chief Dean Baquet announced that the paper needed a replacement for the shredded gonfalon of RussiaGate.

That move by Mr. Baquet has more than a little quality of whistling past the graveyard. When the summer is over, ill winds will be blowing the SS *Resistance* close to the reefs of Durham and Barr, when many of the ship's officers — Ensigns Brennan, Clapper, Comey, Lynch, McCabe, and many others, perhaps even Admiral Obama — start perp walking around the deck. What a mighty embarrassment that will be. The cry that "mistakes were made" won't salvage the party's reputation as it founders and sinks. Glug glug.

THE G-7 BLUES

August 26, 2019

What's at stake in all these international confabs like the G-7 are the tenuous supply lines that keep the global game going. The critical ones deliver oil around the world. China imports about 10 million barrels a day to keep its operations going. It produces less than 4 million barrels a day. Only about 15 percent of its imports come from next door in Russia. The rest comes from the Middle East, Africa, and South America. Think: long lines of tanker ships traveling vast distances across the seas, navigating through narrow straits. The Chinese formula is simple: oil in, exports out. It has worked nicely for them in recent decades. Things go on until they don't.

That game is lubricated by a fabulous stream of debt generated by Chinese banks that ultimately answer to the Communist Party. The party is the Chinese buffer between banking and reality. If the party doesn't like the distress signals that the banks give off, it just pretends the signals are not coming through, while it does the hokeypokey with its digital accounting, and things appear sound a while longer.

The US produces just over 12 million barrels of oil a day. About 6.5 million of our production is shale oil. We use nearly 20 million a day. (We're not "energy independent.") The shale oil industry is wobbling under the onerous debt load that it has racked up since 2005. About 90 percent of the companies involved in shale oil lose money. The capital costs for drilling, hauling a gazillion truckloads of water and fracking sand to the rig pads, and sucking the oil out exceed the profit from doing all that. It's simply all we can do to keep the game going in our corner of the planet, but it's not a good business model. After you've proved conclusively that you can't make a buck at this using borrowed money, the lenders will quit lending you more money. That's about where we are now.

Europe is near the end of its North Sea oil bonanza and there's nothing in the on-deck circle for them. Germany tried to prove that it could run the country on "renewables" and that experiment has flopped. They have no idea what they're going to do to keep the game going in their patch of nations. They must be freaking out in their charming capital cities.

The next economic bust is going to amount to the crack-up of the oil age, and the "global economy" that emerged in its late stage. It was all about moving fantastic quantities of things around the planet. The movements were exquisitely tuned, along with the money flows that circulated freely, like blood carrying oxygen to each organ. All of that is coming to an end. The nations of the world must be feeling desperate, despite the appearance of good manners at meetings like the G-7. What's at stake for everybody in the dark background is the ability to maintain high standards of living only recently attained. And the fear behind that is not knowing just how far backward these high standards of living may have to slide.

A lot of people still alive in China must remember a daily existence on par with the twelfth century. In the USA, where democracy is mostly represented by low-order thinking skills, the memory of life before electricity and running water is long gone. We've been living in Futurama since the end of the last world war. That war, by the way, is not entirely forgotten in Europe, despite all the charm currently on display and the tourists swarming with their selfie sticks. The place was a charnel house for centuries and the Euro folk will do about anything to suppress conflict. Lately, it looks like they're willing to give up on Western civilization itself to keep the peace.

Lord knows what Mr. Trump's strategy is with these so-called trade talks. He has explicitly enough pushed for the reindustrialization of America, and that implies — among other things — decoupling from the China's torrential merchandise supply lines, cutting off its revenues. Closing off China's access to US markets itself might be enough to finally blow up China's deeply fraudulent banking system. Maybe the aim is to just disable China, derail it from its seeming aim of becoming the next world hegemon. Does Mr. Trump think he can do that without blowing up the rest of the world's financial arrangements? The stock markets haven't been digesting that story very well lately. Could the US government be collectively dumb enough to think that shale oil will permit this country to reindustrialize while the rest of the world stumbles back into a dark age?

More likely, all the advanced nations will make that downward journey together. The US is well on its way, despite all the MAGA bravado. The country is reeling in bad faith, delusion, official corruption, porno-pharmaceutical vice, and ethnic rancor. The people who live in Flyover Land style themselves like Visigoths, all tatted up and armed to the teeth, moiling angrily at the edge of the Rome-like coastal enclaves. The elites want to stuff themselves inside their phones and live there. Guess what: that won't be a "safe space."

A View from the Brink

September 16, 2019

Welcome to the world where things don't add up. For instance, *some people did some things* to the Saudi Arabian oil refinery at Abqaiq over the weekend. Like, sent over a salvo of cruise missiles and armed drone aircraft to blow it up. They did a pretty good job of disabling the works. It is Saudi Arabia's largest oil processing facility, and for now, perhaps months, a fair amount of the world's oil supply will be cut off. President Trump said, "[We] are waiting to hear from the Kingdom as to who they believe was the cause of this attack, and under what terms we would proceed!" Exclamation mark his.

How many times the past few years has our government declared that "we have the finest intelligence services in the world." Very well, then, why are we waiting for the Kingdom of Saudi Arabia to tell us who fired all that stuff into Abqaiq? Whoever did it, it was unquestionably an act of war. And, of course, what are we going to do about it? (And what will *some people* do about it?)

Let's face it: the USA has had a hard-on for Iran for forty years, ever since they overthrew their shah, invaded the US embassy in Tehran, and took fifty-two American diplomats and staff hostage for 444 days. On the other hand, the Arabians and Iranians have had a mutual hard-on for centuries, long before the Saud family was in charge of things, and back when Iran was known as Persia, a land of genies, fragrant spices, and a glorious antiquity (while Arabia was a wasteland of sand populated by nomads and their camels).

The beef was formerly just about which brand of Islam would prevail, Sunni or Shia. Lately (the past fifty years) it has been more about the politics of oil and hegemony over the Middle East. Since the US invaded Iraq and busted up the joint, the threat has existed that Iran would take over Iraq, with its majority Shia population, especially the oil-rich Basra region at the head of the Persian Gulf. The presence of Israel greatly complicates things, since Iran has a hard-on for that nation, too, and for Jews especially, often expressed in the most belligerent and opprobrious terms, such as "wiping Israel off the map." No ambiguity there. The catch being that Israel has the capability of turning Iran into an ashtray.

The world has been waiting for a major war in the Middle East for decades, and it might have one by close of business today. Or perhaps *some people will do nothing*. The Iran-backed Houthi rebels of Yemen supposedly claimed responsibility for the attack. That's rich. As if that ragtag outfit has a whole bunch of million-dollar missiles and the knowledge and capacity to launch them successfully, not to mention the satellite guidance mojo. A correspondent suggests that the missiles were fired from a pro-Iranian military base in Iraq, with the Houthis brought in on flying carpets to push the launch buttons.

President Trump is trumpeting America's "energy independence," meaning whatever happens over there won't affect us. Well, none of that is true. We still import millions of barrels of oil a day, though much less from Saudi Arabia than before 2008. The shale oil "miracle" is hitting the skids these days. Shale oil production has gone flat, the rig count is down, companies are going bankrupt, and financing for the debt-dependent operations is dwindling since the producers have demonstrated that they can't make a profit at it. They're trapped in the quandary of diminishing returns, frontloading production, while failing to overcome steep decline curves in wells that produce for only a couple of years.

It's also the case that shale oil is ultra-light crude, containing little heavier distillates such as diesel and aviation fuel (basically kerosene). Alas, American refineries were all built before shale oil came along. They were designed to crack heavier oil and can't handle the lighter shale. The "majors" don't want to invest their remaining capital in new refineries, and the many smaller companies don't have the ability. So this makes necessary a high volume of oil swapping around the world. Without diesel and aviation fuel, US trucking and commercial aviation have a big problem, meaning the US economy has a big problem.

With the new crisis in the Middle East, benchmark West Texas Intermediate oil is up from around $55 a barrel to just over $60 at the market open (European Brent crude is just above $70). That's a pop, but not a spectacular one, considering that a whole lot more damage might ensue in the days ahead. China, Korea, and Japan stand to lose bigly if the players in the Middle East really go at it and bust up each other's assets. If that happens, the world will never be the same. You can kiss the global economy goodbye for good. Let's hope some people don't do something.

THE FUMES OF FANATICISM

October 28, 2019

Judging by the volume of intemperate emails and angry social media blasts that come my way, the party of impeachment seems to be inhaling way too much gas from the smoking guns it keeps finding in the various star chambers of its inquisition against you-know-who. You'd think that the failure of Mr. Mueller's extravaganza might have chastened them just a little — a $32 million effort starring the most vicious partisan lawyers inside the Beltway, 2,800 subpoenas issued over two years, 500 search warrants exercised, and finally nothing whatever to pin on Mr. Trump — except the contra-legal assertion that now he must prove his innocence.

When you state just that, these frothing hysterics reply that *many* background figures — if not the Golden Golem of Greatness himself — were indicted and convicted of crimes by Mr. Mueller's crew. Oh yes! The Russian troll farm called the Internet Research Agency was indicted for spending $400,000 on Facebook ads (and never extradited or tried in a court of law). Pretty impressive victory there! The hacking of Hillary Clinton's emails by "Russia"? Still just alleged, never proven, with plenty of shady business around the search for evidence. Paul Manafort, on tax evasion of money earned in Ukraine, 2014? We'll see about that as the whole filthy business of the 2014 Ukraine regime-change op under Mr. Obama gets reviewed in the months ahead. George Papadopoulos for lying to the FBI? Stand by on that one, too; still a developing story. General Michael Flynn, for ditto? You may have noticed that General Flynn's case is shaping up to be the biggest instance of prosecutorial misconduct since the Dreyfus affair (France, 1894–1906, which badly educated Americans most certainly know nothing about).

To set the record straight I'm forced to repeat something that these New Age Jacobins seem unable to process: you don't have to be a Trump cheerleader to be revolted by the behavior of his antagonists, which is a stunning spectacle of bad faith, dishonesty, incompetence, and malice — and is surely way more toxic to the American project than anything the president has done. Every time I entertain the complaints of these angry auditors, I'm forced to remind myself that these are the same people who think that "inclusion" means shutting down free speech, who believe that the US should not have borders, who promote transsexual reading hours in the grammar schools, and who fiercely desire to start a war with Russia.

That's not a polity I want to be associated with, and until it screws its head back on I will remain the enemy of it. In fact, in early November I'm traveling to New York City, where the Jacobin city council has just made it a crime to utter the phrase *illegal alien* in a public place, with a $250,000 penalty attached. I challenge their agents to meet me in Penn Station and arrest me when I go to the information kiosk and inquire if they know what is the best place in midtown Manhattan to meet illegal aliens.

The volume of Jacobin hysteria ratcheted up to "11" late last week when the news broke that the attorney general's study of RussiaGate's origins was upgraded to a criminal investigation, and that a voluminous report from the DOJ inspector general is also about to be released. What do you suppose they're worried about? Naturally the Jacobins' bulletin board, a.k.a *The New York Times*, fired a salvo denouncing William Barr — so expect his reputation to be the next battle zone for these ever more desperate fanatics. Talk of preemptively impeaching him is already crackling through the Twitter channels. That will be an excellent sideshow.

Meanwhile, how is Rep. Adam Schiff's secret proceeding going? Last week he put out a narrative that the US chargé d'affaires to Ukraine Bill Taylor fired a gun that smoked *fer sure* in testimony. Except, of course, as per Mr. Schiff's usual practice, he refused to issue any actual transcript of the interview in evidence, while there are plenty of indications that Mr. Taylor's secondhand gossip was roundly refuted under counterquestioning by the non-Jacobin minority members of the House intel committee. Mr. Schiff's pattern lo these many months of strife has been to claim ultimate proof of wrongdoing only to have it blow up in his face. It's a face that many Americans are sick of seeing and hearing from, and I am serenely confident that before this colossal scandal is resolved, the congressman from Hollywood will be fatally disgraced, as was his role model, Senator Joseph McCarthy, before him.

THE TURNAROUND

November 29, 2019

At yesterday's Thanksgiving table, fifteen adults present, there was not one word uttered about impeachment, Russia, Ukraine, and, most notably, a certain Golden Golem of Greatness, whose arrival at the center of American life three years ago kicked off a political hysteria not witnessed across this land since southern "fire eaters" lay siege to Fort Sumter.

I wonder if some great fatigue of the mind has set in among the class of people who follow the news and especially the tortured antics of Rep. Adam Schiff's goat rodeo in the House's intel committee the past month. I wonder what the rest of Congress is detecting among its constituents back home during this holiday hiatus. I suspect it is that same eerie absence of chatter I noticed, and what it may portend about the nation's disposition toward reality.

The dead white man Arthur Schopenhauer (1788–1860) famously observed that "all truth passes through three stages: first, it is ridiculed; second, it is violently opposed; and third, it is accepted as self-evident." America has been stuck in stage two lo these thirty-six months since Mr. Trump shocked the system with his electoral victory over She Whose Turn Was Undoubted, inciting a paroxysm of rage, disbelief, and retribution that has made the Left side of the political transect ridiculous, and repeatedly, ignominiously so, as their fantasies about Russian "collusion" and sequential chimeras dissolve in official proceedings.

The astounding failure of Mr. Mueller's report did nothing to dampen the violent derangement. There was no rethinking whatsoever about the terms of engagement in the Left's war against the populist hobgoblin. The solidarity of delusion remained locked in place, leading to Mr. Schiff's recent antics over his false "whistleblower" and the enfilade of diplomatic flak catchers tasked to ward off any truthful inquiry into events in Ukraine.

But then, with the Thanksgiving shutdown, something began to turn. It was signaled especially in the Left's chief disinformation organ, *The New York Times*, with a weeklong salvo of lame *stories* aimed at defusing the Horowitz report, forthcoming on December 9. The *Times* stories were surely based on leaks from individuals cited in the IG's report, who were given the opportunity to "review" the briefs against them prior to the coming release. The stories gave off an odor of panic and desperation that signaled a crumbling loss of conviction in the three-year *narrative* assault on the truth — namely, that the US intel community organized a coup to overthrow the improbable President Trump.

From this point forward, the facts of the actual story — many of them already in the public record, one way or another, and sedulously ignored by the news media — will be officially detailed by federal authorities outside the orbit of the coupsters, and finally beyond the coupsters' control. The facts may include the uncomfortable truth that Mr. Mueller and his helpers were major players in the bad faith exercises of the intel community against the occupant of the White House.

I'm not so sure that the Resistance can keep up the fight, since their enemy is reality as much as reality's mere personification in Mr. Trump. The *violent opposition* Schopenhauer spoke of in his three-stage model was just procedural in this case, moving through the courts and committees and other organs of the state. I don't think the Left can bring the fight to the streets. They don't have it in them, not even the Antifa corps. The hard truths of perfidy and treachery in the upper ranks of government will rain down in the weeks ahead, and when they do, there's an excellent chance that they will be greeted as self-evident. The *Times*, the *WashPo*, and the cable news networks will have no choice but to report it all. My guess is that they will display a kind of breathlessly naive wonder that such things are so. Most remarkably, they might just assert that they knew it all along — a final twitch of bad faith as the new paradigm locks into place.

I expect that we will see something else happen along with that: a loud repudiation of the Democratic Party itself, a recognition that it betrayed the mental health of the nation in its lawless and demented inquisitions. I expect that sentiment will extend to the party's current crop of candidates for the White House, to the delusional proposals they push, and perhaps even to the larger ethos of the wokester religion that has programmatically tried to destroy the common culture of this country — especially the idea that we have a duty to be on the side of truth.

Christmas in Flyover Land

December 22, 2019

Last year, a local guy started renovating a restaurant on Main Street that has been shuttered for at least fifteen years. He'd retired from the army and started a company that made a fortune clearing land mines in faraway lands where US nation-building plans went awry. Wasn't that a ripe business opportunity! He's from here and loves the village and married his high school sweetheart — and would like the place to come back to life.

He's partnered up with another guy who intends to open a bistro with a bar, a fireplace, and supposedly a boutique distillery operation in the back. That would give some people in town a reason to leave the house at 5 o'clock in the afternoon, when the day's work is done — people like me who work alone all day. It could also give the citizens of this community a comfortable place to talk to each other about their lives and the place where we all live, and what we might do about things here. That's called local politics.

I'll refrain from tossing off judgments about the exterior treatment for now. Draw your own conclusions. I haven't seen the inside and there's butcher paper taped up on the windows while they finish in there. It looks like they'll open early in the new year. There hasn't been a comfortable public gathering place on Main Street in a long time. There's a "tasting room" at a local small brewery down the block, but it's hardly bigger than a couple of broom closets and the New York State Liquor Authority has an asinine regulation that forbids comfortable seating in such a designated establishment. Stools only. And only a few of those. What kind of culture does that to itself?

Ours apparently. When you get down to it, the sickness at the heart of our nation these days is the result of countless bad choices, large and small, that we've made collectively over decades, including the ones made by our elected officialdom. The good news is that we could potentially move in the opposite direction and start making better choices. However deficient and unappetizing you think Mr. Trump is, and how crudely unorthodox his behavior, that equation is what got enough people to vote for him. The strenuous efforts to antagonize him, disable him, and get rid of him by any means necessary — including police-state tactics, bad faith inquisitions, and outright sedition — have prevented the nation as a whole from entertaining a realistic new consensus for making better choices. In fact, it has achieved just the opposite: a near civil war, edition 2.0.

All the people of America, including the flyovers, are responsible for the sad situation we're in: this failure to reestablish a common culture of values most people can subscribe to and use it to rebuild our towns into places worth caring about. Main Street, as it has come to be, is the physical manifestation of that failure. The businesses that used to occupy the storefronts are gone, except for secondhand stores. Nobody in 1952 would have believed this could happen. And yet there it is: the desolation is stark and heartbreaking. Even George Bailey's "nightmare" scene in *It's a Wonderful Life* depicts the supposedly evil Pottersville as a very lively place, programmed only for old-fashioned wickedness: gin mills and streetwalkers. Watch the movie and see for yourself. Pottersville is way more appealing than 99 percent of America's small towns today, dead as they are.

The dynamics that led to this are not hard to understand. The concentration of retail commerce in a very few gigantic corporations was a swindle that the public fell for. Enthralled like little children by the dazzle and gigantism of the big boxes, and the free parking, we allowed ourselves to be played. The excuse was "bargain shopping," which actually meant *we have sent the factories to distant lands and eliminated your jobs, and all the meaning and purpose in your lives — and cheap stuff from Asia is your consolation prize. Enjoy.* The "bones" of the village are still standing but the programming for the organism of a community is all gone: gainful employment, social roles in the life of the place, confidence in the future. For a century starting in 1850, there were at least five factories in town. They made textiles and, later on, paper products and, in the end, toilet paper, ironically enough. Yes, really. They also made a lot of the sod-busting steel plows that opened up the Midwest, and cotton shirts, and other stuff. The people worked hard for their money, but it was pretty good money by world standards for most of those years. It allowed them to eat well, sleep in a warm house, and raise children, which is a good start for any society. The village was rich with economic and social niches, and yes it was hierarchical, but people tended to find the niche appropriate to their abilities and aspirations — and, believe it or not, it is better to have a place in society than to have no place at all, which is the sad situation for so many today. Homelessness in America runs way deeper than just the winos and drug addicts living on the big city sidewalks.

I've written a ton about the bad choice of suburbanizing the USA and all its subsidiary ill effects, and yet it's a subject so rich that you can hardly exhaust it. It has produced an entropic wasting disease on our country so complex in symptoms that all the certified PhD economists and sociologists of the Ivy League and the land-grant diploma mills can barely diagnose the illness, or calculate the pain it has caused. Not a small part of this is the utter and abject absence of artistry expressed in the places we've built since 1945.

Our Main Street flaunts that boldly. The 1960-vintage post office looks like a Soviet lunch counter — or, more specifically, the box that it came in. What were they thinking? The video store looks like a muffler shop. The graceful four-story hotel that stood at the absolute center of town, and burned down in 1957, was replaced by a one-story drive-in bank. The facade redos of the 1970s and '80s display a mindboggling array of bad choices in claddings, colors, proportioning, and embellishment. It's as if the entire world of aesthetics had died in the canebrakes of the Solomon Islands in 1944, and afterward nobody realized that something in America had gone missing. It's particularly dismaying when you see the efforts that earlier generations made to instill some beauty in the things they built, with a few examples still standing for all to wonder at and dote on.

The damage done can be undone. It's really a question of what it might take and that's a big question because it will almost surely take a shock to the system. That shock could come as soon as the next two weeks — as not a few observers have predicted — in the form of a gross financial dislocation. The ongoing mysterious action in the "repo" markets suggests that some kind of black hole has gaped open in the banking cosmos and is sucking literally hundreds of billions of dollars into an alternative universe. Guess we'll have to stand by on that. The shale oil orgy is probably peaking, and the aftereffects of that will be pretty harsh, but it might take a couple more years to play out. The weak leg of the stool these days seems to be our politics, the dangerous deformities of which I set forth in this blog regularly. (Some readers object to hearing about it, of course, for reasons I must regard as peevish and specious.) Most likely, the shocks will come in combinations from banking, from the rest of the actual economy, and from these deadly "gotcha" politics.

You can see the humble beginnings of change around here, or at least an end to some of the practices and behaviors I've described above. The Kmart shut down last March. It left the town without a general merchandise store — besides the dollar store, which sells stuff that fell off a truck somewhere in China. But the chain stores will have to go down if we're ever going to rebuild networks of local and regional commerce and bring Main Street back to life. And you must be aware that chain stores *are* going down by the thousands all around the country, the so-called *retail apocalypse*. These things have to die for a new economic ecosystem to emerge, and it looks like the process is underway. I hope the fast-food joints are next. At least we're getting a new independent bistro in town.

The landscape around here is composed of tender hills and little hollows that precede the Green Mountains of Vermont, ten miles down the pike. Apart from its stunning beauty, it's not bad farmland, either, and the rugged topography lends itself to small-scale farming, which is a good thing because that's the coming trend. I maintain that farming will eventually become the center of the next economy here as life in the USA is compelled to downsize and relocalize. We could make a few things again, too, because a river runs through town with many hydro sites — waterfalls where small factories once stood — and that river leads to the mighty Hudson four miles downstream. The Hudson can take you around the world or deep into the interior of North America via the Erie and Champlain canals that run off the Hudson.

For the moment, though, the country faces that set of convulsions I call the Long Emergency, with politics at center stage just now. The locals, myself included, have strung up the colored lights and set out the effigies of Santa and his reindeer. I love Christmas, the trappings, the music, and the sense that we're obliged to bring some enchantment into our lives when the days are shortest and darkest. I doubt we can *Make America Great Again* in the Trump sense, but we can reanimate our nation's life, and reenchant our daily doings in it, and learn to care about a few things again.

Merry Christmas, readers! And thank you for being here!

Evidence of Absence

December 27, 2019

What is most perilous for our country now would be to journey through a second epic crisis of authority in recent times without anybody facing the consequences of crimes they might have committed. The result will be a people turned utterly cynical, with no faith in their institutions or the rule of law, and no way to imagine a restoration of their lost faith within the bounds of law. It will be a deadly divorce between truth and reality. It will be an invitation to civil violence, a broken social contract, and the end of the framework for American life that was set up in 1788.

The first crisis of the era was the Great Financial Crash of 2008 based on widespread malfeasance in the banking world, an unprecedented suspension of rules, norms, and laws. GFC poster boy Angelo Mozilo, CEO and chairman of Countrywide Financial, a subprime mortgage racketeering outfit, sucked at least half a billion dollars out of his operation before it blew up, and finally was nicked for $67 million in fines by the SEC — partly paid by Countrywide's indemnity insurer — with criminal charges of securities fraud eventually dropped in the janky "settlement." In other words, *the cost of doing business*. Scores of other fraudsters and swindlers in that orgy of banking malfeasance were never marched into a courtroom, never had to answer for their depredations, and remained at their desks in the C-suites collecting extravagant bonuses. The problems they caused were papered over with trillions of dollars that all of us are still on the hook for. And, contrary to appearances, the banking system never actually recovered. It is permanently demoralized.

How it was that Barack Obama came on duty in January of 2009 and got away with doing absolutely nothing about all that for eight years remains one of the abiding mysteries of life on earth. Perhaps getting the first black president into the White House was such an intoxicating triumph of righteousness that nothing else seemed to matter anymore. Perhaps Mr. Obama was just a cat's-paw for banksterdom. (Sure kinda seems like it, when your first two hires are Robert Rubin and Larry Summers.) The failure to assign penalties for massive bad behavior has set up the nation for another financial fiasco, surely of greater magnitude than the blowup of 2008, considering the current debt landscape. Not a few astute observers say they feel the hot breath of that monster on the back of their necks lately, with all the strange action in the repo market — $500 billion "liquidity" injections in six weeks.

But now we are a year into Attorney General Bill Barr coming on the scene — the crime scene of RussiaGate and all its deceitful spin-offs. The Mueller investigation revealed itself as not just a thumping failure, but part of a broader exercise in bad faith and sedition to first prevent Mr. Trump from winning the 2016 election and then to harass, obstruct, disable, and eject him from office. And six months after Mr. Mueller's faceplant, out comes the Horowitz Report tracing in spectacular detail further and deeper criminal irregularities in the US Justice agencies. What's more, tremendous amounts of evidence for all this already sits on the record in public documents. The timelines are well understood.

And so an anxious nausea creeps over the land that Mr. Barr and Mr. Durham are dawdling toward a goal of deflecting justice from the sick institutions behind the three-year coup — that our polity is so saturated in corruption nothing will be allowed to clean it up. Personally, I don't subscribe to that hopelessness, and I will say why. But I must also say that if Barr & Durham fail to deliver a bale of indictments, they will be putting a bullet in the head of this republic. There will be no hope of restoring trust in the system and the hopelessness will inspire serious civil violence.

It ought to be obvious that we are well into Strauss and Howe's *Fourth Turning*, the generational climax of a grand political cycle tending toward darkness and ruin (and eventually the birth of a new cycle). But the God of History in the Making is a prankster. For instance, in the Fourth Turning there is the archetypal figure they call the "Gray Champion," specifically a baby boomer who emerges as the national leader to turn back the gathering darkness. Well, you order up a Gray Champion and cosmic room service sends up a New York real estate grifter with a twenty-three-word vocabulary, an impulse control problem, and a mystifying hairdo. It becomes extremely difficult to defend this ludicrous character — except that the conduct of his antagonists has been much much worse, and probably more destructive to the long-running American experiment in liberty.

Exactly because the misconduct against Mr. Trump was so deep and broad, bringing actual cases to court will require extreme care, especially if these cases are folded into a RICO rap. Mr. Barr has been surprisingly transparent in his procedures and his motives. He made it quite clear in speeches last fall at Notre

Dame and the Federalist Society that he deplores the lawless anarchy of "Resistance" efforts to engage "in a war to cripple, by any means necessary, a duly elected government." He stated recently that he expects Mr. Durham to act by late spring. Many are discouraged that he did not bring a case against James Comey on an earlier referral by IG Horowitz in the Hillary email server matter. Mr. Barr averred that it was not the strongest case against the former FBI chief. I took that to mean that graver charges await and there was no point going through the motions with a weaker Mickey Mouse count — and possibly losing in court. Point taken. We'll have to wait and see.

In the meantime, there is the impeachment ceremony, connoting a trial in the Senate to resolve the charges. Just days after it was voted out in the House — and in the limbo between Christmas and the New Year — nobody seems to know what will come out of all that. The president seems eager for a Senate trial. His counselors could call witnesses until the cows come home, and probably do a great job of humiliating and disarming the rabid forces of the Resistance. But hauling in the likes of Brennan, Comey, Strzok, McCabe et al. might only queer any cases to be brought against them by Mr. Durham. Limiting the witnesses to the Ukraine "whistleblower" scam that provoked the impeachment — Eric Ciaramella, Michael Atkinson, Adam Schiff — would be a capital entertainment, but it might also queer federal cases against them, a necessary corrective in the big picture.

On balance then, whatever happens in the Senate, the briefer the better, and the most obvious tack would be a simple summary dismissal of the House's charges as devoid of merit. And then a season of patience while events are allowed to play out. What's at stake beyond the fog of concerted deception and bad faith is whether we'll return to the principle that actions bring consequences, which is also the basic principle of reality. The departure from that since 2008 has just about wrecked the foundations of this country.

❧ 2020 ❧

GRAVE TENDINGS

January 17, 2020

So titanically self-unaware is the Democratic Resistance that it failed to grok it was actually signing the party's death warrant Wednesday, complete with official Nancy Pelosi commemorative black-and-gold signature pens. And that their *solemn, prayerful* journey from one side of the Capitol building to the other was actually the conveyance of that death warrant in what amounted to the party's funeral march. Remember this eternal paradox of the human condition: *people get what they deserve, not what they expect.*

Could you look at the lineup of Democratic impeachment managers without laughing? Was there ever such a band of hapless, misbegotten ninnies assembled for a suicide mission? Led by the waddling homunculus Jerrold Nadler, side by side with Adam Schiff, oozing a flop sweat of falsehood, a rank cloud of bathos trailed the procession to the Senate side with its pathetic bill of particulars.

Could they actually be so dim as to proffer "abuse of power" and "obstruction of Congress" as articles of impeachment? These two figments would be laughed out of a second-year law school mock court. Legal necromancers of the future, with all the time in the world, may never unpack the intended meaning of these charges besides "we hate you" and "you hurt our feelings." But it's up to the Senate of today to dispose of them procedurally one way or another, and the exercise is sure to be a high order of entertainment.

In a sane world of rational adults, these charges would be coolly dismissed out of hand as lacking any discernible malfeasant substance. As we live in a time of hysteria, the normal rules don't apply. That being the case, the defense should spare no mercy in unmasking the bad faith and fraud on offer by doing what the House Democrats have asked for, calling witnesses, so as to walk the Democrats into the fiery furnace of humiliation and infamy they so richly deserve.

Wouldn't you like to hear from the legendary "whistleblower," since his actions provoked this chapter of the three-year orchestrated coup to oust Mr. Trump? If it's a basic tenet of law that a defendant has a right to face his accuser, can there be any further excuse for concealing this person's identity — whose supposed right to anonymity, by the way, has been one of the signal frauds of the whole episode. Would it not be instructive to seat his mentor and former boss John Brennan in the witness chair and give him another opportunity to perjure himself? We must also hear from Michael Atkinson, the "whistleblower's" enabler and lawfare warrior Mary McCord, Atkinson's former boss at the DOJ national security desk, who apparently stage-managed the "whistleblower's" doings through Adam Schiff's House intel committee. Mr. Schiff would be the ripest witness of all, of course, since he has left a trail of falsehoods and fabrications longer than the Pacific Trail — but it's unclear just now whether the Senate rules will allow a manager to be called to testify.

There is also much to be unraveled about the American mischief in Ukraine — which includes, but goes far beyond, the arrant grift of Hunter Biden. For example, the relationships between the George Soros–backed NGO Atlantic Council and Burisma, the natgas company that put Hunter B. on its board, and Ukrainian oligarch Victor Pinchuk, board member of the Atlantic Council (and $25 million contributor to the Clinton Foundation), and Dmitri Alperovitch (also Atlantic Council), cofounder of Crowdstrike, the company that "examined" the supposedly "hacked" DNC servers, and Hillary Clinton herself, the self-dealing secretary of state behind the international pay-for-play charity fraud she operated while in office. Also bring back former US ambassador to Ukraine Marie Yovanovitch to 'splain the actions she took to conceal all these machinations, as well as her role in operating the 2016 Kiev Hillary campaign office.

What would soon be obvious is that the precipitating "whistleblower" caper was an effort to divert attention from a network of Americans that used a politically captive Ukraine — following the Maidan Revolution of 2014 — to protect an enormous racketeering operation threatened by the candidacy, and then the election, of Mr. Trump. Naturally, they are desperate to get him out of the way. So many of the facts are already publicly known and documented about these matters that the legal machinery has yet to catch up with it all. And when it does, the Democratic Party will have driven a wooden stake through its own depraved heart.

EXECUTIVE ORDER

February 10, 2020

In this pause between past and future Deep State seditions, and the full-blown advent of coronavirus in every region of the world, we pause to consider Mr. Trump's executive order requiring new federal buildings to be designed in the classical style. The directive has caused heads to explode in the cultural wing of progressive wokesterdom, since the worship of government power has replaced religion for them and federal buildings are their churches — the places from which encyclicals are hurled at the masses on such matters as who gets to think and say what, who gets to use which bathroom, and especially whose life and livelihood can be destroyed for being branded a heretic.

Federal Building San Francisco by Thom Mayne

The religion of Progressivism (under various names) has been growing for over a century, based on the idea that the material abundance of techno-industrial societies should be centrally managed by national bureaucracies, finally leading to a nirvana of perfect fairness. The part that's always left out is that this is accomplished by coercion, by pushing people around, telling them what to do and how to think, and by confiscating their property or docking their privileges if they seem to have too much of either. You can observe the operations of this doctrine in the current crop of Democratic Party aspirants to the White House.

The architecture that expressed all that is loosely called "modernism" mostly because it was supposed to represent the distilled essence of everything that is up-to-date, and the idea of coercing an unfair world toward universal fairness has ruled the elite managerial class ever since Karl Marx lanced his boils of social grievance on the printed page. The First World War really sealed the deal for modernism. The industrial-scale slaughter — well depicted in the recent movie *1917* — so horrified the elites that the architecture branch of elitedom decided to shitcan all the offensive claptrap of history as expressed in buildings and replace them with bare boxes of one kind or another. A whole metaphysical theology was constructed to justify this attempt at a totalistic do-over for the human race. "Less is more" et cetera.

Meanwhile, along came Stalin and Hitler who persisted in the dirty business of neoclassical architecture, and they screwed the pooch on that theme for all time, while the Second World War reaffirmed the urge to cleanse the world of all that *filthy* symbolism. By the 1950s modernism ruled the scene as the architecture of decency and democracy. It very quickly became the architecture that glorified corporate America, viz., the rows of glass box skyscrapers hoisted up along the grand avenues of midtown Manhattan, and then every other city center in America. Before long, as the old government buildings of yore grew obsolete, they too were replaced with confections of modernism, and then the university libraries, and finally . . . everything.

The trouble with being up-to-date in architecture is that buildings last a long time and dates fade into history, and if you hate history you have created a problem. The world is a restless place. The main feature of this particular moment is that techno-industrial society has entered an epochal contraction presaging collapse due to overinvestments in hypercomplexity. That hypercomplexity has come to be perfectly expressed in architecture lately in the torqued and tortured surfaces of gigantic buildings designed by computers, with very poor prospects for being maintained, or even being useful, as we reel into a new age of material scarcity and diminished expectations — especially the expectation for reaching that technocratically engineered nirvana of fairness.

Of course, the mandarin uber-class among the elite, especially the poohbahs in the architecture schools, can't bear the thought that things are tending this way. Their theology of up-to-dateness, of "the cutting edge," is all about fashion. That things go out of fashion has given them the opportunity to create and cash in on ever more new fashions, to keep up the pretense of perpetually surfing that *cutting edge* from which they derive their status. And this incessant reach for status, and the power it confers, belies and betrays the whole business of representing the ultimate *nirvana of fairness*, revealing them to be the mendacious frauds they are.

The Trumpian reach backward toward classicism is certainly a quixotic move, even though one can make a case for it being a national style, at least in the early years of the USA when that mode of building was supposed to represent the democracy of ancient Greece and the dignity of the Roman republic — hence, Greco-Roman architecture. Some things to consider. We're going to have to reduce the scale of the things we build. The *cutting edge* grandiosity of today is about to go out of style. National bureaucracies will shrink, if they don't vanish altogether, and so will the buildings that house their operations.

We're going to need buildings that don't go out of style, so you can forget about the *cutting edge*, and classicism does have the virtue of timelessness — or at least it did, *for a long time*. These new buildings ought to have the capacity for adaptive reuse over generations, even centuries. They will probably have to be made out of nonexotic materials, namely, masonry and wood, since the scarcities we face will include a lot of modular fabricated materials ranging from plate glass to aluminum trusswork to steel I-beams to Sheetrock — all things requiring elaborate, complex mining and manufacturing chains.

A virtue of classicism is that it employs structural devices that allow buildings to stand up: arches, columns, colonnades. These are replicable in modules or bays along scales from small to large. These devices honestly express the tectonic sturdiness of a building within the realities of gravity. A hidden virtue of classicism is that it is based on the three-part representation of the human figure: the whole and all the parts within it exist in nested hierarchies of base and shaft and head. This is true of columns with capitols set on a base, of windows with their sills, sashes, and lintels, and the whole building from base to roof. Classical architecture follows proportioning systems universally found in nature, such as the Fibonacci series of ratios, which are seen in everything from the self-assembly of seashells to the growth of tree branches. Thus, classicism links us to nature and to our own humanity.

University of Virginia by Thomas Jefferson

Classical ornaments — the swags, moldings, entablatures, cartouches, corbels, festoons, and what have you — are not mandatory but, of course, they also provide a way of expressing our place in nature, which is a pathway to expressing truth and beauty.

Modernism doesn't care about truth and beauty; it cares about power, especially the power to coerce. Many people detect that dynamic, and that is one reason they loathe modernist buildings. The main imperative of modernism was to separate us from nature, since it was human nature that brought about all the horrors of the twentieth century and so revolted the intellectual elites. The result of that was a denatured architecture of the machine and an animus against what it means to be human located in nature.

We're probably not going back to anything like formal classicism because the contraction ahead will leave us in a world of salvage, of cobbling together whatever we can from the detritus left over. But sooner or later — surely well after Mr. Trump has decomposed into his constituent molecules — we will get back to an architecture that is based on our place in nature, so don't set your hair on fire over this new executive order, no matter how much *The New York Times* wants you to.

JAMES HOWARD KUNSTLER

IMPURE THOUGHTS

February 14, 2020

What if the coronavirus turns out to be a genuine pandemic with *legs*, not some punk-ass, flash-in-the-pan bug like SARS . . . and it infects hundreds of millions around the world? And what if it happens to go logarithmic in the USA, as in China now? And what if takes a few months, or half a year, to do that? And what if Americans will not get on airplanes when that happens? Or gather together in large numbers? Or if government imposes quarantines ? Will the parties hold their nominating conventions? Might the November election have to be postponed?

Just sayin' . . . since nobody else seems to be talking about it. A few months ago, nobody was thinking about a disease that would virtually lock down China's economy, either. And now here we are. Speaking of which, that lockdown of China's economy is already generating serious damage to global GDP, after only a few weeks. But nothing shows our detachment from reality like the recent surge in financial market indexes while the Chinese economy was busy shutting down. In particular, one must wonder: what supports the global daisy chain of debt obligations while all this is going on?

After all, companies doing business need a revenue stream to service their revolving debts. They have to make stuff, and move stuff, and get paid for it. What happens when there is no revenue stream? The workings of this hypercomplex financial system depend utterly on the velocity of these revenue streams. They can't just . . . stop! Everybody who follows these things understands that China's banking system is 1) a hot mess of confabulated public and private lending relationships, 2) completely opaque as regards the true workings of its operations, and 3) shot through with fraud, swindling, and Ponzis. Did China's ruling party just put its banking system in an induced coma while the coronavirus plays out? How can that possibly not affect the rest of global finance, which is plenty janky, too?

The USA gets everything from car parts to pharmaceuticals from China. How long will it take for the manufacturing lockdown to show up in American daily life? What if it continues for some months going forward? You can easily draw your own conclusions.

Here's another interesting angle on that: coronavirus might give President Donald Trump an easy out from being the *bag holder* for a stock market crash and banking train wreck. The signal weakness of Mr. Trump's term in office was his taking *ownership* of a magical mystery stock market that climbs ever higher day after day, defying all known rules of physics as applied to money. This longest "expansion" in US history (if that's what it was, and I'm not so sure about it) seems to have hit a speed bump last September when something broke in the short-term "repo" lending markets, at which time (and ever since), Jay Powell's Federal Reserve began jamming hundreds of billions of dollars into them to smash down zooming interest rates and prevent a heart attack in the system. That creation of "liquidity" — money from thin air — *appears* to have stabilized the situation. But then, it is a peculiar feature of our times that a lot of things have an *appearance* that doesn't sync with reality.

In short, if coronavirus and its side effects do substantially knock down the stock markets, Mr. Trump gets off scot-free on the one thing that has been really propping him up. Not only can he blame a looming market calamity on this black swan pandemic, he can then turn around and play the Franklin Roosevelt role in attempting to rescue the nation from a depression. And then, if the election has to be postponed, we will see a for-sure discontinuity in US political history, consequences as yet unknown.

Meanwhile, schemes continue apace to overthrow Mr. Trump by hook or by crook before the election, with Sedition Release 4.0 just breaking in the Roger Stone sentencing affair and four prosecutors (three of them Mueller alumni, imagine that!) staging a phony-baloney resignation huff to stir up useful idiots like Rep. Eric Swalwell on the House's intel committee for the next *go* at impeachment. Understand, this wicked business is just another ploy engineered by the same combined Deep State / lawfare scoundrels that ran RussiaGate, MuellerGate, and UkraineGate, and the real purpose of it is to stave off efforts to prosecute a pretty broad network of those same former and current officials in the FBI, DOJ, CIA, State Department, Pentagon, Obama White House, and the Clinton Foundation for seditious conspiracy and, yes, possibly even treason. Personally, I believe that the attorney general is honestly trying to smoke out the truth in this morass of nefarious intrigues, and that neither attempts to block him by the perps and their allies nor a visitation of coronavirus across the land will thwart him.

STRENGTH AND WEAKNESS

March 20, 2020

Happy Colorectal Awareness Month, everybody — in case you're wondering why it feels like fate shoved a four-by-four up your nether region where the sun don't shine. Millions around the country must be stunned at how bad this suddenly is. And every new morning seems worse than the last: *Friday the Thirteenth* meets *Groundhog Day*. Jobs and incomes instantly gone. Businesses staring into the abyss. Retirements vaporizing. Everyone stuck home alone with nothing to think about but going broke and hungry. And the final indignity: the possibility of death if you stray outside to get something you need, or just seek the comfort of other people.

This is our hard time. If you ever needed God, or some human representation of *the good father*, this would be the occasion — someone to guide and reassure you and inspire you to do your best under difficult circumstances. For the time being, America has Donald Trump. To the agnostical thinking class, with its obsessive loathing of men, white men especially, and white men in the father role most of all, Mr. Trump represents the ultimate grotesquerie. To that class of scribes, professors, assorted "creatives," virtue signalers, and social justice seekers, even Tennessee Williams could not conjure up a more fearsome and detestable *Big Daddy* than Mr. Trump. Hence, their nonstop underhanded attempts to get rid of him the past three years — which had all the earmarks of a neurotic adolescent rebellion. ("The Resistance" was actually a good name for it.) And yet there he stands at the podium in our hard time. You can call that a lot of things, but one of them has got to be: strength.

Yes, he is peculiar-looking: the strange blond helmet, the orange face. Note, back in one of America's earlier hard times, a lot people thought Mr. Lincoln looked like a great ape, and had much sport with that image of him in the newspapers. It's also a fact that the decisions he made led to the deaths of hundreds of thousands of mostly young men in the bloodiest slaughters then imaginable. Yet those young men going to their deaths called him Father Abraham in their songs around the campfire. I'm not saying that Donald Trump is another Lincoln

— certainly not in sheer rhetoric — but I am saying we don't know yet what his mettle will show in this crisis, and where it might take us. One thing for sure: he's been subjected to more political abuse than any character on the scene in my lifetime, and it's amazing that he didn't fold or quit or lose his shit as it went on and on and on.

And so you now have the strange and ironic spectacle of his organized opposition, the Democrats, hoisting up onto their pinnacle of leadership absolutely the weakest candidate possible to oppose Mr. Trump in the election: Joe Biden. There was something certainly supernatural about his ascent in the recent cluster of primaries, as if some gang of someones worked strenuously behind the scenes to make it happen. If Mr. Biden ever had any charisma even in his prime as a young senator, there was no sign of that now, either in his own bumbling behavior or in the sparse crowds that were flushed out of the DNC's voter registration thickets to show up at his rallies. In fact, he emanated the exact opposite of charisma, a faltering flop-sweat odor of weakness, and of every kind of weakness: physical, mental, and ethical.

His role was not *the good father*, it was the half-crazy old uncle in the attic — the kind who puts on his threadbare best suit every day to go down to a corner bar and sip beers until it's time to stagger back home, where a dutiful niece-in-law might give him supper, if he could manage to ask for it politely. The kind who, until his forced retirement due to incompetence and blundering, had worked as an errand boy for the local mob, picking up receipts from the numbers racket, and was then cast off like a banana peel in a drainage ditch when his usefulness ended.

Of course, Joe Biden's eminence in government, as vice president, afforded him grander opportunities for grift than that. He went into the anarchic mess of Ukraine — engineered by US agencies, by the way — as Mr. Obama's "point man" and came away from it with at least several million dollars in a guaranteed revenue stream for his hapless fuckup of a son Hunter, and there's hard evidence that many millions more found its way into Joe's pockets, too, via Ukrainian oligarch money laundered through the banks of Estonia and Cyprus — who would look there? (Rudy Giuliani, actually.)

That is the sort of president America would get if they happen to elect Joe Biden. The Democratic Party could not elect a strong and stupendously corrupt woman in 2016, and they have reeled in disbelief at their own failure ever since. Now they are marching forward into a national election — if that election can even be held, and we don't know that yet — with a nominee who looks and acts like a wax figure of a president in one of those eerie hushed chambers of Disneyland. But please understand, this is exactly what the Democrats have wished for lo these several years that have taken us into America's hard time: weakness and their own death, by suicide. Let's not go there with them.

PEOPLE GET READY!

March 30, 2020

The cable news announced the other day that Covid-19 patients placed in critical care may have to be on ventilators for twenty-one days. Only a few years ago, I went in for an ordinary hip replacement. A month or so later, I got the hospital billing statement. One of the line items went like this: room and board: 36 hours . . . $23,482.79. I am not jiving you. That was just for the hospital bed and maybe four lousy hospital meals, not the surgery or the meds or anything else. All that was billed extra. Say, what?

Now imagine you have the stupendous good fortune to survive a Covid-19 infection after twenty-one days on a ventilator and go home. What is that billing statement going to look like? Will the survivors wish they'd never made out of the hospital alive?

Right now, we're in the heroic phase of the battle against a modern age plague. The doctors, nurses, and their helpers are like the trembling soldiers in an amphibious landing craft churning toward the Normandy beach where the enemy is dug in and waiting for them, with sweaty fingers on their machine guns and a stink in the pillbox. Some of the doctors and nurses will go down in the battle. The fabled fog of war will conceal what is happening to the health care system itself, while the battle rages. After that, what?

One thing will be pretty clear: that the folks in charge of things gave trillions of dollars to Wall Street while tens or perhaps hundreds of thousands of Covid-19 survivors got wiped out financially with gargantuan medical bills. Do you think the chargemaster part of the hospital routine will just stop doing its thing during this emergency? The billings will continue — just as the proverbial beatings will continue until morale improves! In the aftermath, I can't even imagine the 'splainin that will entail. The rage may be too intense to even get to that. For some, it may be time to lubricate the guillotines.Meantime, of course, the global economy has shut down, which suggests to me, anyway, that any prior frame of reference you may have had about money and business and social normality goes out the window. The world is still here. We're just going to have to learn to live in it differently. The American portion of the world is in need of a severe retrofit and reprogramming. We waited too long to face this in a spell of tragic complacency and the virus has forced the issue. Here are the main things we have to attend to.Reconsider how we inhabit the landscape. Do you think $20-a-barrel oil is a boon to the Happy Motoring way of life? It's going to at least bankrupt most of the companies producing shale oil, and that's where way more than half of our production came from in recent years. How many ordinary Americans will be able to finance car payments now? To say suburbia will not be functioning too well mere months from now is a merciful way to put it.

The big cities will not recover from the trauma and stigma of the virus, but that is only the beginning their problems. What, exactly, will the suffering poor of the ghettos do, under orders to remain cooped up until the end of April? These are people who are unlikely to have laid in supplies ahead of time, and a month from now they are sure to be very hungry. How will the big cities be able to manage their infrastructures with municipal bonds massively failing? How will they provide social services when tax revenues are down to a trickle? The answer is, they won't manage any of this. They grew too big and too complex. Now they have to get smaller, and the process will not be pretty.

What will the business of America be after Covid-19? If we're lucky, it will be growing food and working at many of the activities that support it: moving it, storing it, selling it, making an order of smaller-scaled farm machinery, including machines that can be used with horses and oxen, breeding the animals. I'm not kidding. Growing food happens in the countryside, where the fields and pastures are. There are towns there, too, associated with the farming, where much of the business of farming and the activities that support it transact. I believe we'll see impressive demographic movements of people to these places. There are opportunities in all that, a plausible future. The scale of agriculture will have to change downward, too. Agribiz, with its giant "inputs" of chemicals and borrowed money, is not going to make it. Farms have to get smaller too, and more people will have to work on them. Farewell to the age of the taco chip!

If we want to get around this big country of ours, and move food from one place to another, we better think about fixing the railroads. Try to imagine what six trillion dollars might have done for that crucial venture. And I'm not talking about high speed and high tech; I mean the railroads that were already here. Where I live, the tracks are still in place, rusting in the rain. How did we let that happen?

Then there is the question of how do we behave? You may not think that matters so much, but we've become so profoundly dishonest that it's impeding our relationship with reality. On top of that we're surly, impolite, clownish, blustering, greedy, and improvident. Believe me, that is going to change. Hardship is a great attitude adjuster. When Americans awake from the corona coma like millions of Rip Van Winkles, it will matter again to be upright and to act in good faith. This will be a different country.

Ruin Nation

April 13, 2020

The ruins of Mary McClellan Hospital stand on a hill overlooking the village of Cambridge, New York, in what was a "flyover" corner of the country until the planes stopped flying. The hospital cornerstone was laid July 4, 1917. The USA had entered the war against Germany a few months earlier. The "Spanish" flu pandemic kicked off in January 1918. The hospital opened in January 1919. The flu burned out a year later. The hospital shut down for good in 2003.

I've lived around here for decades and never actually got a look at the place until I went up there on a blustery spring Saturday before Easter to look around. I like to read landscapes and the human imprint upon them. This one is a ghost story, not just of the bygone souls who came and went here, but of an entire society, the nation that we used to be and stopped being not so long ago.

This is the old main building today. It's astounding how quickly buildings begin to rot when the human life within them is gone. The style was Beaux Arts Institutional, seen everywhere across America in that period in schools, libraries, museums, and hospitals, an austere neoclassicism that radiated decorum in a confident and well-run society — because that is what we were then. Note especially the entrance and the beautiful bronze marquee above it. The message is this: *You enter through a portal of beauty to a place of hope and trust.*

This is Mary McClellan Hospital not long after it opened. The site itself, on its hill, with views east across the state line to the Green Mountains, speaks of authority and command. The America of 1919 was a deeply hierarchical society. Today we regard hierarchy as a bane and a curse. The truth is, it is absolutely required if you expect to live in a well-run society, and proof of that is the disordered mess of bureaucratic irresponsibility we live in today, with virtually every institution failing — well before the Covid-19 virus arrived on the scene — and nobody called to account for anything anymore. Hierarchy must be fit to scale to function successfully. In small institutions like this, everybody knows who is responsible for what. That's what makes authority credible.

These are the ruins of the nursing school associated with the hospital (and also associated with Skidmore College in Saratoga Springs, 25 miles west). The nurses lived here, in Florence Nightingale Hall. In the early twentieth century, the profession favored young, unmarried women whose allegiance and attention to the patients would not be distracted by the needs of a family. Was that exploitation? Or was it simply an intelligent way to organize a hospital subculture? The nurses lived here very comfortably. The institution cared for them, literally.

JAMES HOWARD KUNSTLER

There's no record available of what exactly these buildings were for. The one in the foreground has a cut stone sign that says "The Junior" on it. I infer that this may have been where a couple of staff resident physicians lived, young men probably, just out of their internships, close at hand and on call for emergencies. The building in the background is a rather grand country cottage, possibly the residence of the chief surgeon or the hospital director. The hospital was, after all, a community unto itself, and it was important that authority have a visible presence there all the time. Both buildings display architectural grace notes that humanized and dignified that resident authority. We no longer believe in grace notes for the things we build, so is it surprising that we live in a graceless society?

This is the power plant for the whole operation, on the premises, ensuring that the electricity would stay on at all times. In the early twentieth century, electric power was the new sine qua non of advanced civilization. America's rural electrification program really didn't get underway until the 1930s, so it's likely that many of the farms outside the village were not hooked up to a grid. The hospital generators must have been driven by coal, or perhaps oil. Somebody had to attend to all that machinery. The laundry — hospitals produce a lot of that — was also on the premises, as was all the meal preparation. The hospital maintained a large garden to furnish some of the food. All these tasks required crews of people working purposefully and getting paid. The hospital was a complex organism, a world within a nation within a world.

BIRDSEYE VIEW MARY McCLELLAN HOSPITAL CAMBRIDGE, N.Y.

Things rise and self-organize beautifully into fully formed systems and after a while they run down, even while they overgrow; authority starts working more and more for its own sake and its own benefit; hierarchy breaks down into disrespect, lack of trust, fear; and then society loses its vital institutions, which is exactly what happened at Mary McClellan Hospital in little Cambridge, New York. It dwindled and then quickly collapsed. The town lost a part of itself, the part that welcomed people in a particular kind of trouble and cared for them, as it cared for those who did the caring. By the way, in 1919, a private room was $7 a day (a bed on a ward was $3). Imagine that! The town also lost a vital component of its economy. And that was all of a piece with its decline into the flyover place it became in our time.

American health care, as we call it today, and for all its high-tech miracles, has evolved into one of the most atrocious rackets the world has ever seen. By racket, I mean an enterprise organized explicitly to make money dishonestly. This is what we've become, and the fact that we seem to be okay with that tells you more about what we have become. The advent of Covid-19, along with the extreme economic disorders it has triggered, will probably be the beginning of the end of that racket. We have no idea how medicine will reorganize itself, but I'd guess that it will happen at a much more primitive scale — because that's usually what happens when human societies overshoot badly. Alas, history is not exactly symmetrical.

But read these photos and meditate on what we were once capable of putting together in this land, and maybe you will find some clues about what was truly admirable about the American condition before we stopped caring.

The Great Conundrum

April 27, 2020

Don't it always seem to go, that you don't know what you've got 'til it's gone, Joni trilled half a century ago. Another song, by CSN, went, it's been a long time coming, it's gonna be a long time gone. Boomers. Back in the day — before they invented the hedge fund, glyphosate, and political correctness — they had a way with the deep vision thing. And now, here we are! Just like they saw it.

"Open up" is code, of course, for return to normal. You're kidding, right? Where I live, the future happened ten years ago. Main Street is nothing but consignment shops, that is, old stuff people got rid of, mostly for good reasons. The one thing you can't get there is food, unless there's a bowl of mints next to the cash register. Oh, and the Kmart in town shuttered exactly a year ago, so the supply of new-stuff-waiting-to-be-old-stuff has been cut off, too. Welcome to America, the next chapter.

The public is understandably frantic to bust out of their quarantine bunkers. Seven weeks of jigsaw puzzles bears an interesting resemblance to the old Chinese water torture. (Can you even say that? There, I said it for you.) What will they find as they emerge blinking from the doleful demi-life of the sequester? It's liable to be a society in which just about everything no longer works the way it was set up to work.

For instance: work itself. A lot of it has gone missing. Despite the feel-good propaganda broadcast on CBS's *60 Minutes*, converting General Motors' Kokomo plant into an emergency respirator manufacturing operation is not going to save that company, or the greater mission it serves: US suburban life per se. The car industry was on the ropes before the Covid-19 virus landed. Car dealers were so desperate to move the merch off the lot last year that they attempted to induce folks who had already defaulted on their car loans to come sign up for another car and a new loan. And that was after they'd tried seven-year loans for preowned vehicles. General Motors sold 7.7 million vehicles last year, while the whole US auto industry sold 17 million. They are not going to survive as boutique carmakers.

Which leads to the Great Conundrum of the moment. Reality is telling us that things organized on the gigantic scale are entering failure mode; but so many Americans are employed by exactly those activities organized on the gigantic scale. Or were, I should say. The humungous joint effort by the federal government and its caporegime, the Federal Reserve, to flood the system with dollars is precisely a desperate effort to prop up the giant-scale activities that defined the prior state of things. Those giant enterprises even did an end run around the truly small businesses that were supposed to get scores of billions in grants, loans, and bailouts so Congress is attempting a do-over of that play.

The question, then, is how do you go through a swift and dramatic rescaling of a hypertrophic, excessively complex, ecologically fragile economic system in a way that doesn't produce a whole lot of damage? I can't answer that satisfactorily except to say this: at least recognize what the macro trend is (downscaling and relocalization), and support that as much as possible. Don't knock yourself out trying to save giant, foundering enterprises that need to go out of business. Don't bankrupt the society or destroy the meaning of its money to prevent the necessary bankruptcy of things that must go bankrupt. Remove as many obstacles as you possibly can to allow smaller-scaled enterprises to thrive and especially to support the rebuilding of local networks that smaller-scaled businesses play their roles in.

Apart from the insane spending orgy of the fed gov and the Fed, a lot of this is already underway organically and emergently. Few have failed to notice the death throes of national chain retail, for instance. Macys, JC Penny, Neiman Marcus, and many other outfits like them are whirling around the drain. By the way, even the holy sainted Walmart will not be immune to this trend. Its supply lines have been cut. And, as I have averred, Amazon's dumbass business model will sink with the oil and trucking industries. Realize, too, commerce will persist in human life. It just won't be the Blue Light Special, credit-fueled phantasmagoria we got used to for a few decades. Commerce, i.e., the trade in goods, will have to be reorganized differently. There are huge opportunities for young people who recognize this.

All this remains to be worked out, and quite a workout it is apt to be before we get to it. Even with those glorious $1,200 checks, millions of people know just how broke and how probably screwed they are. They are being let out of confinement just as fine spring weather sweeps across the land. It will be momentarily exhilarating. Then, the rage and resentment will percolate up and the bile will rise. Before you know it, they'll be singing that other old boomer refrain of yesteryear (the Rolling Stones): summer's here and the time is right for fighting in the street . . .

WHEN THE BIRDIES SING
LIKE THE FAT LADY

May 4, 2020

Spring is popping now with a ferocious energy that can only remind the sullenly sequestered masses that life is going on without them. Every living thing is busy making and doing *out there,* except the poor humans, idled without work or purpose. That won't last long. People don't submit automatically to zombification when some pissant bureaucrats issue them $1,200 checks. They yearn to bust out like everything else on this living planet. And if they can't do it in a good way, well . . .

The megamachine we constructed to drive this society has sucked a valve and thrown a rod. The machine is broken, no matter how much more fuel the mechanics pump in. (One suspects somebody may have topped it off with Karo syrup.) Anyway, the machine got too big and too complex, with too many extraneous bells and whistles, and with way too much computerized cybernetic control built in, so the mechanics barely noticed it was coming apart (they were too busy partying). That big machine is smoldering in a ditch for the moment. The dazed and bloodied passengers realize that the ride is over, and now they must march on to get somewhere, anywhere, away from this miserable ditch and the wreckage in it. The fine spring weather is their only consolation.

And so here we are at a fraught moment in the convergent crises of coronavirus and the foundering economic system that it infected, with all its frightful preexisting conditions. Of course, it isn't *capitalism,* so called, that is failing, but the perversions of capitalism, starting with the appendage of the troublesome term *ism.* It isn't a religion, or even a pseudoreligion like Zoroastrianism or communism. It's simply the management system for surplus wealth. In a hypercomplex society, the management of wealth naturally grows hypercomplex, too, with lavish opportunities and temptations for chicanery, cheating, fraud, and swindling (the perversions of capital). It's in the interest of the managers to cloak all that hypercomplex perversity in opaque language, to make it seem okay.

How many ordinary Americans have a clue what all the Municipal Liquidity Facilities, Primary Dealer Credit Facilities, Primary and Secondary Market Corporate Credit Facilities, Money Market Mutual Fund Liquidity Facilities, Main Street New Loan Facilities and Expanded Loan Facilities, Commercial Paper Funding Facilities, currency swap lines, the TALFs TARPs, PPPs, SPVs represent — besides the movement, by keystrokes, of "money" from one netherworld to another (both conveniently located on Wall Street), usually to the loss of nonelite citizens generally and to their offspring's offspring's offspring?

Real capital is grounded in the production of real things of real value, of course, and when it's detached from all that, it's no longer real capital. Money represents capital, and when the capital isn't real, the money represents . . . nothing! And ceases to be real money. Just now, America is producing almost nothing except money, money in quantities that stupefy the imagination — trillions here, there, and everywhere. The trouble is that money is vanishing as fast as it's being created. That's because it's based on promises to be paid back into existence that will never be kept, on top of prior promises to pay back money that were broken or are in the process of breaking. The net result is that money is actually disappearing faster than it can be created, even in vast quantities.

All this sounds like metaphysical bullshit, I suppose, but we are obviously watching money disappear. Your paycheck is gone. That activity you started — a brew pub, a gym, an ad agency — no longer produces revenue. The HR department at the giant company you work for told you: *don't bother coming into the office tomorrow, or possibly ever again.* Your bills are piling up. The numbers in your bank account run to zero. That sure smells like money disappearing. Wait until the pension checks and the SNAP cards mysteriously stop landing in the mailbox.

There's going to be a lot of trouble. Ordinary Americans are going to get super pissed if money doesn't disappear from the stock markets, too. They've seen this movie before. They will know for sure that they were played, that the class of people who hold most of the stocks are doing just fine while everybody else stares into that old abyss staring back at them. I wouldn't want to be anywhere near the Hamptons on that fateful day.

All this because we just can't face the task of reorganizing our national home economics to suit new circumstances. So nature will do it for us. Nature will furnish us with a marvelously efficient black hole where we can conveniently stash our fake money so that we'll never have to see it again. Nature will bust up our giant institutions, our giant corporations, our giant networks of financial obligations. And after a period of confusion and social disorder, some clever humans will aggregate into smaller networks and reorganize their activities on a smaller scale that actually supports truthful relationships between the production of things deemed to hold value and money that represents those things.

The beauty of springtime is sublime and, as Edmund Burke noted, that very beauty provokes our thoughts of pain and terror.

When Giants Fall

May 22, 2020

It was only a few decades ago that Walmart entered the pantheon of American icons, joining motherhood, apple pie, and baseball on the highest tier of the altar. The people were entranced by this behemoth cornucopia of unbelievably cheap stuff packaged in gargantuan quantities. It was something like their participation trophy for the sheer luck of being born in this exceptional land, or having valiantly clawed their way in from wretched places near and far — where, increasingly, the mighty stream of magically cheap stuff was manufactured.

The evolving psychology of Walmart-ism had a strangely self-destructive aura about it. Like cargo cultists waiting on a jungle mountaintop, small town Americans prayed and importuned the gods of commerce to bring them a Walmart. Historians of the future, pan-frying possum cutlets over their camp-fires, will marvel at the potency of their ancestors' prayers. Every little burg in the USA eventually saw a Walmart UFO land in the cornfield or cow pasture on the edge of town. Like the space invaders of sci-fi filmdom, Walmart quickly killed off everything else of economic worth around it, and eventually the towns themselves. And that was where things stood as the long emergency commenced in the winter of early 2020, along with the Covid-19 coronavirus riding shotgun on the hearse wagon it rolled in on.

We're in a liminal, transitional moment of history, like beachgoers gawking at the glassy-green curve of a great wave in the throes of breaking. Such mesmerizing beauty! Alas, most people can't surf. It looks easy on TV, but you'd be surprised at the conditioning it takes, and Americans are way, way out of condition. (All those tattoos don't give you an ounce of extra mojo.) And so, in this liminal moment, the people still trudge dutifully to Walmart with their dwindling reserves of cash money to get stuff, going through all the devotions that we took for granted before the wave welled up and threatened to break over us.

Which is happening. Despite all the fake-heroic blather from the Federal Reserve, from Nancy Pelosi, from Mr. Trump and Mr. Mnuchin — from everybody in charge, to be really fair — and in the immortal words of another recent president — *this sucker is going down.* Specifically, what's going down is the aggregate of transactions we call "the economy." Meanwhile, the people in charge struggle to prop up the mere financial indexes that supposedly represent economic activity, but more and more just look like a shadow play on the wall of some special slum where the street-corner economists peddle their crack. Eventually, the people don't even have money for the crack, and to make matters worse, whatever money actually remains on the street is worthless.

The wave is breaking now, and a lot of things will be smashed under it — are getting smashed as you read. As in any extinction event, it will be the smaller organisms that survive and eventually thrive and that's how it will go in the next edition of America, whether we remain states united or find ourselves organized differently. Accordingly, the giants must fall. When the communities of America rebuild, it will be the thousands of small activities that matter, because they will entail the rebuilding of social capital as well as exchanges that amount to *business.* Social capital is exactly what Walmart and things like it killed in every community from sea to shining sea. People stopped doing business with their neighbors. It took a cataclysm for them to finally notice.

If you think Walmart will survive the same cataclysm that's killing chain-store retail generally, you're going to be disappointed. Everything about it is over and done, including the Happy Motoring adjunct that allowed the cargo cultists to haul their booty those many miles home. (And, ironically, it wasn't the oil issue that determined this, but the end of the financing system that allowed Americans to buy their cars on installment loans, when it ran out of credit-worthy borrowers.) Amazon will be the last giant standing perhaps, but it will go down, too, eventually, on its ridiculous business model, which depends utterly on a doomed trucking system. It will be like the last dinosaur roaring at the dimming sun — while the little proto-mammals skitter to their hidey holes beneath it.

One thing remains constant: human beings are very adept and resourceful at supplying each other's needs, which is what business amounts to. Young people, freed from the fate of becoming serfs to corporate giants, can start right now at least imagining what they can do to be useful to others in exchange for a livelihood. The earnest and energetic will find a way to do that at a scale that makes sense when a new order emerges from the wreckage. After a while, it won't matter much what any government thinks about it, either. Like all the other giants, it will fall, too.

THAT CHANGE YOU REQUESTED...?

June 1, 2020

All the previous incidents of white cops killing blacks were just too ambiguous to seal the deal. Michael Brown in Ferguson, Missouri (a murky business); Tamir Rice in Cleveland (waving the BB gun that looked like a .45 automatic); Trayvon Martin (his killer George Zimmerman was not a cop and was not "white"); Eric Garner, Staten Island (black policewoman sergeant on the scene didn't stop it); Philando Castile, Minneapolis (the cop was Hispanic and the vic had a gun). Even the recent February killing of jogger Ahmaud Arbery in Brunswick, Georgia, had some sketchy elements (did Arbery try to seize the shotgun?) — YouTube has scrubbed the video (?) — and then it took months for the two white suspects (not cops) to be arrested.

The George Floyd killing had none of those weaknesses. Plus, the video presented a pretty much universal image of oppression: a man with his knee on another man's neck. Didn't that say it all? You didn't need a Bob Dylan song to explain it. The Minneapolis police dithered for four days before charging policeman Derek Chauvin with Murder 3 (unpremeditated, but with reckless disregard for human life). The three other cops on the scene who stupidly stood by doing nothing have yet to be charged. Cut it, print it, and cue the mobs.

The nation was already reeling from the weird twelve-week Covid-19 lockdown of everyday life and the economic havoc it brought to careers, businesses, and incomes. In Minnesota, the stay-at-home order was just lifted on May 17, but bars and restaurants were still closed until June. Memorial Day, May 25, was one of the first really balmy days of mid-spring, 78 degrees. People were out and about, perhaps even feeling frisky after weeks of dreary seclusion. So, once the video of George Floyd's death got out, the script was set: take it to the streets!

Few Americans were unsympathetic to the protest marches that followed. Remorse, censure, and tears flowed from every official portal, from the mouth and eyes of every political figure in the land. The tableau of Officer Chauvin's knee on Mr. Floyd's neck was readymade for statuary. Indeed, there are probably dozens of statues extant in the world of just such a scene expressing one people's oppression over another. And yet the public sentiments early on after the George Floyd killing had a stale, ceremonial flavor: *The people demand change! End systemic racism! No justice, no peace!* How many times have we seen this movie?

What is changing — and suddenly — is that now it's not just black people who struggle to thrive in the USA, but everybody else of any ethnic group who is not a hedge fund veep, an employee of BlackRock Financial, or a K Street lobbyist — and even those privileged characters may find themselves in reduced circumstances before long. The prospects of young adults look grimmest of all. They face an economy so disordered that hardly anyone can find something to do that pays enough to support the basics of life, on top of being swindled by the false promises of higher education and the moneylending racket that animates it.

So it's not surprising that, when night falls, the demons come out. Things get smashed up and burned down. And all that after being cooped up for weeks on end in the name of an illness that mostly kills people in nursing homes. Ugly as the Antifa movement is, it's exactly what you get when young people realize their future has been stolen from them. Or, more literally, when they are idle and broke and see fabulous wealth all around them in the banks' glass skyscrapers, and the car showrooms, and the pageants of celebrity fame and fortune on the boob tube. They are extras in a new movie called *The Fourth Turning Meets the Long Emergency* but they may not know it.

Hungry for change? You won't have to wait long. This society may be unrecognizable in a few months. For one thing, there's a good chance that the current violence in the streets won't blow over as it has before. There hasn't been such sudden, massive unemployment before, not even in the Great Depression — and we're not even the same country that went through that rough episode. Just about every arrangement in contemporary life is on the rocks one way or another. Big business, small business, show business . . . it's all cratering. The great big secret behind all that is not that capitalism failed; it's that the capital in capitalism isn't really there anymore, at least not in the amounts that mere appearances like stock valuations suggest. We squandered it, and now our institutions are straining mightily to pretend that "printing" money is the same as capital. (It's just more debt.) Note, the stock markets are up this morning at the open! Go figure.

Change? We're getting it good and hard, and not at a rate we were prepared for. It's hugely disorienting. It produces friction, heat, and light, which easily becomes violence. There's, for sure, plenty we can do to make new arrangements for American life without becoming communists or Nazis, but a lot of activities have to fail before we see how that could work. The overburden of obsolete complexity is crushing us, like Derek Chauvin's knee on George Floyd's neck. They were both, in their way, common men, caught in the maelstrom of metaphor. That proverbial long, hot summer we've heard about for so long? It's here.

HISTORY LESSON

July 3, 2020

Now I am going to tell you why BLM is a hustle, and how it came to this. Here is an opening to that honest conversation about race everyone's been pretending to ask for. That's been a hustle too, so far, because when anybody actually ventures to launch it, the cries of "racist" shut it down.

The BLM hustle has turned into a violent insurrection supported by a body of bad ideas geared to driving the nation insane. The action on the ground is like the Jacobin phase of the French Revolution seasoned with the murderous derangement of Mao Zedong's Cultural Revolution. As biologist Bret Weinstein said in his podcast last week with linguistics prof John McWhorter: "If you attempt a Maoist takeover of the US, you'll get a civil war."

What we're seeing in the looting and burning, the "canceling" of careers and lives, the toppling of statues and the attempt to rewrite history, the pathetic obeisance of political leaders to raging mobs, and the lives lost in senseless acts of violence is the unfinished business of the civil rights movement. That business was the full participation of black citizens in American life. The main grievance now is that black Americans are still denied full participation due to "systemic racism." That's a dodge. What actually happened is that Black America opted out and lost itself in a quandary of its own making with the assistance of their white dis-enablers, the *well-intentioned* "progressives."

Let me take you back to the mid-twentieth century. America had just fought and won a war against manifest evil. The nation styled itself as *Leader of the Free World*. That role could not be squared with the rules of Jim Crow apartheid, so something had to change. The civil rights campaign to undo racial segregation under law naturally began in the courts in cases such as *Brown v. Board of Education* (1954). So-called public accommodations — hotels, theaters, restaurants, buses, bathrooms, water fountains, etc. — remained segregated. By the early 1960s the clamor to end all that took to the streets under the emerging moral leadership of Martin Luther King and his credo of nonviolent civil disobedience.

Many acts of nonviolent street protest were met by police using fire hoses, vicious dogs, and batons to terrorize the marchers. This only shamed and horrified the rest of the nation watching on TV and actually quickened the formation of a political consensus to end American apartheid. That culminated in the passage of three major federal laws: the Public Accommodations Act of 1964, the Voting Rights Act of 1965, and the Fair Housing Act of 1968.

Meanwhile, something else was going on among black Americans: not everybody believed in Dr. King's nonviolence, and not everybody was so sure about full participation in American life. Altogether, Black America remained ambivalent and anxious about all that. That *full participation* implied a challenge to compete on common ground. What if it didn't work out? An alternate view emerged, personified first by Malcolm X, who called MLK an "Uncle Tom," and then by the younger generation, Stokely Carmichael, the Black Panthers and others retailing various brands of Black Power, black nationalism, and black separatism. It amounted, for some, in declining that invitation to participate fully in American life. "No thanks. We'll go our own way." That sentiment has prevailed ever since.

So the outcome to all that federal legislation of the 1960s turned out not to be the clear-cut victory (like World War Two) that liberals and progressives so breathlessly expected. The civil rights acts had some startling adverse consequences, too. They swept away much of the parallel service and professional economy that blacks had constructed to get around all the old exclusions of everyday life. With that went a lot of the black middle class, the business owners especially. In its place, the liberal and progressive government provided "public assistance" — a self-reinforcing poverty generator that got ever worse, especially in big cities where deindustrialization started destroying the working-class job base beginning in the 1970s. The catch was that Black America did not ask for or demand an end to those poverty-generating "welfare" programs. Rather, it objected loudly to changing them. It was, of course and unfortunately, a form of addiction.

How did white liberals and progressives react to all that? Increasingly with shame, disappointment, consternation, and amazement that the civil rights campaign had worked out so imperfectly. Despite all their idealism, American life had not become a nirvana of equality, fraternity, and amity. In the most troubled places, the urban ghettos, the statistical markers of out-of-wedlock births, crime, drug use, failure in school were getting demonstrably worse year by year. It was embarrassing, confusing, galling to the sociology professors, the congressional staffers, the school boards, the media pundits, the arts community, the literati, the clergy . . . really everybody who had hoped to right all the wrongs of history in their lifetime.

The solution was *multiculturalism* and *diversity*. These credos declared that a society didn't require a common culture, a consensus about behaviors, manners, and values. *Multiculturalism* and *diversity* (M & D) provided a rich repertory of rationales for moral grandstanding, not to mention countless well-paid jobs administering institutional policy, without requiring anything of anyone. But, contrary to good intentions once again, that didn't work. It only increased friction between groups of people and induced more failure.

For example, the language problem. Black children in the centers of poverty were not learning how to speak English coherently. Their poor language skills were arguably a greater impediment to success in school, and in adult life later on, than the color of their skin. Yet the dogmas of M & D militated against fixing that. And, of course, it is still a deep taboo to broach the subject. Really, America, if you want to begin somewhere, require the teaching of language skills in the schools. If you continue to deny it, you are condemning people to failure.

Eventually, M & D evolved into the identity politics that turned the universities into lunatic asylums and finally infected the already badly fragmenting culture at large. The figments and phantoms that preoccupy "woke" revolutionaries are products of that still-vibrant shame, disappointment, and hysteria that progressive America feels about the outcome of the long civil rights campaign. That is what all those Ivy League Maoists are acting out in the streets now, abetted by their elders in the Democratic Party establishment, the city halls, and the statehouses.

The economic collapse underway is intensifying these quandaries, paradoxes, and predicaments because from now on life is going to get much more difficult for everybody in the USA. It will require everybody to get more serious about what actions they can take, what behaviors they can follow, in order to remain civilized. Do we really want it to become a fight over the table scraps of history, or can we clear the phantoms out of our heads and play it straight for a change?

"Good Trouble" and Not-Good Trouble

August 21, 2020

And so, the party of the Resistance has completed its solemn four-day confab of info ceremonials and sent forth its *primero ingenioso hidalgo*, Joe Biden, on his limping horse of platitudes, armored by news media hosannahs, a saintly woman of color at his side to assist, tilting onward with his lance of moral instruction to bring love, hope, and light to a world darkened by the shadow of *MAGA Diablo*, Trump the Terrible. Plus, Joe promised to stop Covid-19 and cure cancer.

The convention organizers contrived a schedule Thursday night that did not put Mr. Biden before the cameras until eleven o'clock, preceded by a cavalcade of his former primary election rivals and family members pouring on soporific encomiums to a tinkly-treacly musical soundtrack — aiming, apparently, to lull as many viewers as possible to sleep before the speech. But, finally, the candidate appeared out of the studio mists, and acquitted himself ably reading from the jumbotron teleprompter, while his handlers cringed offstage in little pools of flop sweat.

The speech itself was wholly an invocation of righteousness in opposition to the manifest evil as represented by the current occupant of the White House. The question is: how many voters actually believe that when the party of the Resistance tacitly supports mobs looting, shooting, and burning across the land? Earlier that day, the Terrible Trump sallied forth diabolically to Joe Biden's place of birth, Scranton, PA, where he inveighed against "the crazy people on the other side."

He had a point. The Democrats are crazy people with a mostly crazy policy program — which a large number of noncrazy Americans actually see for what it is: the drive to run America on sheer coercion, pitting the supposedly underprivileged against the supposedly overprivileged, telling everybody what to think and punishing all noncorrect thinkers. The catch is that life in this country has gotten a whole lot harder for everybody economically and, before long, matters may turn quite desperate. So will the months and years just ahead become a fight over the table scraps of the bygone twentieth-century banquet, with dreadful racialist overtones, mobs rioting and battling in the streets?

The Democrats have not called off their war dogs and really everybody is aware of that. Antifa rioters have insulted the public order for eighty-some nights in Portland, Oregon, while the Democratic mayor, Ted Wheeler, and the Democratic governor, Kate Brown, do absolutely nothing to stop it. Similar campaigns against civil order are run by Democratic mayors Lori Lightfoot in Chicago and Bill de Blasio in New York City to the degree that these places may never return to the old normal. Mayor Jacob Frey allowed "social justice" mobs to burn down Minneapolis, leading the city council to logically propose abolishing the city's police force. The Democratic regime in California uses hordes of the mentally ill homeless to prod its productive citizens to flee the state. Baltimore, Philadelphia, St. Louis, Richmond, Louisville — all yield to Democratic Party–inspired violence and anarchy.

For Mr. Biden, the party's Don Quixote, and his sidekick Kamala Harris, yesterday with all its infomercial glitz will be the apogee of the campaign. Antifa is promising a big Saturday night of "good trouble" in Portland to end the week. The NFAC black paramilitary gang is promising a show of armed "resistance" at the Louisville racetrack on the rescheduled Sept. 5 Kentucky Derby day. Last time the group came out, in late July, they accidently shot three of their own troops. Just a week before the Democratic Convention, looters on Chicago's ritzy Michigan Avenue announced that their robberies should be written off as "reparations" for slavery. Mr. Biden and Ms. Harris haven't said a word about any of it. The voters are not supposed to notice, or care.

Personally, I don't see how this amounts to a winning election strategy. And the Democrats themselves may not either. Rather, their aim may be to generate as much disorder as possible from the election process itself to paralyze governing the USA at every level and paint Mr. Trump as hobgoblin in chief in order to keep their hustle going: the mau-mauing of America. It's a really dumb and reckless game and it will bring on a whole lot of not-good trouble for a country reeling into full-blown economic collapse.

When There Are No
Consequences for Anything

September 11, 2020

The Democratic Party with its Deep State auxiliaries begins to look like a monstrous hybrid of Matt Taibbi's fabled Vampire Squid and the skulking kraken of the maelstrom, devouring the innards of our republic in its deep, dark depths one institution at a time while a storm rages on the surface and citizens' eyelids flutter in horror, frozen like sleepers in the paralysis of a nightmare, at the rising havoc and ruin. Or to put it plainly: what the fuck is going on in America?

Ongoing sedition is the answer, with fetid slime trails across the political landscape everywhere you look. We're informed hours ago, for instance, that the top lawyers in Robert Mueller's special counsel operation wiped all the records from their cell phones before the DOJ inspector general could collect evidence of their communications from the SC team's three-year exercise in overthrowing a president. How is that not an obstruction of justice, and who will answer for it?

That's on top of many other bits of essential evidence in the RussiaGate coup and other perfidious acts mysteriously gone missing — Special Agent Joe Pientka's original "302" document from the Flynn interrogation, thousands of Strzok-and-Page text messages, official verifications of the Steele Dossier submitted to the FISA court, communications between the FBI "small group" (Comey, McCabe, Priestap, Carlin, McCord, Baker et al.) plus CIA Chief John Brennan and DNI James Clapper with Senators Burr and Warner on the Senate intel committee, communications between "whistleblower" Eric Ciaramella, Col. Alexander Vindman, and House intel committee chair Adam Schiff, records of CIA prop Stephan Halper's doings with the Pentagon's Office of Net Assessment, all communication records between State Department official Jonathan Winer and British ex-spy Christopher Steele . . .

And now, like a fever building to climax, comes the news right out front that the Democratic Party intends to foment insurrection if the election goes against them. They're supporting the coming siege of Lafayette Square set to kick off fifty days of "protest" across from the White House beginning Sept. 17 as a warm-up for anarchy in the streets across the nation following the Nov. 3 vote. Behind us is the summer of riots, arson, and looting, and who paid to support all that? Who paid for flying Antifa and BLM personnel from city to city, feeding and housing them, paying for their "commercial grade" fireworks, pallets of bricks, gas masks, lasers, bullhorns, black riot outfits? Why is it hard to find out who bought the plane tickets, booked the hotels? Months have gone by since all that started. Is someone in the DOJ following the money? And following their communications (especially considering the crimes against property they've committed)?

Why is Christopher Wray still director of the FBI? Why is Bruce Ohr still collecting a paycheck from the DOJ? Why is Eric Ciaramella still keeping a seat warm at the CIA? What exactly was US attorney John Huber doing for two years? Why is Mark Esper still running the Pentagon? Why is General James Mattis not facing a military court of inquiry for proposing a coup against the president? Why is the federal judge Emmet Sullivan still defying the DOJ's motion to dismiss the case against General Flynn? Why is it taking years to resolve the legal issues around Julian Assange while he rots in jail? Where exactly does William Barr stand with all this? And is it possible that John Durham's efforts to unravel the giant hairball of sedition begins and ends with one lame guilty plea of petty fall guy Kevin Clinesmith?

It may sound paranoid, but I feel compelled to ask: is Barack Obama running some kind of shadow government from his Kalorama fortress —that is, issuing suggestions (or instructions) to scores of loyal high officials in federal agencies for opposing and undermining everything the current president attempts to do — such as Mr. Trump's executive order this week to cease and desist the depraved "critical race theory" and "white privilege" struggle sessions run all over DC by obscenely highly paid "diversity and inclusion" consultants? And what role is Hillary Clinton playing behind the scenes these preelection days, since her foundation is so heavily invested in the DNC and she is issuing directives on subverting the election through a complicit news media?

How on earth can responsible adults pretend that the empty shell of Joe Biden is a plausible candidate for president? What will Joe do in the two scheduled debates without his teleprompter or an earpiece? He can't possibly perform without them (and barely even with them, it appears lately). When was the last time Joe Biden took impromptu questions from reporters? When has he stood before a crowd of actual voters, not live-action role players picked by his handlers? Who is trying to hustle the USA out of existence and what are you going to do to stop them?

Last Roundup at
the Wokester Corral

October 26, 2020

I have some questions for former friends who have dumped me on account of my support for Mr. Trump's reelection — which is mostly a vote to prevent the Democratic Party and its fellow travelers from running the government. On the whole, these former friends are college-educated, mature in experience, and cultured. Some of them are well acquainted with history, which is to say, they ought to know better than to support the obviously illiberal motives of the political Left.

Are you against the principle of free speech? The Democratic Party is. It used to be the champion of the First Amendment; now Democrats want to make it conditional on ideas and sentiments they support. Contrary ideas are to be labeled "hate speech," and suppressed, along with anything that might hurt somebody's feelings. How did you come to such a complete misunderstanding of what free speech means? Namely, that a free society is obliged to tolerate the expression of disagreeable ideas up to the limit, as the Supreme Court put it, of "crying 'fire' in a crowded theater."

I will answer my own question partially by saying: you have been programmed against free speech by what used to be the very vehicles of it, the newspapers and TV news channels, which have, amazingly, come out against freedom of the press and turned into propaganda outlets for Woke Progressivism and its illiberal agenda — thereby inadvertently committing suicide of the entire profession. We've seen this acted out most vividly just the past week in the social media companies' efforts to suppress all news of the Biden family's global business operations, along with *The New York Times*, *The Washington Post*, CNN, NPR, and other leading news organizations that Americans used to depend on to know what was happening in the nation. This is especially unforgivable during a national election.

Did you support the movement on campus in recent years to shut down events featuring speakers such as Charles Murray (*The Bell Curve*), Heather Mac

Donald of *City Journal*, Dinesh D'Souza, and many others who represented not-so-woke ideas that "offended" you? Since when are your feelings so special that they negate the open exchange of ideas in the places that used to be dedicated to it, the universities? Should higher education only entertain ideas that you and your cohorts approve of? What if, in some future, a different cohort gains control of higher education and seeks to exclude your ideas on the grounds that they're "offensive" (i.e., they just don't like them)?

Are you in favor of a politicized Department of Justice and CIA? That is what the Democratic Party's Resistance League deliberately brought about during the 2016 election, and they continue to promote it. Is it okay for bureaucrats to break the law to disable their political adversaries? That was the essence of the RussiaGate ruse. Former employees of those agencies, such as ex-CIA chief John Brennan and Andrew Weissmann, who ran the Mueller investigation, to this day still hype "Russian collusion" falsehoods to deflect attention from their own misdeeds. You let them get away with that.

Is it okay for these government agencies to spy on US citizens without any legal predicate, except their being political adversaries? Would it be okay if that were used against you in some future disposition of things? Is it okay for the FBI to withhold exculpatory evidence in federal court proceedings, thereby obstructing justice? Is it okay for the FBI and CIA to "leak" falsehoods to news reporters for political advantage? Do you not understand how by failing to oppose these actions you undermine the basis of political rectitude in a republic — bearing in mind the literal meaning of the word *republic*, from the Latin, *res publica*, the public thing, where civilization lives?

Are you against reason itself? For all your talk about the primacy of science, your agenda militates furiously against it: math is "racist," there's no biological basis for understanding sex, all science is a "white colonial way of knowing," masculinity is "toxic," women can have penises and men can menstruate. Do you really believe these absurd fantasies manufactured in the graduate schools in the service of academic careerism at all costs — or do you just go along with them for the sake of protecting your own careers and perquisites?

Are you in favor of Antifa riots and the BLM hustle? They are staunchly supported by elected Democratic mayors and governors. These organizations looted and burned down shopping districts in many cities, and Democratic leaders did nothing to stop them. In Portland, Oregon, the nightly riots have continued for over 120 days under Mayor Ted Wheeler and Governor Kate Brown. The nightly riots have ceased to have any genuine political purpose or meaning; rather they've degenerated into a party space for energetic young people who can't otherwise go to clubs, parties, concerts, cafés, or raves during the Covid-19 shutdown. So, rather, they're enjoying a long-running game of Cops and Robbers out in the streets, busting things up, setting fires, getting chased around, and waking people up in their homes late at night with bullhorns and heavy metal music. They're obviously having fun. The police have been forbidden to effectively disperse them, and the Multnomah County DA refuses to prosecute any of them — all of which just inspires the Antifas and BLMs to keep the game going. They have no real stake in the public interest. The net effect is terrible destruction of the city as a functioning civic organism. The Democratic Party has made it all possible. Wait until it comes to your town or city.

Are you in favor of cancel culture? The Democratic Party is addicted to it. Should livelihoods and reputations be destroyed for expressing an opinion, or telling a joke? Is asking someone for a date in the office a firing offense? Were Christine Blasey Ford and Michael Avenatti unimpeachable witnesses during the Brett Kavanaugh SCOTUS hearings? Or was that just an instance of *anything goes and nothing matters*? How much sadistic pleasure do you suppose has been involved in the professional ruination of men in the media, the arts, and politics? How much of cancel culture and the MeToo movement has been based on simple coercion, the wish to push other people around, and on vengeance for personal losses and slights?

By the way, did you notice that Jeffrey Toobin has *not* been fired from his positions at *The New Yorker* magazine and CNN for jerking off on-screen during a Zoom meeting of his professional colleagues last week? None of them have even publicly criticized him. Why do you suppose that is? I suppose it's because he is a favored member of the Woke Journalists club and enjoys special protection from professional ruin — though the truth is he's thrown away his credibility as a legal commentator, whether the *wokerati* like it or not, especially on matters of public conduct. But that's just one example of the hypocrisy that wokesterism is full of, and reveals its chronic disingenuous insincerity.

The Democratic Party supports all this pernicious mendacity and bad faith, and more. Joe Biden is the current figurehead of the party. Mr. Biden pretty clearly has insurmountable defects of his own, first as an international grifter while holding national office, as well as the misfortune of his cognitive decline, which is not his fault but disqualifies him for high office. As for everybody else in the party, I don't want such a reliably dishonest gang to be in charge of running the American government. So I'm voting for Mr. Trump. He's far from my idea of an ideal candidate, but despite his defects he's managed to hold the country together during the greatest disruption of normal life since World War Two. I've also come to admire his resilience and, yes, his bravery, in the face of an opposition that has spared no effort of foul play to destroy him.

I'm under no illusions that Donald Trump will Make America Great Again in the way that many of his supporters understand that slogan. The USA is headed into a terrible ordeal of economic disorder that I call the Long Emergency. Mr. Trump won't stop it, and it may yet make a fool out of him. But the Democratic Party's agenda would add an extra layer of tyrannical and sadistic insanity to the process that will only bring more suffering to more people, and I don't want that to happen. I believe that Mr. Trump will probably win the election, but we'll have to see what kind of nefarious dodges his opponents will employ to prevent any resolution of that outcome.

THE MANY LAYERS OF TRAVAIL

November 20, 2020

One thing you could say about the three Trump campaign lawyers' joint press conference at high noon, Thursday: it sure wasn't slick. But then, are we now such a nation of lobotomized chumps that our chief criteria for any public acting out of an acute national melodrama is slickness of presentation? I guess we like our crises fluffed, like a Caitlyn Jenner spot on *The View*. This one, though, is raw and savage.

And so there stood Rudy Giuliani in that cramped briefing room, with dark rivulets running down both temples as if he were sweating blood (more likely hair dye), cracking jokes at times, and laying out some rather harsh predicates for pending election fraud lawsuits. Next up, the usually demure Sidney Powell appeared boiling over with grief and rage at the hijacking of American democracy, and the Deep State's long-running connivance with all that, yielding nearly to tears at moments as she sketched out the sinister history and associations of the Dominion and Smartmatic vote systems — and the utter failure of public officialdom to monitor any of it for many years. Then Jenna Ellis, much in command of herself, emphasized perhaps half a dozen times, and quite sternly for the obdurately seditious news media, that the actual evidence would be revealed in court and that the day's presentation was a mere overview. Got that? *In court.*

The news media didn't get the message — on purpose, as usual — and so the stories flew all over the internet's gaslit echo chambers that the three lawyers failed to make a case. Later that night, Tucker Carlson piled on Sidney Powell for not sharing what she intends to present in a court of law. Apparently, she hung up the phone on him. Let's face it, the lady has had a hard month, and a hard year, having to battle the malevolent and depraved Judge Emmet Sullivan over the dismissal of the case against General Flynn (as ordered by the DOJ), and now this colossal hairball of a momentous and historic election fraud case. (If I were her, I'd be deep into the George Dickel No. 12 Sour Mash by eight o'clock that night, Tucker Time.)

All right then, Mr. Trump's lawyers have set the table for this epic political food fight with just a few weeks to file and proceed, and we'll have to stand by like grown-ups and see how it all plays out in the courts. There may be other sideshows and shenanigans in the various state legislatures over electoral college slates and such, along the way, but meanwhile I want to remind you that there are many other layers in this burgeoning megacrisis worth being mindful of.

One, of course, is the train of tyranny that would follow the crooked and demented Ol' White Joe Biden into power, should he manage to be sworn in (more on that below). From the actions so far of his, *ahem*, transition team, Mr. Biden (or the shadowy gang behind him) is aiming to bring on an official regime of speech suppression, news suppression, cancel culture, race hustling, gender warfare, and other portfolios of wokesterism to the federal agencies. Do you have any idea how much anger and opposition that will provoke? Do you suppose that half the population will sit still for struggle sessions over *white privilege*?

Another layer is the Deep State itself. This evil empire is close to prevailing in a final act of sedition after four years of contemptible, serial intrigues. The Justice Department, the FBI, the CIA and all the other spook agencies will have a free hand in surveilling US citizens and attempting to control whatever they do. The whole RussiaGate case (such as it might be under John Durham) will get towed out to sea and dropped overboard in cement slippers. Comey, Brennan, Clapper, McCabe, Strzok, Gina Haspel, Andrew Weissmann, and the rest of the gang will all skate — some of them possibly pirouetting back into federal offices. Facebook, Twitter, and Google will be enlisted as social controllers (this has already happened, of course) to guard against the sharing of *undesirable* information. Gawd knows what sort of misadventures in foreign lands this gang will blunder into. I won't even bother to outline the possible economic perversities and experiments the new regime might attempt to try because of the following...

...which is the king-hell financial fiasco that will attend a Joe Biden presidency and the monumental unwind of activity that will present as implacable depression. The global banking system is ten months pregnant with Rosemary's baby. The Covid-19 winter lockdowns will put a bullet in the brain of any remaining small businesses, and the giant zombie companies are next to fall. Rent, mortgage, and loan forbearances run out in December. If they are not renewed, many families stand to lose their homes; if they are extended, many creditors and landlords will be screwed, unable to meet their own obligations. Few in the media or in officialdom seem to comprehend that unpaid debts thunder through the system, and eventually undermine the whole system, especially the currencies that circulate like the system's blood supply. Not only will there be no money for progressive economic experiments, there will not be enough money to arrest the fast-sinking standard of living in America. Biden & Company, so triumphal in these days of dwindling daylight, are in for shock with 2021.

In the looking-less-likely event that Mr. Trump prevails in this election quarrel, he and his people will be subject to exactly the same thing, which is the onset of the epic crisis or "fourth turning" that I call the Long Emergency. It will include an additional layer of Antifa/BLM anarchy in the streets on top of epochal economic hard times. How America manages to emerge from that will be the $64 trillion question of the ages. Neofeudalism, a dark age, a new stone age . . . who knows?

As a kind of PS, and per what I mentioned above, there are the lingering questions as to whether Ol' White Joe Biden can manage to make it to the inaugural podium in any case. Apart from his failing mental faculties, there are the matters around his and his family's shady business dealings in foreign lands over recent years, especially the money garnered from ventures in China linked to China's intel services. There are legitimate concerns about Mr. Biden being a security risk as president. They are not going away.

Finally, a few words of encouragement to those of you almost terminally disgusted with the dishonesty and bad faith of the people who have been running things in our country: this is not a place like Russia in 1989. The Soviet overlords had a captive press, of course, but the internet was barely a larval presence in world culture then. All the Russian people had to fight the immersive milieu of lies they lived in was the mimeograph machine and the verbal grapevine. We have much better resources for distributing information in America today, despite our tribulations with the corporate news media and their Silicon Valley cadres. We have a pretty sturdy alt news network and many diligent entrepreneurial reporters who are able to get the news out. It will get out, and it pays to remember that truth has godly powers of its own.

SOMETIMES LIFE REALLY
IS LIKE A BAD DREAM

December 11, 2020

When you think of the US Supreme Court, it's probably the image of its august Greco-Roman facade, expressing the conjoined ideas of *democracy* (ancient Greece) and a *republic* (classical Rome). Or else, you might imagine the grand courtroom inside — always featured in drawings, because photos aren't allowed — which is the ultimate performance space for the law of the land. But there must be quite a backstage area, offices for the justices and their clerks, and surely some kind of boardroom, or even a comfy lounge full of overstuffed leather club chairs, a fireplace, and a sideboard with the cut-crystal sherry bottle. Would you suppose that the nine justices, or at least the two divisions of them, get together there and palaver informally over dockets and cases? I would.

Now imagine they are palavering over the current case at hand brought by Texas with what . . . eighteen other states now, plus the president, in for backup? Is the court really reluctant to take the case, as the media gossip says? Maybe. But if they do take it, would they eventually rule to not disturb the current disposition of the election — even as alleged to be rife with ballot fraud — out of fear of venturing into a constitutional wilderness, as other gossip has it? Maybe. But what happens then?

Hey, whatever you think of Donald Trump, he has been POTUS for four years, with access to a whole lot of nonpublic information about his colleagues in government, including who among them have been playing footsie with the tentacles of China, and lots more. Accordingly, and prompted by four years of nonstop seditious harassment by a deranged Democratic Party, would you suppose he had a plan to meet some version of what played out on November 3? I would.

I would suppose, for instance, that Mr. Trump's military intelligence allies saw, in real time on election night, all the packets of internet data that Dominion vote tabulation machines in the USA sent across the Atlantic to the Dominion server lodged in the CIA's Frankfurt, Germany, cyberwarfare station. This, you understand, when those Dominion machines in the USA were forbidden by law to be connected to the internet. If you're a regular reader here, you will recall the recent report of a US Army special forces operation going into the Frankfurt CIA station directly after the election and seizing servers there. Assume that they underwent forensic dissection afterward. If you were President D.J. Trump, would you suspect that the CIA might be playing dangerous games with you (and, by extension, the nation)? Are you aware that China has a 75 percent investment stake in the holding company that now owns Dominion? Are there grounds to suppose that China somehow interfered in the election? With assistance from an eager Democratic Party and the CIA?

Would Mr. Trump, of all people, let such a thing stand? Especially considering the evidence that the putative "winner" of the election, Joe Biden, *the kid from Scranton, PA*, was up to his eyeballs, with the rest of his family, in Chinese funny money? (Not to mention money from Ukraine, Kazakhstan, Russia, and other lands?) Note: information about this evidence gleaned from Hunter Biden's forgotten laptop was deliberately suppressed in October by the major newspapers and cable news stations, with help from Facebook, Twitter, and Google, along with a claque of "fifty former and current intel officials" led by John Brennan, who denounced the reports from *The New York Post* in a public letter as "Russian disinformation" — yet another seditious conspiracy among the swamplings.

Are you aware that in the weeks since the election there have been unusual movements of US military aircraft around the country, including C-130 Hercules troop carrier planes? And that the navy has two carrier groups out along the Pacific Coast and three strung along the Atlantic coast? That's what I hear. Remember, the president cleaned house at the top of the Pentagon this fall, and probably not for nothing. Sounds like preparation for something . . . some extraordinary executive action to prevent the national security risk known as Joe Biden from being sworn in as president — in the absence of anything else in a strictly constitutional way that would keep that from happening, like a Supreme Court decision that would order the rare passing on of the disputed 2020 election to the House of Representatives for resolution, with a strong statistical likelihood that the body would reelect Mr. Trump.

These are the sorts of things I imagine the Supreme Court justices might be palavering about and weighing over their sherry in the comfortable back room of their august clubhouse. There is, of course, the likelihood that such a momentous decision to send the vote to the House would provoke a violent, batshit crazy response from the Democratic Party's street warriors BLM and Antifa — thus the

C-130 flights perhaps deploying troops around the country. This time, expect the Black Blocs to get their asses kicked, and swiftly. Expect also a mind-blowing raft of arrests of political celebrities on charges like treason. Does it sound like a bad dream? Yeah, kind of does. But there it is.

IN DARKNESS VISIBLE

December 28, 2020

The signals from the political establishment to Donald Trump ring pretty clear now: *get thee hence, thou big-bottomed orange menace to order and sanctity!* Has ever a president been lonelier at 1600 Pennsylvania Ave? Lincoln's "team of rivals" in the drear winter months of 1864 seem downright chummy in retrospect and, of course, poor Richard Nixon stayed swozzled on scotch whiskey during the darkest nights of Watergate, when he reputedly wandered the West Wing halls conversing with portraits of his predecessors.

The other power centers of America, especially the news media, insist that there is no evidence of fraud in the recent election and it's time to get on with the hallowed ceremonies of transition. The post-Christmas suspense is killing them. Mr. Trump will not be moved to declare that he lost the election — probably for the excellent reason that he really didn't, if there had been anything like an honest tally of the ballots. They hear murmurings of *martial law* and *the Insurrection Act*, and it all sounds to them like an imperial *Nightmare on Elm Street*. They can hear the tinkle of their lucrative perquisites shattering in the creases of their temporal lobes.

It's said in the alt media that the president wishes to exhaust all the formal alternatives before possibly moving on to the novelty steps of contesting this final act of the four-year coup against him, which brings us all the way to January 6, when the electoral college slates are toted up in the House chamber, Vice President Pence presiding. One popular fantasy has the veep tossing out "certified" votes from states where irregularities were starkest in favor of alt slates submitted by Republican-majority state legislatures — with Hieronymus Bosch–style Antifa chaos to follow all over the land. Sounds like a low percentage deal to me, but then . . . what's actually at stake here?

Not to be too melodramatic, but something kind of like a *Manchurian Candidate* situation. How okay is it, actually, for Joe Biden, with a record of accepting large sums of money from China's intel apparatus, to move into the Oval Office, especially after they laid the Covid-19 trip on the world? *No prob-*

lemo, the DNC and its vast network of apparatchiks answer. *There's no evidence of Ol' Joe colluding for pay!*

Oh, but there's plenty of evidence, and quite a bit of it is in the public annals already, what with Hunter B.'s laptop having been partially dissected since, at least, October, and a great tangle of slime trails clearly revealed in the email logs and his corporate memoranda. And one must wonder if there is additional evidence in John Ratcliffe's DNI files — you know, the place where every electron of recorded information ever transmitted on the internet sleeps. You might have forgotten that something a little screwy is going on there, since the ODNI was supposed to issue a public report on the election (and its adumbrations) by December 18 and the fateful report was indefinitely postponed for reasons so far unknown.

Maybe the president's antagonists are acting superanxious to get rid of him — and constructing yet another media campaign to agitate public opinion — because there is evidence that other persons in government, persons of both parties, have been importuned by CCP largesse to perform services in recent years, not to mention other incriminating hijinks they'd hoped would fade harmlessly into history with tags such as the Clinton Foundation, the Open Society Foundations, Skolkovo, Uranium One, the Maidan Uprising, the Steele Dossier, the Mueller investigation . . . you get the picture . . . a vast sepulcher of unholy rot where the Deep State has tried to entomb its most shameful secrets, including now the dark deeds of election 2020.

Problematical, also, is the likelihood — in the event that he actually does concede and agree to exit the scene — that Mr. Trump will transition into post-presidential life with a bale of secret knowledge so huge, reeking, and damaging to his enemies, gathered over four years of access to the nation's intel files, that not a congressman, senator, or high-up bureaucratic lifer will be left standing as the information dribbles out strategically in the months to come of the as yet hypothetical Biden-Harris (or Harris-Biden) administration. Imagine what Ol' Joe, Kamala, Nancy, Chuck, perhaps even "Cocaine" Mitch and the rest of the Beltway gang are fretting about as they chug down their midnight Zolpidems. The Golden Golem of Greatness is not fading away from the swamp crime scene no matter which way this thing turns out. And don't forget, he is not exactly alone. Tens of millions of extremely pissed-off Americans are standing by pretty quietly, for now, from sea to shining sea, behind him.

❧ 2021 ❧

INSURRECTION VERSUS INSURRECTION

January 11, 2021

In the dark hours of Sunday, the Big Tech–government alliance showed its hand in its massive purge of *the public square* — which is what social media became in a nation of strip malls, parking lots, and nonstop propaganda — shutting down all voices countering the constructed narrative du jour: that the Democratic Party stands for defending Americans' liberty against a rogue president. There have been many "shots" fired so far to kick off a civil war, but that action was an artillery blast.

Remember, the Left's playbook is to accuse their opposition of doing exactly what they are doing. And so, of course, House Speaker Nancy Pelosi has launched a last-minute impeachment on grounds of the president inciting "insurrection." By a strange coincidence, reports on as yet still-live web channels say that the president has actually invoked the Insurrection Act against seditionists in our government, including, perhaps, Ms. Pelosi. If it is true — and I can't confirm it — then the nation has blundered into an epic political battle.

Some facts may suggest the truth of the situation. The Washington DC airspace was shut down for hours on Sunday afternoon, and 6,000 National Guard troops have been moved into the District of Columbia as well as other cities controlled by Democrats with Antifa/BLM mobs at their disposal. What does that signify? The news media couldn't be troubled to find out. Mr. Trump is reported to be in "a safe location." As of last week, that was Dyess Air Force Base outside Abilene, Texas. Maybe he is somewhere else now. *The New York Times*, *WashPo*, and *CNN* would like you to think that Mr. Trump has been pounded down a rathole. That's one possibility. Another possibility is that the Democratic Party is unnerved and desperate about what's liable to come down on them in the days ahead, which resembles a colossal hammer in the sky.

Mr. Trump is still president, and you've probably noticed he has been president for four years to date, which ought to suggest that he holds a great deal of accumulated information about the seditionists who have been playing games with him through all those years. So two questions might be: how much of that information describes criminal acts by his adversaries — most recently, a deeply suspicious national election based on hackable vote-tabulation computers — and what's within the president's power to do something about it? I guess we'll find out.

Or, to state it a little differently, it is impossible that the president does not have bargeloads of information about the people who strove mightily to take him down for four years. At least two pillars of the intel community — the CIA and the FBI — have been actively and visibly working to undermine and gaslight him, but you can be sure that the president knows where the gas has been coming from, and these agencies are not the only sources of dark information in this world. Also consider that not all the employees at these agencies are on the side of sedition.

By its work this weekend, starring Jack Dorsey (Twitter), Zuck (Facebook), Tim Cook (Apple), and Jeff Bezos (Amazon *and* the *WashPo*), you know exactly what you would be getting with the *Resistance* taking power in the White House and Congress: unvarnished tyranny. *No free speech for you!* They will not permit opposing voices to be heard, especially about the janky election that elevated America's booby prize Joe Biden to the highest office in the land.

Now there's a charismatic, charming, dynamic, in-charge guy! He's already doing such a swell job "healing America." For instance, his declaration Tuesday to give $30 billion to businesses run by "black, brown, and Native American entrepreneurs" (*WashPo*). Uh, white folks need not apply? Since when are federal disbursements explicitly race-based? What and who, exactly, comprise the committee set up to operate Joe Biden, the hypothetical, holographic president? Surely you don't believe he's spirit cooking this sort of economic policy on his own down in the fabled basement.

And so, here we stand at the start of what's liable to be a fateful week for the United States. There is a lot of chatter on the lowdown that the current president — that would be Mr. Trump, for those out there who are confused — is about to act to take down the scurvy party that enabled and condoned six months of rioting, arson, and looting in at least a dozen cities — cadres of whom may have actually instigated that incursion into the US Capitol building on Wednesday. The president appears to understand his duty to preserve, protect, and defend the Constitution of the United States against all enemies, foreign and domestic. He had plenty of opportunity to be a quitter from 2017 to 2021 and he hung in there, against every cockamamie operation the Deep State threw at him. Odds are he's not quitting now.

FLYING BLIND

January 25, 2021

Events are in the driver's seat now, not personalities. Gil Scott-Heron was right way back in the day when he said, "The revolution will not be televised." Only what he called "revolution" turns out to be collapse, led by the disintegrating news business, so that the people of this land are flying blind into a maelstrom of hardship. Everything is going south at once here, and you probably don't know it.

If you think we're headed into a transhuman nirvana of continuous tech-assisted orgasm, social equity, and guaranteed basic income, you are going to be disappointed. Our actual destination is a neo-medieval time-out from all the techno dazzle of recent decades. It's not as bad as you might think. The human project will continue at a lower pitch, probably for a good long while, but minus most of the comforts and conveniences we're used to, and with very different social arrangements. You can waste your energy hand-wringing and wailing over all this, or summon the fortitude to go where history is taking us and make something of it.

The old economy is wrecked. Many Americans already know this because they've lost their businesses and their livelihoods. What used to be there isn't coming back. But there will always be ways to make yourself useful providing things and services that other people need, just not within the crumbling armature of the economy we're leaving behind. There will be a lot of debris left in the way to overcome, especially the crap we've smeared all over the landscape.

One business you can begin to organize right now is a salvage industry, sorting out the reusable components of all that crap — the steel I-beams, the aluminum trusses and sashes, plate glass, concrete blocks, copper and PVC pipe, and dimensional lumber. A lot of this stuff we just won't be making anymore, certainly not at the former scale. Think of all the shopping malls to be disassembled.

Growing food and getting it to markets is the most critical activity. Poor Bill Gates, addled by his fortune, has bought up something like a quarter-million acres of farmland. His grandiosity prompts him to believe he can organize farming on the super-giant scale — Walmart for corn and turnips. Nothing could be further from the real coming trend: a reduction of scale and scope of farming and of the distribution supply lines that serve it. Poor Bill doesn't seem to realize that the oil and gas–based "inputs" (fertilizers, pesticides) won't be there for him, nor will the million-dollar diesel-powered combines. Nor the trucking industry. He could do more good for mankind getting into the mule business. (He won't. Lacks razzle-dazzle.)

The transition between the old giant agribiz model of farming and the emergent system of small-scaled farms based on human and animal labor will be arduous and disorderly in the early going. A lot of people will miss a lot of meals, and you know what that means. Working on a farm will be one way to make sure you get enough to eat. But also consider all the businesses that have to be created from scratch on the local level to serve the logistics of farming. You are already seeing many food products unavailable in the supermarkets. That will become more distressingly obvious in the disorders of 2021. When food deliveries to the supermarkets get really spotty, the farmers' markets will not just be for schmoozing over lattes and almond croissants.

For those perhaps not paying attention, Covid-19 has destroyed what remains of education, especially the public school system. It was already moribund, waiting to crash, reduced to a pension racket for teachers. Going forward, the money won't be there to operate these giant centralized schools and their yellow buses (while paying out pensions). The virus has kick-started exactly the kind of home-schooling pod system (several families combining) that can be reorganized into small-scale schooling for people who want it. People who don't want it can move into their future without knowing how to read or do arithmetic. We'll finally get a good test of the *noble savage* hypothesis. As for the colleges and universities, their business models are toast. They'll be downscaling and shuttering as far ahead as the eye can see. Whatever remains will be more like finishing schools for neo-medieval ladies and gentlemen — and, by the way, the distinction between men and women will be reestablished. Why? Because reality insists on it. There will be plenty of work for former professors of *intersectionality* in the sorghum fields.

A central theme of *The Long Emergency* is that government becomes increasingly impotent and ineffectual as our manifold crises deepen. Is Joe Biden not the perfect avatar for this feature? He's spending his first week in office laser focused on policy that supports transsexuals, about 0.42 percent of the population. When the applause dies down, he'll be unable to act on anything that might get the people moving on what they need to do and where they have to go.

Meanwhile, we get an exciting show trial: Donald Trump's impeachment in the Senate. Not a bright idea. Mr. Trump would get to defend himself, of course. What if his attorneys produce solid evidence (i.e., proof) that the incursion into the Capitol building was actually launched by Antifa / BLM cadres? Could happen. What if the Democratic Party gave them some aid and comfort in organizing the event? Wondering what is on Nancy Pelosi's purloined laptops?

President Joe B. may not even be in office a month from now. Justice Amy Coney Barrett will rule shortly on the lawsuit against the state of Wisconsin for ignoring constitutional requirements in changing its voting rules. Unlike so many other cases tossed out on procedural grounds, there's a pretty good chance this case will stand, and the outcome could end up nullifying last November's national election, canceling Joe Biden. That will birth a whole new political crisis on top of the cratering economic picture. There are no road maps for any of that.

THE GAME IS ON

February 1, 2021

The hijinks playing out in financial markets instruct us that politics finally comes back to the soundness of our economic arrangements, no matter how far out into the asteroid belt of psychopathic ideology the nation veers. For instance, we're about to find out how little race-and-gender hustling actually matters to the common good of this land. After their successful prank with GameStop, the subreddit vigilantes are aiming to send the price of silver to the silvery moon now, and, in the process, drive hedge-fund privateers and bankster short sellers into insolvency, even if it wrecks the financial system.

Do you doubt that the system, led by the clueless and feckless Federal Reserve, was already beating a path to financial suicide? Two decades of trying to paper over America's broken business model with money-from-nowhere, and failure of the authorities to regulate the games being played around that, switched off the price discovery mechanism of markets. Does that sound abstruse? I'll explain. Price discovery is the main function of markets: to send correct signals as to the true price of everything, soybeans, iron ore, stocks, what have you, and, most important, the exact price of money itself, borrowed over a period of time: that is, term interest rates, meaning the cost of debt.

The price of silver (and of gold, too) has been among the most manipulated, suppressed, and perverted for many years because the rising price against paper currencies would signal the falling value of money, which would inform the people that their standard of living is falling — and nothing stirs up political anger like that. So the regulatory authorities looked the other way when their cronies in big banks such as JPMorgan played games to suppress precious metal prices with a revolving short-selling scheme that regularly knocked down the price to discourage buyers from investing in precious metals.

It's been fifty years since precious metals enjoyed any official peg with the US dollar, but for five thousand years previously gold and silver were money itself and paper currencies became mere representations of that *money*. That relationship ended in 1971 when President Nixon closed the "window" that allowed foreign countries to redeem gold in exchange for dollars they accumulated from the commercial trade of goods — and, our dollar being the world's supreme reserve currency, the rest of the world's currencies followed.

Despite all efforts since then by banking authorities to denigrate the value and the role of gold and silver in financial affairs, the "barbarous relics" retained a persistent influence in men's minds because of their intrinsic qualities. These were: the vested energy they represented from mining and refining, their physical durability, portability, and divisibility, their freedom from counterparty obligations, and, especially in modern times, their vital usefulness in electronics and other industrial applications. The latter quality is greatly reinforced by the powerful wish to transition from a fossil fuel economy to an alt-energy economy of solar cells and wind turbines — a wish that probably won't come true.

And so, as promised by the subreddit vigilantes, the silver price was up around $3 or 10 percent in overnight trading going into the week's Monday open. It looks like they mean bidness. And that could mean many things. The most obvious is a very conscious effort to punish the high hats of Wall Street for years of lawless game playing that made them ultra rich and left everybody else in the country impoverished. Some of the vigilantes frankly express the desire to wreck the degenerate banking system altogether, a great purge of evil to restore something like god-fearing accountability, moving toward a fresh and honest restart of markets and banking. I'm not convinced that we would get any such orderly restart in the sense that global banking could be reconstructed along pre-2020 lines.

Rather, wrecking the banks in a daisy chain of shattered obligations would be an express ticket to the Palookaville of neo-medievalism I've been warning about, and probably in a sharp, disorderly, violent, and deadly episode of losing everything that has made us civilized. In any case, the country has already prepped itself for some kind of spectacular failure with all the social mind fuckery of the past four years that eventuated with the empty shell of Joe Biden in the White House, and millions of his supporters swept into an epic hysteria of manufactured moral outrage over pseudorealities initiated by academic racketeers and then weaponized by our politicians. But the game is on, whether you like it or not. This may be a last opportunity to get your minds right before you lose your country and your future.

PREVIEWS OF COMING ATTRACTIONS

March 12, 2021

How reassured were you by Joe Biden's speech to the nation Thursday night? The more his managers pretend that he's in charge of anything, the more unlikely it actually seems. So they wound him up — Adderall would be my guess, to fortify the attention span — and rolled him out like the mummy of Amenhotep III, and one could just imagine the leaders of this and that foreign nation cringing (or cackling) in their seats to see this embodiment of collapsing America go through his spiritless ritual motions.

Mostly what did not fly is the idea that the Covid-19 virus can still be used as a cattle prod for herding citizens into feedlots of compliance — Americans are buffalos, not steers. They are determined now to take care of business, and the main business of people with any initiative will be to rig up some sort of gainful occupation while the lumbering old systems break down. They will do it despite orders to operate at fifty percent capacity, or close at nine o'clock, or be hand-cuffed by rinky-dink regulations. They'll have to get creative to figure out ways around all the official impediments to making a living. This group of the not yet undead will resist further attempts to restrict their liberty and to steal the fruits of their own enterprise to pay for other people's failures or lack of enterprise.

The federal government is one system visibly working to destroy itself with epic giveaways of money it pretends to command and the Covid-19 stimulus bill will only accelerate its loss of credibility. A $1,400 check won't "solve" the problem of someone a year behind on mortgage payments or rent. It sure won't solve the problems of their creditors and landlords. And if you think shortchanging that class of people is a good idea, you're beating a path straight to the death of credit per se, and then of our money, the dollar, which is based on credit.

Taxpayers are not so stupid that they'll fail to notice who is being asked to bail out bankrupt states, irresponsible cities, and pension funds and there's going to be trouble over that. The trouble will express itself both in political strife and in the further decay of the relationship between work and wealth. It means a collapsing standard of living for most people. Turning the one-shot $1,400 into a monthly Guaranteed Basic Income can only be a short-term shuck and jive when a loaf of bread goes from $5 to $15 to $50 — which can happen easily, and quickly, too, as lots of "free" money chases crashing productivity. Wait for it.

Meanwhile, the party in charge of things is squandering the last of its moral authority in stupid and tyrannical woke crusades against free speech and free thought. They went after Washington and Jefferson last year. This month, it's a purge of cartoon characters, starting with an auto-da-fé over at the Warner Brothers' Loony Tunes lot. Disney better watch out because they'll be coming after Mickey Mouse next — for "acting white." Which brings us to the 800-pound gorilla in the room: the abysmal condition of race relations in the USA, expressly sponsored by the Democratic Party.

The Left's promotion of the supreme conspiracy theory du jour, that "white supremacy" stifles and suppresses people of color in everything they endeavor, has inspired provocations so dastardly that they are driving the country to racial war. The rioting and looting season is upon us again, and the perfect stage set for the opening offensive is Minneapolis, where the trial of officer Derek Chauvin just kicked off this week. Black Lives Matter is marshaling its troops outside the courthouse to intimidate jurors and threaten mob violence against an outcome they may not like.

The facts of the case suggest that former officer Chauvin has a sturdy defense, starting with the Minneapolis police training films that show officers how to apply the same knee restraint that Chauvin used on George Floyd. It was in their instruction manual, too. Add to that the forensic reports that show fentanyl levels in Mr. Floyd's bloodstream several times above what would likely kill a normal person, plus meth, plus marijuana. He had an enlarged heart and was Covid-19 positive at the time of his death. And, of course, he was not complying with the cops' orders during his arrest, which is exactly what led to him being physically subdued.

None of that will matter to BLM because the video of Mr. Chauvin kneeling on George Floyd's neck was such a perfect poster for the white supremacy meme, whatever the reality of the situation was, and it's just too rich in coercion value to let go of. I'd predict trouble in the streets no matter which way the Chauvin trial ends up, just because energies are up and the weather is good. It will be infectious in cities across the nation again because the dividend of getting to loot is such a temptation, and last time that happened the authorities did nothing to stop it.

How will it go this time? By now, shop owners in Minneapolis (and elsewhere) must have gotten the message that the police are not interested in defending their places of business — their bosses, the politicians, ordered them not to. Some business owners may opt for defending their property themselves. Imagine the cognitive dissonance that will make for as Nancy Pelosi's Congress tries to pass new gun control laws. If Joe Biden is even around, will he step up and tell BLM and Antifa to cut it out? Or will he just ignore all that as he did during the election campaign last year? Half the country, at least, won't stand for it anymore.

In the meantime, gawd knows what will be happening in financial markets and banks as all that new money floods an economy that can't produce enough to absorb it. Racial war and runaway inflation . . . not a good recipe for political continuity.

PEAK NATIONAL DYSFUNCTION

April 23, 2021

No need to argue anymore about defunding the police. The police across America have been successfully disarmed and castrated. Why would any cop with a sense of self-preservation interfere in the commission of a crime now? Just assume that the social contract is canceled. You're on your own.

Interesting factoids, by the way: rape reports are up 322 percent in New York City over the past year, shootings were up 97 percent, and murders up 44 percent — a good start to the new era of all against all, where life is solitary, poor, nasty, brutish, and short. But don't worry, Benjamin Crump and his legion of superhero personal injury lawyers stand ready to enforce the suspension of law, seeking multimillion-dollar payouts in civil suits, such as the $27 million recently settled on the family of George Floyd, which is $27 million more than Jesus of Nazareth got for somewhat harsher treatment years back, though, according to House Speaker Nancy Pelosi, George Floyd has by far outpaced the old lord and savior in sheer saintliness mojo. Looks like George and Jesus will soon be vying for Speaker of Kingdom Come in the new, revised cosmos of American Wokery.

Anyway, New York's City Council voted last month to end qualified immunity for police officers, which formerly shielded them from personal lawsuits in the performance of their duties. Predictable result: they will no longer perform their duties. This is on top of Mayor Bill de Blasio ending the age-old practice of posting bail for charged felons pending disposition of a criminal case. Meanwhile, the city's main jail, Rikers Island, is scheduled to be closed down in 2026. Abolish incarceration! Well done, Big Apple!

For the moment, Derek Chauvin is on ice, having served his purpose as sacrificial goat in a trial that had all the fateful velocity of the Chattanooga choo-choo. No need to rehearse the prejudicial actions of Rep. Maxine Waters (D-Calif.), Oval Office occupant Joe Biden, sidekick Kamala Harris, the *Minneapolis Star-Tribune* newspaper, Minnesota AG Keith Ellison, and other workers on the railroad of justice. The case will surely go on to appeal and by the time it is finally adjudicated the old USA will be on ice, too — in the mortuary of lost civilizations.

Minneapolis police officer Kim Potter is teed up next in the death of multiple felony suspect Daunte Wright, who was *turning his life around* when he made the impulsive decision to evade arrest on an outstanding warrant for gun possession. And on deck: Columbus, Ohio, police officer Nicholas Reardon, who (it's said all over Twitter and cable TV) unfairly interfered in a knife attack between a couple of girls just going about normal teenage girl stuff in, like, their normal, playful way.

Critical race theory and its enforcement arm systemic racism have got America in a full nelson, having put over the idea that any regulation of behavior among 13 percent of the US population is a crime against humanity — effectively rendering lawlessness a new social entitlement. Waiting to see how that works out as 2021 rolls forward. The weather didn't cooperate much this week of the aforesaid events, so there was little action in the streets after the Chauvin verdict and all — except in Portland, Oregon, city of masochists, where the nightly riots continued as usual.

Is there a problem with all this? Only that the remaining 87 percent of the folks who live in the USA have so far failed to identify these operations for what they are, an epic hustle — by which I mean the seeking and acquiring of advantage, including large sums of money, by underhanded means. Sorry to tell you: the responsibility for this is on the 87 percent who are craven and feckless enough to allow themselves to be hustled. What's the payoff for them in this game? A sense of radiant, self-informed moral purity for consenting to be coerced by the hustlers. The endorphin rush must really be something, a little like a snootful of fentanyl and meth.

Notice, too, how all this racial psychodrama is an effective smoke screen for other nefarious actions afoot by the Democratic Party. I refer to the various bills moving through Congress now to pack the Supreme Court, turn the District of Columbia into the fifty-first state (to gain two more Senate seats), and institutionalize voting fraud across all the states (HR-1). Not paying any attention to that? It's just a gang of power-hungry maniacs trying to destroy your country. That is, unless Joe Biden & Co. manage to start World War Three in Ukraine or Taiwan before that bidness comes to a vote. Oh, and here's the moral of the story: life is tragic. Sometimes things don't turn out . . . they just turn.

Happy Birthday

May 24, 2021

We step back from the disorders and idiocies of the moment to wish Bob Dylan a happy eightieth birthday. He entered the scene in a previous moment of national disorder, the sixties, as we call that wild era when we boomers came of age and turned the world inside out for a while, flinging our ids into a raging zeitgeist. Bob was actually a little older, not quite a boomer, born seven months before the US entered World War Two.

This is important because he was poised perfectly on the front end of that breaking wave in a particular way that I will try to explain. When he stole into New York City from his Midwest Nowheresville in the winter of 1961, he was unformed, ambitious, intelligent, cunning, and not yet grown up. He did his growing up in public over the next decade. He acted it out in the songs he wrote. It was the essence of what he meant to those of us who trailed behind him. He instructed us in the mystery of what it means to come through adolescence into consciousness, and he did it with a matchless artistry that, once he got traction, made his competitors look barely adequate. It's easy to understand how being cast in that role irked him, but that's how it was.

It was Bob who turned the long-playing record album into the art form of my generation. Before that, the pop music scene in America just amounted to different sorts of adolescent fluff, clichéd hormonal yearnings of boys and girls for each other. It was a long way from the Everlys' "Wake Up Little Susie" to Bob's "Visions of Johanna." He was twenty-four when he wrote it in late 1965 (and then recorded it in February 1966). Twenty-four is about the age when the judgment region of the human brain finally develops, and the song spells out vividly the jarring wonder of becoming a fully equipped adult — and recognizing it! The subject of the song isn't a girl anymore, she's a woman, with such cosmic ramifications that "the ghost of electricity howls in the bones of her face."

Lyrics like that — and Bob generated them by the bale then — just made everybody else's songs seem a little lightweight and silly. The Beatles came close around exactly the same time with their venture into songs of full-fledged adulthood in the album *Rubber Soul*, but they were not able to bring the focus of a single sensibility to it the way Bob did, and they knew it.

Anyway, Bob had been leading up to that for years lyrically. He had a comfortable childhood back in Minnesota, but it was a harsh place. He absorbed that and summed it up with dazzling concision and specificity in songs like "North Country Blues" about a failing family in a failing town where the iron ore mines are shutting down and there is no such thing anymore as the future. Similarly, "The Ballad of Hollis Brown," which is the story of a despairing farmer who kills himself and his family of six out on the lonesome South Dakota prairie. These were stories about other people and other lives, reportage from the scene, with more resonance than Walter Cronkite could ever hope to bring to it.

When Bob wrote about himself and his own strange journey, more and more he populated that dreamscape with a hallucinatory cast of characters: dwarves, madonnas, hermit monks, cowboy angels, drunken politicians, Napoleon in Rags, the mystery tramp . . . Imagine how weird it was to be Bob in those few years. He barely had to struggle to become famous, was rolling in dough before he was twenty-five, and had every jerkoff workaday Johnny journalist tugging at his sleeve whenever he left the house begging him to explain how the world worked. No wonder he played cute with them, claimed he was "just a song-and-dance man," when everybody knew better. And, amazingly, he pulled it off.

Once he completed that transformation into adulthood, he had pretty much done his duty, and everything after that has been a long coda, with not a few flashes of the old brilliance like these stupendous lyrics from his 1985 song "Dark Eyes":

A cock is crowing far away and another soldier's deep in prayer,
Some mother's child has gone astray, she can't find him anywhere.
But I can hear another drum beating for the dead that rise,
Whom nature's beast fears as they come and all I see are dark eyes

Sounds like what's going on "out there" right now, don't you think? He deserved that Nobel Prize. I'm glad he's persevered through all these years and still goes on stage and keeps putting out tunes. I met him once back in 1975 when I worked for *Rolling Stone* magazine. It was after a benefit concert in San Francisco in the Fairmont Hotel. I couldn't help greeting him like an old friend, and was foolishly surprised to realize that he didn't know me from a hole in the wall. Anyway, I'm glad we shared these decades together on this marvelous planet and I salute him on his birthday for what he gave that has lived inside me all these years.

Thinking Out Loud

June 21, 2021

Events are tending toward an unfortunate convergence that may leave the USA in a very reduced condition before the end of this year, while the "Joe Biden" government cripples all our institutions, especially the military, with race and gender mind fuckery as a distraction from its own coming and untoward collapse. The "president" is back from his toilsome travels through Europe, which included a summit meeting to butter up Vladimir Putin, hoping to possibly use Russia as a buffer against an increasingly hostile China.

In a kind of comic reversal of George W. Bush's first meeting with Vlad Putin — "*I was able to get a sense of the man's soul*," W said — this time, Vlad looked into "Ol' Joe's" eyes and probably saw the ghost of Konstantin Chernenko. You may recall Ol' Konstantin led the foundering Soviet Union for about a year, his final months from Moscow's Central Clinical Hospital, where emphysema, congestive heart failure, and cirrhosis of the liver laid him low. "Joe Biden" did not start smoking cigarettes at age nine, as Chernenko had, but when Vlad P. looked into his eyes, he probably saw a 15-watt bulb flickering within, and played him accordingly. After the summit, Vlad sized up the "POTUS" as "professional" for the press — a witty snark, if ever there was one.

You can see a procession of events now marshaling up toward an epic storm of bad karma for this exceptional nation of ours turning the corner into summer and then the fall. Of course, the friendly news media are not fully reporting the latest institutional failure, that is, the perfidious behavior of US chief health official Dr. Tony Fauci, who, either with stupefying naïveté or by some other motive, assisted China in the development of a bioweapon, which China then loosed upon the USA (and everybody else). Net result: millions dead around the world, and an awful lot of people here now extremely suspicious of the vaccines being aggressively touted by the government. Meanwhile, the roughly half of the US population who took the vaxes now have to worry about what the active ingredient, a toxic spike protein, is doing to their hearts, blood vessels, brains, and other organs, and whether something worse awaits down the road. Has a trap been set? (We'll get to that below.)

Just now, we have news of the strange case, revealed last week, of a "top Chinese counterintel official," a vice minister of state security, name of Dong Jingwei, defecting to the USA back in February. The strange part is that he came in from the cold to the Defense Intelligence Agency (DIA) because he did not trust the CIA or the FBI to be outside China's influence, and Dong sought protection from them. More American institutional failure? This raises a whole bale of questions, including whether Dong is a double reverse disinfo agent, or what? It is rumored that he is proffering even more sordid dirt on "Joe Biden's" son Hunter than is already known from the memo-and-email cache lodged on his infamous laptop from hell — not just sexual escapades while in China, but details of big money deals made for the Biden family business. And not just that, but heaps more dirt on other prominent political figures paid off by China. As if the US government is not already in a bad odor with at least half the country's citizens.

This Chinese spy tale is ripening at exactly the same time that the Maricopa County, AZ, election audit concludes phase one of its operations — scaring the panties off of the DNC and its PR staff at MSNBC, CNN, and the *Wash-Po* — with a lot of noises coming in from Georgia and Pennsylvania about likewise conducting vote audits. All that, plus Dong's garbage barge of toxic political dirt, suggests that "Joe Biden" will have an even shorter run than Konstantin Chernenko did. We may find ourselves in an intense constitutional crisis by midsummer. Hold that thought . . .

While all that is cooking on one front burner, we also have the case of the US equity markets burbling away at bubblicious highs on another burner, and therefore primed for a nauseating boilover. Would a new and lethal government scandal supply the few extra therms for that? And by *scandal* I mean something more like a broad loss of legitimacy and paralysis of the "Joe Biden" government. Also, how would a market train wreck affect the credit markets? The US dollar? Whatever is left of the on-the-ground economy? Let's just say it sure won't act as a tonic for any of that; more like a slug of ethylene glycol. So now we're talking about a simultaneous government crisis and financial crisis.

Now, consider what might happen in the fall if a potent new strain, or "third wave," of Covid-19 virus wafts across America. We've already seen speculation in the medical media that the residual action of mRNA "vaccines," if exposed to yet another novel coronavirus, might tend to whack out the immune response of those who got vaxed, killing them, as well as killing a new cohort of victims among the unvaxed, adding up to many millions of dead Americans.

How would the country manage any of this along with a twin crisis of economy and government? We couldn't even manage the pandemic when our institutions were supposedly still functioning.

And now, consider what might happen if China decides this is a good time to gain control of Taiwan (and the world's leading chip manufacturers). A savvy friend of the blog writes:

"They'll hit Taiwan, Guam, Vietnam, South Korea, Philippines, Australia. Iran would move to secure the overland route from China to Africa. The Israeli/Saudi coalition could stop Iran but only if China didn't help Iran. (Iran/China are far ahead of us in drone swarm warfare.)

"China could overrun all of it in a matter of weeks and establish a deep defensive perimeter before we could effectively respond. More importantly they'll hit our infrastructure so hard we'll have a hard time hitting back effectively for years.

"Last year pretty much exposed our weakness; now they'll move to exploit it. They'll not wait till 2030, as our fearless leaders are touting, otherwise we might have time to mend our ways. Sun Tzu dictates they act now. My bet is they follow his guidance. It is the one area they are most predictable. Xi is following *The Art of War* to the letter so far."

Kind of makes you take a deep breath and say, Whoaaaa . . . ?

Those are *known unknowns*, as Mr. Rumsfeld liked to say. Add to that the *known known* of the megadrought that has already developed in the American West and its implications for the food supply (not to mention the electric supply from the great western dams and the water supply to the western megacities). And add to that the extremely bad mood the various ethnic and racial groups remain in, due to the years-long DNC-Marxist fermentation of hatred among us. It all boils down to something that looks like an American collapse. Just sayin'. Also sayin' it might be a really good time to lay in a few extra bags of rice, dried beans, and chili powder to make it edible.

THE ICE-CREAM FLAVOR
NEXT TIME

July 5, 2021

A nation mesmerized by its own weakness wanly celebrated the long-ago and far-away memory of standing up for itself, while it passively endures the current orgy of tyrannical cancellation and suppression of anyone talking back to the present folks in charge. Over just a few years, this tyranny has grown like a toxic slime mold from such an unlikely place, the internet social app ecology of Facebook, Twitter, and Google, as they took over the public arena — where the battle of ideas is supposed to live — and did the government's dirty work, complete with adorable emojis. *You're fired!* 😐

Who will stand up to Zuck, Jack, and Sundar Pichai? Who elected these megalomaniacs boss of the USA? What will it take to end their reign of terror? Some sort of . . . revolution? (Shhhh! That must be a dirty word, even considering we just celebrated the high point of the American Revolution: the Declaration of Independence, signed July 4, 1776.)

Don't look to "Joe Biden," the nation's putatively elected leader — about whose election back in November 2020 you are liable to hear more about as the summer stickily unspools. Zuck, Jack, and Sundar managed to protect "Joe Biden" from the stupendous depredations of his offspring Hunter Biden, recorded in explosive detail on a laptop the public was not allowed to hear about. Don't look to the Department of Justice, supposedly "investigating" that horde of memos and emails detailing the Bidens' influence peddling to the CCP and others — they're busy surveilling "white supremacists" on the apps run by Zuck, Jack, and Sundar. And for sure don't look to the news media, that coalition of sellouts and quislings, busy decoding the foreign policy moves signified in "Joe Biden's" ice-cream flavor choices. (Rocky Road means: *Oh, let China have that . . .*)

Wondering who is actually running the "Joe Biden" government? Some of us out here are. (Do you think we're allowed to say that?) For instance, have you tried googling the name Susan Rice lately? Remember her? Maybe not. "Joe

Biden" appointed her director of the White House Domestic Policy Council. From the looks of things across the country, you'd think her plate would be heaped mighty high, what with "insurrection" and other white mischief threatening to take down the republic. Anyway, I googled "news" for her. Hardly a gosh darn thing came up that wasn't from months ago, and most of that was sheer puffery about how accomplished she is, and what a fabulous person. Don't you wonder what her phone log looks like? All those calls to the Obama residence, day after day, hour after hour?

All of which raises the question: is the USA just floating merrily merrily down the stream of events under the beneficent reign of "Joe Biden" (Susan Rice, Barack Obama & Co.)? Or are we, rather, freefalling? I suspect it is the latter. And toward what? It being midyear, I will venture a few guesses. Enjoy the summer while you can because coronavirus is coming back in the fall and watch out for people who are vaccinated getting sicker than the unvaxed. That will be a mind bender, as if Americans are not already utterly perplexed and bewildered by one political swindle after another. The whining will drown out even the news of more "white supremacy." *But they told us . . .*

An autumn wave of Covid-19 (one "variant" or another) would take out whatever remains of the service economy, the restaurants struggling just now to return to normality (ha!), the hair salons, the gyms, the florists, booksellers, sports, theaters, live music venues, what have you. Since we no longer have much of a manufacturing economy, the only thing left would be Wall Street — which was originally designed to raise money for the manufacturing and service sectors but now raises money only for itself via the seemingly magical mingling of "leverage" with "liquidity" to conjure profit from black holes where the ghosts of productivity howl.

It's some trick but, let's face it, it's still just a trick. Also in that picture is the weird three-legged race of deflation tied to inflation running both uphill and downhill at the same time like a nightmare out of M. C. Escher by way of Stephanie Kelton. The USA will be toting up a $3 trillion–plus deficit just for the current fiscal year at the same time that debt becomes ever more obviously unpayable. How does debt even mean anything if there is no prospect of paying it back? Especially in the form of financial instruments, namely: bonds. And how does a financial system based on debt behave when all that is the case? I guess we're going to find out.

My guess would be a price collapse in financial instruments — abstract things represented by money — and then a collapse of money itself. You may be thinking: *not a pretty picture*. I know. And we thought the last days of the Soviet Union were bad in 1990. Hooboy, are we in for a rough ride. One can hardly imagine the social side effects of all that, but it would seem to imply people having a rather hard time finding something to eat, or getting anything else they need. Remember good ol' Ross Perot talking about "a giant sucking sound"? Think of that against a background of things on fire. What flavor ice cream will "Joe Biden" be ordering on Halloween?

Throwdowns and Showdowns

August 23, 2021

Notice, there are two sets of hostages in this phase of what looks like an engineered US collapse: the thousands of stranded Americans who can't get out of Afghanistan thanks to the history-rockin' ineptitude of "Joe Biden," Tony Blinken, and General Mark Milley, and the millions of We the People back home whose minds are hostage to the narratives concocted in a shadowland of sinister governance. Welcome to a week of throwdowns and showdowns, a force majeure of mind change.

A strange paralysis in the Pentagon has prevented the use of US power to clear an escape corridor to Kabul's airport and establish order in the facility — this, after the tactically mystifying decision to abandon the US's Bagram military airfield, a good twenty miles outside of festering Kabul, and surrounded by more easily securable empty desert. Britain and France managed to get their nationals out last week, only to be rebuked by American brass for "making us look bad." That helped, I'm sure.

And then how long can the stranded Americans even stay hidden and alive? They have to eat. Either they come out of their hidey holes and get to some market or they would (theoretically) have to send some Afghani servants to fetch them supplies, But what Afghani in his right mind would want to be caught in service to the Americans by the Taliban? That quandary must have a pretty short time horizon on it. Standing by to see how it works out.Next in this week's throwdown parade is the FDA's imminent approval of Pfizer's Covid-19 vaccine, without any of the usual extensive trials. How does that even happen, with an efficacy rate of 39 percent maximum and a runaway train of vicious side effects ranging from brain and heart damage to infertility? The so-called mRNA vaccines are also implicated in the ongoing mutation of the disease, producing a cavalcade of variants. Is that, perhaps, on purpose, to keep the pandemic going, preventing it from burning out?

Covid-19 is an expedient device for exercising the most severe control over the daily life of Americans, and it is being used liberally once again in the "blue" cities to make ordinary business as difficult as possible even unto shutdown and ruin. FDA approval will further enable the mandatory "vaccination" of schoolchildren, government workers, and corporate employees. About half the country still refuses to get jabbed. You are about to see them go hardcore when the FDA makes its move.

The shadow cabal behind "Joe Biden" will, accordingly, destroy what is left of public education as millions of parents withdraw their kids from the system. You will then see the rapid assembly of home-schooling networks that aggregate informally into small private academies — and, of course, the biggest losers will be the minorities who lack the cultural mojo to home school. Well done, "Joe Biden" and the FDA! While you're at it, why not destroy higher ed, too? (That sound you'll hear is plywood getting nailed up on the windows of countless insolvent small colleges.)

The school revolt will be only one part of a greater uproar against the confabulated hysteria of Covid-19. Throwdown will lead to showdown as the alienation of We the People from a tyrannical rogue government bangs the crisis gong. Next up: the release of the Arizona election audit's preliminary findings. Rumor is that they show the grossest possible, and probably criminal, mismanagement of the balloting, pointing to a conclusion that "Joe Biden" did not win that state's election. Additional rumor has it that the ballots carried hidden, traceable serial numbers, or something like that, showing conclusively how the paper vote was rigged. Rachel Maddow's nightmare — "*They* have *the ballots*!!!" — comes true . . . a wake-up for the woked-up.

As predicted here, John Durham is back in the news. The captive news media — that is, the mainstream orgs *owned* by the intel community — put stories out last week that the RussiaGate special prosecutor has actually made some trips to the grand jury. That implies some kind of criminal prosecution. Their spin was that he had only netted a few small fry, characters mostly outside government such as Igor Danchenko of the Brookings Institution, said to be the chief source for Christopher Steele's nefarious "dossier." Don't believe it. Durham is going for the sharks and whales: Andrew McCabe, Peter Strzok, John Brennan, Bruce and Nellie Ohr . . . and, really, how can James Comey be excluded from that gang, since he was running it?

This week marks the beginning of the Deep State's hard time. Its narratives are shredding. Its mind-control measures are slip-sliding away. Half the country has been on to their game for years, and the other half is about to feel their heads explode as a corrective reality elbows into the scene. That is, the *real and only* reality, not the one confabulated backstage for you by skulking quislings. See how you've been played? They have taken your country. Maybe you should start caring about that.

Ordeal by Narrative

September 13, 2021

Has doctor Anthony Fauci booked passage to Paraguay yet? Like, on a smallish container barge registered in Côte d'Ivoire, conveying a six-month backlog of cars stolen out of Essex County, New Jersey, for detailing and resale way up that lazy river to Asunción? The captain has a comfortable guest cabin, price negotiable, but better bring your own food. The US intel community will not find the good doctor down there because they will not bother looking for him. And so, the distinguished American public servant will live out his last days in exile among the swooping fruit bats and grinning crocodiles, to the music of toucans screeching in the silk floss trees (*Chorisa speciosa*).

Anyway, that's my fantasy du jour. Walt Disney had it right: America's fate would be a descent into pure fantasy as the final product of our many twentieth-century triumphs. It is increasingly difficult, for instance, to sort fact from fantasy in Dr. Fauci's magnum opus: the Covid-19 pandemic, starting from the premise that it actually exists. There was some kind of rumpus in Wuhan, China, in January of 2020 . . . folks dropping dead in their tracks on the sidewalks (captured on closed-circuit TVs) . . . folks getting the doors to their apartments welded shut . . . and then what?

Not much indication of further freakouts inside China since back then. Perhaps the virus has been raging over there all the while, but a million here, a million there, do you really notice the attrition in a land of 1.4 billion? Or did they just switch off that groove on their narrative machine? The CCP can do that, I hear.

Back in the USA, where you'd have to subtract a billion and then some in population, something was surely killing folks, though, overwhelmingly, most of those folks were already sick, and old, pretty much in the checkout zone. In 2020, the death of old and sick people was declared . . . impermissible! Death suddenly had no place in the *exceptional* order of things American. (Ask old Uncle Walt, who reportedly had his head and its gelatinous contents cryogenically frozen, in expectation of future reanimation via science magic! Still waiting for him to come back.)

Of course, the new medical rules of engagement circa 2020 included the denial of early treatment with known common antiviral drugs for folks coming down with early symptoms of the mystery illness. So while pretending to object to the implacable fact of death — a certainty of the human condition, according to *science* — we killed a whole bunch of people by withholding treatment. And concurrently, we rolled out the vaccines promising to "protect everybody" only to learn that it provided other, even more diabolical, routes to death.

And so we're left as of last week with the putative leader, "Joe Biden," of a fantasy cult formerly known as the United States, barking at the populace to line up and get vaxed . . . or else! Did you flash on Jonestown, Guyana, 1978, the Peoples Temple, and the Rev. Jim Jones exhorting his deranged followers to "drink the Kool-Aid"? Is this whole extravaganza starting to look like a two-year-long bad dream that you're finally waking up from?

It was heartening to see those football stadiums this weekend filled to their superspreading parapets with good folks chanting the magic words of exorcism: "Fuck Joe Biden." And with such exuberance! As if returning home to genuine and familiar consciousness after a hypnotic journey to a weird plane of existence where anything goes and nothing matters. They are finally unimpressed after eight months of this gibbering empty suit who so ineptly fronts for a shadow administration operating wholly outside the law. We are going to get to the bottom of just how they put us through this wringer of the national soul, and exactly who was behind it.

After the initial flush of liberation, though, things get real. The hard work resumes and you start to feel pain again. I have a hunch that the weeks ahead will be doozies as the collective national mind undergoes reconstruction and narratives fall away with the season's blazing leaves. A great sorting out of the real from the unreal lies ahead. Illusions will dissolve. The fog will lift. Some will be blinded by the light, even as we head into the darkest time of the year.

In a Dark Wood

October 1, 2021

Behold the photo (above) showing President "Joe Biden" getting his booster shot of the Covid-19 "vaccine," with the news media clustered to the left of what is apparently a stage set built in a larger chamber. Do you possibly ask yourself: why bother to build a set for this event in or under the White House somewhere — including even fake daylit windows — when there are any number of actual rooms in the White House perfectly suited to holding this grand event in real daylight? What is going on here?

And, by the way, how do we know that "JB" is getting an actual mRNA booster? Or is it just 3 cc's of saline solution? Is not the syringe, after all, just another prop in the show? The video of this event was broadcast on cable TV channels and corporate media websites everywhere. None of them commented on the strange artificiality of the staging. And so, the mystery abides.It only reinforces the creeping suspicion that absolutely everything about the "Joe Biden" regime is fake. And malevolently so. How else could it be that so many bad things are happening at the same time in this country if there was not some faction seeking to destroy it?

For instance, the vaccine mandates for medical personnel. In upstate New York, WNYT-TV reported yesterday that two hundred employees of Albany Med, a large, regional teaching hospital, are placed on seven days' unpaid leave prior to getting fired for refusing the vaccine. Andrew Cuomo's replacement, new governor Kathy Hochul, has blocked unemployment benefits for fired nurses and technicians if they persist in evading the vax. Doctors are included in the mix, too.

Of course, large numbers of health care workers getting kicked out of their jobs will only make it more difficult to care for patients — with Covid or any other health problem — so how does this policy help anyone? (Unless you consider that, with fewer staff on duty, fewer Covid in-patients will be subjected to the medical malpractice of being placed on ventilators and treated with the killer drug remdesivir.) Not only has effective early treatment with other drugs been banned from the official medical standards of practice across the USA, but mere talk about it has been banned, notably by Google's YouTube app.

This coercion of health care workers is going on all over the country, of course, not just in New York state. These nurses and techs have been working around Covid patients for going on two years, and many of them have gotten the disease, with symptoms or without, conferring natural immunity. So what is the point of forcing the vaxes on them? It is also a fact that vaccinated people are susceptible to catching the disease, and that, in any case, the vaccinated carry heavier viral loads than the unvaxed, making them more efficient spreaders. It is also a fact that mass vaccination in the midst of a pandemic promotes the mutation of new variant viruses that increasingly are not affected by the vaccines.

Thursday night, CNN ran a segment with its house doctor Sanjay Gupta, hectoring one Andrea Babinski, a La Crosse, Wisconsin, nurse who is quitting her job at Gundersen Hospital there rather than take the vax shot. Dr. Gupta, acting all perplexed, asked her why. Ms. Babinski said she was concerned about blood clotting. Dr. Gupta dismissed her concern, saying, "If you've got a clotting disorder, you should get the vaccine." Really?

After the segment, Dr. Gupta and Anderson Cooper shook their heads in amused puzzlement over the nurse's obdurate foolishness. They are apparently uninformed that the spike protein produced by the vaccine is known to bind onto the endothelial lining of blood vessels and promote blood clots, leading to a range of lethal events such as myocardial infarction and cerebral hemorrhage — heart attack and stroke — plus a broad array of organ damage and neurological disorders.

The Medicare Tracking System states that 48,465 people have died within fourteen days of receiving a vax shot. Many had comorbidities, of course, so not all the deaths can be directly attributed to the vaccines, but the public health authorities are averse to autopsies that might establish the truth of the matter.

Anyway, the CDC has ruled recently that it will only count people more than fourteen days out from a shot as being considered officially vaccinated — so none of those aforementioned deaths would have counted as vaccinated persons under the rule. Do you see how they are gaming the statistics to keep Americans as misinformed as possible?

Despite all the efforts to bamboozle the public, the "Joe Biden" regime has about run out the string on Covid paranoia, and wrung all of the political usefulness out of it. Going forward, it will only backfire on them. Do they think that wrecking hospital services while depriving thousands of health care workers of their incomes is a winning strategy? These are existential threats to US citizens.

Everything else under "Joe Biden's" watch looks like a pyromaniac seeking to burn down the country. Over 10,000 Haitian interlopers have been surreptitiously dispersed from Del Rio, Texas, to nether regions of the USA. The government made no effort to vaccinate them — what does that tell you? Over 100,000 more invading opportunists from all over the world are reportedly heading to the southern border. A month after the fall of Afghanistan, and after this week's hearings in both the House and the Senate, still nobody knows who gave the insane order to surrender Bagram Air Base outside Kabul. The Democrats' dishonest "infrastructure" bill is wilting in Congress. Food and energy prices are rising fast, with shortages on the horizon. The capital markets are wobbling. And Special Counsel John Durham is back on the scene with more actions against Hillary Clinton's favorite law firm, Perkins Coie, facilitators of the seditious RussiaGate campaign. Put it all together and you have a mechanism that looks like a "Joe Biden" toaster.

Off in a far corner of the News-o-Sphere, someone affecting to be John McAfee dwells on a Telegram channel labeled "OfficialMcAfee." John McAfee, for those who don't know, was the wealthy inventor of antivirus computer software who found himself at odds with the US government, went rogue, and supposedly committed suicide in Spain last June. Now, he has apparently turned up on this social media app in a series of videos and cryptic info drops. Whether he is actually still alive, or perhaps recorded these videos before taking his life, is not known. But he had threatened to release terabytes of digital evidence against his antagonists, including video of sexual misconduct among well-known political figures connected to the late Jeffrey Epstein, as well as incriminating documents from the DNC and the Hillary Clinton campaign files from 2016. Those info dumps have commenced and the figure who appears to be John McAfee in the Telegram videos says that the dumps will contain incrementally more shocking material for weeks to come.

All of this activity is obviously weird to an extreme never before seen in national affairs prior to the deep fake era — to the degree that reality is almost impossible to establish for now. We are a people lost in a dark wood. When you are lost, the first thing you must do is stop your useless, self-defeating locomotion, hunker down in place, and carefully assess what's around you. Even if everything else is murky and perplexing, one thing is known: there is a way out of these dark woods. Remain calm and alert and it will reveal itself.

CHILLING BIGLY

November 1, 2021

Is it so, as some wags say, that industry no longer makes money; only finance does? That's been the operating theory for much of the West lately. Of course, that invites the question: what then is finance supposed to finance, that is, put money into? Why, industry, of course, and in the broadest sense of the word: the production of goods . . . goods being things that have value (that's what's *good* about them). How quaint! But most of the industry that used to be here has gone to other lands.

What about all that money (capital) flowing into technology: Facebook, Google, Amazon? Hmmmm. What does Facebook produce, besides conflict between its users? Okay, it harvests data about them to sell to advertisers. And what are the advertisers advertising? Their products. Who produces the products? Mostly those people in other lands. Facebook users, then, are increasingly not employed, at least not in the production of goods. Perhaps in services like nursing, trucking, garbage pickup, food prep, police, firemen, prison guards, government bureaucracy (is that a service or a dis-service?) *and* et cetera.

Anyway, those service people are being fired left and right now because they refuse to be coerced into taking a vaccine that was never properly tested and has many scary side effects. By the way, as of Sunday, the "newspaper of record" (*The New York Times*) finally had to come clean, after months of whistling past the graveyard, and admit what the public already knows: mRNA vaccines are dangerous.

While we're on the subject, what does Google produce? Supposedly, answers to questions, plus, like Facebook, it harvests information about the people who ask the questions and then sells the info, blah blah. And whutabout Amazon? Doesn't it sell a lot of products? Yeah, mostly produced by those people in other lands. What Amazon really produces is a phenomenal amount of motion — trucks going hither and thither, at increasing cost now as the price of gasoline and diesel fuel shoots up. To me, that looks like a problem for Amazon's business model. Another problem is the growing number of people without gainful employment who have little money to buy stuff from Amazon, wherever it comes from.

The F.D.A. is assessing whether the Moderna vaccine can cause heart problems in adolescents.

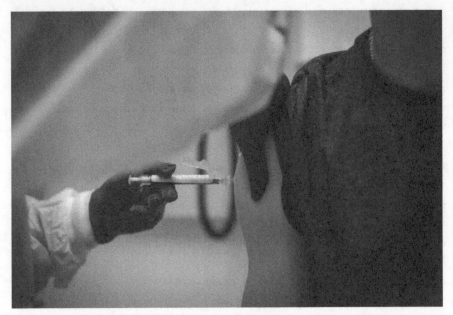

Several European countries have paused use of the Moderna vaccine in young people, citing concerns about myocarditis — an inflammation of the heart muscle. Brandon Thibodeaux for The New York Times

That last problem has been papered over for two years by "helicopter money" from the federal government — direct payment to *the people* for doing nothing, producing neither goods nor services. This has been an impressive trick. The money comes from nowhere and for nothing. The trick is based on simple accounting fraud. The second law of thermodynamics, a.k.a. entropy, suggests that eventually this process will degrade the value of the money (or "money") issued by the fraudsters.

The hand in play for the moment is the spending legislation proposed by "Joe Biden." It would generate a whole helluva lot more helicopter money from nowhere for nothing, and would theoretically keep the game going a little bit longer — except the process will only generate more unwanted entropy, causing decay in the value of that "money" and canceling the desired effect of spreading it around. That's called inflation. If the value of money drops hard and fast, that is called hyperinflation. It would be politically and socially devastating, and probably lead to the downfall of the government. The net effect would be a nation bankrupt at all levels and that will segue into an epic economic depression.

If the legislation doesn't get passed, the USA will perhaps skip the hyperinflationary intermezzo and move straight into a deflationary depression, which is what you get when nobody has any money. When that happens, especially in a system with money actually based on debt creation, debts do not get paid (mortgages, car payments, credit cards, perhaps even coupons on US Treasury bonds), and when debts are not paid, money disappears. *Poof!* No money! It's a vicious cycle. The more money disappears the more money keeps disappearing. None of this bodes well for the winter ahead.

Add to that the growing breakdown in global trade operations. Even many of those goods produced in other lands aren't making it to the docks, and the reduced flow of goods that happened to already land on the docks can't get unloaded and delivered to its various destinations because of disruptions in the US trucking sector. To some degree, those disruptions are caused by bonehead government regulations, especially in California, where most of the stuff from Asia lands. The bonehead regulations (like, outlawing trucks more than three years old) can be thought of as typical government "dis-services."

Now add to that the rising cost of oil, natural gas, and coal — the global economy's primary resources — and disruptions in the industries that produce these vital resources and you've got another layer of disorder being introduced into the system (entropy again). For the moment, government propaganda tries to divert your attention to a possible shortage of Christmas presents as the nation's main concern. Don't be fooled. It's more about total systemic economic breakdown, as in US citizens having no heat and no food. Also, no gasoline and no parts for fixing broken cars (and trucks).

Do you suppose the capital markets will keep rising as all this spins out? I would suppose that the capital markets will lose 80 to 90 percent of their value when all is said and done. The fabled "One Percent" will finally feel the pain that was previously distributed among the rest of us. Don't make the mistake of thinking the One Percent can control the situation. They are mere Wizards of Oz, barfing into their laptops. If working from home wasn't a thing, they'd be jumping out of windows on Wall Street.

It's a grim outlook, I admit, but you could see it coming over the horizon from a thousand miles away. Where I differ from other observers is that I doubt that any sort of extreme government surveillance state can be imposed on the public under these conditions. The people will be too pissed off and, anyway, the current regime will be broke and out of mojo — possibly to the degree that it has to be shoved aside. "Let's Go Brandon" is serious business. It's the end of something.

In the background lurks this virus thing, and the insane vaccination program it prompted. We know that people have been harmed by the vaccinations, but not how many people altogether will be affected moving forward. The possibility, though, is for a nation both broke and sick struggling to get through a dark passage of history. Stay nimble, stay local, stay reality based, be helpful, be honest, be brave, and be kind to each other. We'll get through it.

DECOLONIZE THIS!

November 26, 2021

Now that Thanksgiving with all its *racist* trimmings is put to bed, will Americans be able to "decolonize" their minds? Not if the masters of universal hysteria can help it. Here it comes, just in time to reignite the limbic channels in your brain with pulses of cosmic terror on the runway to Christmas: the B.1.1.529 Covid-19 variant out of Botswana. It's a beauty, with thirty-two mutations on its decorative spike protein, supposedly making it a deadly hazard to the already vaccinated.

Except the already vaccinated were already catching the boring old Delta variant that so energized the year 2021, with its Fauci-inspired affronts to the Bill of Rights, working needle-in-arm with the mystery managers of "Joe Biden," the cigar-store Indian who has decolonized the Oval Office from the brutish grip of Western civ and all its dastardly legalities.

Yes, I am sorry to tell you that the mRNA "vaccines" are just not working that well. The already-vaccinated millions, marinated in the goodness of their obedience to authority, live in terror of the unvaccinated, who so knavishly spread disease to those vaccinated against it. Say, what? Something ain't workin' right here.

Half the nation can't think straight, and for a good reason. The relentless mind fuckery abroad in this land courtesy of your politicized news media, the despotic social networks, the bottomless greed of the pharmaceutical makers and their errand boys in the CDC, plus the malevolent generosity of sponsors like the Bill and Melinda Gates Foundation and George Soros. Thus, the blue mommies of America follow Pied Pipers like NPR and Sanjay Gupta holding hands with Big Bird to vax up the kids.

It's just a cult initiation ceremony, you understand. Vaxing the kids reinforces the psychotic mass formation intoxication of the blue mommies. It does absolutely nothing good for the kids, who realistically have a near zero chance of being harmed by Covid-19 — but have a fair chance of being harmed by the mRNA "vaccines," which will mess with their still-developing immune systems and their various organs. All the authority of Anthony Fauci's officialdom presses remorselessly toward the ever receding horizon of max vax. It begins to look like enough parents are on to the game and will refuse to go along with it.

Dr. Fauci and his evil network are in the process of being smashed at long last. First, there is Robert F. Kennedy Jr.'s book just out, *The Real Anthony Fauci: Bill Gates, Big Pharma, and the Global War on Democracy and Public Health*. I was up reading it at two-thirty in the morning. The Kindle version is $2.95, cheap. Get it. It's a seamless, gripping, and lucid legal brief against a bureaucratic monster who was allowed to run amuck in forty-plus years of power seeking, malicious moneygrubbing, and death dealing, and who has capped that career by destroying the economies of the Western world and our accustomed liberties with it. RFK Jr. lays out exactly what Dr. Fauci has done, footnoted to the max with fact and numbers to back it all up, so that the people still capable of thinking cannot avoid the conclusion that they have been viciously played.

But events themselves are dispelling the cult psychosis that infected the blue half of the public consensus. The not-guilty verdict in the Kyle Rittenhouse case confirmed at least one remaining constitutional principle: that you have a right to defend yourself even with a firearm against forces of anarchy. Rack up an "L" for blue Marxists whose ultimate yearning is to disarm American citizens so that they would have no say in the further destruction of this society (accomplished by manufactured anarchy). Those forces of anarchy are on notice now, despite all the funding by George Soros and the perfidious operations of Merrick Garland at DOJ and Christopher Wray at the FBI.

The vehicular mass homicide at a Waukesha, Wisconsin, Christmas parade, carried out by a walking stereotype of a dangerously deranged antisocial maniac named Darrell Brooks, who advertised his racial animosities lavishly on public video and Twitter, is taking the starch out of the popular "white supremacy" meme brandished by the likes of President "Joe Biden" and his dwindling corps of admirers. That trend was reinforced by the flash-mob robberies all over the country last week. Observers couldn't fail to notice, for instance, that the eighty or so folks rampaging out of Nordstrom's in Walnut Creek, CA, their arms full of stolen merch were not a manifestation of "white supremacy." Could be we have turned the page on that hustle.

Up ahead on this runway to Christmas we'll be waiting to see how many people get sick in the heralded latest Covid-19 surge, but especially how many of these are among the "vaccinated" and revaccinated. Many of the really old folks who got their shots early on in the January to March 2021 period have by now lost whatever immunity those shots conferred, since the alleged protection dribbles away after six months. Dr. Fauci and his CDC will do whatever they can to confound the statistics on their illnesses, probably referring to this cohort as "unvaccinated" — which they have already been doing in their campaign to force the latest boosters. Don't put it past them to simply not report it.

Among the non-old "vaccinated," it remains to be seen how much their immune systems may have been damaged by the invasive mRNA magic, and whether they will meet with severe contagion as a result. On a quite separate track from the immune system issue is the question as to how much the spike proteins prompted by the vaxes have damaged people's bloodstreams and organs, meaning, whether we'll see a spooky uptick in non-Covid deaths from heart attacks, strokes, embolisms, and other typical vascular dysfunction as the winter wears on. In the face of all this, how do the organs of our body politic come through? And will anybody pay for the many harms done?

FURY, RISING

December 3, 2021

If anything, political pressures may prevent the White House from going far enough, Binghamton University political science professor Olga Shvetsova argued.

In order to halt the virus, she said vaccines must not only be mandated but that fully vaccinated people need to be tested regularly to stop the emergence of new variants.

"We cannot allow people to be sick but not too sick," Shvetsova said. "That's what created delta, and that's what created omicron. It's not only about preventing people from being terribly sick. It's about preventing them from being sick in invisible ways."

— as reported in the Washington Examiner

Of course, Ms. Shvetsova is not a medical doctor, and it's reasonable to doubt that politics represents any kind of *science* at all, but just a pretense of it in order to affect some academic respectability. Which prompts one to wonder: what shreds of respectability remain in the universities run by Jacobin maniacs? (Answer: almost none, and zero cred, too, lately, and note that having surrendered entirely to this kind of intellectual racketeering, higher ed is just another major institution whirling around the drain.)

There's a lot to marvel at, though, in the manifold insanity of Ms. Shvetsova's quoted views, starting with her overall totalitarian gusto. No ambiguity there about the need for coercion, for pushing people around, with no reference to legal niceties. (Note, political *science* is a field apart from the study of law, which doesn't pretend to be *science*.) The bit I love most is: "It's about preventing [citizens] from *being sick in invisible ways*." Huh? You know what else is invisible? Your thoughts. You could be harboring hostile thoughts about the folks who seek to push you around, which could lead to the accusation that you are an enemy of the state!

Prof. Shvetsova was not the only one out of her lane in the Covid thunderdome this week. Wall Street shill Jim Cramer took a few minutes off of pimping stocks on his CNBC-TV show to declare that the US Army should be used to force vaccinations on the vax resistant. "Acting President" Anthony Fauci and his political adviser "Joe Biden" used the hatching of Omicron to beseech the multiply vaxed to booster up — overlooking the perhaps embarrassing reality that the mRNA vaccines do nothing to stop the spread of Covid, though they do have quite a downside in relative harm from adverse reactions.

For instance, a new study and warning from the American Heart Association concluded that mRNA vaccines dramatically increase risk of developing heart disease between 11 and 25 percent. Twitter slapped an "unsafe" warning on anyone attempting to transmit this news on its sacred app. Unsafe to whom, or what? Why, to the sacred *narrative*, of course, which is that the USA must be kept in a never-ending paranoid uproar over Covid — certainly until at least past the 2022 elections, in order to maintain all the emergency mail-in ballot provisions that enable voting fraud.

Meanwhile, the emerging reality of Omicron is that it has a much lower transmission coefficient than its predecessor the Delta variant, and produces only mild symptoms of illness. Someone should tell Acting President Fauci that Halloween is over and he can stop trying to scare everybody. Anyway, two federal judges rendered decisions striking down Acting President Fauci's vaccine mandates. The second ruling, penned by U.S. District Judge Terry A. Doughty of Louisiana's Western District, featured a particularly lusty and detailed diagnosis of the mandate's constitutional impropriety, and extended the injunction against vax mandates to all fifty states.

This leaves the USA in a distinctly *exceptional* position among the other nations within the loose confederation of Western civ. Thanks to manifestations of sanity on the federal bench, the vax mandates appear DOA here now, while Austria and Germany have rushed into full-blown psychotic fugues over Omicron, announcing harsh punishments for their unvaxed and, coincidentally, wrecking another Christmas season among people whose Teutonic devotion to the ancient pagan solstice rites runs hot and deep. There is obvious awareness among German vax protesters, as seen on their T-shirts and placards, that 2021 is looking like a nauseating rerun of 1933. Is it not amazing that the German politicians don't see that in their diktats?

The Covid psychosis is just a reassignment of the Trump derangement, which was provoked by the generalized anxiety about collapsing industrial societies. The reasons for the collapse are not hard to grok: a declining resource base, especially affordable, economically plausible oil, a financial system purposefully detached from on-the-ground material reality, and sets of grossly foolish overinvestments in complexity in the techno-narcissistic effort to work around all that.

The epic Trump and Covid hysterias (with a side dish of climate neurosis) managed to distract the masses from those essential economic quandaries. But now the breakdown in all the channels of production, trade, and money is roaring in our faces, and just at Christmas time, too, when the sore-beset people seek just a few weeks' respite from their travail and despair. Don't be surprised by their rising fury over this in the days ahead.

☙ 2022 ❧

No Time for Crybabies

January 17, 2022

Do you know what most of America wants? I will tell you: America wants Daddy to step up and say, "Okay, you can stop being insane now. Really, enough is enough." Trouble is, America is short on daddies these days. That's what happens when you throw *The Patriarchy* on the old garbage barge. Mr. Trump was a kind of daddy, but to many women, especially, he was the wrong kind, *Bad Daddy*, the worst kind of daddy, the kind who makes you clean up your room and come home before midnight. They traded him in for demented Grampa. He just wants to fondle you — and not in a good way — but family decorum requires that we don't talk about that. In the meantime, we can do whatever we *feel* like.

It's a fact that more-educated folks are most susceptible to mass delusion, and the reason will surprise you. It's because of status seeking. Yes, even more than money. We're hardwired for it. And status is liable to send money in your direction, anyway. Among the educated managerial class, going along with everybody else is crucial because careerism in a bureaucratic system, public or private, demands it. If you seek to rise in the hierarchy, or are just angling for brownie points, you must appear to subscribe to the reigning beliefs of the moment, no matter how crazy, and the punishments are severe for appearing to not go along— like losing your career and livelihood, and all prospects of a comfortable life.

The main belief of the moment is that battling the invisible menace called Covid-19 requires the most extreme measures, and anyone against that is an enemy, a *domestic terrorist*! Thus, it is most urgent to "vaccinate" every human being in the nation. Why? Because Dr. Tony Fauci, America's doctor, says so. Why does he say so? Because the Covid-19 "vaccines" are the crowning achievement in his long vainglorious quest to bring forth a world-saving magic cure for a dread disease. And since Dr. Fauci is *The Science* incarnate, and *The Science* must be followed (because . . . come on . . . we are modern people in a modern world ruled by *The Science*), we must follow Dr. Fauci!

But it's obvious now, after a year on the scene, that the vaxes work poorly at best to protect against infection or control the spread, and, at worst, induce terrible long-term damage to organs, blood vessels, and the immune system. The vaxes can kill you or gravely disable you. The statistics in the CDC's VAERS registry show this in no uncertain terms: 1,003,992 Covid vax adverse event reports including 21,745 deaths linked to them through January 7 — and these figures are said to be deeply understated due to the poor design and difficulty using the VAERS website with its clunky, outdated code that the CDC refuses to fix.

Dr. Fauci has avoided addressing these adverse reactions and the negative efficacy of the "vaccines." He simply states that the vaxes are "safe and effective." That so many Americans believe him, despite all the evidence, and go along with the crusade to vax up everybody, is proof that they are insane. But now that the whole story is unravelling, they are ever more determined to stick to the script. Covid-19 has been their security blanket for two years. As long as it was in the picture, raging and killing as an invisible demon, it could be the focus of all their free-floating terror.

Terror of what, you might ask? Of the meaninglessness, alienation, and debility induced by the managerial class in its own sick institutions and corporations . . . in short, the twenty-first-century America that the managers evolved in and supported — a culture of junk food, junk work, junk art, junk environments, junk government, junk economics, and, lately, junk science . . . a sickening panorama of systems out of control and entering failure mode. Confronting the disaster of its own incapacity to sustain a healthy culture and an economy with a future, the managerial class went nuts. Its insane actions now are killing people while seeking to punish those who refuse to walk sheepishly into America's version of the gas chamber, the Anthony Fauci "vaccines."

One way out of a trap like this is to follow your insanity into all-out Götterdämmerung, chaos and destruction. That's the Hitler way (preceded by a period of psychotic totalitarian social control and sadistic scapegoating). I don't recommend it. When it's over, there's not much left to assist the continuity of the human project. But we are led, at the moment, by a very Party of Chaos that is making all those moves. Check the boxes: social control freakery, check . . . punishment unto the unvaxed, check . . . loony war drumming, check . . . The cries for more lockdowns and punishments grow shrill as Omicron burns across the land, presenting a fair chance of putting a stop to Covid-19. We'll know in a couple weeks where this is going. Will those telltale "all-cause deaths" mount in the insurance companies, suggesting that the "vaccines" seeded millions with lurking illness? Will the public turn on Dr. Fauci and run him from public health to rough justice? Will the inept "Joe Biden" regime start World War Three in Ukraine, a place of no real interest to us, or the South China Sea, just to *change the channel*?

You can feel the paradigms straining to shift under your feet now. For that degenerate managerial class, and its psychotically woked-up minions on the campuses and in the newsrooms, this thing would likely go the Schopenhauer way: the new paradigm is at first ridiculed, then violently opposed, then accepted as self-evident. Snap your fingers and they'll come out of it, just like that.

The managerial class will try to pretend that they never did the things they did. A few will offer weak apologies. But the damage is done. Before long, an economic riptide takes the drowning out to sea. The rest of us left on dry land have a lot of work to do. It'll be no time for crybabies.

DEATH WISH

February 4, 2022

Reality is the kryptonite of the Left, sapping its superpowers of coercion and persecution, which — get this — are the *only* abilities it cares about. The Left only pretends to want to make the world a better place. It doesn't care about governing, y'know, managing national affairs, and it wouldn't know how — as no one has demonstrated better than "Joe Biden" and the shadowy wrecking crew running him behind the scenes. The Left actually just seeks to punish its adversaries, and it generates ever new adversities and animosities in its quest to lay on more punishments, the more sadistic the better. Thus, the never-ending Covid-19 melodrama, which provides such an excellent excuse for torturing the populace. The Left's motto: *the beatings will continue until morale improves!*

Reality is intruding now, though, with the help of its twin sister, Truth. Particular truths are emerging to fortify reality and weaken the Left's efforts to beat down the peoples of Western civ. For instance, the implacable truth that the mRNA vaccines don't work and that they gravely injure people. In the face of this obvious reality, government and corporations persist in their irrational campaigns to vax up every last man, woman, and child. Why, at this point, despite all the free Kit Kat bars you could stuff down your craw, would any sane employee of the Hershey's chocolate empire opt for a vax that could make you stroke out at your desk? The ridiculous official answer, of course, is *to protect the already vaccinated*. Sshh-yeah, right . . .

Ditto, the unfortunate, put-upon citizens of Austria, such a tidy little country, too, and so hopelessly lost in its daze of mass formation psychosis. This week, Switzerland, Finland, Sweden, the UK, and Ireland are dropping all Covid-19 restrictions and impositions, while Austria makes its vax mandate a national law. (How many Austrians are secretly studying Hungarian now?) The cognitive dissonance must be unbearable, like a kind of 5G-induced tinnitus that afflicts an entire population, making them want to bang their heads against the nearest wall.

Likewise, the absurd government of Canada, led by the clueless ponce Justin Trudeau, who refuses to take his patent-leather go-go boot off the neck of Canadian truckers. The truckers aren't having it anymore, of course, and neither are the towing services that the government is trying to enlist to get rid of the truckers' trucks. Meanwhile, the premiers of Saskatchewan and Alberta provinces have thrown in the towel on Covid-19 restrictions, leaving Mr. Trudeau in his fortress of solitude, exact whereabouts unknown, desperately hurling objurgations at the "racists, Islamophobes, and transphobes" seeking to end his career as a turbaned, cross-dressing, blackface political entertainer.

And also likewise, the "progressive" sadists on the Loudoun County, VA, school board, who refuse to lift their cruel and stupid mask mandate on schoolchildren, despite Governor Glenn Youngkin's recent executive order to cut it out. The school board sadists surely don't care about the kids. Everybody from the Johns Hopkins med school to the *Atlantic* magazine — to even the lost-in-space CDC —have admitted that wearing face masks is pointless. Not to mention that Covid-19 has been reduced to the wimpy Omicron variant, plus the truth that the incidence of serious illness in children from Covid-19 of any kind is near zero. So why keep the kids in masks? For the pleasure of making them miserable and flaunting their power over the kids' parents. This is how the Left rolls.

Now, as a general proposition, you can bet that the reason the Left wants to keep the Covid-19 scare going as long as possible is in order to keep in place the "emergency" mail-in voting allowances that so easily enable ballot harvesting and other election frauds. Alas, the timing on this doesn't look good for them. The rapid Omicron upspike has turned into a rapid downspike. The goldurned thing is vanishing in the winter mist. By early March there may be no actual Covid on the scene . . . *omigosh*, and then what? The midterms are yet months away, and if there's no emergency . . . Well, I dunno. It's not beyond imagining that the Left and its mysterious sponsors out there in the mythical matrix of sinister global interests will send yet another new coronavirus variant down the chute to keep the worldwide scare going so as to complete the ruin of Western civ. It'd have to be a humdinger, though, something, say, that made folks bleed out of their ears, nostrils, and eye sockets — because otherwise, at this point, the people are done with lockdowns, forced vaxes, mask mandates, green passes, and other social control nonsense, and would opt to just get on with what remains of normal life in this twilight of empire.

Looks like the backup plan is for "Joe Biden's" geniuses in the foreign affairs and intel bureaucracy to start a war with Russia over Ukraine, our dearest ally in the whole wide world (not). Yesterday, State Department spox Ned Price floated up a raggedy balloon about Russia pulling a "false flag" stunt in Ukraine's

Donbass frontier to get things going. It sounded like he was just making shit up. And he was conspicuously short on details. *"Our intel people something something, blah blah ..."* Skeptical reporters shot the balloon down with a few barbed remarks — the darn thing just zinged around the press room with the air rushing out and crashed on the spox's podium — suggesting that even the news media is tired of its role in the controlled demolition of our country.

More likely, though, the financial scaffold of late modernity gives way under the burden of rackets and Ponzis it has been asked to support. This week, Facebook (a.k.a. Meta) scored the world record for biggest single-day market value drop ever, shedding $232 billion in capital losses. You go, Zuck! The Everything Bubble has achieved supernova scale and everybody knows she's gonna blow as soon as Jay Powell lifts the Fed funds rate 25 basis points. When that finally happens, things get realer than real and Truth comes marching in like the saints with bells on. It'll be the Left's *Masque of the Red Death ... ashes, ashes, all fall down.*

The actual global economy itself — the thing that sends, you know, *products* from one place to another — is seizing up like the engine on a beater 1998 Buick Regal. Long about right now, lots of things are *not* going from point A to point B, including stuff of a food nature. It's starting to irk the home folks. When all that goes south, you'll hear no more about Covid-19, systemic racism, the patriarchy, the drag queen story hour, and all the other hobgoblins that infest the Left's gospel garden of Wokery. The kryptonite is coming on hard. They are done ... and for the moment we are stuck with them running the country.

THE UNMASKING

February 18, 2022

We're in the midst of a tremendous shift of public opinion. Winter is not over but the truth is budding now in a thousand places.

O Canada, the Great White North, hovering ominously above Niagara Falls somewhere, is a winter wonderland, and one of the great pleasures of the season there, apparently, for Prime Minister Justin Trudeau, is skating on thin ice. Why is that? Perhaps in all the hollering you have forgotten how Mr. T has kicked off a civil war: by forcing government-mandated shots on his country's working class of an alleged "vaccine" that doesn't work and harms people, at the dwindling end of a worldwide disease scare that *scientists in Canadian labs may have helped to create.*

The great truckers' convoy that converged on Canada's capital city, Ottawa, has exposed the ugly truth at the heart of this historic moment for Western civ: that governments have declared war on their own citizens. It happens that PM Trudeau represents his country's Liberal Party, which is suddenly the party of unchecked government power to interfere in the lives of citizens, the party of speech suppression, news management, forced unsafe vaccinations, and the seizure of citizens' property outside due process of law.

Under the Emergencies Act, Mr. Trudeau's police have now arrested the leaders of the truckers' revolt, Tamara Lich and Chris Barber, on charges of "counseling to commit mischief" (O, dear!), and seized their bank accounts, while also freezing the bank accounts of anyone who donated money to the truckers' cause. That action led, naturally, to runs on Canada's major banks, leading to bank shutdowns on Wednesday — duh . . . what do you expect when the authorities send the message: *your money is not safe in Canada's banks, and might not even be your money if we say it's not?*

And now everybody — including alert citizens watching from many other countries — waits to see what the next moves are. Let's also note that it's not just the truckers in revolt against insane government mandates; it's also at least half the population of Canada who stand behind the truckers and against the new fashion for tyranny in what used to be called the Free West. I'd venture to guess that the next move will be a general strike that paralyzes Canada and forces its parliament to overrule the Emergencies Act and get rid of PM Trudeau.

Meanwhile, like a coronavirus itself, the trucker protest movement has infected America. A "People's Convoy" is assembling around Barstow, California (the capital of the Mojave Desert, where there's plenty of room to assemble), with a launch date of February 23, next Wednesday, destination: Washington, DC. Won't that be . . . interesting? What will the government of "Joe Biden" do? Likewise invoke some sort of emergency powers? Declare yet another "insurrection" as with January 6, 2021? Mess with the truckers' bank accounts, and those of the people who support them? Do they want to inspire a run on US banks at a juncture where the extreme fragility of the global banking system threatens to blow up financial markets? Standing by on that.

The US government, like Canada's, has likewise been at war with its citizens. At least half the country has awakened to this unappetizing reality — even while somewhat less than half the country still catatonically follows whatever idiotic diktat the despotic bureaucracy spews out. Why, for instance, do so many still go about in face masks even where local regulations are lifted? (And especially in light of the overwhelming evidence that masks don't work?) Answer: to signify that they are *still against Trump*, the evil leviathan said to be responsible for all the woes and injustices in the world and who threatens their "safety"— meaning, their status as oppressed victims of "white supremacy," including the guilty and penitent self-oppressed white people of the Left themselves. Yeah, it's just that simple because we are in an epic episode of human social hysteria.

Except that the hysteria is dissipating for all except the most psychotic or the most politically cornered due to their record of perfidy and bad faith — the David Frums, Max Boots, and Rachel Maddows of our world, the cable news outfits, the Democratic Party hierarchy, the criminally psychopathic swine running the US public health agencies, and the craven doctors who have fecklessly murdered patients at the behest of Dr. Anthony Fauci & Company. Despite the sedulous efforts to suppress the data (O, the sacred data!) about the failure of their "vaccines," the real news is getting out: the "vaccines" don't prevent transmission or infection of Covid-19, and they pose lethal side effects for the vaxed. There it is, in plain English. And yet, "Joe Biden," putative president of the US, is still telling the country to "*go out and get vaccinated, get boosted*" — ???

The companies who produced the "vaccines" are even on the run. Pfizer withdrew its application for an emergency use authorization in India, where the public health agency insisted on seeing the safety records Pfizer was obliged to furnish — and refused to. India is a big market for pharmaceuticals, some 1.39 billion. Pfizer's stock has crashed nearly 10 percent the past two weeks. By the way, some of the states of India are notable for having battled Covid-19 with the mass distribution of early treatment kits containing cheap antivirals such as ivermectin, hydroxychloroquine, vitamin D, etc. The program was famously successful in reducing deaths there.

The CEO of Moderna, Stéphane Bancel, has sold off $400 million of his own stock in the company and deleted his Twitter account on rumors that all-causes deaths reported by US life insurance companies show a shocking and mysterious rise in mortality that just may be attributed to the "vaccines" causing strokes, heart attacks, cancer cases, and immune system failures. (Moderna's stock is also sinking.) Neither the mainstream news media nor the US public health agencies are making any effort to investigate this now well-documented occurrence.

We're in the midst of a tremendous shift of public opinion. Winter is not over but the truth is budding now in a thousand places. The people are done kneeling docilely to be silenced and killed. They will not let this country, and many other nations in the Western civ club, be destroyed without a fight. The unmasked are unmasking their masked antagonists. Stand by, now, to find out who has been behind all this deadly mischief. We will rip off their masks and the rule of law will be restored.

National Assisted Suicide

March 21, 2022

The defining moment last week in America's ongoing mental health crisis was U Penn swimmer Lia Thomas's record-setting win in the NCAA women's 500-yard freestyle championship race. It was celebrated in the sports news as *a thing* — that is, an alleged feature of reality. Lia Thomas began "transitioning" in 2019 when "she" was a full-grown male human being, otherwise known as a "man," and was already competing in men's NCAA swimming events. One thing you can conclude from this is that the board of the NCAA is insane.

It's not the only institution in our country that has lost its mind. Are you comfortable with that? Outside of certain fairy tales involving naked emperors, there is but one greater instance of a people being so willingly insulted by falsehood, namely, the still-continuing campaign to "vaccinate" and "boost" the public against Covid-19 with a genetic cocktail that doesn't work to prevent illness or transmission of disease and has already killed or injured many thousands of people.

Yet they're still out there pimping for the vaxes: Rochelle Walensky of the CDC, Dr. Anthony Fauci, Mary Basset (New York's commissioner of public health), and many other officials in other lands. This is a major part of the scripted suicide of the USA, along with the rest of Western civ. Our government's own Vaccine Adverse Event Reporting System (VAERS) now lists a total of 24,177 pericarditis and myocarditis cases for all of year 2021, and 11,829 cases for just January and February of 2022. Do you see an ominous trend there? Those are but two deadly conditions linked to the vaxes; there are over a thousand more.

The deluded people getting boosted now are taking on board additional toxic spike proteins to the ones they already acquired in the first two shots. Might one predict that quite a few of them will develop a horrifying array of bodily disorders and die or become disabled in the next two years? It might soon even get hard for the woked-up, vaxed-up, Trump-maddened "blue" multitudes to ignore the impending mass murder they have been subjected to.

Such an unappetizing prospect might account for America's reckless poking of the Russian bear over the future of Ukraine, a distraction from the developing picture of national assisted suicide here at home. The prospect of World War Three is apparently more compelling than the emerging information that indicates the US government is killing off its own population, and lying its face off in the process.

"Joe Biden" and company might have prevented Russia's "operation" there by simply reiterating what NATO itself had declared: that Ukraine would not be invited to join the alliance. But Ukraine has been a special client of the USA since 2014, when we changed out a pain-in-the-ass government there. Since then, we've used Ukraine as an international money laundry, a proxy forward base for NATO, and, apparently, a place removed from the USA to set up bioweapons labs when our own government called an at-home moratorium on gain-of-function research in 2014.

Part of the forward base activity in Ukraine since 2014 was the training and arming of the 600,000-troop Ukrainian army, one of the biggest armed forces in the world, which Russia now feels constrained to disarm and neutralize. How successful Russia might be in that endeavor, with an operational force of about 200,000, is the subject of a propaganda war being waged one level removed from the action on the ground.

The reality, as one might expect from such basic troop numbers, has been an onerous grind for the Russians. American javelin missiles have proven deadly to Russian tanks and armored vehicles. But, contrary to the narrative script of CNN and *The New York Times*, Russia is hardly "losing" the contest. Russian forces are in the process of kettling up Ukraine's most potent units, the notorious Azov battalions, along the Donbass line in the east. There are a lot of them. They are surrounded, cut off from their central command, and now given the choice of surrendering or being slaughtered. For the moment, it is Ukraine's choice.

For the Russians, this is, as they say, an existential matter, something they have faced before and understand the stakes of — think Napoleon and Hitler. The US has shown, at least, an exorbitant will to antagonize Russia using Ukraine. This, too, is yet more insanity. In Mr. Putin's early years as head of state, Russia asked to join NATO, in Russia's quest to be treated as a normal European nation after overcoming seventy-five years of Soviet insanity. Request rebuffed.

Twenty years later, and many instances of antagonism in the meantime, Russia had enough. It is doing something America no longer can do: establishing boundaries. Ukraine will not be used as a platform for further antagonisms. Our response: wreck the global economy starting with the international money system, and possibly bring on a world famine by destroying supply lines for fossil fuels and things made from them, such as fertilizer.

Our country is interested only in dissolving boundaries — geographical, as in our boundary with Mexico, behaviorally, as in the boundary between male and female, psychologically, as in the boundary between reality and fantasy, and existentially, as in being alive or dead. And now Russia, at considerable cost, has to teach the USA a lesson in the importance of boundaries. They are going to complete their operation in Ukraine and they'll likely work around the "sanctions" heaped on them. Their part of the world these days has all the production, a great many valuable commodities, and most of the world's population.

Our part of the world seems bent on submitting to self-imposed tyranny and suicide. At least that has been the trend until now. Suddenly information is busting out from all angles penetrating and shattering the dome of unreality we've lived under for years. Yes, those vaxes are killing a lot of people . . . yes, the intel community and the DNC overthrew the previous president . . . yes, every US intel bigwig in the land lied to you about Hunter Biden's laptop . . . yes, that laptop is crammed with hard evidence of bribery and, arguably, treason involving the current president . . . yes, the US economy is tanking because we've borrowed more money than we can ever pay back and we don't produce enough stuff of value . . . and no, Russia is not losing in the Ukraine — rather, Russia is showing the commitment and fortitude of a nation interested in self-preservation. You think we might learn something from that?

A Theory of the Case

April 4, 2022

There was Scott Pelley of CBS's *60 Minutes* on Sunday night — the prime-time slot of the new week — all cued up to run interference for the US State Department (and other Deep State "actors") in the propaganda war over Ukraine. Let's be brutally frank and get this out of the way: can you really trust either the US news media or the US government to tell you the truth?

Of course, you can't. You have been boldly lied to by them with absolute consistency for years now. Common knowledge, which is common sense's twin sister, has it that the CIA "owns" *The Washington Post*, the FBI owns *The New York Times*, and the State Department owns CBS News. All are conduits for official narratives. And since the State Department is most of all responsible for the Russian cleanup operation now underway in Ukraine, you can bet that CBS News is in on the info grift to protect State, its patron.

What Russia had to clean up was the long-building aftereffects of now Under Secretary of State Victoria Nuland's 2014 engineered Maidan coup against the elected government of President Viktor Yanukovych. The issue of that bygone day was a tug-of-war between the US and Russia, with Ukraine as the flag in the middle of the rope. Russia wanted Ukraine in the orbit of its economic "customs union" and the US was affecting to pull Ukraine into the Eurozone and NATO — or, at least, use Ukraine as a forward base for NATO, in order to antagonize Russia.

Russia has been the all-purpose hobgoblin that every US agency and many political personages turn to when they are caught doing something nefarious. When Hillary Clinton's email trove was purloined through her poorly defended illegal home server, Russia was to blame. That fiasco spawned the multiyear RussiaGate operation that bamboozled half the nation and ended up tainting the FBI, the DOJ, the FISA court, and both the House and Senate intel committees.

Then, along came Hunter Biden's laptop, infamously labeled "Russian disinformation" by every retired senior intel spook still drawing a fat pension. The news about the laptop and its lurid contents was strenuously suppressed by every mainstream media company except *The New York Post*, and its coverage was banished from Facebook and Twitter, which so many Americans rely on for news — an obvious and true conspiracy between government, high tech, and the news media.

All this coincided, you understand, with the horror-show official response to Covid-19 coming on the scene at exactly the same time: winter of 2019–20. By then, half the country had already been groomed into a mass formation psychosis over the RussiaGate narrative that declared President Donald Trump was a stooge for Vladimir Putin . . . thus, Trump derangement.

There is the possibility that Covid-19 was hauled onstage deliberately to terrorize the American public, confound Mr. Trump, and prevent his reelection in November 2020. Hence, the panicky scramble ever since spring 2020, among Anthony Fauci, Peter Daszak of the shadowy EcoHealth Alliance, and other public health officials, to ward off the suspicion that Covid-19 was created in the Wuhan lab with American sponsorship, and released for the aforesaid purpose of queering the election. Mr. Daszak notoriously put together a paper for the preeminent British medical journal *The Lancet*, using a roster of medical luminaries to denounce the "lab leak" theory. *The Lancet* eventually had to withdraw the paper. Its reputation will be diminished for years to come, merely one manifestation of medicine's more general moral collapse and eventual total collapse.

Meanwhile, in the winter of 2020 came impeachment number one of Mr. Trump, provoked by CIA White House mole Eric Ciaramella and his companions in sedition Lt. Col. Alexander Vindman of the NSC and intel community inspector general Michael Atkinson. At issue, you recall, was Mr. Trump's phone call with Ukraine's president Volodymyr Zelensky, inquiring about rumored grifting operations among the Bidens in that foreign land. Managing Ukraine, you remember, was in veep "Joe Biden's" assigned portfolio of duties. The impeachment segued seamlessly into the Covid panic, distracting the public's attention from the issues behind the impeachment, namely: what exactly was the Biden family up to in Ukraine, with crackhead Hunter pulling in millions in walking-around money from the Burisma oil and gas company? That turned out to be just the tip of the griftberg.

Ten days before President Trump declared a national emergency over Covid-19 and the ensuing lockdowns, on March 3, 2020, the Super Tuesday primary was held. Joe Biden trailed badly with support in single digits. Somehow, he miraculously trounced the rest of the field. The narrative constructed afterward attributed the miracle to a single endorsement from Congressman Jim Clyburn of South Carolina. (Dominion vote-counting machine hijinks, anyone?)

Voilà: there is your Democratic Party nominee, the former veep "Joe Biden," not altogether sound of mind, compromised by already revealed foreign influence peddling, a malleable figure fronting for a Deep State cabal. Special Covid-19 election procedures (mail-in ballots) shooed him straight into the White House (thanks for your "help," Mark Zuckerberg).

What you have here is an interesting chain of circumstance: Ukraine 2014 . . . the astounding flop of Hillary . . . RussiaGate . . . the mystifying Democratic primary race . . . the Ukraine-based impeachment . . . the Covid-19 fiasco (including deadly mRNA vaccines) . . . the election of "Joe Biden" . . . and now Ukraine again. The American Deep State is in a heap of deep trouble. It's impossible anymore to hide its turpitudes. Even *The New York Times* and the *WashPo* have been forced to confess that Hunter Biden's laptop is for real, including the thousands of incriminating memoranda and emails on it, along with all the selfie-porn and drugging. It's obvious that the "president" of the US is corrupt and compromised. Doesn't look too good.

Additionally, the Deep State must now try to hide the emerging attempted mass murder of the US population via the side effects of the Covid-19 "vaccines." But the information can't be hidden anymore and is, in fact, bursting out from unexpected places, for instance, from the life insurance quarterly actuarial reports, which show unprecedented "all-causes" deaths and injuries among people under sixty years old. We know how this happened. On top of the deadly "vaccines," introduced with falsified trials, the Deep State suppressed early treatment medications (is still at it, in fact), and instead forced protocols with the deadly drug remdesivir. In sum, America's government has capped years of lying and conniving via high tech and the news media by killing its citizens. Rochelle Walensky & Company are still urging the public to vax up and "boost." How is that not criminal?

So Ukraine is back onstage and the Deep State made sure it would be by refusing to rule out Ukraine joining NATO and by arming and subsidizing a large army that has spent eight years shelling and terrorizing the Russian-speaking population of Donbass in eastern Ukraine. Mr. Zelensky apparently was led to believe that NATO would come to his rescue, the poor chump, wherever he really is. CBS News would have you believe that Russia is perpetrating war crimes by bombing hospitals in Ukraine. What they don't tell you is that the hospitals were turned into fortresses by the Nazi-inflected Azov brigades.

They also would like you to believe that the Russian operation is a flop. That is not so, though it surely was not a cakewalk. What's left of the Ukraine army (including its Azov brigades) is cut off from communication, out of diesel fuel, out of ammo, out of food, and soon to be shut down altogether. When that happens, Ukraine will not be used to make needless trouble in the world. The sanctions imposed on Russia have successfully destroyed the financial scaffold of the global economy so that an economic collapse of the nation states in Western civ is a sure thing. The lingering question: will the hardships to come only reinforce America's mass formation psychosis, or will it compel us to wake up and pay attention to the attempted suicide of our country?

NAUSEA RULES

May 6, 2022

The way financial markets puked this week they must have started reading the news. Let's face it, the headlines are a little short of reassuring. The $6.49 price on a gallon of diesel is enough alone to tell you that the nation can't do business the way it's set up to do, and there isn't a new model for running things ready to launch — not even Klaus Schwab's utopia of robots and eunuchs.

What's *out there*, rather, is a model of breakdown and collapse that the woked-up, globalist neo-Jacobins are doing everything possible to hasten. US-inspired sanctions on Russia have quickly blown up in America's face. How's that ban on Russian oil working? Do you understand that US shale oil — the bulk of our production — is exceptionally light in composition, meaning it contains not much of the heavier distillates like diesel and aviation fuel? Tis so, alas. Truckers just won't truck at $6.49 a gallon, and before long they'll be out of business altogether, especially the independents who have whopping mortgages on their rigs that won't be paid. The equation is tearfully simple: no trucks = no US economy.

Europe, the old original homeland of Western civ, isn't just losing face, it's blowing its head clean off going along with "Joe Biden's" economic war. Are Germany, France, and the rest of that bunch really so dead set on jamming Ukraine into NATO that they're willing to go full medieval for it? By which I mean sitting in the cold and dark with empty plates. That's a hard way to go just to prove somebody else's point.

The war in Ukraine itself was apparently losing its sex appeal for the click-hungry news media. No matter which way *The New York Times and friends* tried to spin it, they failed to grok both Russia's determination to neutralize Ukraine and its ability to get the job done, even if it takes a longer than expected grind to finish. That's how important it was to Russia that Ukraine not become a forward missile base and bioweapons lab for its adversaries. When that operation concludes, the West will be left economically crippled and humiliated — which are conditions that historically portend regime change. Will America cough up "Joe Biden" like a hairball to get those trucks running again? Might the Dems themselves resort to releasing the kraken known as Hunter's laptop just to send the old grifter packing?

In the meantime, the leaked *Roe v Wade* cancellation ruling shoved the Ukraine fiasco offstage so as to provoke more useful histrionics for the dreaded midterm elections upcoming. The poorly understood truth is that said ruling will only send the abortion question back to the individual states. But let's get real: places like New York, Massachusetts, Maryland, and California are not going to enact any new anti-abortion laws, and that's where most of the people having hebephrenic breakdowns over the issue live. Which is to say there's little danger that the shrieking denizens of these blue states will lack abortions. So how much has the party only been pretending that *Roe v Wade* is its primal touchstone?

The strange parallel question has been raised: might laissez-faire abortion be a cover for the evident new problem that Covid-19 vaccines have made a shocking number of *birthing people* incapable of reproducing? There's a buzz about it, anyway. It's a fact that Pfizer excluded pregnant and breastfeeding women from all phases of its mRNA trials. Among the various harms now ascribed to the mRNA shots are infertility, miscarriage, and newborn abnormalities. But, of course, that sort of rumor — here coming from cases among vaccinated military personnel and not so easily hushed up — is just what the many lurking censors want to slap down in any forum where ideas could be exchanged. It's *misinformation*!

And so, the derangement volume knob over Twitter changing ownership stays up at 11. Imagine what will happen if the supposedly 70-odd percent of Americans who got vaxed learn in a reliberated Twitter Zone that the Covid-19 vaccines are not "safe and effective." According to Zero Hedge, twenty-six globalist NGOs with ties to George Soros signed a letter saying, "Elon Musk's takeover of Twitter will further toxify our information ecosystem and be a direct threat to public safety, especially among those already most vulnerable and marginalized."

They are, as usual, projecting — since what is a greater threat to public safety than inducing tens of millions of frightened citizens to accept multiple shots of a poorly tested pharmaceutical cocktail that can kill you six ways to Sunday? The folks in charge (and others who would like to be the boss of you) don't want you to know any of this. The pharma companies, the doctors, the hospital administrators, and the politicians must be frantic with terror of being found out.

Altogether, the scene looks like a multidimensional nightmare. Broken economy . . . sinking Western civ . . . police state tyranny . . . vaccine death and injury . . . starvation . . . So, there it is. Oh, look, those markets, they're puking again!

We're in It Now for Sure

May 23, 2022

When I wrote *The Long Emergency* nearly twenty years ago, I never thought that, once it got going, our government would work so hard to make it worse. My theory then was just that government would become increasingly bloated, ineffectual, impotent, and uncomprehending of the forces converging to undermine our advanced techno-industrial societies. What I didn't imagine was that government would bring such ostentatious stupidity to all that.

Obviously, there was some recognition that ominous changes are coming down. Otherwise, we wouldn't have heard so much chatter about alt energy, "sustainable growth," "green" this and that. But the chatter was more symptomatic of wishful thinking for at least a couple of reasons: 1) mostly it ignored the laws of physics, despite the fact that so many people involved in enterprises such as wind and solar energy were science-and-tech mavens; and 2) there was a dumb assumption that the general shape and scale of daily life would remain as it had been — in other words, that we could still run suburbia, the giant cities, Disney World, Walmart, the US military, and the interstate highway system just the way they were already set up, only by other means than oil and gas.

Now, we're finding out the hard way how much daily life must change, and is changing, and how disorderly that process is in every way from the imperative personal adjustments to our spiritual attitudes about them. As with so many things in history, this disorder expresses itself strangely, even prankishly, as if God were a practical joker. Who would've imagined that our politics would become so deranged? That there would be battles over teaching oral sex in the fifth grade? That the CDC would keep pushing vaccines that obviously don't work (and that so many people would still take them)? That stealing stuff under a thousand dollars in value wouldn't merit prosecution? That riots featuring arson and looting are "mostly peaceful"? That we'd send $50 billion halfway around the world to defend the borders of another country while ignoring the defense of our own borders? That financially beset Americans would spend their dwindling spare cash on . . . tattoos?

Notice that all of these strange behaviors have really nothing to do with making practical adjustments to the way we live. The collective psychology of all this is bizarre. Of course, mass formation psychosis accounts for a lot of it. Groups of people under duress, suffering from loneliness, purposelessness, helplessness, and anxiety, will fall into coordinated thought and action if presented with some object or someone to fixate their ill feelings upon.

Donald Trump was such an object. He galvanized about half the country into an intoxicated fury aimed at destroying him. It actually managed to drive him off the scene via a fraud-laced election that many in power (local officials, judges) deemed a means justifying the desired end. That success reinforced their mass formation psychosis. Alas, having succeeded against Mr. Trump, they were left without a galvanizing object to focus on. So they adopted one of the devices of Trump riddance, Covid-19, as the next object of all their distress and anxiety, adopting the mRNA vaccinations as their next savior du jour.

Unfortunately, the vaccination scheme has gone very much awry, and now millions face a future with damaged immune systems. The horror of that is too awful to comprehend, especially by government, which caused the problem in the first place and can't possibly admit it without demolishing its legitimacy ... so it presses on stupidly and heinously with the vaccine program. Already all-causes deaths are substantially up, and in time the recognition of how and why this happened will reach a point of criticality.

It will be too obvious to ignore. But by that time (probably not far away), the economy will be so wrecked, the people of America so deranged, and our circumstances so desperate that the government will resort to a supremely stupid act of national suicide, say, starting a nuclear war. The government under "Joe Biden" seems perfectly disposed to that possible outcome. Which brings us to the spiritual part of the story: those unused to consorting with alleged "higher powers" might consider getting used to prayer.

Lately, a new derangement is overtaking Western civ, for the excellent reason that Western civ gave birth to techno-industrial societies and is now first to undergo the alarming demise of that system. I speak of the World Economic Forum (under one Klaus Schwab) and its stated ambition to *Build Back Better* — based on its unstated premise that the current system must be nudged to its death sooner rather than later, and on purpose. All the governments of Western civ nations seem coordinated on this.

But it's not going to happen as Mr. Schwab and his followers hoped, for at least a couple of reasons. First, as already stated, God is a prankster and likes to throw knuckleballs at the human race. Anyway, the "better" that Mr. Schwab expects is an ultra-techno-industrial "transhuman" scheme that is unlikely to come about if the support system of the older techno-industrial system is no longer available to support it. As currently conceived, BBB depends on electric power, and that is one of the major subsystems of our system that already looks like it's going janky.

You get the idea, I'm sure, so I'll cut to the chase for now. About a year ago I had my French easel set up on a country road nearby and was busy painting a motif at hand when along came a horse-drawn wagon filled with four men in severe black-and-white clothing, wearing beards. They were apparently a bit surprised by the strange sight of me painting a picture and they stopped to chat. They were Amish and had lately moved to the county from down in Pennsylvania, which was running out of farmland for their fruitful people. Not a half hour later a second horse-drawn wagon passed by. I admit, the incident gave me a thrill — not just the sensory pleasure of the horses' ripe animal smell and the gentle rhythm of their clip-clopping along. But since I had lately been writing a bunch of novels about life in a post–economic collapse town like my own (the *World Made by Hand* series), I enjoyed the strange delight of being transported briefly into a scene of my own imagining — the prequel of my own books.

Many more Amish are landing in the county these days. I hear they go around to the failing or inactive farms with bundles of cash and make an offer, just like that. Evidently the method works. It's given me a business idea: to start an Amish skills school, buy a few acres with a barn and hire some Amish men to teach all us non-Amish how to do a few things that might be good to know in the years ahead, like how to harness horses to a cart or a mule to a plow. (The Amish like to make a bit of cash money when they can.) That's my idea of how to build back better. What do you think?

CHILDHOOD'S END

May 27, 2022

The phoniest trope in American life goes like this: we must find the cause of X *so that it never happens again*. Of course, it will happen again. We only pretend that the cause is a mystery. Let's count the ways that school massacres happen.

American schools are fantastically depressing places. They are designed to look like medium security prisons and insecticide factories. They send the message: *Enter here and be psychologically brutalized*. They are too big, overwhelmingly alienating, ugly, devoid of visible symbolism signaling the value of being human. The interiors of the schools are designed for the convenience of janitors, hard surfaces of tile and linoleum that can be hosed down easily like the quarters of zoo animals. Children act accordingly.

The "facilities," as we call them, are deployed in the illegible landscape of a demolition derby, separated from all the other activities of daily life, which themselves have reached a culminating state of meaninglessness: big box shopping, national chain franchise food installations, strip malls of empty storefronts, parking lot wastelands, nothing that will excite a child's imagination with emotions other than bewilderment, anxiety, and aversion.

The "teaching" that supposedly goes on in schools is a broken remnant of preparation for an economy that no longer exists. We're no longer a society of people who do things, but rather a society of people to whom things are done, many of them harmful, humiliating, and arbitrary. America's demoralized teaching corps is so unhinged by their own anomie that they resort to imposing sadistic fantasies on the children in their charge.

Thus, all the inappropriate curricula around adult preoccupations with sex, such as the Drag Queen Story Hour, for which mentally ill men are invited to act out impersonations of women as monsters for young people who can't possibly be expected to make sense of the spectacle. (I suspect that even six-year-olds, hardwired to function as successful animals in this world, understand it as some kind of affront to reality.) Otherwise, American teachers are out of ideas, and are themselves damaged by the same forces in culture that they are now asked to direct.

America has become a malfunctioning pageant without feasible roles that children can realistically project themselves into. What ten-year-old longs to become the Burger King fry-o-later boss in a brown apron and an asinine cardboard crown? Rather, they are prompted to aspire to become sports star millionaires, of which there are perhaps fewer than five thousand positions in a land of 340 million. By age twelve, they probably comprehend the unlikelihood of that outcome, or of becoming the next Kardashian . . . or Spider-Man. (Superheroes are supplied by the entertainment cartels to occupy the imaginative realm of children because American culture is bereft of reality-based roles worth aspiring to.)

In this tumult of cultural impoverishment, psychotic grandiosity creeps in. Be big if you can't be anything else. Hence, one achievable role for young persons in American life is mass murderer. It is a way of becoming important, of having an effect on other people and society in general. Your name may be forgotten, but the act itself will endure in the collective memory of a people. It will be some kind of a mark in history, even better remembered, perhaps, than whoever played third base for the Atlanta Braves in 1994 . . . or the woman who once capered down the red carpet at the Oscars in a dress fashioned on a slaughtered swan.

The mayhem unleashed in a school shooting is just the rectified essence of the manifold derangements in our national life. Everything is out of whack, including our perception of what's going on and what it means. There is almost nothing left of childhood in this land, in the way of young, unformed creatures assisted by adults who love them into a future worth being part of. We have forgotten how to be grateful for coming into this world at all, leaving us unworthy of being here. The quality of virtue, meaning that some things and some doings are recognizably better than others, was deceitfully replaced by the *equity* of nothing being allowed to be better than anything else. Truth and beauty have gone outlaw. Bad faith and wickedness rule, led by a Party of Chaos. So, really, what do you expect? And what do you deserve?

Get Your Monkeypox On

June 10, 2022

The made-for-TV January 6 Capitol riot hearings kicked off last night with tribute video of a whole lot of pissed-off ordinary Americans marching on the stately building where, that fateful day, the final certification ceremony of a blatantly dishonest election was underway after, mind you, four years of seditious machinations by a weaponized bureaucracy aimed at disabling and destroying the sitting chief executive — in case it's unclear why the huge crowd flocked to the capital city in the first place.

The Party of Chaos is playing its hand: a select committee of seven deuces and two jokers. Do they look like they're going to get through this extravaganza without humiliating themselves? You never know what might come out of some witness's mouth, despite the orchestrations of former ABC's *Good Morning America* producer James Goldston, brought in to cement the narrative in the collective public brain, presoftened with years of manifold media mind fuckeries.

It's the centerpiece of their midterm campaign. And I submit that it may be just a little premature as it becomes increasingly clear that the Party of Chaos, led by the "winner" of the 2020 election, "Joe Biden," and unseen handlers, have nearly completed their mission of destroying the USA as an ongoing enterprise. Broken economy, broken health, broken military, broken law enforcement, broken culture, broken morale. They sure got'er done. Do they think nobody noticed?

If the January 6 Committee show is short and sweet, say a few weeks, it will be quickly forgotten in the welling summertime heat as the great masses of America groan under $5 . . $7 . . . maybe $10-a-gallon gasoline prices (or maybe no gas at all) while diesel prices at $6.50 today are already destroying the trucking industry — and thus the entire system for delivering all goods around the country. The zeitgeist is quivering with intimations of food shortages and the philosopher reminds us that any given body politic is just nine missed meals away from bloody rebellion. Have another look at that motley January 6 Committee group photo and consider the lampposts along Pennsylvania Avenue.

It's a dangerous game trying to beat down the population this way, and to what end, exactly? I doubt that even the Blue Team could articulate it — or would dare to — because at this point their sole aim, really, is to hide their many acts of criminality over a span of the past six years and escape prosecution, a compelling motive. And it's getting harder and harder to conceal all that, especially their campaign to physically harm over 200 million people with mRNA "vaccines." The body count is rising — way higher even than deaths from the hypothetical "pandemic" that the "vaccines" were supposedly concocted to vanquish, and spectacularly failed to.

And was this Covid-19 "pandemic" itself cooked up tacitly to disorder the 2020 election with mail-in ballots so easily replicated, harvested, and stuffed by the bale into drop boxes under cover of night? Kind of looks like it, more and more. And now, the Party of Chaos is so keenly desperate to stay out of prison that they apparently seek to repeat the trick in the fall midterm, which is otherwise quite certain to sweep them ignominiously off the game board like so many misplayed quoits.

Thus: monkeypox, the visitation of weeping pustules far more visually horrifying than was Covid-19 in all its spikey iterations, if actually hardly lethal. The hopelessly corrupt CDC has already gotten into the act with its guidance to mask up on airplanes against this new plague. Perhaps travelers would do better wearing condoms on their noses. Apparently, monkeypox spreads by means of intensely intimate flesh-to-flesh contact. The current outbreak popped up following a giant sex rave in the Canary Islands, men having rough sex with other men. Suspicions abound that this monkeypox bears the earmarks of something engineered in a lab. Jeez, d'ya think?

If there is a God, when judgment is at hand, a jury in the court of the angels will bum-rush this Party of Chaos into a special hell of an eternal drag queen story hour, featuring Rep. Adam Schiff (D-Calif.) reading *Uncle Remus* to an assembled multitude of howling Jacobins, Bolsheviks, and Maoist Red Guards. Refreshments will not be served. Ever.

It's Not Working

July 11, 2022

This summer's weather is perfect now in the Hudson Valley: warm, sunny days for primping the garden and cool nights that invite deep sleep. Zucchini and cukes are coming on, along with currants, gooseberries, blueberries. Unseen underground, the potatoes swell. The chickens range happily over their daily smorgasbord of bugs. At midnight, fireflies blink in the orchard. On the human side, though — commerce, culture, and politics — nothing works. At least not here in America. Sigh.The solar electric I installed on the house nine years ago is down. It's supposed to feed that monster called the grid. Since April, I noticed that the electric bill is creeping up way beyond the usual seventeen bucks that the electric company charges home solar producers for the privilege of feeding their system — which, let's face it, has a downside for them because the intermittency of so-called alt energy disorders their operations.

It's counterintuitive. Many people, I'm sure, assume that the more solar units feeding the grid, the better. Strangely, not so. Electric companies work much better when the production and flow of current is absolutely predictable and under their control — like, when *they* decide to fire up the natgas on generator number three or tune down the hydro turbines. It's much harder to run the system with little dribs and drabs of electricity trickling in from hither and yon. But alt energy is good PR for the government, so it does whatever it can to promote or even compel its use.

I got a whopping folio of tax breaks and subsidies from the state and federal government when I decided to put solar electric on my house in 2013, though it finally still cost a lot: $35K. I had intimations of living through a chaotic period of history, and the decision was consistent with my general theory of history, which is that things happen because they seem like a good idea at the time. Getting a home solar electric rig seemed like a good idea.

So, last week, after considerable hassle with my solar company setting up an appointment for a techie to visit and evaluate the problem here, the guy came up (at $150 an hour) and informed me that my charge controller was shot. The charge controller processes all those chaotic watts coming from the solar panels on the roof into an orderly parade of electrons. He also told me that my backup batteries — for running critical loads like the well pump during grid outages — were at the end of their design life. Subtext: you have to get new batteries.

There are four big ones in a cabinet under the blown charge controller and the inverter (for turning direct current into alternating current that is the standard for running things). The techie had some bad news, though. New building codes forbid his company from replacing the kind of batteries I have, which are standard "sealed cell" lead-acid batteries. Some bullshit about off-gassing flammable fumes. Now the government requires lithium batteries, which would cost me $16K more to replace than new lead-acid batteries.

Now, it's theoretically possible for me to replace the less expensive lead-acid batteries — they're still manufactured and sold — but the catch is: I'm on my own getting them and installing them. I'm in the middle of that learning curve right now. These particular batteries cost about $850 each for the four of them, plus a hefty charge for "drop shipping" about three hundred pounds of lead and plastic. I will almost certainly go that way, though. A new charge controller will run about $2K. All together, replacing these components represents a big chunk of change.

At the risk of sounding like some kind of pussy, I confess that this whole business of repairing my solar electric system has put me into a welter of anxiety and fury. I am trapped in the cage of *sunk costs*, a.k.a. *the psychology of previous investment*. Not only do I have $35K (in higher-value 2013 dollars!) tied up in all this equipment — the solar panels themselves, the wall of electronic devices, the conduit, control panels, and digital readouts — but now I have to dump thousands more into it after only nine years. It pisses me off because I should have known better. I walked with eyes wide shut into the pit of techno narcissism.

The hypercomplexity of a home solar electric system is extreme. There are hundreds of little integrated components that can blow, all of it adding up to a case of guaranteed fragility. There are no easy fixes or duct-tape workarounds for any of it. I can't make any replacement parts in my garage. They come from faraway factories via supply lines that get sketchier every day on trucks that don't operate profitably at $6.50-a-gallon diesel fuel.

In a low-grade epiphany while going through this ordeal last week, I realized that back in 2013, instead of getting the solar electric system, I could have bought the Rolls-Royce of home generators and buried a 500-gallon fuel tank outside the garage, *and* had a manual water pump piggybacked onto the well, *and* maybe even purchased a fine, wood-fired cookstove — and had enough money left over for a two-week vacation in the South of France. Silly me.

Of course, these travails with my home solar electric system are a metaphor for the complexity and fragility that is, all of a sudden this year, causing the operations of Western civ to fly to pieces. My investment in solar was as dumb as what the entire nation of Germany did in attempting to run itself on "green energy." (Not to mention its more recent dumbass decision to forgo imports of Russian natgas in order to please the geniuses at Tony Blinken's State Department, the dumb bunnies.)

Of course, even when I get the solar electric back up and running again, something else is sure to go wrong. And in another ten years, the solar panels will be at least half dead. So, if you're reading this personal lamentation, consider bending toward simplicity. Wish I had.

PLAYING CHICKEN
WITH THE FATES

July 29, 2022

Who is surprised that the US government's war on the American people is not going any better than its sponsored war in Ukraine? The only thing the government is really good at is covering up its crimes, which mainly requires them to do nothing — don't investigate anything, don't furnish documents to anyone, don't answer official letters, slow-walk every required action, and otherwise dodge, duck, deny, deflect, and dissemble.

Now, even that game plan is falling apart. Some senior officials in the FBI turned whistleblower this week, perhaps desperate to preserve their self-respect, and finally cleared up one of the great mystifications of our time, namely, how is it that the Hunter Biden laptop, stuffed with incriminating memoranda of bribery, treason, and diverse felonies, and in the FBI's possession for two and a half years now, just sat gathering dust in some sub-subbasement cubby hole — while "Joe Biden," the putative president (or, more likely, the enigmatic claque behind him), was allowed to carry out a demolition of America's economy and culture?

The answer is one Brian Auten, FBI senior analyst, who engineered a scheme to label Hunter's laptop "Russian disinformation," which allowed FBI Director Christopher Wray to throw a switch that turned off any further inquiry in the matter beginning in August before the 2020 presidential election. In turn, other senior FBI officials had all the documents pertaining to the decision process on that matter locked up in a special file that would never see the light of day. Auten's action led to the release of a letter signed by "fifty former intelligence officials" labeling the laptop as a Russian disinfo op — which became the basis for social media to conspire to censor any discussion of the laptop and its contents. And so it was that a political puppet deeply in the pay of foreign interests got shoehorned into the White House. Well, that and widespread election fraud.

Turns out that Agent Brian Auten was also involved in favorably vetting the Steele Dossier when it was used to justify FISA court warrants against figures in Mr. Trump's 2016 campaign, part of the RussiaGate operation that disordered and disabled President Trump's entire four-year term. Well now you know. Perhaps Special Counsel John Durham knows this, too. (If he didn't before, he must now.) Eventually, Mr. Auten will have to answer for all this, maybe after the midterm elections. We must imagine that he will implicate many other familiar figures in the process who were on the scene at the time, including Peter Strzok, Andrew McCabe, and James Comey, comfortably sitting on the sidelines lo these many years enjoying their book royalties and cable news salaries.

Senator Chuck Grassley (R-Iowa), ranking member of the Judiciary Committee, says he will hold hearings about this. When? The Senate is scheduled to be in recess August 6 to September 6 for politicking back home. Maybe after that Senator Grassley will actually produce his whistleblowers in open session — unlike the 2019 first impeachment of Donald Trump, in which chief whistleblower CIA agent Eric Ciaramella, amazingly, never made an appearance. That will be refreshing.

It would also be nice to hear from FBI Director Wray. Did he approve of the decision to label Hunter's laptop "disinformation"? Was he familiar with the contents of the laptop, the emails between Hunter and his business associates and agents of the CCP? Did Mr. Wray happen to examine any of the pornographic videos of orgies with Hunter's stable of Russian whores plus the crack smoking? Did Mr. Wray wonder whether equally bad or worse material was in the hands of Uncle Xi's regime? Did it occur to Mr. Wray that all this might compromise "the Big Guy" in the Oval Office?

It also would be edifying to hear from Mr. Wray's boss, Attorney General Merrick Garland. During his twenty months on the job, has he ever inquired of his FBI what's up with that Hunter Biden laptop? Was he acquainted with the contents? Half the country has seen the videos of Hunter cavorting naked in hotel rooms and lighting up the crystal meth, but not Mr. Garland? There's rumored to be more depraved material on the laptop involving minors that even conscientious auditors outside of government have seen and deemed too atrocious to release. (Copies of Hunter's hard drive are in possession of many people outside government.)

I hope Senator Grassley also calls Lisa Monaco, the deputy attorney general, now at Mr. Garland's right hand, who was formerly President Barack Obama's White House homeland security advisor — a fancy way of describing her role in weaponizing the apparatus of the security state against the Democratic Party's political opponents. Lisa Monaco's current role is *the DOJ fixer* — the person who makes sure that federal law enforcement does nothing about the crimes carried out by Mr. Obama, former CIA Director John Brennan, former Director of National Intelligence James Clapper, and many other now well-known names in the RussiaGate cosmos, as well as continuing to squelch any inquiry on the Biden family's criminal operations.

All of this is going to blow open, of course, and all at the same time that two other big things blow up: 1) the realization that the government lied about everything in the Covid-19 story, including especially covering-up the harmful effects of their vaunted mRNA shots, and 2) deepening US economic chaos, including the implosion of markets, derivatives, banks, and the US dollar.

Some observers say that "Joe Biden" has nothing left except to shove the USA into a hot war. Kind of looks like he's trying — sending US Special Forces to Ukraine's border, and all. I don't think he'll dare cross that line, though. To me, it's more likely that our government will summon, shall we say, a special sort of doctor from the intel community to administer a permanent sleeping med to the Big Guy. Did you see how bugeyed he was on video the other day? Didn't even blink for the longest time. Looks like he badly needs sleep . . . a big sleep . . . the biggest sleep there is. Wait for it.

CRAZYLAND

August 22, 2022

Economic and cultural suicide is hardly the only option, and certainly not the best...

In a confab of friends on a warm evening this weekend, someone asked: Do you think what's going on is due to incompetence or malevolence? The USA is certainly skidding into a great and traumatic reset featuring a much lower standard of living for most citizens amidst a junkyard of broken institutions. But so are all the other nations of Western civ. If it's not being managed by malign forces, such as der Schwabenklaus and his WEF myrmidons, then it sure looks like some sort of controlled demolition. The big question hanging over the 2022 election, then, is: Must America commit suicide?

What provoked the mental illness of the Left? What turned the Democratic Party into the Party of Chaos? It seemed pretty sane in 1996 when President Bill Clinton declared — to much surprise — in his State of the Union address that "the era of big government is over." Of course, few understood back then how cravenly corrupt the Clintons were, even especially as Hillary launched her own political career once Bill's *turn* was over. Few, I daresay, thought at the time that Hillary would come to eclipse Bill in influence — though more came to suspect that the first lady operated as the demented megalomaniac she has proved to be.

Gawd knows what went on in that Shakespearean marriage . . . but the Democratic Party in the post-2000 Hillary years discovered that its very existence required the government to get ever bigger because the American economy — the real, on-the-ground economy outside Wall Street's financialization hall of mirrors — was withering away with the offshoring of industry and something was needed to replace it. And, by the way, let's stipulate that the Republican Party mostly abetted all that, even despite transient rumblings from its Tea Party renegades.

Forgive me at this juncture for repeating my oft-stated theory of history: *Things happen because they seem like a good idea at the time.* Offshoring seemed like a good idea at the time. Fob off all those filthy, polluting factories onto other countries, and pay the natives three bucks a day to make all the stuff we needed.

Plus, pay for the stuff with US treasuries (IOUs). What a racket! But then every activity in America was turning into a racket — which is to say, making money dishonestly — until it became the immersive economic milieu of the land. Even the two most noble endeavors in our society, education and medicine, disgraced themselves with shameless moneygrubbing.

Something weird happened starting in 2004 when one Barack Obama came onstage at the Democratic convention that nominated the haircut in search of a brain called John Kerry. The new star lit up the joint posing as a Great Uniter. And four years later he made a fool of Hillary, cutting her off at the pass from seizing her supposedly ineluctable *turn* — and supreme glass-ceiling breakthrough triumph — as president. Where'd he come from? This pavement-pounding community organizer with the thousand-watt smile?

In retrospect, Barack Obama appears to have been manufactured out of some misty Marxist cabal of the Far Left that infested a subbasement of the Democratic Party. He came onboard in 2009, just as all that skeezy financialization blew up the banks and launched the era of government rescue operations that heaped previously unimaginable quantities of debt on the USA's already unmanageable burden. Republican George Bush II got the blame for all that and Mr. Obama proceeded to make it a lot worse.

Barack Obama served as liberalism's bowling trophy, the capstone of the great civil rights crusade: a black president, proof of America's moral uprightness. He managed to do next to nothing to change the conditions that had wrecked black America — namely, the paternalistic policies that shattered families — but he put up a good front while the country teetered economically. And notice that his DOJ, under Attorney General Eric Holder, managed to avoid prosecuting anyone but mortgage vampire Angelo Mozilo for all the banking crimes of the day. Meanwhile, President Obama *took care* of Hillary by anointing her secretary of state, from which perch she grifted tens of millions of dollars into the coffers of the janky Clinton Foundation. Smooth moves there. In the end, Mr. Obama remained an enigma, passing the baton to Her Inevitableness in 2016 — which she commenced to blow utterly in overestimating her own political charm — she had none — and underestimating the appeal of her opponent, the Golden Golem of Greatness, Donald Trump.

Mr. Trump's astonishing victory apparently disordered Hillary's mind. She was reportedly too drunk late that election night to even appear at the podium to make the excruciating concession speech. But her Russian collusion operation ginned up months earlier had already set in motion a great vengeance machine that partisans in the DOJ, FBI, CIA, and State Department ran with through the whole of Mr. Trump's term in the White House, climaxing in the orchestrated election frauds of 2020, which installed Barack Obama's empty vessel of a stand-in "Joe Biden" as president.

The amalgamated pathologies of Barack Obama's reign — which includes the birth of Wokery, the Jacobin-Marxist crusade to trash culture and economy — and Hillary Clinton's psychotic thirst for revenge has transformed the Democrats into the Party of Chaos, presiding over the suicide of America, and Western civ with it. Which, of course, prompts the question: Who exactly is running Barack Obama? I don't pretend to know at this point. Many people I know are sure it is an international banking claque. The part that doesn't add up is the supposed banking claque's utter lack of political charm. Nobody in Western civ is for them, in the sense that they offer any salvation program from either the disorders of woke culture or the disorders of crumbling economic globalism.

Mysteries abound now, and they are disconcerting to an extreme. How did the polite and rational society called Canada fall under the punishing sway of Justin Trudeau? Ditto the apparently insane Australia and New Zealand? Ditto the Europeans, who followed America's absurd campaign to make Ukraine a war zone, and who now face a winter with no fuel for industry or home heating — and possibly a descent into new medievalism. Perhaps the Covid bamboozle did that, just drove them over the edge. (And they will soon learn what a deadly con that was, especially the "vaccine" feature.)

Personally, I think we underappreciate the tendings of history per se, and that tending these days is the set of circumstances adding up to a Long Emergency, a.k.a. the Fourth Turning, a.k.a. Mr. J. M. Greer's Long Descent. In plain English, we're exiting the techno-industrial fiesta of the past two hundred–odd years and entering the uncharted territory of what-comes-next, and that is driving the immense anxiety of the age. Our business model for everything is broken, mostly because the fossil fuel situation has become so uncertain, and it is driving us nuts. Understand that and you will have enough mental equipment operating correctly to stay sane.

Suicide is hardly the only option. Resist those who want to drag you into it. We are going to carry on one way or another. We're going to make it through this bottleneck. Let the insane bury the insane. Keep your eyes peeled, keep your hearts open, and keep your powder dry.

Soul Man

September 2, 2022

I knew Abe Lincoln, and that was no Gettysburg Address . . .

I knew we were in for *the business* with that "soul of the nation" buildup ballyhoo, but I didn't exactly expect Independence Hall to be decorated in blood red and sepulchral black à la the mouth of hell for a sermon by the Lord of the Flies himself. Somehow his staff managed to get the Old Trickster to the fiery podium on time, where, in his trademark inside-out and upside-down mode of argument, he inveighed wrathfully against the "grave threat to democracy" posed by an opposition laboring to undermine "our personal rights . . . the pursuit of justice [and] the rule of law." Roger that, Kemosabe.

I confess, I was hoping to see MAGA superhero Homey D. Clown materialize in a puff of rainbow-colored smoke right up there beside the sulfurous incarnation of "Joe Biden."

"MAGA Republicans have made their choice," the hypothetical president shouted. "They embrace anger . . . they live, not in the light of truth, but in the shadow of lies."

"I don't think so," Homey would have surely retorted. Upon which, Homey whaps the Party of Chaos's front man upside his hair-plugged noggin with a sock full of Milk Duds. "Homey don't play that."

So much for reveries of true righteousness.

And thus went this watershed moment in our floundering nation's politics du jour. Did you catch an odor of desperation in that marvelous spectacle? A politician does not declare war on half the country in a spirit of comity. Something's up in this land and it don't feel all comfy cozy as we turn the corner on our election season. A lot of things are up, in fact, all of them kind of sketchy and dark.

"Joe Biden's" guardian of the rule of law, the DOJ under Merrick Garland, is on a rampage, not just seeking long prison sentences on J6 misdemeanor defendants, but now going after their very attorneys, officers of the court, for daring to represent them. There is the recent Mar-a-Lago caper, of course, in which the FBI snatched a bale of documentary evidence Donald Trump had collected detailing these agencies' four-year campaign to overthrow him. And, having gotten their mitts on it, the AG declared all the material part of a bogus "ongoing investigation" in order to prevent the docs being introduced in Mr. Trump's just-opened defamation and racketeering lawsuit against HRC, her posse of lawfare ninjas, and most of the people who worked in leadership of the FBI and DOJ circa 2016–2021. In short, the FBI stole evidence of their own prior crimes to evade prosecution. Something tells me that's not going to work out so well for AG Mr. Garland and Chris Wray of the FBI.

You realize, don't you, that all of "Joe Biden's" scripted maundering about "democracy" and "justice" and "the rule of law" is a smoke screen sent up to hide the many crimes committed by his shadowy managers just now breaking into disclosure, and they are running out of dodges and distractions to divert the pliable center of the voting public from seeing it all.

Following Mark Zuckerberg's epic mistake telling Joe Rogan that the government used his company, Facebook, and Jack Dorsey's Twitter, to squash the First Amendment, the wheels came off any pretense that this was not direct interference in the 2020 election by activists in government. For a whole year, the FBI sat on evidence that candidate "Joe Biden's" family was running an international grifting operation fronted by his son Hunter, and when news reports about the notorious laptop began to leak out, the agency used its considerable powers of intimidation to make the news disappear. Now the FBI fears the next step: who exactly in the agency managed that operation along with supervisory agent Timothy Thibault — hustled into retirement days ago after lawyering up — and who, in that exceedingly hierarchical org, approved of it? It's all coming out now.

Thursday night, "Joe Biden" heralded a US economy firing on a gazillion cylinders. "American manufacturing has come alive across the heartland, and the future will be made in America, no matter what the white supremacists and the extremists say," he declared. Is that so? Of course not. The country is verging on an economic catastrophe more consequential than the Great Depression of the 1930s, and the harbinger of it, a financial market crash, is sure to occur before November 8. Everybody and his uncle on Wall Street knows that. The shadow regime behind "JB" knows that. He didn't dare mention the word "inflation," as if no one has noticed it. (Anyway, white supremacists did that.)

The regime is backpedaling so hard on its Covid-19 bullshit that it has burst clean through the looking glass it rode into in 2021, when, in the name of "choice," it mandated that millions of Americans submit to forced shots of unsafe and ineffective pharmaceuticals. They know we are entering another flu season with those millions of people tragically left with wrecked immune systems courtesy of the vaxes. They see the numbers of mystery deaths happening right now in this country and the rest of Western civ and they're working furtively to attempt to change the story. Guess what? It's not working. Too many people have seen the damage firsthand. We know exactly who is responsible for all that, and it's not white supremacists.

The war in Ukraine instigated by "JB" & Company hasn't panned out so well on any grounds — as a distraction from problems at home, as a geopolitical gambit against Russia, or as anything remotely beneficial to Ukraine itself. The endgame on all that approaches as Germany and the rest of NATO are forced to the negotiating table, with or without the USA's cooperation, or else face a rapid return to the thirteenth century. The terms will end up being more embarrassing than the exit fiasco a year ago from Afghanistan. The voters will notice it had nothing to do with white supremacists. Yes, they will.

"I give you my word as a Biden, I've never been more optimistic about America's future," the old faker intoned last night. His word as a Biden? So sayeth the *Soul Man*.

LABOR DAY ASSESSMENT

September 5, 2022

Uncertainty rules at the top of our slide into the dark half of the year.

There will be a Great Reset, of course, but it's not exactly the one that Western civ is blabbering about — a mere shuffling of political and financial protocols. It's happening with or without "Joe Biden," the EU, and der Hoch Schwabenklaus, though the aggregate stupidity they represent is surely making the entry process worse. The Great Reset is what happens when the business model goes bust for powering the world with oil and other fossil fuels — even if there is quite a bit of all that stuff left in the ground. Years ago, I called it the Long Emergency.

Everything emanates off of that, including the astonishing bouts of mischief made in attempts to work around it, assign the blame for it, grub money off it, and shift the effects of it from one group of people or one region of the world to another. Steve St. Angelo says it neatly: "Energy drives the economy; finance steers it." That's so. When the oil business model broke in 2008, industrial society lost its mojo and, after that, finance steered it into a ditch.

The Great ReSet is an emergent phenomenon. It unspools naturally out of circumstances that reality presents. It goes its own way and we have to adapt to it, like it or not. Is our climate changing? Maybe. But so what? The climate has changed many times since the Bronze Age. If preventing that is actually out of the question, which it is, then what else are you going to do? The answer is: adapt intelligently to new conditions. When you clear away all the mental resistance to that — which amounts to a titanic struggle to keep things just the way they are — you're going to have to make changes anyway.

America was, for a time, the greatest industrial society and now that appears to be over. The disorder in all the moving parts of it is probably too gross to arrest at this point. We shoved it into disorder by making some very bad choices, like getting rid of our factories and squandering our wealth on an absurd suburban living arrangement. Shale oil was a financial stunt to keep our setup going a little longer. It was part of the colossal debt rollup — the *steering* function of finance — that was used to compensate for our actual loss of mojo, and now that gambit has hit the wall. You can't pretend to issue more debt when everyone knows it can never be paid back.

Europe, the old home base of Western civ, never got around to shale oil, and its financial structure was such — reckless bond issuance with no fiscal accountability whatsoever — that now it is collapsing faster and worse than America. Europe's leadership is clearly insane and it will likely be overthrown before long. The foreign minister of Germany, the winsome Annalena Baerbock, promised last week to keep demonizing Russia to support Ukraine's black hole of racketeering "no matter what my German voters think or how hard their life gets." Stand by to see how that goes over.

The angst around these circumstances is expressing itself in a generalized political nervous breakdown featuring the sort of tragicomic behavior previously confined in lunatic asylums. Have you ever seen anything more patently insane than the sexual confusion acted out in American schools? Drag queen story hours? Litter boxes in the bathrooms for students who *identify* as "furries"?

That was the funny part. The Covid-19 event is no joke — rather a psychopathic mass murder. Obviously, it was no accident. We have a pretty good idea who made it, and set it loose into the world. And the "vaccine" response looks plainly malevolent at this point. Yet the Covid episode is shot through with mystery. How did all those sedulously trained doctors get so mind-fucked as to persist in saying the "vaccines" were safe and effective, when the vaxes were obviously killing and maiming people? They're still stuck in that disgraceful posture, busy punishing their colleagues who demur, and dishonoring medicine — not to mention the thousands of public health officials still pushing vaxes and boosters to this day. We can attribute that to mass formation psychosis, but even that reeks of mystery. Maybe, as the old American hymn goes, *farther along we'll understand why*.

Anyway, and in the meantime, we're obliged to see where all this is taking us and what we have to do about it. The survivors of this disorder will be living in a world of generalized contraction, facing much-reduced standards of living. All the giant enterprises will be gone, including probably the federal USA government as we know it, and all the supports it offered. We'll be gravely disappointed by the failures of advanced technology to mitigate any of this, and much of that technology will disappear, including reliable electric service and the internet. Whatever you do will have to be much more local and, in one way or another, these activities will revolve around growing food.

I called it a *World Made by Hand* in the cycle of four novels I churned out between 2008 and 2017. You can look there for a detailed, graphic description of how this new disposition of things might work. The society depicted is still recognizably *an American culture*, and the people still find joy, purpose, and meaning in being here on this planet, despite the reduction in comfort and convenience. In many ways, it is a world in recovery from the ravages of the super high velocity way of life we're leaving behind, and because of that it is shot through with grace. That is our destination.

Keep that in mind — if you still have a mind — as you witness the unravelings ahead. This is not the end of the world or the end of the human project in this world. Not everybody will be violent or insane and the number of reality-based people with their emotional equipment intact will, oddly, grow in proportion as the others depart this plane of existence. For some of us, this is a movie with a happy ending. Make some popcorn while there is still some corn, and some electricity to pop it with.

HERE IT COMES

September 9, 2022

The frolics of summer are done, the day shortens, the sky darkens, the suspense deepens . . . Labor Day is in the rearview mirror and the long, sickening slide into we know not what (but it can't be good) commences! Well, there are a few things we know, but only in the shaggy outlines because the folks who are supposed to inform us — the news media, the public health gang — like to keep the real action behind a scrim of unicorns cavorting through a rainbow-lit candyland. Of course, we are not all the idiots they want us to be.

Here's one thing we sort of know: you-all vax-happy woksters are about to have a new BA-5 bivalent booster laid on you. The Darwin Award season has been extended at least another six months! You'll be glad to hear it's been tested in a trial involving eight lab mice, and quickly approved by our FDA. The bad news is that all eight mice got Covid. The worse news is that the booster was wildly inconsistent in producing antibodies among the eight identical mice, meaning the ultimate effect on their immune systems is a crap shoot — but, hey, they're only mice.

Thus, some more good news: humans were so far spared any testing for this new miracle treatment. Pfizer and Moderna didn't hurt anyone in any cobb-job trials, like they did the first time around (hiding the results). The not so good news is: nobody, especially no one in the FDA, has any idea what effect the new booster will have on humans. The best news is that our beneficent government will only make the new vax available to people who are already vaxed. You have to be "eligible," in the club, so to speak. Aren't you special! I never joined that club, so it works for me.

I'd suppose, though, that a lot of people who originally joined the vax club will demur from pharma's latest offering. Actually, most of them. Perhaps they've heard that each shot drains more mojo from your immune system. Perhaps they've heard about friends and relatives who developed sudden vicious cancers, neurological difficulties, vascular disasters, or lingering, unshakable Covid symptoms. Suppression of news has been epic, of course, but surely you're aware that Justin Bieber lost the use of half his face six months ago. No world tour for Justin.

Another thing we know (this one for certain): a new leading cause of death throughout Western civ in people under sixty is "cause unknown." At least that's the official designation because the officials running public health and the medical establishment don't want to know what's killing people. Or, more precisely, they don't want you to know, so they pretend not to know.

If they suddenly felt the itch of curiosity, they might discover that the mRNA shots were behind the spread of Sudden Adult Death Syndrome (SADS) — the interchangeable and equally ambiguous tag for this mystifying phenomenon. That might suggest to a Nancy Drew–level medical sleuth that mRNA vaccines are not good for you, not "safe and effective," that is, meaning that the entire two-plus-years of vaxing up roughly 260,000,000 Americans has been a fraud, which would vacate Moderna's and Pfizer's liability shield for these products. Cue every lawyer born after 1940.

Another thing we know for sure now is that people who are vaccinated are far more likely to catch Covid and also more likely to be hospitalized for it. One in fourteen Brits are currently infected with it, mainly the vaxed-and-boosted. The media propaganda is full of people bragging that their bout of Covid, or several bouts of Covid — from which they were supposedly immune — "could have been much worse." Actually, for many of the vaccinated, it is much worse. They don't hear about it because the news media won't tell them, and the news media executives do what their commissars in government and pharma tell them to do. "Jump!" ("How high?")

A federal judge this week ordered the White House, Anthony Fauci, Secretaries Becerra and Mayorkas, and a slew of other US officials to surrender their email correspondence with social and news media companies in the matter of government working to suppress the First Amendment and, in the censoring, deplatforming, and defaming of many individual citizens who attempted to present views of the Covid melodrama contrary to the official narratives. This was in a suit brought by state Attorneys General Eric Schmitt (MO) and Jeff Landry (LA). From it, a million more lawsuits for personal injury may bloom. Mark Zuckerberg let the cat out of the bag days ago as to how the FBI leaned right on him.

Prepare for an avalanche of unwelcome news evading the censors as we slide out of summer into the *cold and flu* season, as it's called. Hundreds of millions throughout the highly vaxed nations will be walking around with crippled immune systems. The life insurance companies may require a bailout, from all those "unknown causes" that killed people. But so will every other institution in Western civ.

Alas, the money for that is fated to go up in a vapor later this fall as history's greatest margin call gets underway. Let's face it, Europe and North America are sloughing off their industrial economies and the financialization racketeering underneath all that doesn't produce anything of value. Seventy percent of the pubs in the UK are shuttering because they can't pay the electric bill. Germany is just flat out hanging itself the basement. The euro is going to trash.

A little birdie told me to expect a last gasp stock market rally the next ten days, with the Dow nearing 35,000. What a setup. Markets are truly diabolical the way they prey on human wishes. God help the suckers watching CNBC.

Following his Mouth of Hell speech last week, declaring war on half the country, "Joe Biden's" prospects are dimming along with sclerotic circuits in his brainpan. The Party of Chaos is desperate to survive the midterm election. Therefore, look for it to grudge up an excuse to make them not happen. They need a "national emergency" and they'll manufacture one if necessary. Wait for it.

A postscript. The seemingly everlasting presence of Queen Elizabeth has peacefully departed this plane of existence. The old girl had a mighty good run, perhaps the best that will ever be, temporally at least, for any sovereign outside the sci-fi movies. This leaves Britain and its chattel domains with a king, Charles III. I've long identified, in a halfassed way, with this quirky fellow. We were born only a month apart, and I've witnessed all of his agonizing endless wait for the electric moment when he would rise to the crown and scepter.

Charles was very active in midlife in the New Urbanist movement, as I was. I gave some talks in those years to the Prince's Charities Foundation, though I never met the guy. He did some really nice work, notably building the walkable town of Poundbury, Dorset, which he sponsored as a demonstration project to show that England would benefit from quitting its mode of suburban sprawl — which it most surely must do now with all its oil and gas problems.

There is chatter that King Charles has lately become a tool of der Hoch Schwabenklaus and his World Economic Forum, with its satanic program for revising the human project into a nanobot horror show. I hope that is not so. The world needs a lot of help right now, and not from that gang. Here's wishing Charles an upright and valiant go at the kingship thing, at least lending some honest moral support to his floundering country.

We're Coming for You

October 14, 2022

*Slip slidin' away . . . Slip slidin' away . . . You know the nearer your
destination the more you're slip slidin' away*   —Paul Simon

Have you noticed, as the election looms, the Party of Chaos trips deeper into its own self-created chaos? Turns out that the effort to make Ukraine the fifty-first state is not going over so well with the voters. Nor is the campaign to convince children to switch sexes. Or the crusade to sell ever more mRNA "vaccines" that the CDC knows good and gosh darn well are killing and maiming credulous citizens by the millions. Or the program for importing limitless alien "vibrance" across the open border with Mexico. As the venerable Rolling Stones sang more than a half century ago: "*Rape . . . murder . . . it's just a shot away!*" This is the kind of country that the Party of Chaos has been grooming you up for.

It's not working. We are coming for you: leaders, mesmerized minions, and obliging tools of this satanic faction that seized the levers of power in America and turned them into wrecking bars. After the nervous hiatus from November to January, we're coming for you in 2023. You are going to answer for the decisions you took and the rules you made that drove our country to its knees and half out of its mind. We are storming you in your Kafka's Castle of lies and malice, and we are going to drag you out of there kicking and screaming. Preserving your decorum will not be our first consideration, Rochelle Walensky, Tony Fauci, Alejandro Mayorkas, Merrick Garland, Christopher Wray, and the people who work for you.

There's a lot of loose talk about some as yet unknown Party of Chaos ploy to stave off the November 8 reckoning — say, drag out the vote count for weeks and confabulate the results . . . declare some emergency to shut down in-person voting . . . or somehow postpone the vote altogether. Nothing like that will go over successfully this time around. The lampposts in the Walmart parking lots could be decorated with dangling local election officials who get caught churning phony ballots, tweaking Dominion machines, and taping up the polling places' windows with cardboard.

You're getting no help, meantime, from the folks who run the maundering flunky you installed as president. They just flipped off Sergey Lavrov's invitation to negotiate some reasonable end to your $60 billion–plus orchestrated fiasco in Ukraine. These are the people that party apostate Tulsi Gabbard identified lately as "an elitist cabal of warmongers driven by cowardly wokeness." She got that exactly right, and at exactly the right moment in history, too.

Did you actually propose, Secretary of Defense Lloyd Austin, that the purpose of our misadventure in Ukraine was "to weaken Russia"? How's that working out? I'll tell you: Russia is fixing to wipe up the floor with its Nazi antagonists in Kiev (and their NATO helpers). Russia is proceeding with prudence and determination to neutralize our country's foolish provocations, even despite "Joe Biden's" admission that "Armageddon" is an option. Here's some news for you, Party of Chaos: Russia is not insane, but you surely are. You, Lloyd Austin, are busy destroying the American military with your deranged sexual boundary bamboozle, and your sinister "vaccine" policies that have led, among other disasters, to a tripling of cancer rates in the ranks. What, exactly, have you succeeded in weakening?

Do you think the American people have failed to notice this? How are those financial sanctions working against Russia, Tony Blinken, Victoria Nuland, Jake Sullivan, and Susan Rice? Here's how: they energized trade relations and financial settlements between Russia and the 70 percent of the economic world that is outside the orbit of Western civ. Meanwhile, they drove the birthplace of Western civ (Europe) to its knees, upon which it is sliding headlong back to the twelfth century. Who told you to do that? George Soros? Klaus Schwab? (Oh, by the way, we're coming for the two of them also, if they're still alive in 2023 — are you listening Bill Gates?)

We've also had enough, Party of Chaos, of your "Green New Deal" and climate change bullshit. The former is a sheer shuck and jive. You propose to mandate the end of gasoline-powered cars in favor of electric cars that charge off of fossil fuel–fired power plants? That's rich. Ironically, though, the whole mass-motoring matrix is failing not on the basis of whatever powers a car but on the simple fact that a sinking middle class, whose destruction you engineered, can't afford to buy any kind of car anymore, whatever way it's powered.

As for your climate change hysteria, consider that human culture has gone through scores of climate swings since the age of the pharaohs; the main ones being the Bronze Age warming, the Hellenic cooling, the Roman warming, the Dark Age cooling, the medieval warming, the Little Ice Age cooling, and now the present-day warming — with evidence that we are slipping back into another cooling.

The truth is that it has always been difficult for civilizations to adapt to these events, but it's especially difficult for us with our supercomplex, mutually dependent, hypertech systems of daily life, not to mention the giant scale of it all, which pretty much guarantees a hard landing for us. We're not going to run Walmart, Walt Disney World, and the suburbs on any combination of wind, solar, and recycled Frymax oil, so stop pretending, and quit making everything worse than it has to be. We've got to make other arrangements for sure, and that will be hard enough — but no thank you on that transhumanist robot utopia you're trying to sell.

Well, of course, you'd never quit trying. You just have to be defeated. And that's exactly what's going to happen. And after you're defeated, we're going to come for you, and stuff your asses into those witness chairs, and compel you to come clean on why you worked so hard to destroy the USA. Maybe you'll apologize. You should be the first to know, though, that it won't matter. When did anyone's apology ever induce in *you* something besides the demonic lust to inflict more pain on your victims?

COCKAMAMIE STORY

October 31, 2022

All the narratives spun by the Party of Chaos are falling apart now, but this final fiasco, a mere week before the midterm election, is a humdinger with a cherry on top.

It's been several days since San Francisco police interrupted a hammer fight between Paul Pelosi — husband of House Speaker Nancy — and his "friend . . . David," in the Pelosis' Pacific Heights home, and apparently the cops have not asked David DePape why he was there in the first place. Odd, a little bit. Is it possible that a whole chain of authorities from the San Francisco Police Department (SFPD) clear up into the top of the US government and its Democratic Party sidekicks don't want you to know what actually happened?

So far, not much in this cockamamie story adds up. Quite a bit is known now about the attacker, David DePape. He was a colorful character on the scene in radical Berkeley across the bay, a "nudist activist" and BLM supporter. He'd lived there and had a child with one Oxane "Gypsy" Taub, a fellow nude activist and whack job, who has spent time in prison for child abduction. That partnership ended seven years ago and DePape has been homeless on and off since then. Acquaintances and Berkeley neighbors describe him as not mentally healthy, saying he exhibits psychotic delusions and is sometimes incoherent.

So far, police have not disclosed how DePape journeyed from Berkeley to Pacific Heights at 2:00 o'clock in the morning, about fourteen miles. Did he walk from Berkeley across the Bay Bridge and then halfway across town? Mr. DePape is apparently also known to the police as a gay hustler, that is, a person who sells sex for money. Unless I'm mistaken, the SFPD has a detective department — experienced men and women who go around the city seeking clues, evidence, and testimony in order to make sense of perplexing crimes — and then solve them! Shall we assume they are on the job?

Now, Paul Pelosi, eighty-two, who made a $300 million fortune running a car service (also shrewd investments in real estate and the stock market), has been in quite a bit of trouble this year. On May 28, 2022, he was arrested for Driving Under the Influence (DUI) in Napa (near a vineyard estate he owns with Nancy) when his 2021 Porsche crashed into a 2014 Jeep driven by one "John Doe" (as the police identified him). KGO-TV, ABC's affiliate in the San Francisco area, said that there was a second person in the Porsche with Pelosi at the time of the accident. He has never been identified.

In August, Mr. Pelosi was sentenced to five days in jail, a fine of roughly $7,000, a three-month drinking-and-driving course, eight hours of public service, and having an "interlock" device installed on his car that would require him to blow into an alcohol sensor before the engine can ignite. By any chance, were the Napa police or the county court contacted in the matter at some point by the US Capitol Police or the FBI? We may never know.

If David DePape didn't walk fourteen miles from Berkeley to Pacific Heights, or take a cab (expensive), how did he get there? Here's a theory: he rode the BART subway from Berkeley to the Church Street and Mission station in the city, a five-minute walk to the Castro, San Francisco's fabled gay district. Sometime before 2:00 a.m. closing time, he met up in a bar there with Paul Pelosi, who drove DePape to the Pelosi house in a car not equipped with an interlock device. That is to say, David DePape was let into the house by Mr. Pelosi.

The police and the news media have theorized that DePape broke into the place by smashing a glass door in back. Uh-huh. Ask yourself: would there not be an alarm system at least on all the ground-floor windows and doors in the house? Would there not be security cameras on the back side of the house — the side that burglars might prefer, if they could get over the wall? Would the Speaker of the House, with a discretionary budget on top of a $300 million fortune, and in a time of epic political rancor, not have a team of security guards in place at her private home?

Initial news media chatter had both DePape and Paul Pelosi dressed in their underwear, struggling over a hammer, which turned out to belong to Mr. Pelosi. Not until the police entered the house did DePape wrest the hammer from Mr. Pelosi and commence to brain him with it. What does the arrest report actually say about the two men's state of dress? It is not public information. How and why were the police just watching until DePape assaulted Mr. Pelosi — who was hospitalized afterward and had surgery on his cracked skull? (Uh, how did a blow that literally broke his skull not kill the elderly Mr. Pelosi?)

The news media initially suggested that somebody — a third person on the scene — opened the door to let the police in. Now they are saying no such person was there. Was the front door unlocked? (Weird, considering the general threat level for a public figure of Nancy P.'s stature.) Or did police break the glass door in the rear of the house to get in? (However, photos of the door show the glass being broken from the inside and shards spread over the outside.) Odd, also, that such a wealthy and powerful couple would not have hard-to-smash security glass on such a door. (It's easy to buy.) Odd, too, that there was not one human security guard on the premises. The house had security cameras all over the exterior and interior. No mention in the news media or from the SFPD of what might have been recorded by these cameras at the time of the incident.

My assessment of this bizarre episode as follows: Paul Pelosi was out drinking late the night of the incident. He hooked up with David DePape, a hustler he might have been previously acquainted with, and took him back to the house in Pacific Heights. Something went wrong with the transaction. Considering that DePape exhibited psychotic behavior at times, it might have taken little to set him off. All the authorities involved are playing it coy, but failing to construct a narrative that adds up.

The Democratic Party has attempted to convert the sordid incident into a political talking point, painting DePape as a MAGA crazy. That spin apparently failed almost instantly. Their next effort will be to shove the story down the memory hole — the news media will just not report on any developments. Meanwhile, Nancy Pelosi put out a statement that her family is "heartbroken" over the incident. Yes, of course. I'm sure. Nobody knew about Paul Pelosi's peccadillos. Boo-hoo. Cry me a river, you degenerate jade. Don't suppose the truth about this will be successfully suppressed, like Hunter B.'s laptop. And so, the career of Nancy Pelosi comes to an ignominious end in the November 8 election, with a cherry on top of personal humiliation. She deserves every bit of it.

THE FOUR FUCKERIES

November 28, 2022

"We want to save the planet, and the life upon it, but we're not willing to pay the price and bear the consequences. So we make up a narrative that feels good and run with it." — Raul Ilargi Meier

I doubt there is another era in the history of Western civ when the forces in motion acting on society were so mystifying to those acted upon. And isn't it especially galling that this is so in an age *after* rational scientific practice had decoded so many of nature's secrets? Did that project somehow fail in the end? Has the Enlightenment been defeated? How have we become trapped like frogs being boiled haplessly in our own pond water?

I have reduced these forces to four obvious streams of the sheerest seemingly evil fuckery, which is to say nefariously managed events meant to harm us. They are surely all related in some way. Let's try to demystify them to understand what we're up against.

First: Covid-19. How is it that we don't know for sure how this organism came into the world, or understand what ensued after it did? Answer: the people who caused it to happen in the Wuhan lab have been busy covering their asses for three years, and successfully so. Yet we know exactly what Anthony Fauci, Francis Collins, Peter Daszak, Ralph Baric, and others did. The paper trail in correspondence and patents alone is clear. We just can't seem to do anything about it.

We don't know *why* they did it yet, too, but there are plausible guesses. Maybe Dr. Fauci wanted to cap his long, checkered career with a final heroic triumph: the introduction of world-saving mRNA vaccines — incidentally, a great financial boon to himself and the pharma industry he secretly served. Like everything else Fauci worked on for forty years, this experiment ended in disaster: a Frankenstein disease that persists in the population and vaccines that maim and kill people. How did Fauci and company get away with it? Here's how.

Two: Government's war on its own citizens. I'd date this for the sake of simplicity to the DOJ's and FBI's campaign to defenestrate Donald Trump

JAMES HOWARD KUNSTLER

starting in 2016 for the crime of winning an election. What began as the Russia collusion prank morphed into RussiaGate, another ass-covering extravaganza in which public officialdom gave itself blanket permission to lie about everything it was doing. The likes of James Comey, Andrew McCabe, and Barack Obama's girl squad in the White House — to name just a few of many participants — also managed to hook in the mainstream news media under the supposition that they were the good guys fighting a disgusting, pussy-grabbing supervillain, which disposed the news media to go along with all the FBI and DOJ lies, and also stranded the media in an endless loop of ass covering they are still locked in to.

Bottom line: all involved came to recognize that there was no accountability for their wicked deeds and lying about them, and that became an all-purpose license for everyone in public life to lie about everything and anything ever after — including Dr. Fauci and his colleagues, who watched RussiaGate roll out for four years before the debut of Covid-19. This license to act wrongfully and lie about it extends, by the way, to the epic election mischief carried out programmatically by the Democratic Party's lawfare arm in 2020 and 2022, and the installation of a fake president.

Three: Wokery, the Marxist campaign to disorder society in order to overthrow existing institutions and replace them with a utopian dictatorship of the *intersectionally* oppressed — also known as *The Revenge of the Losers*. Its primary tactic is to normalize mental illness. Wokery is often described as a new kind of religion, but that's mainly because all of its proffers and principles are irrational, as is characteristic of all religions. Also, as in many religions, Wokery in practice is preoccupied with coercion and punishment — which is natural for a movement based on vengeance — and often to a sadistic degree. It laughs at the idea of redemption. Its adversaries are never forgiven, only dealt additional punishments for asking.

The mystery here is how Wokery was incorporated into the operating system of the Democratic Party. The answer is the party needed something to replace its erstwhile corpus of organized industrial workers, gone with the winds of globalism, and so it valorized the various categories of the mentally ill, the permanently downtrodden, and sundry persons who had become economic hostages to its corrupt system of payments and grants. High above that ragtag and bobtail of crazies reigned an aristocracy of the so-called *cognitive elite*, people of unquestioned virtue, college professors, the *creative class*, the credentialed echelon — superbusy signaling their good intentions to their vassals to keep them in line.

Wokery, you may have noticed, is also a "religion" dominated by women, and a particular strain of women: those left grossly disappointed by the promises of feminism in its several iterations, that is, the ideal of having brilliant careers minus family and children — producing an implacable, inchoate, and transmissible rage at the world and a fierce wish to punish others not so disposed to woke dogma. So it's no surprise that so much of that dogma emanated from the humanities departments of the universities where such careerist feminist intellectuals flocked and marinated in their disappointments. Thus, too, their avatar: the ever cold-blooded and fiendish Hillary Clinton, forever seeking requital for her life's losses. Hillary leads us to the world stage, and to . . .

Four, the most mysterious of the four fuckeries: globalism as represented by the World Economic Forum (WEF) led by the quasi-comical Klaus Schwab. Supposedly — and I can't endorse this proposition — it is a front for some cabal of exalted international bankers and oligarchs, the proverbial Rothschilds and Rockefellers, Soros and Bill Gates and their various subalterns. There is certainly a lot of money involved and, as the old saying goes, *Money talks and bullshit walks*. There is also a ton of chatter about this selfsame cabal centering around a satanic child molestation cult.

I dunno about this, either. Seems plumb cuckoo to me. And yet, how do you explain Jeffrey Epstein's activities, and how he got it away with all of it, until he was offed right under Attorney General Bill Barr's nose? How to explain the deification of transsexuals by the folks in charge of culture and politics? You are dared to condemn such outrageous insults to human hardwired morality as the Drag Queen Story Hour.

It's hypothesized that the satanic sex module is just of a piece with the WEF's transhumanism project: to engineer a superrace that will manage and enjoy the perqs of life on earth as a previously unseen hermaphroditic genus, and all the performative kink sexuality on display is just a preview of that, to soften us up. More to the point, though, is the idea that this WEF elite will rule a planet of lower-order slaves (us), to mine their lithium and mix their drinks. And along with that is the much heard narrative of the WEF seeking to severely reduce the earth's current human population. I'm not wholly on board with believing any of this; just sayin' it's all "out there" and, crazy as it sounds, it is hard to explain.

Except in this way. Readers know that I have retailed my personal view of a collapsing techno-industrial society as the Long Emergency. My own conviction is this: that the general apprehension of such an event, now ongoing, has generated among the citizenry such terror as to drive society crazy. (Mass formation psychosis is a related interpretation, not necessary to go into here.)

I suppose this has happened to most other civilizations that wobbled and fell. The one best known to me — because I wrote about it in *The City in Mind* (2002) — is the psychosis that overcame the Aztecs 1519 to 1521. It is the weirdest story in history that I know of. Aztec civilization was barely two hundred years old. The great city-state of Tenochtitlan had quickly grown to half a million people when Hernan Cortés and company, representing Spain of the Inquisition, marched in. Cortés, in his gleaming steel helmet, was the personification of the Aztecs' god of dawn, wind, and knowledge Quetzalcoatl, the "feathered serpent," who, in legend, had once ruled the region but went missing and was expected to return from wherever elsewhere the gods reposed and destroy everything. In fact, that's exactly what Señor Cortés and his few hundred soldiers proceeded to do to a half million Aztecs and their culture.

During the two years Cortés sojourned among them, the Aztecs went batshit crazy, ramping up their previously modest program of human sacrifice — a few hapless captives now and again — to a fantastic ritual mass bloodbath, cutting the hearts out of hundreds at a time atop their great pyramid to propitiate their sun god, Huitzilopochtli, and persuade him, by such a bloody performance of their devotion, to not end their world. It ended anyway, though another world (arguably not a better one) took its place: Mexico.

This is the kind of periodic human mass insanity that I see in the Four Fuckeries now loose in the world as Western civ wobbles. The trouble is, having replaced our gods with science, we have no deity to propitiate. Just endless hypotheses of what's to come.

SANTA AND SATAN

December 23, 2022

"Amidst the general call to happiness, the bustle of the spirits, and stir of the affections, which prevail at this period, what bosom can remain insensible?" — Washington Irving (1783–1859) on Christmas

Santa... Satan? Notice, they're spelled similarly. Weird, a little bit. The Santa we know came from a mashup of ancient pre-Christian Teutonic and Norse folk figures (Wotan, Odin) with the fourth-century Greek bishop St. Nicholas, a humble giver of gifts to children. That evolved in nineteenth-century Anglo America, with help from Washington Irving, Charles Dickens, and Clement Moore, into the jolly fat man in a fur-lined cloak, chortling merrily amid the platters of roast goose and baskets of sugarplums.

And then, of course, the Santa character was retooled and stylized by the big advertising mills of mid-twentieth century Madison Avenue into the red-suited icon who functioned as a cosmic deliveryman to suburban houses where the little ones dwell, efficiently distributing Red Ryder BB guns and Barbie dolls from sea to shining sea out of his reindeer-powered express vehicle, circling the entire globe in a single breathless night of glittering snow and shining stars, plangent with countless wishes from little hearts.

Strange to relate, in some corners of Europe, St. Nick acquired a traveling companion named Krampus. The two went from house to house in the dark hours of St. Nick's name day (Dec. 6) interrogating children as to their conduct. Dark and hirsute with horns, cloven hooves, and a darting red tongue, this monster acted the "bad cop" of the roving pair, badgering the little ones about their naughty or nice doings, and whacking them with a birch rod if he didn't like their answers. If especially displeased, he stuffed kids into a basket for transport to Hell.

A Krampus-like character reemerged in America this pre-Christmas week in the figure of Volodymyr Zelensky, president of Ukraine, who flew halfway around the world in a US government–issue magic sled to meet up with his

JAMES HOWARD KUNSTLER

Gruss vom Krampus!

chum "Joe Biden," the new Santa Claus, alleged current president of our land. Mr. Z, still tricked out in his wartime olive-green togs and scruffy beard, was here to lecture the boys and girls of Congress about being naughty or nice vis-à-vis "democracy" in his distant land, lately under a siege of angry bears. Ukraine did nothing to make the bears angry, you understand. They just lumbered in from the forest one day and started busting stuff up, as bears will.

Ukraine has already received many gifts from Santa's workshop, formerly known as the USA, toys much more impressive than any Red Ryder BB gun, for sure: howitzers, Javelin missiles, Stinger missiles, High Mobility Artillery Rocket Systems (HIMARS), Phoenix Ghost tactical drones, Switchblade tactical drones, Puma surveillance drones, Vampire antidrone systems, Mi-17 helicopters, Harpoon coastal defense systems, and much more. (How did Santa fit it all in his sack?)

Mr. Z and fellow officials of the bear-besieged country have also received plenty of "walking-around money," much of which has walked around so far and wide in the world as to park itself in sundry obscure bank accounts, real estate investments, or just plumb vanish into thin air. It wasn't enough, Mr. Z complained upon arrival here. You must pony up more . . . or else! And you must punish the bears harder!

"Joe Biden" promised another fifty billions of dollars to Mr. Z's bear-extermination project, with the further objective of dethroning the king of all bears, the wicked Putin, who glowers at the world from the mouth of his faraway Kremlin Cave. Then, in Congress Wednesday night, before a coast-to-coast TV audience, Mr. Z tuned up our elected boys and girls in the great House chamber, forked tongue darting, to tell heart-wrenching tales of bear-provoked terror. He played them like the very keys of a harpsichord — a trick he has performed before with an interesting twist on Ukrainian television. The elect of our land stood and cheered, ready to proclaim Ukraine the fifty-first state. Mr. Z stole a smooch from the ruler of Congress, the winsome Ms. Pelosi, and then disappeared in a puff of smoke that left a tang of sulfur wafting on the stale air.

To underscore his seriousness, and using his secret powers, Mr. Z arranged for a bomb-cyclone storm to roar out of the North Pole a few days after his departure to give Americans a little taste of what it's like to sit in the cold and dark at Christmastime — because the USA is such a blessed land as to have no problems of its own, and needs to be reminded about the sufferings of the less fortunate. And so it goes this Yuletide of 2022 in our charmed and exceptional country. The elves of Clusterfuck Nation wish you all a merry little Christmas!

❈ 2023 ❈

LOSE-LOSE

February 3, 2023

"The White House has taken the entire West in such a direction and speed of triumphalism, arrogance and 'egregious' imbecility that there is no going back or reversal possible without a total defeat of the official narrative and the consequent eternal shame."
— Hugo Dionisio

The New York Times — indicted this week as a chronic purveyor of untruths by no less than its supposed ally the *Columbia Journalism Review* — is lying to you again this morning.

> *WASHINGTON — The number of Russian troops killed and wounded in Ukraine is approaching 200,000, a stark symbol of just how badly President Vladimir V. Putin's invasion has gone, according to American and other Western officials.*

This whopper is an artful diversion from the reality on the ground that Ukraine is just about finished in this tragic and idiotic conflict staged by the geniuses behind their plaything President "Joe Biden." By the way, it's not a coincidence that Ukraine and "JB" are going down at the same time. The two organisms are symbionts: a matched pair of mutual parasites feeding off each other, swapping each other's toxic exudations, and growing delirious on their glide path to a late winter crash.

The point of the war, you recall, is "to weaken Russia" (so said DoD sec'y Lloyd Austin), even to bust it up into little geographic tatters to our country's advantage — that is, to retain America's dominance in global affairs, and especially the supremacy of the US dollar in global trade settlements.

The result of the war so far has been the opposite of that objective. US sanctions made Russia stronger by shifting its oil exports to more reliable Asian customers. Kicking Russia out of the SWIFT global payments system prompted the BRIC countries to build their own alternative trade settlement system. Cutting off Russia from trade with Western civ has stimulated the process of import replacement (i.e., Russia making more of the stuff it used to buy from Europe). Confiscating Russia's offshore dollar assets has alerted the rest of the world to dump their dollar assets (especially US Treasury bonds) before they, too, get mugged. Nice going, Victoria Nuland, Tony Blinken, and the rest of the gang at the Foggy Bottom genius factory.

All of which raises the question: who is liable to bust up into tatters first, the USA or Russia? I commend to you Dmitry Orlov's seminal work *Reinventing Collapse: The Soviet Experience and American Prospects.* For anyone out there not paying attention the past thirty-odd years, Russia, incorporated as the Soviet Union, collapsed in 1991. The USSR was a bold experiment based on the peculiar and novel ill effects of industrialism, especially gross economic inequality. Alas, the putative remedy for that, advanced by Karl Marx, was a despotic system of pretending that individual humans had no personal aspirations of their own.

The Soviet / Marxist business model was eventually reduced to the comic aphorism: *We pretend to work and they pretend to pay us.* It failed and the USSR gurgled down history's drain. Russia reemerged from the dust, minus many of its Eurasian outlands. Remarkably little blood was shed in the process. Mr. Orlov's book points to some very interesting setups that softened the landing. There was no private property in the USSR, so when it collapsed nobody was evicted or foreclosed from where they lived. Very few people had cars in the USSR, so the city centers were still intact and people could get around on buses, trams, and trains. The food system had been botched for decades by low-incentive collectivism, but the Russian people were used to planting family gardens — even city dwellers, who had plots out of town — and it tided them over during the years of hardship before the country managed to reorganize.

Compare that to America's prospects. In an economic crisis, Americans will have their homes foreclosed out from under them, or will be subject to eviction from rentals. The USA has been tragically built out on a suburban sprawl template that will be useless without cars and with little public transport. Cars, of course, are subject to repossession for nonpayment of contracted loans. The American food system is based on manufactured microwavable cheese snacks, chicken nuggets, and frozen pizzas produced by giant companies. These items can't be grown in home gardens. Many Americans don't know the first thing about growing their own food, or what to do with it after it's harvested.

There's another difference between the fall of the USSR and the collapse underway in the USA. Underneath all the economic perversities of Soviet life, Russia still had a national identity and a coherent culture. The USA has tossed its national identity on the garbage barge of "diversity, equity, and inclusion," which is actually just a hustle aimed at extracting what remains from the diminishing stock of productive activity and showering the plunder on a mob of "intersectional" complainers — e.g., the City of San Francisco's preposterous new plan to award $5 million "reparation" payments to African American denizens of the city, where slavery never existed.

As for culture, consider that the two biggest cultural producers in this land are the pornography and video game industries. The drug business might be a close third, but most of that action is off the books, so it's hard to tell. So much for the so-called arts. Our political culture verges on totally degenerate, but that is too self-evident to belabor, and the generalized management failures of our polity are a big part of what's bringing us down — most particularly the failure to hold anyone in power accountable for their blunders and turpitudes.

This unearned immunity might change, at least a little bit, as the oppositional House of Representatives commences hearings on an array of disturbing matters. Meanwhile, be wary of claims in *The New York Times* and other propaganda organs that our Ukraine project is a coming up a big win, and that the racketeering operations of the Biden family amount to an extreme right-wing, white supremacist conspiracy theory. These two pieces of the conundrum known as reality are blowing up in our country's face. It will be hard not to notice.

The World Has Enough Trouble

February 24, 2023

"[This] is what happens when you invent your own reality. You end up bamboozling yourself. — The Sirius Report on Twitter

If you think about it at all, can you come up with any good reasons why our country has involved itself in the Ukraine war? To defend democracy, many say? An emptier platitude does not exist in the vast slippery lexicon of spin. To thwart Russia's imperial overreach? You apparently have no clue about Ukraine's history, ancient or modern. To incite an overthrow of the wicked Putin by his own people? The Russian president is more popular there now than even John F. Kennedy was here in 1962.

There actually are no good reasons for what we are doing in Ukraine, only bad reasons. Mainly, stoking the war there diverts Americans' attention from our own problems, which is to say the titanic failures of America's political establishment. The USA is falling apart from a combination of mismanagement, malice, and negligence. Our economy is a tottering scaffold of Ponzi schemes. Our institutions are wrecked. The government lies about everything it does. The news industry ratifies all the lying. Our schoolchildren can't read or add up a column of numbers. Our food is slow-acting poison. Our medical-pharma matrix has just completed the systematic murder and maiming of millions. Our culture has been reduced to a drag queen twerkfest. Our once beautiful New World landscape is a demolition derby. Name something that hasn't been debauched, perverted, degenerated, or flat-out destroyed.

And so, the "Joe Biden" show is busy ginning up nuclear war hysteria because that's all it has left for manipulating public emotion. The Covid-19 derangement lost its mojo in 2022 and the population has only just begun to grok the all-causes death disaster underway courtesy of Pfizer and Moderna (and the CDC with the FDA). Did you notice, by the way, that the CDC just added those unapproved, still experimental shots to the childhood vaccine schedule, considered official "guidance" that is followed by virtually every school system in America. Rochelle

Walensky did that despite massive evidence that the "vaccines" damage children's hearts, nervous systems, reproductive systems, and immune systems?

Do you know why Ms. Walensky did that? Because adding the mRNA shots to the childhood schedule *supposedly* confers permanent immunity from legal liability for the drug companies, even after the current emergency use authorization (EUA) runs out. The catch to that cozy arrangement is if there was any fraud committed on the public in the release and administration of those products, the companies lose their immunity and can be sued until there is nothing left of them but the paper clips. Plus, the executives may be liable for criminal prosecution. Hard time.

One Brook Jackson, a technician involved in the sketchy Pfizer drug trials, and who directly witnessed the procedural violations as they occurred, is currently suing Pfizer under the False Claims Act (31 U.S. Code § 3729) saying that the company defrauded the government. Pfizer's lawyers have asked the judge to dismiss the case on the grounds, they said in court, that, "We did not defraud the government. We delivered the fraud that the government ordered." So now, millions of schoolchildren in this land will be subject to compulsory harmful mRNA shots in order to cover the pharma companies' multibillion-dollar asses. Doesn't that sum up our national predicament nicely? Way to go, Rochelle. Don't think nobody noticed.

It's also worth pondering whether we are neck deep in the Ukraine morass because Volodymyr Zelensky is blackmailing "Joe Biden" over the mysterious Biden family business operations that took place there directly following the US-orchestrated Maidan revolution that overthrew Ukraine President Viktor Yanukovych in 2014. Remember "The Big Guy's" earnest efforts to get rid of the Ukrainian state prosecutor who was looking into the affairs of the Burisma gas company that invited Hunter Biden and his associate Devon Archer onto the board of directors. Of all people in Western civ . . . these two Americans . . . with no knowledge of or experience in the natgas industry. Weird, a little bit. Do you suppose Mr. Zelensky still has the prosecutor's files in his possession?

Then, of course, there is the bizarre matter of the Nord Stream pipeline caper, lately disclosed by the scrupulous reporter Seymour Hersh as a US naval operation. We blew them up. Four EU member nations (also US NATO allies) held a combined half-ownership in the pipelines (the other half held by Russia). European industry and households depended on a steady supply of that reasonably priced gas to continue modern life there. Both President "Joe Biden" and his deputy secretary of state for political affairs Victoria Nuland promised the news media (and the American public) that the pipeline would "be no more" if a Russian military operation crossed into the Donbass. Well, *sonofabitch*, the pipelines were "no more" as of last September.

Was that an injury to Russia? Well, yes, though Russia has found workarounds for selling its natgas elsewhere than northern Europe. Do you realize, though, that it was every bit as much an act of war against our supposed allies? None of the NATO countries with a stake in Nord Stream have made a peep so far about the shocking disclosure. Which may lead a casual observer to ask whether Western civ has gone plumb insane. Maybe so, in which case perhaps it deserves to suffer. After a while — not such a long while, either — modern life will be but a memory in northern Europe.

Somehow the specter of unintended consequences looms over all this mischief. My guess is we just haven't seen them yet — and when we do they will be ferocious. For starters, NATO will be another thing that *is no more*. And our country will have to go about our blustering war hawkery without any backup or convenient staging areas for fomenting more shenanigans in a faraway region where we have no real national interest, just a certain zeal for creating unnecessary trouble and hardship in a world that already has more than it requires.

Remember what his old boss Barack Obama said about the former veep: "*You can never overstate Joe's ability to fuck things up.*" What a prophet that man is! Under "Joe Biden," the USA has been slip-sliding sideways and backward into a realm of darkness unimaginable a few years ago. But now, something is heaving through the public sensibility, as spring marches north in America. It feels like a sharp change in attitude, a refusal to continue acting like a reality-optional society. It's crackling through the air like a rumor of liberation in a hostage crisis. Can you hear it?

SVB + FTX + SBF = WTF?

March 17, 2023

"Deny, deflect, minimise & mock your enemies questions. Don't engage them in good faith, they're attacking you with a view to undermining you. Don't fall for it. Don't give them an inch."
— Aimee Terese on Twitter

The net effect of all the lying propaganda laid on the public by the people running things lo these many recent years is a peculiar inertia that makes us seemingly impervious to gross political shocks. Momentous things happen and almost instantly get swallowed up by time, as by some voracious cosmic amoeba that thrives on human malignancy. Case in point: the multiple suicide of several giant banks just days ago that prompted "Joe Biden" to nationalize the US banking system.

As if all the operations around finance in this land were not already unsound and degenerate enough, the alleged president just canceled *moral hazard* altogether. It's now official: from here forward there will be no consequences for banking fraud, poor decision making, fiduciary recklessness, self-dealing, or any of the other risks attendant to the handling of other people's money. Bailing out the Silicon Valley Bank and Barney Frank's deluxe Signature Bank means that the government will now have to bail out every bank every time something goes wrong.

The trouble, of course, is that the government doesn't have the means to bail out every bank. Its only resort is to ask the Federal Reserve to summon new money from a magic ether where the illusion of wealth is conjured to paper over ever greater fissures in the splintering matrix of racketeering that America has become. That will quickly translate into US dollars losing value, that is, accelerating inflation, which is how nature punishes you when your government lies and pretends that it has a bad situation well in hand.

Be advised: the situation is not in hand and is going to get a whole lot worse as new and subsidiary shocks thunder through the weeks and months ahead, until the whole wicked business blows. Likewise, the reactions of our government will only get more tragicomically pathetic. The harder this gang of feckless, wannabe control freaks pretends to control events, the faster events spin out of control.

Money dies when it loses its direct connection to the generation of wealth from the real things of this earth: fuels, crops, metals, materials, labor, and the value-added products made from them. Since that divorce has already happened, the need arises for something else that can function as money (a store of wealth, an index of value, and a medium of exchange). The government will pretend that a Central Bank Digital Currency is that something else. Since banking is now nationalized by the Federal Reserve backstopping everything and everybody, then theoretically all the wealth of the nation is under its command. That would be another illusion.

This CBDC would not be "money" representing wealth because America's wealth is going, going, gone, pissed away, falling apart, delaminating, oxidizing, rusting in the rain, going up in a vapor. Think of all those mortgaged cars on the road racking up the mileage until they're worthless and all those mortgaged suburban houses built out of particle board and vinyl smeared all over the landscape, decomposing into their constituent chemicals — over time, a dead loss. And that's what's left of our American dream: coldcocked by entropy and, by extension, the laws of the universe. The CBDC would just be a computerized tracking apparatus for zombies lurching pointlessly around that dead zone . . . a final insult. The CBDC is already DOA, only the CB doesn't know it.

One big mistake so many commentators and observers are making takes us back to the matter of canceled moral hazard, and of consequence in general: it is the failure to appreciate how much disorder will manifest from the farrago of mind fuckery and misconduct we've been subjected to. By which I mean things stop working, including the elemental things like your ability to get food, fix whatever breaks, and keep the lights on.

The potential disorder is why our government will probably not be able to fix itself. The disorder may go on for quite a while, but eventually the survivors will synergetically fix their circumstances themselves working in step with the *emergent* mandates of reality. Having lived through a reality-optional period of history, it will come as an ecstatic shock to learn that the world requires us to pay attention to what is really happening and to act accordingly. We'll find ways to get food, make some things work, and shine some lights in the darkness, if perhaps not by means we're familiar with now.

In the meantime, expect more disordering tragicomedy from the "Joe Biden"–led psychotic regime ruling over us with its drag queen commissars, lawless lawfare vandals, race hustlers, agents provocateurs, informers, censors, prosecutors, inquisitors, jailers, and propagandists — the worst collection of imbeciles, grifters, and villains ever assembled into political party.

An Eastertime Carol

March 27, 2023

"The true administration of justice is the firmest pillar of good government"
— inscription on the pediment of the Manhattan Criminal Court

After wolfing down a heartburn-inducing Popeye's Shrimp Tacklebox Combo for supper, Manhattan district attorney Alvin Bragg retires to his four-poster Sleep Number bed beset with anxiety about the grand jury he has convened for fulfilling his campaign promise to stuff Donald Trump into a state prison cell. From the wall-mounted flatscreen across from his bed, the specter of a giant rabbit emerges, gaunt and grizzled, draped in chains and weighty padlocks.

"Who are you, spirit?" Bragg asks.

"I am the ghost of prosecutions past," it moans. "This night you will be visited by three other spirits: the ghost of what you wish to be, the ghost of what should be, and the ghost of actually what it is."

"Oh, gawd," Bragg groans, his esophagus on fire with acidified hot-sauce residue.

The DA falls back into a febrile sleep, but wakens minutes later. The bedroom of his condo has transformed itself into a sunny street scene. He is riding an open limousine down Broadway through a blizzard of ticker tape, the sidewalks filled with cheering citizens. Beside him sits a nubile person of the birthing persuasion, with supernaturally large infant-feeding glands, not unlike a certain star of adult films at the center of his brilliant case against the former president.

"I am the ghost of what you wish to be," she says, her breath warm in his ear. "You're a bigger star now than ever I was in life, and without all the mess."

"Yeah? What's that up ahead?" he asks.

"The steps of City Hall where you will receive your Nobel Peace Prize and be handed the nomination for governor, your stepping-stone to the White House."

"We gonna have to change the name of that place," Bragg grumbles.

Suddenly a box appears on Bragg's lap. It contains two McDonald's Sausage, Egg, and Cheese McGriddles® plus an apple fritter and a caramel macchiato. No sooner do his teeth close on that first delicious bite when the confetti in the air turns to pixels, which dissolve along with the street scene, and then Bragg is back in his bed. Laughter rings across the big room, but with a demonic dissonance. A large white man with a silvery mane of hair and a nose like an Appalachian dulcimer, draped in black judicial robes, sits up behind a lofty bench, wearing a scowl of privilege.

"What do *you* want?" Bragg asks.

"Your law license, asshole."

"Who do you think you are?"

"I am the spirit of what should be," the judgelike figure growls.

"This is a racist ploy!" Bragg barks back. "Plus, you got no standing!"

More fiendish laughter from the bench, joined suddenly by a chorus of a million other laughers, people of all sizes, genders, and colors, a collage of Manhattan humanity, each one pointing a finger at Bragg, who retreats in terror under his king-size duvet. The laughter dissolves into Bragg's own blubbering wails of despair.

The DA wakes a third time, trembling, to the sound of the doorbell, which he tries to ignore, but it keeps on ringing and ringing. Finally, Bragg kicks off the duvet, plods over to the door, and throws it open. A tall, stout white man with a mystifying platinum hairdo stands framed within.

"DoorDash, at your service," the ghost of actually what it is says.

"Oh, no . . ." Bragg cries out, as he is handed a paper bag. He opens it and peers in, only to loose a nauseating stench that instantly fills the room. "Hey, this is not the Build Your Crème Brûlée Pancake Combo from the IHOP," Bragg complains.

The DoorDash looks at his phone. "It says here you ordered the shit sandwich."

Bragg feels like his head will explode. He reaches out to strangle the malevolent specter but wakes up choking his Saatva premium pillow instead. Eventually, he comes back to his senses, but feeling utterly drained from the night's visitations. He washes the night sweats away in the shower, dons a fine chalk-strip suit the size of a Coleman six-person tent, and meets his driver waiting at the end of his building's canopy. In the backseat of his city limo there is a bag with his usual breakfast: two Starbuck's Double-Smoked Bacon, Cheddar & Egg Sandwiches, a blueberry scone, a glazed donut, and a Starbuck's Reserve® Hazelnut Bianco Latte. He horses it all down in traffic on the way to the DA's headquarters on Hogan Place.

It is Monday morning, of course, roughly a week after the world was expecting him to issue an indictment against former president Donald Trump for writing off payments to a porn star as a campaign expense. But there was much to think about as the week marched along, much to mull over, many options to consider ... the future to assess. The office is spookily quiet as Bragg strides in. An attractive blonde of a certain age approaches him warily.

"Ready to rock and roll, boss?" asks Lisa DelPizzo, chief of the Trial Division, expecting Bragg to make his historic announcement shortly to the dozens of assembled reporters waiting in the press lobby.

"Get me a ham sandwich," he grunts. "And bring it down to the grand jury chamber. We got work to do!"

THE HERO'S JOURNEY

April 7, 2023

"If I run, my top priority will be to end the corrupt merger between state and corporate power that has ruined our economy, shattered the middle class, polluted our landscapes and waters, poisoned our children, and robbed us of our values and freedoms." — Robert F. Kennedy Jr.

More proof — as if you needed more — that we live in a mentally ill society is the apparently broad acceptance of the idea that "Joe Biden" will run for president again. It's so obviously preposterous that you have to wonder whether mRNA "vaccines" really do (as rumored) switch off activity in the frontal lobes. Did you happen to see this degenerate cat's-paw step up to the White House microphone to deliver scripted remarks on the Nashville school shooting only to drift into several minutes of unscripted badinage about how he came downstairs looking for chocolate chip ice cream? There's your current *Leader of the Free World*.

We need not belabor the trail of destruction "Joe Biden's" regime has cut through our country in just over two years. But you must sense nervously that we're about to reap what this cabal has sown. America is falling apart. "JB" has allowed a rogue bureaucracy to make us a viciously unfree country. Our sleazy Ukraine project is wrecking Western civ. The rest of the world has noticed and is fast dissociating from us, especially from using our dollar for trade and investment.

"JB's" Party of Chaos is engineering an economic smashup worse than the Great Depression. They've torpedoed the rule of law. The woke Marxist social nuttery they've unleashed has disordered millions of young minds. They work overtime to destroy language so that we don't know what we're talking about. Their race and gender hustles have transformed us into a clown nation. The worst of us is valorized and the best canceled. They've perverted the election process. And it's increasingly clear that they've disabled and killed at least a million people with their medical tyranny.

You may have noticed that Robert F. Kennedy Jr. announced he is running for president as a Democrat. I might be wrong, but just now it seems to me that this changes everything. First, let me tell you something interesting about RFK Jr. Despite the family name and all the baggage that comes with it, he is not the least bit imperial. He's unpretentious. He communicates in plain English (and with a damaged larynx). I doubt that he entertained any idea of running for office until the current moment. Sometimes the zeitgeist calls, though, and you have to step up, even understanding very clearly that you might get killed for doing so.

Mr. Kennedy's life has been a rocky hero's journey. He was a troubled young man, at times lost in drugs. He had a marriage end as badly as possible (wife's suicide). He's dedicated the past twenty-five years to fighting the growing menace of Big Pharma and doing it pretty valiantly, considering the US government and mainstream media assists all of Big Pharma's depredations. He wrote *the* book about Dr. Anthony Fauci, and it is a helluva book. He's running in opposition to just about everything that the Democratic Party stands for these days. This must seem strange, but I suspect a substantial portion of rank-and-file Democrats may be secretly anxious to cast off the woke / Deep State despotism that cloaks the party like a smallpox blanket. For many, it will be like waking from a nightmare.

Now I'm going to tell you something that might blow your mind, something that maybe lurks in a quiet corner of your own brain, something which for my generation has been hiding inside there for decades, and it is this: there is a deep, primal wish in the American psyche to correct the damage to our country caused by the murders of John F. Kennedy and his brother Robert. November 22, 1963, was exactly when this nation went off the rails, and many Americans understand that. RFK Jr. has stated unambiguously that he believes the CIA killed his uncle, the president. And he recently supported the parole of his father's killer, Sirhan B. Sirhan, suggesting that there was a whole lot more to Bobby's assassination than that patsy.

Here's the heart of the matter: that wish to correct the abominations of history is a sentiment much stronger than anything else currently whirring in the fog of emotion that grips a nation in extremis, certainly stronger than all the bullshit embedded in *equity, diversity, and inclusion* and the bad faith aspirations of the climate change / Great Reset claque. RFK Jr. represents a way out of all that. He may be strong enough and honorable enough to make that our new national reality.

Then there is Mr. Trump. He's been on his own even stranger hero's journey, considering his origins in real estate and showbiz, and his personal peccadillos. Mr. Trump also recognized the evil afoot in our country and he set out to correct all that. He was attacked unfairly and incessantly by people of bad character and ill intent, even to this day as he faces an absurd political prosecution in Manhattan. You have to admire his fortitude and resilience in the face of such massed official bad faith.

His first time around in the White House, though, Mr. Trump kind of muffed the job. He had many opportunities to disarm and fire antagonists like Christopher Wray and the perfidious generals who kept backstabbing him, but he just didn't do it. He got played on the whole Covid fraud and still hasn't renounced the killer "vaccines" developed in the Warp Speed flimflam.

While I consider the New York case brought by DA Alvin Bragg to be a disreputable shuck and jive, over which Mr. Trump will prevail, and while I recognize him as the current leader in the battle against a globalist putsch, I think Mr. Kennedy would be a far better choice to clean up the mess that has been made of us. I was particularly unnerved by Mr. Trump's speech at Mar-a-Lago the night of his indictment. I know many find his manner charming, but to me his mode of speaking seems childish and weirdly inarticulate — and the last thing this country needs is more rhetorical confusion. And I'm also disturbed by the histrionic trappings that went with it — the grandiose music, the myriad flags and seals. It actually has a banana republic flavor.

Mr. Kennedy, on the other hand, brings a solemn humility to the scene. Even in his quavering voice, he speaks clearly and with insight. He's an excellent writer. He reminds me much more of what was good about our country and the men it once produced than the flamboyant Golden Golem of Greatness. I'm aboard for the ride. It's going to be gosh darn interesting and I hope the bastards don't try to kill him, because that will really be the end for us.

In his own words:

Robert F. Kennedy Jr ✔
@RobertKennedyJr   •••

The collapse of U.S. influence over Saudi Arabia and the Kingdom's new alliances with China and Iran are painful emblems of the abject failure of the Neocon strategy of maintaining U.S. global hegemony with aggressive projections of military power. China has displaced the American Empire by deftly projecting, instead, economic power. Over the past decade, our country has spent trillions bombing roads, ports, bridges, and airports. China spent the equivalent building the same across the developing world. The Ukraine war is the final collapse of the Neocon's short-lived "American Century." The Neocon projects in Iraq and Ukraine have cost $8.1 trillion, hollowed out our middle class, made a laughingstock of U.S. military power and moral authority, pushed China and Russia into an invincible alliance, destroyed the dollar as the global currency, cost millions of lives and done nothing to advance democracy or win friendships or influence.

ECON 101, A FABLE

May 1, 2023

"Much of the social history of the Western world, over the past three decades, has been a history of replacing what worked with what sounded good."
— Thomas Sowell

Historians of the future, poaching possum snouts in sorrel sauce over their camp-fires, will trace the fall of Western civ in the 2020s to the dissolving hallucination that was called the financial economy. It was a phantom parasitical organism that thrived on the back of a real economy based on making and doing things derived from the natural world, turbocharged by fossil fuels.

The orgy of making and doing went on for two hundred–plus years. Even with cyclical "recessions," the making and doing always increased in the aggregate, while its products got ever more plentiful, elaborate, and complex. The phantom financial parasite clinging to its back got used to this "growth" and it, too, developed ever more ingenious ways to suck the life out of its host organism, until it became a greater entity than the host itself, breaking its back.

The whole of this chapter in the long-running human project had strange effects on human minds that had not changed much since the late days of hunting and gathering. After the first hundred years of fossil fuel plentitude, humans had a hard time telling the difference between the host and the parasite. Both of them seemed to thrive equally. The real economy produced food and useful things and the financial economy produced money, which could buy food and useful things.

People made things incessantly, especially better and better tools and engines. That allowed people to grow more food and make more useful things that provided comfort and convenience. The financial economy made more and more money. It also produced myriad new ways for money to represent itself. At first, these things such as stocks and bonds (ownerships and loans at interest) were firmly attached to activities in the real economy — that is, they were sucked directly out of the host's makings and doings.

Later on, the things that represented money became more numerous and more detached from real makings and doings, more abstract, more based on promises, hopes, and wishes than on things derived from nature. That is to say, these newer representations of money tended ever more to a realm of the unreal. After a while, it became very hard to tell the difference between money things that were real and unreal. The financial economy furnished plenty of mystification to blend the two. This confusion prompted plenty of fraud, a brisk commerce in unreality that produced winners and losers.

Every story has a beginning, a middle, and an end, of course. As the fossil fuel supply drew closer to its end and further from the long, happy middle time of plenty, the business model for making and doing started to shudder and crack. It didn't fall apart all at once, but it put many makers and doers out of business. They stopped making and doing. By then, the financial economy was a colossal phantom parasite that dwarfed its host. It was burdened with so much unreality, so many workings dissociated from nature, that it could no longer pretend to be anything but a phantom.

To keep the host alive, it upchucked some of what it had sucked out of the host, adulterated with money based on unreal promises, hopes, and dreams. This turned more and more into a spewage of money so debased by broken promises, hopes, and dreams that making and doing just about stopped altogether. That is when the phantom parasite of finance began to dissolve and humans began to regard it as a hallucination that had gone away, dissolved into mist. What remained were a lot of humans embedded in nature.

And that is the place where the humans of Western civ find themselves in the 2020s. Western civ was the first region of the world that tapped into the fossil fuel orgy and it is now the first region exiting this phase of history. Even when the financial hallucination melts into air there will be a lot of real things around that were made before the great age of making and doing stopped.

Humans are ingenious animals, enterprising and resilient, though there will surely be fewer of us around. These fewer humans will likely be healthier, working more directly in nature and no longer compromised by the pernicious by-products of all the bygone making and doing. We will figure out how to use the leftover useful things to get food out of nature and keep making other useful things. The new making and doing will happen at nothing like the former pitch or scale. It may represent a time-out from the lost experience of the old, ever more elaborate and complex makings and doings. After a while, humans may discover a new way to get more out of nature. Or maybe not.

In the meantime, lodged as we are in the present, in the moment of this epochal transition, anxiety besets many millions of minds. Not a few minds have grown disordered watching all this go on around them, dreading the journey from one disposition of things to the next. Some have made themselves obnoxious. Let them do what they will until they tire themselves out. Keep your own well-ordered minds on the tasks ahead, your own makings and doings within the bounds of what is real. Take some time out to make some music. There are still plenty of good instruments around, and you can always sing. Put a meal together with your friends and loved ones and sing out. *It's all right, Ma*, Bob sang out long ago, *it's life and life only*.

JAMES HOWARD KUNSTLER

The Next Big Thing

May 8, 2023

"Psychopaths and narcissists aren't 'mentally ill,' they're just horrible people, and they get worse with age, not better."
—Aimee Terese on Twitter

Now that the charm has worn off the transsexual craze — the idea that a person's emotional distress can be cured by identifying as the opposite sex — we await the next ploy out of the woke transhumanist game plan to destabilize the human project on earth. People of color, brown, indigenous, Pacific Islander, gay, lesbian, plus-size, differently abled, all women (of course) have taken their turn in the batting order of intersectional oppressed minority groups, and each has walked off with a participation trophy. Who's left now?

The dead! Their needs have not received sufficient attention. Inclusion has not come to them . . . yet. They are systematically kept out of all current activities and ceremonies. They are segregated in ghettos of grass and granite. The legal system stigmatizes them. Numerically, taking in the whole of human history, they are by far the largest demographic. Yet they are routinely ignored, overlooked, disrespected. If anyone deserves to be woked-up from the sleep of oppression it's them.

Don't despair, a great grooming is underway. The next new thing will be for most of us to transition into the dead. Do you think it's an accident that Hollywood has churned out zombie movies by the morgueful in recent years? Obviously, more and more Americans have come to identify as the walking dead. (And, judging by the behavior in our land, a lot of people's brains have been eaten.) Even our businesses and banks have a walking dead kind of look to them.

Our project in Ukraine has been a tremendous grooming aid in preparing people to become dead. But that experiment is nearly complete now. Hence, we must seek a much bigger global project for transitioning humanity into the satisfactions of being dead. A war with China would be the ideal grooming opportunity. They outnumber us about four to one. They've developed hypersonic missiles that can deliver nuclear payloads anywhere in our country, with the potential of transitioning millions of Americans at a pop. And when they're done with that, they can send an army over here to work the luckless survivors to death out in the soybean fields and the corn rows.

Perhaps in anticipation of strange turning, America elected (so they say) a president in midtransition to being dead. "Joe Biden" is celebrated for staying mostly out of sight, underground; for speaking a dead language that resembles twentieth-century American vernacular English; for lurching one way and another, zombielike, on his way offstage in fleeting public appearances; and for taking large sums of money from Chinese officials who support America's transitioning program. Best of all, the president personally empathizes and identifies with the dead, encourages more Americans to become dead, offers cash incentives to hospitals that expedite death, and makes pharmaceuticals available — both legal and illegal — for inducing efficient transitions to the bliss of nonbeing.

In fact, there seems to be a rush now to transition, with the pace being set by professional athletes in their twenties and thirties who keel over in midplay on the football pitches, by movie actors who undergo conversion as the cameras roll, TV news readers who drop away from the mic with eyes rolling down like window shades in full view of multitudes, and other celebrities who surprise their loved ones by simply waking up dead in the morning. These are the edgy avatars of the next big thing. So hallowed are their transitions from living to dead that the process is spoken of only in whispers, as in a church or a sepulcher. Doctors who come upon the scene are mesmerized to the point of silence, too much in awe to speak of what brought on the fateful transition — certainly nothing they did.

As the people go, so goes the nation. The USA is transitioning from a dynamic system of economic liberty, endeavor, and law into an entropic dystopia of chaos, corruption, and inertia. As suits a country of the walking dead, nothing works: telephone calls go dead, the bank won't give you any money, your duties on the job have been eliminated, your food store has closed down, there are no parts available for your broken things, your flights are canceled, your Facebook archive has been erased, your opinion is not wanted, your vote is meaningless, your children no longer need your permission to do anything, and, final insult, a martini now costs fifteen dollars.

Death is everywhere in America now, hovering over everything we do. Don't fight it — celebrate it! Foster it wherever you go, among all you consort with! Welcome it as you slough off all the annoyances of being here and rise to your blessed platform in the perfect gnostic Elysium promised by the theurgists of Wokery. Become the dead you long to be!

Teachable Moment

June 23, 2023

"In the wake of the Hunter Biden sweetheart plea deal, calling D.C. a swamp is an insult to swamps and frankly to all wetlands in general. We need to redefine the Clean Water Act to include all Biden adjacent areas." — Margot Cleveland, lawyer and legal analyst

"I'm proud of my son" — Joe Biden

I hope you agree this has been an instructive week for our republic, sinking to the bottom as fast as the *Titan* submersible on its way to consort with its grandmama the RMS *Titanic*. Here's what I learned, for instance, from Special Counsel John Durham's visit to the House Judiciary Committee. When asked why he did not seek grand jury testimony from the primary culprits in the Russia collusion hoax — Comey, McCabe, and Strzok — he told the room it would have been "unproductive" because they habitually claimed to "not recall" anything when testifying in Congress.

That's an interesting legal theory. If it is so, we must suppose that any witness in a criminal inquiry may decline testifying on the grounds of claiming a defective memory. I'm not a lawyer, of course, but is it not the case that witnesses can be prompted to recall events when presented with evidence? E.g., "Here is your smartphone text of July 29 saying, 'Don't worry, we'll stop him [Trump].' What means did you have in mind to accomplish that, Mr. Strzok?"

In the four-year lead-up to his personal appearance in the House, many of us were fooled into thinking Mr. Durham was a serious dude. (I sure was.) Turns out the ferocious facial hair masked a rather timorous persona. Mr. Durham apparently did not dare test the boundaries of the narrow lane laid out in the scoping directives set forth by then Attorney General Barr. Mr. D. *did* find a line of criminal conduct between lawfare artist Michal Sussmann, the Fusion GPS disinfo company, the DC law firm Perkins Coie, and candidate Hillary MyTurn in the creation and marketing of the Steele Dossier — yet he never called Hillary to do any 'splainin about it (or anything else she did in 2016). Weird, a little bit.

While his omissions and missteps were spotlighted by the Republican members, Mr. Durham was mugged, kicked to the curb, stomped, and peed on by the committee Democrats, who still labor to prop up the dead-letter Russia collusion fraud against all evidence and reason. As usual, the lead attack dog on that was Rep. Adam Schiff (D-Calif.). He was rewarded the next day with a censure vote for seven years of shameless lying about said fraud, and stripped of his seat on the House intel committee, which he used, as then chairman, to launch Trump Impeachment #1 in 2019 with fake "whistleblower" (and CIA goblin) Eric Ciaramella, whom Mr. Schiff naturally lied about never meeting prior to the proceeding.

We are treated in these twilight months of the "Joe Biden" regime to a cavalcade of revelations laying out the degeneracy of a federal justice system at war with the American people and its shady machinations in service to the Biden family global bribery operation. Late Thursday, the House Ways and Means Committee, chaired by Rep. Jason Smith (R-MO), released the affidavit of IRS supervisory special agent Gary Shapley from testimony given in closed session May 26. It disclosed a concerted program by the DOJ to impede, obstruct, delay, divert, and bury a massive tax evasion and fraud case against Hunter Biden, involving millions of dollars garnered from foreign persons and entities for no discernible services performed in return.

"I am alleging, with evidence..." Mr. Shapley testified under oath, *"...whatever the motivations, at every stage decisions were*

made that had the effect of benefiting the subject of the investigation. These decisions included slow-walking investigative steps, not allowing enforcement actions to be executed, limiting investigators' line of questioning for witnesses, misleading investigators on charging authority, delaying any and all actions months before [the 2020] elections to ensure the investigation did not go overt well before policy memorandum mandated the pause."

Hunter Biden was code-named "Sportsman" as the case opened in 2018. Red flags in bank transfer records of Hunter B. and associates involving millions of dollars triggered the IRS inquiry. It wasn't until a year later that Hunter's laptop turned up, crammed with deal memos of bribes paid along with vivid documentary evidence of sex and drug crimes. The FBI verified its authenticity in November of 2019 by matching the device number against Hunter Biden's Apple iCloud ID.

By the way, note that this was the exact same time that the House intel committee under chairman Adam Schiff commenced its impeachment inquiry against President Donald Trump. AG William Barr and FBI Director Chris Wray therefore knew then that Hunter's laptop existed and that it contained evidence of suspicious money transactions with Russia, China, and most particularly Ukraine — since Mr. Trump's impeachment case was based on a telephone query he made to Ukrainian president Zelensky, regarding the Biden family's operations there. Neither Mr. Barr nor Mr. Wray alerted Mr. Trump's lawyers about the evidence contained in the laptop — which would have provided exculpatory proof of a reasonable motive for Mr. Trump's phone call. How was that not an obstruction of justice?

Mr. Shapley's testimony is just one thread in the much larger tapestry of Biden family corruption now achieving clarity. Rep. James Comer's Oversight Committee continues on its deep dive into the Biden family bank transfer records — with its evidence of money laundering through Biden shell company cutouts — and the direct voice recording evidence of "Joe Biden" discussing his family's financial arrangements with Petro Poroshenko, then president of Ukraine from 2014 to 2019, plus other damning evidence connected to a "trusted" (and well paid) FBI human confidential source in the much fought over FD-1023 document recently surrendered to the Oversight Committee.

In short, the tide is going out even as the sun sets on "Joe Biden" as president. He and his handlers may believe they enjoy the protection of a compliant news media, but even that has its limits. Impeachment is coming, even if not as fast as Rep. Lauren Boebert wants it to, and if and when it does, there will be no ignoring the stark presentation of hard evidence — no matter how much MSNBC's Joy-Ann Reid snorts and cackles.

Meanwhile, please understand that "Joe Biden" is only pretending to run for reelection and his party is pretending along with him just for the present desperate moment. Before long, their whole reeking, creaking edifice of lies and bad faith will come crashing down. "Joe Biden" will have to resign or the nation will be treated to the spectacle, this time, of a trial in the Senate for *real* cause, bribery and treason, not just fake animus. And then, not even Gavin Newsom will be able to save the Democratic Party in its present alignment and foul habits. If it survives at all, Robert F. Kennedy Jr. will have to rebuild it from the ground up and expel the demons infesting it.

COUP COO

June 26, 2023

"At exactly the point of the AFU's weakest moment and near-collapse on the battlefield he chose to strike Russia in the back as if obviously driven by a hidden hand." — Simplicius on Substack

You'd think that the hapless DC neocons Antony Blinken and his boss Victoria Nuland, plus the gang at Spook Central, would have learned a lesson about the diminishing returns of color revolutions: namely, that these bold pranks blow back . . . and not in a good way.

The New York Times informs us that US intel was well aware weeks beforehand of the developing coup attempt by Yevgeny Prigozhin and his personal army, the Wagner Group. Congressional leaders were briefed a day prior to its rollout. Well, golly, can you suppose for a New York minute that Russia's intel agency didn't know all about it, too?

A vast array of explanations for this bizarre wartime vaudeville can be found in every corner of the internet. I'll go with this one: Prigozhin came to bethink himself a Napoleonic figure. Just as Bonaparte wowed revolution-weary France with his military exploits against her enemies, and seized leadership of the nation, Prigozhin's mercenary army carried the brunt of the action in Ukraine this year, culminating in the heroic victory at Bakhmut. Priggy regarded the Russian Ministry of Defense as oafish, and by extension his longtime friend and mentor Vlad Putin, indecisive about it. The moment was ripe to seize power! As a recent US president might have said: he misoverestimated.

It looks like the neocons, the CIA, and Britain's MI6 did, too, if they helped nudge the event to fruition with assurances and cash — say, some of that $6.2 billion the Pentagon happened to find recently via an "accounting error." What better time to destabilize Russia than during Ukraine's vaunted spring offensive (which, let's face it, was not going too well)? In fact, Ukraine's whole NATO-assisted project from the get-go looked like a bust. The Bakhmut "meat grinder" was just the latest fiasco. But then, the irascible, disgruntled, and grandiose field marshal Priggy seemed like the perfect instrument to jazz things up for the demoralized West.

Pretty darn quick, on the road from Rostov-on-Don to Moscow, Priggy learned the hard way that he had no support in the government, the military, or among the Russian public. The coup fizzled before sundown the very day it started. Some say, any way you cut it, the result is Vlad Putin left looking weak and vulnerable. I don't think so. His speech to the Russian people that day appeared, if anything, resolute. And the way he seemed to spit out the words "a stab in the back," you couldn't think he was playacting. By evening, with the whole psychodrama concluded, the people of St. Petersburg crowded the quay along the Neva River and busted into patriotic song.

Let's address one nagging question: why did Mr. Putin allow the Wagner Group private army to play the leading role countering the Ukraine offensive? Answer: because he was saving and building up the regular Russian army to strength in the further event that NATO might finally jump into Ukraine with all its multinational feet when all else fails.

We're left, of course, with the manifold mysteries of the coup's hasty resolution. Mr. Prigozhin, we're told, will be turned over to the custody of the Belarus president Lukashenko to . . . to be done what with? To be put on the shelf like a bowling trophy? I'm sure . . . If they can even find the bugger now. (I'd look in Africa, where sundry Wagner units have been operating — Priggy must have had a plane standing by in Rostov.) In any case, we know the rest: Wagner troops who did not participate in the coup get folded into the regular army, and said regular army takes over duty along the front in Ukraine. Mr. Putin, despite all these insults, will continue to seek a diplomatic end to all this nonsense, and he might get it sooner rather than later. Germany and France, among Euro others, must be sick of these shenanigans.

Can Ukraine even carry on much longer? President Zelensky, the comedian, seems to have gone mad dog now. He just canceled next year's election, which makes him . . . what? Dictator? So much for America's democracy export program. He's also issued warnings to the effect that Russia is about to blow up the Zaporozhye nuclear power plant, Europe's largest. Such an act would supposedly trigger direct intervention by NATO, according to the policy promoted by war hawk US senators Lindsey Graham and Richard Blumenthal. The nuclear plant is under Russian control. Mr. Zelensky says they have set mines in it. The scenario is pretty absurd. Nobody believes it. Of course, Mr. Zelensky might use some of his NATO missiles to zap it, but Russia has video surveillance and recording equipment at every angle around the joint and the world will know five seconds after how it was blown up.

From his latest photographs, it looks like Mr. Zelensky is in the terminal throes of a cocaine rapture, and his actions are consistent with that state of mind. He must know that he's not long for this world. And our country, the USA, must know that this Ukraine gambit is another lost cause on our long march of military misadventures. And if the government of our country doesn't know, the people surely do. Have you noticed, the yellow-and-blue flags are not flying anymore? Even the most hardcore anti-Trump Democrats seem to understand what *pounding sand down a rat hole* means when it comes to the many billions of dollars squandered on this stupid project while our cities rot and a whole lot more goes south in our own ailing homeland.

Not to mention the parlous position of the American president himself, the spectral "Joe Biden," skulking in his demon-haunted White House as evidence of his treasonous turpitudes mounts and mounts. Which leaves us to wonder whether our intel community may have stirred up the Russia coup as just another distraction from its own Biden-linked crimes against this nation.

The Blob Begins to Quiver

July 10, 2023

> *"...the Permanent State lacks the courage to take hard decisions – to say to Moscow, 'Let us put this unfortunate episode (Ukraine) behind us. Dig out those draft treaties you wrote in December 2021, and let's see how we can work together, to restore some functionality again to Europe.'"*
> — Alastair Crooke

When you deny what is self-evident, you are at war with reality, and that never ends well. This is the ultimate disposition of our country's years-long misadventure in maximum dishonesty. The American administrative Blob has not just lied about everything it does, but used the government machinery at hand to destroy everything it touches in a terminal-hysterical effort to cover up its misdeeds — including especially its crimes against its own people.

Get this: there is no way that Ukraine can avoid defeat in its US-provoked struggle with Russia. Russia has every advantage. It is next door to Ukraine. It has robust arms production capacity. The terrain of the war is its own historic "borderland," which it has controlled since the eighteenth century, except for the past thirty years when Ukraine functioned as Grift Central for US military contractors and their political enablers. Despite massive arms assistance from the US and grudging contributions from the NATO contingent in Europe, there is almost nothing left of the Ukrainian military in troops, equipment, and munitions. Ukraine will return eventually to demilitarized "borderland" status.

What are NATO's alternatives now? It can try to return to negotiation. Russia has no reason to trust that process, given how the Minsk 1 and 2 accords worked out (NATO and the US willfully and dishonestly voided them). The US and NATO could send their own troops into Ukraine, but that would be suicide, considering the alliance's arms and munitions drawdown and America's feminized army. The US could go a little further and provoke a nuclear exchange (suicide by other means) — and given the level of terminal-hysterical insanity in the US Blob that's not out of the question.

One likely, reality-based alternative is to stand by and let Russia complete its Special Military Operation to pacify and neutralize Ukraine. The prevailing theory is that this would be the end of America's world dominance militarily, and effectively the end of NATO, but also the end financially for the US, as the non-West abandons the dollar. In that scenario, the BRICs dump their trillions in US bond holdings, sending all that putative "money" back to America, stoking a king hell inflation, effectively bankrupting us. It would be the final fruit of the disastrous "Joe Biden" regime imposed on us via election fraud by the Blob: the US reduced in a few short years to a broke, socially disordered, marginalized power susceptible to its own political breakup — not a tantalizing outcome, but perhaps better than turning the planet Earth into a smoldering ashtray.

That outcome would force our country to turn inward and face its own stupendous failures of honor, decency, and integrity. It would be the end of the Blob's hegemony *inside* the USA. The question is whether the Blob sets America's house on fire in the attempt to save itself and escape a legal accounting for its crimes. One kindling stack already burning is the pileup of jive prosecutions aimed at Mr. Trump. You know that the attempt to kick him off the game board using Special Counsel Jack Smith may easily lead to severe civil disorder, and possibly a countercoup, a US first!

The current Mar-a-Lago "Doc Box" case is as much a complete fabrication as were RussiaGate and Impeachment Number One — Mr. Trump's telephone inquiry to Ukraine about the Biden family grifting operations there, now firmly documented to be true. An upright judge would summarily dismiss the Mar-a-Lago case and slam sanctions on the US attorneys involved, including disbarment and criminal investigation for mounting a maliciously fraudulent prosecution. AG Merrick Garland and his deputy Lisa Monaco obviously would have some 'splainin' to do, possibly before juries.

A long list of public figures populating the Blob await a reckoning: Hillary and Bill Clinton and their retainers, Barack Obama and retinue, John Brennan, James Clapper, James Comey, Christopher Wray (plus Rosenstein, Strzok, McCabe, Carlin, Ohr, Mueller, Weissmann, Horowitz, Atkinson, Ciaramella, Vindman), Rep. Adam Schiff, Senator Mark Warner, William Barr, Avril Haines, Marie Yovanovitch, William Burns, James Boasberg, Marc Elias, Michael Bromwich, David Laufman, Alejandro Mayorkas, Xavier Bacerra, Anthony Fauci, Rochelle Walensky, Francis Collins, Lloyd Austin, Mark Milley, Antony Blinken, Jake Sullivan, Ron Klain, Nancy Pelosi, Liz Cheney . . . the list goes way on, but there's a start.

The weeks of summer 2023 are the fulcrum for a great public attitude adjustment. The Blob's psyops are finally failing among just enough of the formerly mind-fucked to tip the national consensus against the gang behind all this treasonous political depravity. Even the so-called mainstream media are running scared. If they happened to turn in a desperate act of self-preservation, it will be all over for the Blob.

JAMES HOWARD KUNSTLER

August Psychodrama

August 11, 2023

"The idea that our Justice Department can indict someone, especially the sitting president's main political rival, over speech that's protected by the First Amendment is simply insane ... Simply put, this indictment is nothing more than a declaration of war against American voters and their constitutional right to free speech."
— Alistair Crooke

In August, the head shrinkers notoriously abandon their posh clientele among the managerial elites, who are left to flounder in the flotsam of their disordered lives while their shrinks go off to body surf and drink mojitos. And so, a month that ought to be a pleasant break from routine business leaves the managers of all that routine business awash in a rising tide of their own personal misery — the job haters, the sexually tortured, the self-subverters, the hopeless obsessive compulsives, the cringing masochists, the unloved and unlovable, the projectionists of animus, rancor, and loathing . . . Among these are *The People of the Blob*, the folks infesting the high ranks of our government's permanent bureaucracy, which has turned so viciously against the governed. Do you doubt any longer that this demographic in the USA is mentally ill? This malady of self-destructive bad faith and enmity afflicting especially the Democratic Party shoves us inch by inch and day by day toward something that looks like national suicide. Must we all follow?

Could this sick polity be better personified than by the tragicomic figure at the head of it: "Joe Biden" along with the Biden family? The scope of this clan's derangements is almost Shakespearean, lacking only that decorum of personal presentation on view in all the Bard's plays. King Lear, tormented as he was, would never faceplant after a speech. His daughters had a lot to worry about, but as far as we know, they were not subjected to showering with the big guy. And there were no known recordings of the Earl of Gloucester smoking crack with naked, underage girls.

Yet in the real life of our nation, "JB's" troubles mount as each day peels off the calendar. Only the most pathologically credulous might fail to notice the slime trail of bribery lately uncovered by congressional sleuths. "JB" obviously put himself in the service of interests outside the United States, and how is that working out now, notably in Ukraine, where he has levered us into the most perilously halfassed war imaginable — the losing of which will dash what's left of America's standing in the world?

One thing that has become clear in this cabbage soup of perfidy is just how blobbed up Volodymyr Zelensky was when President Donald Trump made that fateful phone call to him in August of 2019 inquiring about "JB's" curious doings in Kiev over the years. Did Z follow up that call immediately with one to Alexander Vindman in the National Security Council, who then called Eric Ciaramella of the NSC and CIA? Because, *voilà*, there was something supernatural about how fast we were off to Impeachment Number One!

And now the not insane cohort of Americans is prompted to ask whether this war in Ukraine was provoked in any part to cover up all the nefarious blobbery that preceded it — and not just Hunter and "Joe Biden's" capers, but the machinations, too, of State Department blobette Victoria Nuland and her retinue in the Kiev embassy, Marie Yovanovitch, George Kent, and many others of the Blob persuasion. A review of all this suggests that "Joe Biden" is what has driven the Democratic Party insane. And now, of course, they can't seem to get rid of him, like a demon riding them through an endless nightmare.

Instead, they have bent every last effort to get rid of "JB's" supposed rival Donald Trump, who has been inducted into a lawfare-engineered chamber of horrors designed to slice and dice him into a million pieces and strew the shreds into the Potomac for the blue crabs to feed on. One can't imagine a lamer case than the charges Special Counsel Jack Smith has cooked up against Mr. Trump for verbally expressing doubt about the probity of election 2020. Will Mr. Smith be able to prove any of this, assuming that it is now against the law in America to *believe* something and say so?

Logically, Mr. Trump's defense might present reasons why he believed the election was rife with fraud, by introducing evidence of said fraud, of which there is actually an impressive amount now, despite whatever mendacious bullshit you see in *The New York Times* and on MSNBC. Do you suppose Judge Tanya Chutkan would do anything but allow that evidence to be introduced? And if she disallows it, is that not instantly grounds for a mistrial, since it would prove beyond a reasonable doubt there were good reasons, after all, for Mr. Trump to express what he believed?

Things are getting durned interesting. Rep. Matt Gaetz (R-Fla.) offered a charming plan this week to counter this deceitful DOJ crusade. Here's how it would work. First, the House Judiciary Committee calls Special Counsel Jack Smith to give transcribed testimony in the next fifteen days regarding the weaponization of the First Amendment. If he refuses, subpoena him. If he ignores the subpoena, the committee holds him in criminal contempt of Congress and issues a formal referral to Attorney General Merrick Garland. If Mr. Garland ignores the referral, impeach the SOB forthwith. At the same time, invite Mr. Trump to give testimony to the committee as a whistleblower, conferring congressional immunity to him among the usual whistleblower protections as stated in law (under 18 U.S. Code 6002 and 6005).

Impeaching Mr. Garland would surely have a salutary influence on America's current troubled mental state. And it would be a grand prelude to the more consequential impeachment of "Joe Biden" for selling out his country, a kind of political electroshock therapy for the Democratic Party, leaving them finally clearheaded enough to nominate Robert F. Kennedy Jr. in the coming election of 2024.